Professor McAlindon argues that there were two models of nature in Renaissance culture, one hierarchical, in which everything has an appointed place, the other contrarious, showing nature as a tense system of interacting opposites, liable to sudden collapse and transformation. This latter model informs Shakespeare's tragedy throughout his career. It can be seen in his broad conception of tragic action as a reflection of 'Chaos . . . come again'; in the characterisation of the hero as a man who becomes his own opposite; in symbolically polarised settings; and in the web of elemental imagery which roots the action in the dynamics of universal nature.

A preliminary chapter on Chaucer's Knight's Tale explains the literary antecedents of Shakespeare's model and its manifestation in *A Midsummer Night's Dream*. The following chapters take the tragedies one by one. This approach to the tragedies shows that Shakespeare at his most characteristic was profoundly indebted to the cultural inheritance of his own time.

Shakespeare's tragic cosmos

Shakespeare's tragic cosmos

T. McALINDON

Professor of English,
University of Hull

CAMBRIDGE
UNIVERSITY PRESS

Published by the Press Syndicate of the University of Cambridge
The Pitt Building, Trumpington Street, Cambridge CB2 1RP
40 West 20th Street, New York, NY 10011-4211 USA
10 Stamford Road, Oakleigh, Melbourne 3166, Australia

© Cambridge University Press 1991

First published 1991
First paperback edition 1996

Printed in Great Britain by Athenæum Press Ltd, Gateshead, Tyne & Wear

British Library cataloguing in publication data
McAlindon, T. (Thomas), 1932–
Shakespeare's tragic cosmos.
1. Drama in English. Shakespeare, William, 1564–1616
1 Title
822.33

Library of Congress cataloguing in publication data
McAlindon, T. (Thomas)
Shakespeare's tragic cosmos / T. McAlindon.
p. cm.
Includes bibliographical references.
ISBN 0 521 39041 9 (hardback)
1. Shakespeare, William, 1564–1616 – Tragedies. 2. Cosmology in
literature. 3. Tragedy. I. Title.
PR2983.M37 1991
822.3'3 – dc20 90-32230
CIP

ISBN 0 521 39041 9 hardback
ISBN 0 521 56605 3 paperback

To Mark, Shane, and Mel

So the war of the elements that has raged throughout eternity continues on equal terms. Now here, now there, the forces of life are victorious and are in turn vanquished. With the voice of mourning mingles the cry that infants raise when their eyes open on the sunlit world. Never has day given place to night or night to dawn that has not heard, blent with these infant wailings, the lamentation that attends on death and sombre obsequies.

(Lucretius, *On the Nature of the Universe*, trs. R.E. Latham)

Thou must be patient; we came crying hither.

(Shakespeare, *King Lear*)

Contents

Preface

In *English Renaissance Tragedy* (1986) I examined the tragedies of
Shakespeare's major contemporaries in the light of a broad referential framework drawn from their shared ideas, preoccupations,
and methods, and clarified, where necessary, by reference to their
cultural context. Although I did not deal directly with Shakespeare,
the referential framework was based on Shakespearian as well as
non-Shakespearian texts, it being my conviction that Shakespeare's
tragedies and those of his contemporaries are interdependent and
mutually illuminating. Given the diversity of authors and texts I
was synthesising in this introductory section, the framework was
wide, embracing such common concerns as violence, change, time,
and permanence; the interrelated themes of justice and love, law
and marriage; the problem of personal identity and the theme of
self-loss; Christian and Stoic conceptions of the noble death, and
the pattern of redemption or renewal; the symbolic uses of ritual
and play; the language of tragic reality. A central and pervasive
concern was that of duality and polarity, my argument being that
the ancient model of natural order as a dynamic system of interacting opposites had a much more profound effect on the Renaissance
interpretation and representation of tragic experience than did the
related notion of universal hierarchy. The present study proposes
to examine a range of Shakespeare's tragedies in the light of this
central claim and will be to that extent complementary to the book
on Shakespeare's contemporaries. In dealing with Shakespeare, I
have narrowed my critical focus in this way because no other tragedian of the period wrestled so long with the universal drama of Love
and Strife or dramatised with such power and inventiveness the
experience of confounding contrariety in the inner and the outer
world. My focus, however, is not so narrow as to preclude consideration of other aspects of cosmological tradition (such as the theme

of time and the symbolism of number) which bear on the central phenomenon of confounding contraries and 'Chaos . . . come again'.

The historicist methodology to which this study relates is that of the 'history of ideas'. However, as applied to a method of literary and dramatic interpretation the term is somewhat misleading, for as Paul Bénichou has observed, 'ideas, which are abstract by definition, cease to be so when they are embodied in a literature and given corporal form' (Tzvetan Todorov, 'Conversation with Paul Bénichou', in *Literature and its Theorists: a Personal View of Twentieth-Century Criticism* (London: Routledge, 1988), pp.20–1). It will be obvious, I hope, that traditional ideas about the natural order are of interest to me only insofar as they contribute to a construction of reality which is imaginatively embodied in action, characterisation, symbolism, and style.

It will be equally apparent that speculative, genetic inquiry of the kind undertaken by the 'new historicists' and 'cultural materialists' into the socio-political conditions which lie behind Shakespeare's ideas about conflict and contradiction is not my concern. My purpose is simply to identify those ideas and the world model they constitute, to stress their traditional nature, and to show how fruitfully they have been deployed in the dramatic and poetic exploration of tragic experience.

Both in the text and in the end-notes I have on occasion expressed disagreement with other Shakespearians: with old and new historicists, with Tillyardians and Marxists and the various descendants of the old 'new critics'. But I have also registered my profound indebtedness to the work of critics and scholars of all kinds. Although in a sense this book began in disagreement, it is in no way polemical: I make no claim to having wielded the great Cutting Edge of a combative and radical new theory. My intention has been to present an argument which establishes Shakespeare's intimate rapport with his contemporaries, and in the process to amend, correct, refute, confirm, and refine interpretations arrived at by other means.

Acknowledgements

I should like to thank those friends whose suggestions and corrections have helped to improve the quality of this book – Robin Headlam Wells, Rowland Wymer, Elizabeth Story Donno, Gilian West, and Angela Leighton. Nor must I forget the anonymous publisher's reader who gave invaluable advice on its organisation. The well-worn formula, however, is as necessary as ever: for those flaws which remain, I alone am responsible.

My thanks are due also to the University of Alberta (Edmonton), which honoured me with an invitation to give a series of lectures in September 1987 that formed the beginning and the basis of the book; and to the Fellows and Trustees of the Huntington Library, California, where the award of a Mellon Foundation Fellowship gave me four delightful months in which to complete it.

Abbreviations

Shakespeare's plays and poems

Ado	*Much Ado about Nothing*
Ant.	*Antony and Cleopatra*
AWW	*All's Well That Ends Well*
AYL	*As You Like It*
Cor.	*Coriolanus*
Ham.	*Hamlet*
1H4	*Henry IV, Part I*
2H4	*Henry IV, Part II*
H5	*Henry V*
JC	*Julius Caesar*
Lr.	*King Lear*
Luc.	*The Rape of Lucrece*
Mac.	*Macbeth*
MND	*A Midsummer Night's Dream*
MV	*The Merchant of Venice*
Oth.	*Othello*
R2	*Richard II*
R3	*Richard III*
Rom.	*Romeo and Juliet*
Tim.	*Timon of Athens*
Tit.	*Titus Andronicus*
Tmp.	*The Tempest*
Tro.	*Troilus and Cressida*
WT	*The Winter's Tale*

Periodicals and series

	Archiv für das Studien der Neueren Sprachen und Literaturen
CQ	*Critical Quarterly*

CR	*Chaucer Review*
EIC	*Essays in Criticism*
ELH	*English Literary History*
ELR	*English Literary Renaissance*
HLQ	*Huntington Library Quarterly*
MAE	*Medium Aevum*
MED	*The Middle English Dictionary*
OED	*Oxford English Dictionary*
PMLA	*Publications of the Modern Language Association of America*
PBA	*Proceedings of the British Academy*
REALB	*Yearbook of Research in English and American Literature*
RES	*Review of English Studies*
SEL	*Studies in English Literature*
ShakS	*Shakespeare Studies*
SJ	*Shakespeare-Jahrbuch*
ShS	*Shakespeare Survey*
SP	*Studies in Philology*
SQ	*Shakespeare Quarterly*
SR	*Sewanee Review*
SUAS	Stratford-upon-Avon Studies
TSE	*Tulane Studies in English*
TSLL	*Texas Studies in Language and Literature*

NOTE. Except where otherwise indicated, all citations of Shakespeare's plays in this book are from *The Complete Works*, ed. Peter Alexander (London and Glasgow: Collins, 1951).

Introduction
'Nature's fragile vessel'
(*Tim.*v.i.199)

I

By the middle of *Timon of Athens*, the hero, a man of enormous wealth and popularity, suddenly finds himself bankrupt and friendless. In despair, he abandons the city and takes to the wilderness, where he 'walks, like contempt, alone' (iv.ii.15), grubbing for roots to sustain his wretched life.

There are many references to Fortune in this play, and one can easily detect in it echoes of the medieval idea of tragedy as a steep fall from the heights of prosperity, a lesson on the terrible insecurity of mundane existence.[1] Dramatically arresting and poignant though it is, however, the material change which afflicts Timon is of far less significance than the transformation which takes place in his character and in his whole conception of humanity. Timon has been the bountiful and convivial friend of all men, one who 'outgoes / The very heart of kindness' (i.i.276–7). But now, playing bitterly on the word 'kind', he declares, 'I am Misanthropos, and hate mankind' (iv.iii.54). Leaving the city, he utters a litany of curses against its inhabitants which simply sums up his feeling that human nature is already accursed and can only get worse. Two sentences in this long speech merit special attention, for they are echoed repeatedly in the diction and imagery of the play and can be taken as signals to its controlling ideas. One occurs near the middle: 'Decline to your confounding contraries / And let confusion live'; the other comes near the end: 'Timon will to the woods, where he shall find / The unkindest beast more kinder than mankind' (iv.i.20–1, 35–6). The word 'confound' means to mingle things so that they become indistinguishable, lose form and identity; thus it also means to destroy, and so has become a virtual synonym for 'curse'. Of course 'confounding' or 'confusing' also has a psychological sense; it is not explicitly invoked here, but dramatically it is very relevant. It signifies bewilderment, aporia, or what Shakespeare and his fellow tragedians characteristically referred to as 'amazement' (with an implicit emphasis on the root sense of the word): a state of mind which registers that sign and referent, name and identity, appearance and essence, have become wholly disjoined. What amazes Timon to the point of madness, turning him into the embodiment of hatred, and infecting his speech with paradox and oxymoron, is the discovery that mankind is not kind, not loving: or perhaps worse, men are monsters whose nature or kind is to be both loving and pitiless, humane and bestial: 'Courteous destroyers, affable wolves' (III.vi.95).

Timon of Athens is a late and notably imperfect Shakespearian tragedy (and perhaps not entirely Shakespearian at that); but it does expose with singular clarity certain ideas and patterns which are fundamental to all Shakespeare's tragedies, from *Titus Andronicus* to *Coriolanus*. Tragedy, Eric Bentley has remarked, offers us 'the experience of chaos'.[2] Most critics would agree that this is particularly true of Shakespeare's tragedies.[3] In these plays, the bond which unites the hero with others, and forms the basis of his self-conception and his world view, is violently shattered. He is the victim or agent of some profound personal betrayal. But, above all, he betrays himself, that is, the noble self with which he is identified in his own and others' eyes; indeed his change is so extreme that he seems at times to have become his own antithesis.[4] The phenomenon of psychic and interpersonal chaos is magnified by the hero's intense emotional distress and reflected in society at large, which is torn by civil strife if not civil war; it is also reflected in external nature, where terrible storms and other more 'unnatural' disorders prevail. And implicit in the whole play, but focussed particularly in the agonised consciousness of the protagonist, is an insistent questioning about the nature of men and women and the world we inhabit: in short, about the nature of nature or 'kind'. This questioning often points beyond nature, but when there is a suggestion that mundane happenings are subject to supernatural ordinance, it remains perfectly clear that supernatural power (the gods, divine providence, Fate) operates in complete consistency with the dynamics of nature. In effect, we are always returned to nature as to the heart of the problem.

The intensity with which Shakespeare imagined 'Chaos . . . come again' (*Oth.*, III.iii.93) is inseparable from his profound awareness of cosmos, an awareness shared by his audience. Indirectly, his plays reflect also a keen interest in the socio-political problems of his own time, so that an interpretative method which approaches them by way of Elizabethan–Jacobean politics is entirely justified. But these are also plays which habitually locate socio-political as well as psychological issues in the universal context defined by cosmology, and to ignore that wider context is not only to diminish both the complexity and the grandeur of the plays but also to neglect something that appealed specifically to contemporary audiences. The Renaissance, as S.K. Heninger has recently reminded us in two fine studies, was an age in which cosmography flourished.[5] It was also an age of microcosmography, when the nature of humankind was studied as never before – but almost always in the context of cosmos, and on the assumption that the microcosm and the macrocosm are constructed from the same basic substances, operate on identical principles, and are closely interconnected. Thus Renaissance culture abounded in brilliant emblems of the universe where man is always given a central place, and brilliant emblems of man which emphasise his physical and psychological subjection to cosmic influences. Even the introverted Montaigne did not so much reject the cosmic setting in his meticulous analysis of his own nature as substitute a Heraclitean cosmos (where all is conflict and change) for the traditional Empedoclean cosmos (wherein discord and concord, change and permanence, are reconciled).[6]

It should perhaps be recalled that from 1599 – when the Globe was opened – Shakespeare's audience was literally surrounded by cosmic emblems. On the so-called 'heavens' or extended canopy above the stage were depicted the sun and moon and other planets, whose unceasing influence was held to be responsible for all change in the sublunary world. And apart from this 'brave o'er-hanging firmament' (to which, no doubt, the actors pointed or looked at appropriate moments), there was the name and shape of the theatre itself. The Globe audience would have been encouraged by that name to see in the rectangular projecting stage surrounded by a circular wall the familiar images of the circularised square (an emblem of the cosmic tetrad) and of the squared circle (an emblem of the timeless and the infinite 'rendered finite and timely . . . by transformation into the square of the elemental tetrad').[7] The tetrad was a schema devised to explain the fourfold system of nature, the structure of contrary elements whose balanced interchange constitutes a perfect unity, reconciling change and permanence, motion and stability – what Milton refers to when he speaks of the 'Elements ... that in quaternion run / Perpetual circle' (*Paradise Lost*, v.180–2). Recent investigations into the architecture of the Globe have adduced further evidence of an underlying cosmic conception: an *ad quadratum* method of construction (which partners the square and the circle), orientation as a summer playhouse towards the summer sunrise, and a consequent correspondence with the structure of the universe and the movements of the heavenly bodies.[8] *Julius Caesar* was probably written to grace the ópening of the Globe in 1599, and if my own analysis of that play is correct, its complex symbolic design is elaborately attuned to the cosmic conception of the new playhouse, for it incorporates not only the elements, the stars, and the rising and setting sun, but also the circle, the tetrad, and a basic number symbolism derived from cosmological tradition (chapter 4). Antony's concluding declaration that in Brutus 'the elements/[were] So mix'd ... that Nature might stand up / And say to all the world "This was a man!"' (v.v.73–5) is utterly in keeping with the imaginative method of this play; but it may also be taken as exemplary of the tragedies as a whole. Shakespeare endows his principal characters with cosmic imagination. He makes them speak to and of the elements, the stars, the sun, the moon, and 'all the world'. This trait not only invests their situation with magnitude and intensity, it also illuminates it. It is part of an endeavour to connect the tragic fate of the individual with the structure and dynamics of universal nature.

As I have been implying, Shakespeare's understanding of nature was fundamentally traditional. Although the new science had already begun to change the whole picture of the universe and of humankind's relation to it, there are no signs of this revolution in his work. On the contrary, he made full use of the established synthesis of cosmological ideas derived from Aristotle, Plato, and the Presocratic thinkers Pythagoras, Heraclitus, and Empedocles, a system which had been reinforced over the centuries by Ptolemaic astronomy and Galenic medicine. Fundamental to this system was the correspondence of the macrocosm and the microcosm, and the fourfold structure of binary opposites inherent in all things – the elements (earth, water, air, and fire), the qualities (heat and cold, moisture and dryness), and, in man alone, the humours (choler, melancholy, blood, and phlegm). With its governing ideas of polarity, balance, and correspondence, opposition and interdependence, this system brought under one conceptual umbrella physics, biology, physiology, psychology, chemistry (alchemy), ethics, and aesthetics.

In stressing Shakespeare's use of the traditional synthesis, I do not wish to suggest that his world view coincides with the Elizabethan world picture as described by James E. Phillips, Theodore Spencer, and (most notably) E.M.W. Tillyard.[9] In this account, the cardinal principle of pre-modern cosmology as understood by the Elizabethans was that of hierarchy or degree; they saw the world as a stratified order where everything has its appointed place and identity. Thus Shakespeare always traces the cause of chaos to the disruption of hierarchy or violation of degree in the socio-political and the psychic spheres – to revolt against lawful authority, to the eclipse of reason and will by passion.[10] Beginning with A.P. Rossiter, however, many critics argued that this view greatly simplifies the way in which Shakespeare presents the disintegration of the individual and society.[11] Such a reaction was perfectly justified; but it was not correct to infer, as so many have done, that pre-modern conceptions of natural order are, in consequence, of little relevance to the study of Shakespeare's tragedies and tragical histories. Ignored in this assumption is the fact that the Tillyardian account of the Elizabethan world picture was seriously incomplete; for pre-modern cosmology construed the world not only as a hierarchical structure of corresponding planes but also as a dynamic system of interacting, interdependent opposites. The two conceptions were commonly combined and treated as twin aspects of universal order – most obviously, in the notion of the world as a stratified arrangement of earth, water, air, and fire, each placed above the other in accordance with its degree of lightness or 'nobility'. The two conceptions are logically connected, since every scale of degree is constructed from opposites and constitutes in effect an attempt to mediate between them;[12] looked at from this point of view, the hierarchical conception of the world is essentially a refinement of the contrarious conception. Nevertheless, the two conceptions, although commonly conjoined, could easily be separated, or, when conjoined, priority of emphasis could be given to one of them; for the hierarchical arrangement of the elements was not thought to alter the fact that they *are* opposites with an entirely '*natural* desire to / Combat each with other'.[13] Indeed everything in the sublunary world, including men and women, was thought to change, decay, and die precisely because it is constituted of opposing forces. Thus while it is true that Shakespeare's tragic universe is structured as a hierarchy of correspondent planes, the most striking manifestation of correspondence between the different planes is the violent conflict and confusion of opposites; this, rather than the disruption of hierarchy, is the outstanding feature of the world as seen in the tragedies.

In the contrarious conception of the world, however, conflict is not necessarily the primary force in nature. That was the view of Heraclitus, who argued that the stability of the world is maintained by Strife (War, Hatred): that is, by the continual friction and interchange of the elements.[14] In this he was consciously opposing Pythagoras, who had taught that the blending or harmony of the opposites, both in the macrocosm and the microcosm, is the law of nature. Empedocles combined these two theories to produce the pluralist doctrine that nature is governed by both Love and Strife, sympathies and antipathies;[15] and mainly from this doctrine came the notion of the world as a system of concordant discord or discordant concord.[16] This is the world view defined by Ovid at the beginning of the *Metamorphoses*, by Chaucer at the start of Book III of *Troilus and Criseyde*, and by Spenser in his 'Hymn in Honour of Love'. In this view, the strife which forever agitates the opposites is kept in check by the harmonising force of love, which binds them together in a fruitful union while upholding the justice of separate roles and identities. The whole order of life – unity, peace, and continuity – is founded on this bond of opposites, just as disorder, chaos, and death are caused by its collapse under the pressure of strife. The cosmic doctrine of the two contraries, or reciprocal principles of nature, was world-wide in ancient mythologies (the Chinese myth of Ying and Yang is a well-known Oriental version).[17] Obviously it is a projection on to the universe of the natural law of reproduction; for that reason, the sexual, marital, and familial relationship in the great writers of the Middle Ages and the Renaissance, and especially in Shakespeare of the tragedies and tragical histories, is frequently central to an all-embracing cosmic vision.

It should be emphasised that the Empedoclean model of the world, as elaborated over the centuries, retained a strong Heraclitean component. Uncontrolled strife was held to be the ultimate negation of natural order, but limited strife was viewed positively as something necessary to the scheme of things, a force which contributes towards differentiation and balance. Thus in the following passage Louis le Roy narrowly escapes conceding that the strife of the opposites is just as important in the dynamics of nature as is their concord or 'tempering':

In like manner is the Earth, and every other thing in the world, tempered and conserved by things of dislike and contrary qualitie. It is not then without cause, that nature is so desirous of contraries, making of them, all decency, and beautie; not of things which are of like nature. This kind of tempering is the cause, that such things as before were divers and different, do accord and agree together, to establish, intertain, and embellish one another, the contrarietie becomming unitie, and the discord concord; the enmitie amitie; and contention covenant. Wherefore Heraclitus said, that discord, and concord, were the father and mother of all things. And Homer, that whosoever spake evill of contentions, did blame nature. Empedocles maintayned not of discord by itselfe, but that with concord, it was the beginning of all things; meaning by discord, the varietie of things that are assembled, and by concord, the union of them. But the union in this assemblie ought to exceede the contrarietie. Otherwise the thing should be dissolved, the principles dividing themselves. So we see in the Heavens contrarie movings to preserve the world: Venus placed in the midst neere unto Mars, to asswage his fiercenes, which of his own nature is corruptive.[18]

It is this view of universal nature which prompts so many Renaissance authors to refer to war – 'the humour radicall / Of Violence' – as a necessary form of bloodletting for sick states, a surgical preserver of 'This Equillibrium, wherein nature goes'.[19] It also underlies Machiavelli's remarkable claim – in defiance of every other writer on politics – that discord and contentious violence can actually strengthen a state (by generating laws to protect the liberties of its various groups) (*The Discourses*, i.iv).

What I am suggesting, then, is that pre-modern cosmological tradition offered in effect two world models, each of which could inspire or sanction quite different feelings about the human situation, different habits of thought. The idea of the universe as a hierarchical system of corresponding planes where everything has its appointed place and identity suggests a fundamental stability and rationality in things and induces a mood of metaphysical confidence in every attempt to interpret the facts of experience. But the notion of the universe as a tense system of interacting, interdependent opposites reminds us that every pattern of harmonious order, every structure of identity, is of its very nature susceptible to violent transformation: of a sudden (to recall Timon), bonds collapse, things decline to their confounding contraries, and confusion prevails. Moreover, since it presumes that both subject and object are duplex and changeful, the contrarious model militates against philosophical certainty, fostering modes of thought and expression which are dialectical rather than categorical, relativist and paradoxical rather than absolute and univocal. Finally, since it is rooted in the assumption that the world was created from Chaos, and that the forces of chaos are intrinsic to its functioning, the contrarious model insistently implies that disorder, aggressive egoism, and blind passion are not just blemishes on nature caused by sin and the Fall, but are as natural as order, altruism, and reason. Thus the model stood in potentially subversive relationship to the philosophy of Natural Law which all the ideological orthodoxies of the Middle Ages and the Renaissance took for granted. It acknowledged as natural that side of human nature which Machiavelli and Hobbes were to treat as the whole.

It is not to be thought that universal contrariety is simply another name for mutability, the condition of relentless changefulness which in the Middle Ages and the Renaissance became the principal focus for complaint about human nature and about the sublunary world below the 'changeless heavens' to which we belong. The two are intimately connected indeed, but the relationship is one of cause and effect, mutability being due to the contrary motions of the stars and the influences which these motions have on the elements and the elements on each other. But mutability is only one of the darker aspects of human experience which could be traced to the con-trarious model of nature; as a cosmological idea, it was potentially much less unsettling than its parent concept.

Both in the Middle Ages and in the Renaissance, exponents of the religio-political status quo inevitably made much of the hierarchical model of the universe; it was a convenient way of naturalising the structure of feudal society. Shakespeare undoubtedly made use of it too; in my view, however, he found – like Chaucer, Kyd, and Marlowe before him – that the radically paradoxical notion of nature as a system of concordant discord or 'harmonious contra-rietie', moved incessantly by the forces of love and strife, answered the facts of experience more truthfully.[20] This model satisfied in him the characteristically human need for a unitary frame of reference while at the same time accommodating his sense of the profound contradictions in human nature and the perceived world. In ad-dition, it gave universal validity to human passions and feelings, the stuff of tragedy. Since conflict and dialectic are 'the essence of drama', and division and extremes the essence of tragedy, it was ideally suited to the structure of his medium. It served, too, as a focal point for many of the other great dualisms which were the common coinage of his culture and which he himself probed with uncommon penetration – passion and reason, barbarism and civility, the individual and the community, nature and nurture. (Such indeed was its usefulness as an explanatory model that it had long since been employed to account for the body/soul antithesis;[21] and even the paradox of free will and pre-determination – so fundamental to the tragic vision – was explained in terms of it[22]).

Many critics have argued that the contradictions inherent in Shakespeare's response to tragic experience mirror a fundamental conflict of ideas about the nature of humankind, society, and the physical world that dominated the intellectual life of his time; the polarised world views are variously characterised by scholars as old and new, religious and secular, optimistic and pessimistic, idealistic and realistic, Hookerian and Machiavellian (or Hobbesian).[23] This is a critical position which has won almost universal assent, the only source of disagreement being the question whether Shakespeare inclines to one view of nature or the other, or maintains a position of honest and fruitful scepticism about both. To challenge a position which commands assent on all sides of the critical spectrum seems presumptuous in the extreme; yet it appears to me that this one requires substantial modification. Shakespeare's acute sensitivity to the intellectual, religious, and socio-political conflicts of his own time is beyond question. Clearly he was well aware that the orthodox view of nature (propounded by Hooker) as an orderly system which dictates reason, altruism, benevolence, and community (as well as hierarchy) was being challenged by a conception of nature as dictating violence, egoism, and the destruction or domination of the weak by the strong. My contention is that he regarded these polarised attitudes as polemical simplifications, having already at his disposal an imaginatively liberating and comprehensive world model which incorporated both viewpoints. This was an inherently paradoxical model which allowed him to interrelate and explore without evasion or reductiveness what he considered to be the most fundamental contradictions in humankind and in our experience of the world in general.

I would stress, moreover, that it enabled him to do so in a manner which was fully intelligible to his audience. Shakespeare's bias towards contrariety has been associated by one critic with the work of certain contemporary continental writers (Castiglione, Paracelsus, Giordano Bruno, and Montaigne) and to some extent imputed to their influence.[24] Its intellectual roots, however, were much more homely and familiar, and its literary background was entirely native. The tragedy of confounding contrariety began with Kyd's *The Spanish Tragedy* and Marlowe's *Tamburlaine the Great*;[25] its original source of inspiration, moreover, was probably the first and most philosophical of *The Canterbury Tales*. In the Knight's Tale, Chaucer consistently, and with immense subtlety, associates the contradictions of chivalric heroism (a twin ideal of valour and love, aggression and courtesy), and so also the contradictions of civilised human nature and society, with the discordant concord of a natural order whose governing forces are Love and Strife, Mars and Venus (see chapter 2). The chivalric sentiments, splendid pageantry, and formal complexity of this tragi-comical romance made it perhaps the most popular of all Chaucer's works during the Renaissance. Shakespeare's special interest in the poem is apparent both at the beginning of his career, when he borrowed its story of quarrelling lovers and friends for *A Midsummer Night's Dream*, and at the end, when (with John Fletcher) he dramatised it as *The Two Noble Kinsmen*; both plays show an enthusiastic appreciation of its dialectical vision and proliferant paradoxes. None of Shakespeare's tragedies, of course, discloses any concrete link with the poem (no more than did the Kyd and Marlowe tragedies); but my claim that there is a fundamental affinity and an almost certain indebtedness involved here will seem much less improbable if we reflect on the fact that Chaucer's narrative, like *A Midsummer Night's Dream* and *The Two Noble Kinsmen*, operates throughout on the verge of tragedy, and might easily have ended as such. The conception of natural order which guides Chaucer (in this poem) and Shakespeare (in all his work), that of a precarious balance of contrary forces, insistently implies that comedy (love and union) is potential tragedy, and that tragedy (division and violence) is comedy *manqué*.

The model of world order which Shakespeare acquired from the past not only encouraged ambivalent, paradoxical, and subversive responses to many of the official pieties of his own time. It also links him very concretely with nineteenth- and twentieth-century thinking. The notion of reality – of nature, history, society, or the self – as a dynamic system of interacting opposites has acquired a whole new life in this period: consider its various formulations in Hegel, Nietzsche, and Marx; in Blake, Yeats, and Lawrence; in Jung, Freud, and Lévi-Strauss. To a large extent, twentieth-century responsiveness to the contrarious and dialectical character of Shakespeare's work (especially the tragedies) has been due to the influence of Hegel and Nietzsche, who chose to apply their life-philosophies to the interpretation of tragedy. Hegel and Nietzsche, however, in seeing life, history, and tragedy as a dialectic of opposed principles or forces, were quite consciously going back to the roots of pre-modern cosmology. 'The way Heraclitus and Empedocles thought is alive once more', wrote Nietzsche in 1878; and Hegel had been of the same view.²⁶ But it was certainly not alive in the way it had been in the early seventeenth century, when Sir Thomas Browne declared that 'this world is raised upon a mass of anti-pathies', and that man himself is 'another world of contrarieties';²⁷ then, it was a mode of thinking bred in the bone.

The various manifestations of philosophical scepticism in twentieth-century thought – culminating in the poststructuralist revival of Nietzschean perspectivism ('Facts there are not ... only interpretations') – have exercised a substantial influence in Shakespearian criticism. In combination with Marxist dialectic, the sceptical temper has greatly reinforced general awareness of the contradictions and instabilities of the Shakespearian text. The plays are praised because they offer no conclusions but rather a heightened awareness of problems; because they are 'ambivalent', 'open-ended', 'complementary', 'disjunctive', 'dialogic', 'polyphonic'. Recent Marxist and poststructural analyses of Shakespeare have foregrounded the oppositional form which the Shakespearian complexity so often assumes; nevertheless, it can still be said that the kind of interpretation which has done most to emphasise and illuminate this aspect of the plays stems from the old New Criticism, with its privileging of ambiguity and ambivalence. Among the key texts here are John Lawlor's *The Tragic Sense in Shakespeare* (1960), Norman Rabkin's *Shakespeare and the Common Understanding* (1967), and Bernard McElroy's *Shakespeare's Mature Tragedies* (1973). Lawlor speaks for the other two critics when, echoing A.P. Rossiter's seminal essay, 'Ambivalence: the Dialectic of the Histories' (1951),²⁸ he indicates that the key to understanding the tragedies is not Tillyard's monolithic world picture but rather Shakespeare's 'dual vision'. The 'dialectical habit', he observes, 'is the greatest single factor in forming the Shakespearian outlook'; 'the centre of his drama is the overburdened human creature, placed between mighty opposites, working out his salvation or damnation'.²⁹ Although all three critics admire Shakespeare for the way in which he balances and controls the opposed elements in his plays, they do not believe that he ever reconciles these elements in any kind of final unity. Rabkin and McElroy are notably emphatic on this point. Citing Rabkin's definition of Shakespearian complementarity as the presentation of equally valid, equally desirable, and equally contradictory ethical ideals or theologies, McElroy insists that 'there is no final merging into oneness, no relaxation of the dialectical tension', no 'Hegelian synthesis': both 'thesis and antithesis remain finally distinct, both are equally persuasive'.[30] This claim surely imputes to Shakespeare's endings a degree of uniformity which they do not possess; and it seems to imply that the only alternative to irresolvable contradiction in ethical and axiological matters is a pseudo-resolution which simply ignores complexity. Although it issues from a desire to liberate the text from univocal, doctrinaire interpretations, the claim is itself doctrinaire and results in a fair amount of unconvincing manipulation of the texts to fit the thesis. Rabkin, for example, argues that *Othello* dramatises an irresolvable conflict between reason (represented by Iago) and love's faith. But this opposition is easily deconstructed on the basis of a point conceded by Rabkin himself in a footnote: namely, that Iago's reasoning is not rational at all but rather a perversion of rationality governed by mere hatred.[31] Othello falls, not because he is seduced by Iago into using reason in the realm of love, but because his reason is enslaved, muddled, and perverted by Iago's and his own blind passion.

The claim that Shakespearian complementarity resists all resolution is due in part to a belief that it is essentially phenomenological rather than ontological, a product of consciousness rather than of nature.[32] If my argument in this book is correct, however, most of the major contradictions in Shakespeare's tragedies are referred to nature as their source and model; they are at root conflicts of natural forces and of feelings rather than of ideas. As such, they are by definition capable of some kind of resolution. And indeed, although the tragedies leave us with many unanswered questions, ethical, axiological, and metaphysical, they do include in their endings a measure of reintegration and harmony – psychic (within the hero), or interpersonal, or social, or all three. This note of unity is always muted and qualified, it varies in degree and kind from play to play, and it never undermines the overriding impression of violent strife and calamitous loss (except, perhaps, in *Antony and Cleopatra*); but it is real and significant nonetheless. It is not an inorganic addendum aimed at the soft-minded or the censor; nor is it a mystifying device for evading the political or philosophical significance of the contradictions which have been exposed in the course of the play. It is entirely consistent with the underlying dialectical conception of nature as a dynamic, unstable system which not only begets hate out of love, war out of peace, and tragedy out of comedy, but the reverse:

> Bring me into your city,
> And I will use the olive, with my sword;
> Make war breed peace, make peace stint war, make each
> Prescribe to other, as each other's leech. (*Tim.*, v.iv.81–4)

II

One very important feature of Shakespearian tragedy to which modern intellectual conventions do not make us properly responsive is the role of time. Although much that is critically very perceptive has been written on the subject, there has been a notable failure to perceive that time is an intrinsic part of Shakespeare's contrarious universe, or even to link it with cosmological tradition. There are two fundamental and closely connected principles relating to time in that tradition. First, an understanding of time is held to be a basic prerequisite for comprehending the whole natural order; as Plato explained, it was by observing the cycle of day and night, the lunar months, and the revolutions of the year, and developing in consequence a conception of number and time, that men acquired 'the power of inquiring about the nature of the universe'.[33] This attitude to time was expressed for the Middle Ages and the Renaissance in a widely disseminated emblematic diagram of the universe as a complex temporal unit. Essentially an expanded tetrad, the diagram consists of a series of three concentric circles. The outer circle encloses the heavenly bodies (represented by the signs of the Zodiac); the second encloses the twelve months of the year, each figured by an appropriate seasonal activity; and in the upper and lower halves of the (evenly divided) inner circle are Summer and Winter – Summer is personified as a young woman, Winter as an elderly man, so that the whole system mirrors the opposition and union of the sexes and the human cycle of birth, death, and reproduction (and vice versa).[34] Second, in the spatio-temporal order of the cosmos, time and space are perceived in a very precise sense as correspondent cosmoi, twin aspects of the same dynamic structure.[35] Time is the measured movement of the material world and, like it, discloses a cyclic pattern of binary and quadruple opposites: day and night, spring and autumn, summer and winter.

Man himself, whose life is usually construed as a cycle of four ages (childhood, youth, maturity, and age), is conceived as a temporal microcosm.[36] Almost every almanac and calendar published in the Renaissance carries an emblem of this conception. The most famous form of the emblem connects the different parts of the body with the signs of the Zodiac. Another connects the parts of the body with the seven planets; others identify man with the annual cycle of the four seasons, or with the diurnal cycle of day and night.[37]

Clearly indicated in such emblems is the idea that the heavenly bodies are not only the determinants of time but also forces which act upon human nature, not randomly but at specific times, and in accordance with the principle of correspondence between qualities, elements, and humours. *The Shepardes Kalender*, for example, an immensely popular work throughout the sixteenth century (the shepherd of the title is an archetype of humankind), explains how the sanguine, choleric, melancholic, and phlegmatic humours successively dominate in the four seasons and the four six-hour phases of the day; how when certain planets are in the ascendant corresponding modes of behaviour are likely to prevail, corresponding psychological and physiological types are born, and certain actions are to be undertaken or avoided by particular individuals.[38] We may be inclined to dismiss such arcane lore as an inessential or insignificant part of sixteenth- and seventeenth-century culture; but if we ignore astrology we must also ignore psycho-physiology and medicine, which were dependent on it; and we are then well on our way to constructing a picture of Renaissance science constituted only of elements which point to the future. It is appropriate to recall here the insistence of a recent historian of science that the tradition of neglecting the mystical–occult world view (which actually acquired new impetus in the Renaissance with the discovery of lost Neoplatonic and Hermetic texts) in favour of the emergent mathematical–observational approach to nature gives an entirely false impression of the mental life of the period. It also overlooks the intricate and often fruitful relationship which existed (in, for example, the work of Kepler and Paracelsus) between the old science and the new.[39]

The notion of the macrocosm and the microcosm as interdependent components of a complex temporal system inevitably had profound effects on people's thinking about the human drama (or 'Zodiake of Man's Life').[40] It follows from such a conception that men and women are creatures of time in a very special sense. They are 'Time's subjects' (*2H4*, I.iii.110), and as such must continually endeavour to 'obey the time', responding to its requirements with 'prompt alacrity' (*Oth.*, I.iii.300, 232) or due patience if they are to enjoy their allotted span and fructify within it. Like any powerful ruler, too, Time can seem both terrible and reassuring. It signifies change, decay, and death; and it may often seem inscrutable – perceiving and interpreting its signs can require preternatural vigilance and wisdom. But, being cyclical, Time also represents a stable order which accommodates both change and permanence. The heavenly bodies are not only agents of mutability but also clocks, images of order and constancy: thus 'most of the first clocks were less chronometers than exhibitions of the patterns of the universe',[41] and in turn the clock or dial becomes a favourite metaphor for rule and self-rule: 'The lives of princes should like dials move, / Whose regular example is so strong, / They make the times by them, go right, or wrong'.[42] Timeliness in human affairs ('ripeness', 'seasonableness', 'opportunity') figures logically as an all-important pragmatic and ethical concept. This goes back to Plato's association of virtue with εὐκαιρία (the well-chosen moment), and to Cicero's praise of *opportunitas* (in the *De Officiis* or *Of Moral Duties*); but no age was more committed to timeliness as a behavioural ideal than was the Renaissance. Timeliness was held to be a prerequisite for all action which is effective, socially proper, and just. Of special significance for the student of Renaissance tragedy is the association of time with justice. In English law-courts, as in Renaissance culture generally, this association was proverbial ('Time is the author of truth and right'); so too was that of injustice and haste.[43]

Shakespeare's rich engagement in the tragedies with the theme of time seems to have been generated initially by his attention to the ironies of peripeteia. There are no allusions to time in the first tragedy, *Titus Andronicus*, but there is a dramatic structure which shows with piercing eloquence how the whirligig of time brings in its revenges. Present anguish echoes past errors in Act III when the kneeling Titus pleads fruitlessly to the Senate to spare the life of his sons, just as in Act I Tamora had knelt and prayed in vain to him to spare her son. However in subsequent tragedies, tragic reversal and tragic (i.e. violent) change in general begin to be related with notable clarity to the metaphysic of time. In essence, tragic action is identified as conflict with time's order; so that if one were to attempt to answer A.C. Bradley's question, What is the ultimate power in Shakespeare's tragic world?,[44] one might not be far wrong if one were to suggest that, if there is such a power, it is time: that being the order of nature in the dimension which most absorbs the practising dramatist, conscious as he has to be at every moment of the limits of time, and of what is past and passing and to come. The deeds which generate the tragic action in Shakespeare are untimely or mistimed in the sense that they are dilatory or (much more often) either rash or cunningly swift. 'All this done / Upon the gad', exclaims the horrified Gloucester at the beginning of *King Lear*, commenting on the behaviour of the King (I.ii.25–6); and then he himself, provoked by the quick-thinking Edmund, sets the tragic subplot in motion by behaving in exactly the same manner. Tragic death, too, figures as a brutal truncation of the temporal cycle, a blasting of natural hopes and reasonable expectations. Lear does not spend his last years as he had intended in Cordelia's 'kind nursery' (I.i.123), happy amidst new life (note the sunken metaphor of the garden). Wedding becomes funeral in *Romeo and Juliet* and *Othello*, even in *Hamlet*: 'I thought thy bride-bed to have deck'd, sweet maid, / And not have strew'd thy grave' (v.i.239–40). Brutus does not 'find time ... find time' to mourn the loss of Cassius (whose death is premature in a double sense, being prompted by his erroneous interpretation of the signs as meaning that Brutus has met with defeat: 'Alas, thou hast misconstrued everything!') (*JC*, v.iii.103, 84). The confusion of night and day, too, is a characteristic feature of Shakespeare's tragic universe. Violent action being often nocturnal either in conception or execution, night is conceived as a time of rest and peace violated, and as a symptom of chaos. The imagery of *Julius Caesar*, *Othello*, and *Macbeth* involves the mythical identification of Night and Hell (Erebus) as the children of Chaos, a myth which Plato projected (in part) into cosmology when he explained that there was no sun and moon and therefore no time in the state of primal Chaos.[45] For Shakespeare, chaos is not only hellish; as for Plato, it is featureless, restless, violent duration: nature without time, and so de-natured.

Shakespeare's tragic catastrophes reveal the corrective action of time. It is corrective first of all in the sense that it is retributive: untimely acts, whether tardy or rash, are punished in kind. Richard II 'wasted time', then abruptly took from Hereford and 'from Time / His charters and his customary rights'; 'and now doth time waste' him (II.i.195–6; v.v.49). Cassius kills Caesar 'in the shell' (II.i.34) (that is, before he has committed his presumptive crime), but has to kill himself on his own birthday, saying: 'Time is come round, / And

where I did begin, there shall I end; / My life is run his compass . . .
Caesar, thou art reveng'd, / Even with the sword that kill'd thee'
(v.iii.23–5, 45–6). There is a comparable sense of symmetrical
justice in Macbeth's grim recognition: 'Time, thou anticipatest my
dread exploits' (iv.i.144). Variously accented, the pattern of time's
justice can be detected in most of the tragedies. This is not to
suggest, however, that there is any neat over-all distribution of de-
serts. Nor can it be said that tragic characters are always responsible
for what befalls them; nor even that the issue of responsibility is a
major concern. Indeed it can reasonably be argued that the dispro-
portion in Shakespearian tragedy between culpable error (where
there is any) and consequent suffering, and between the sufferings of
the noble and the wicked, is so huge as to preclude any idea of justice
and rationality. But that surely is too simple (although it may
coincide with how we ourselves would interpret such events). It
would be more appropriate to say that time – much like Bradley's
undefined 'ultimate power' (*Shakespearean Tragedy*, p.36) – acts
retributively through a convulsive reaction which sweeps away all
but the most fortunate and the most astute. Its corrective order is
both impersonal and, from the purely human perspective, cruelly
imperfect. But the purely human perspective is itself incomplete,
since it entails wrenching the individual at the centre of the cosmic
picture out of a vast network of relations.

Time's action is corrective also in the sense that it is restorative.
The close of *King Lear*, as everyone acknowledges, is heart-rending;
but it could have been infinitely more depressing, since the action
very nearly ended with Queen Goneril and King Edmund on the
throne. Instead, Lear is succeeded by his godson, 'He whom my
father nam'd' (ii.i.92), a nobleman who has learned wisdom before
he is old and who declares that 'Ripeness is all' (v.ii.11). In considering the significance of time in the tragedies we might profitably
widen our canonical perspective and remember that in the comedies
and romances time unties knots and looks kindly on things newborn (Time's scythe is an emblem of destruction within a regenerative cycle). I may perhaps be exaggerating the positive aspect of
time in the tragedies, and the note of renewal in their endings; but
some over-emphasis may be necessary, since it concerns an aspect
of these plays which we seem programmed by our cultural prefer-
ences not to acknowledge. The positive undertone in Shakespeare's
tragic endings, it should be stressed, is a necessary and logical
counterpart to the negative undertone in his comic endings.

To conclude my remarks on time at this point, however, would be to get the balance quite wrong. The overall impression in the tragedies is of a world where time is put disastrously out of joint with terrifying ease, and can only be set right again at huge cost. It is painfully clear too that human passion and fallibility make it extremely difficult to respond to time's exacting demands. And (as already suggested) the vigilance necessary to perceive, and the wisdom to interpret, the signs of the time seem in the tragedies to be beyond the scope of mere mortals. Prospero failed in this respect when rapt in his studies, but succeeded on his island (*Tmp.*, I.ii.177–84). There are, however, no second chances for the tragic protagonists. They exist in 'a strange disposed time' where 'men . . . construe things after their fashion, / Clean from the purpose of the things themselves' (*JC*, I.iii.33–5), and with immediately fatal consequences. George Chapman's 'sentence', '*the use of time is fate*',[46] is most apt in relation to Shakespearian tragedy, especially if we stress the ominous note in the phrasing. Viewed in the abstract, the temporal cosmos is a marvel of intricate and orderly movement. Viewed in relation to the fury and the mire of human veins, it becomes a magnificent metaphor for the overwhelming and remorseless complexity of life.

III

Shakespeare's tragedies could be said to constitute a continuing paradoxical pun on the word 'kind' (signifying both natural and loving). Kind, or nature, is kindly, compassionate, binding, creative, as the word implies and many assume; but nature is also pitiless, divisive, violent. 'Commend me to my kind lord', says the dying Desdemona (kindly). She had protested, 'That death's unnatural that kills for loving', but in truth it *was* natural and in kind for 'the noble Moor' (the title itself is oxymoronic) to hate and kill the wife he loved (*Oth.*, v.ii.128, 45; iv.i.261). For Othello's 'I that am cruel am yet merciful' (v.ii.90), we might substitute Hamlet's, 'I must be cruel only to be kind' (*Ham.*, iii.iv.178). The far-reaching imaginative inquiry conducted in the tragedies and crystallised in this paradoxical pun is focussed primarily on the hero, and in particular on his 'noble nature' (*Oth.*, ii.ii.283; iii.iii.203). Shakespeare's conception of nobility has its roots in the chivalric code, with its twin ideal of violence and civility, devotion to war and to ladies. Like Chaucer's Theseus (who appears, of course, in *A Midsummer Night's*

Dream and *The Two Noble Kinsmen*), Shakespeare's noble characters
when seen at their best exhibit the twin forces of nature in a powerfully developed and finely balanced form. The ideal which they
embody is explicitly defined in the description of the young princes
in *Cymbeline*:

> O thou goddess,
> Thou divine Nature, thou thyself thou blazon'st
> In these two princely boys! They are as gentle
> As zephyrs blowing beneath the violet,
> Not wagging his sweet head; and yet as rough,
> Their royal blood enchaf'd, as the rude wind
> That by the top doth take the mountain pine
> And make him stoop to the vale. (IV.ii.170–7)

The dualistic conception of human nature involved here is quite
different to the familiar Christian conception of human nature as
characterised by a psychomachia or battle between virtues and
vices, or between its angelic and its bestial dimensions. Although
the striving, assertive, violent side of the tragic hero's character is
usually instrumental in precipitating disaster, the twin forces in his
nature are not identified with good and evil. The fiery, striving side
of his nature accounts not only for his cruelty and destructiveness
but also for his sense of honour, his 'divine ambition' (fire is the
noblest element because it is the lightest and mounts upward), his
furious hatred of injustice, and his martial role as defender of society. In combination with such attributes, his capacity for love
makes him the hero that he is, a complete man. Love, on the other
hand, can flow by way of grief into a hunger for revenge that knows
no bounds; or by way of jealousy into hatred. It can resort to the
tyrannous misuse of authority, or be exploited by another for in-
human ends, or degenerate into extravagance, sensuality, and
misrule. The perspective in this view of the self is horizontal rather
than vertical, the danger lying not so much in the rebellion of the
lower faculties against the higher as in a state of confusion which
results from the overflowing of limits and boundaries. Not hierarchical order, but a fine balance or mingling which maintains both unity
and distinction is the psychic ideal here. Relevant too is the idea
of the mean, with all its suggestions of musical and mathematical
proportion, and without any of its modern association with medioc-
rity. The bond which simultaneously unites the opposites in nature
and keeps them apart was thought of as a mean between extremes;[47]

thus Aristotle founded his whole ethical theory on the idea of virtue as a mean between the opposites of excess and deficiency.

With Shakespeare as with Chaucer, 'gentle' was a favourite synonym for 'noble', since it could so easily be used in a punning manner to indicate that humanity is no less an attribute of the great man (the 'parfit gentil knyght') than prowess. For that reason, the word 'gentle' can function, like the word 'kind', as part of a fierce oxymoron. Immediately after the brutal murder of Richard II, for example, Bolingbroke enters addressing two of his enthusiastic supporters as 'kind uncle York' and 'gentle [i.e. noble] Percy' (*R2*, v.vi.1, 11): but the Duke of York has just betrayed his own son to the usurper, and the Earl of Northumberland has briskly beheaded four of the King's loyal followers (lines 8–10). The moral chaos which characterises Bolingbroke's world is encapsulated in that emergent tragic hero, Brutus. To his wife and friends he is simply 'gentle Brutus' (*JC*, ii.ii.279; cf. line 273). But when he kills his best friend because he loved honour, valour, and Rome more (iii.ii.13–33), Antony's apostrophe, 'O judgement, thou art fled to brutish beasts, / And men have lost their reason!' (iii.ii.104–5), begins to transform the meaning of '*gentle Brutus*'. For the benefit of those who have missed the grim sunken pun on the proper name, Shakespeare provides a retrospective elucidation in Hamlet's teasing of Polonius–Caesar (killed by Brutus in the Capitol): 'It was a brute part of him to kill so capital a calf there' (*Ham.*, iii.ii.102–3).

This bold piece of wordplay on the name of 'gentle Brutus' is pertinent here, since it illustrates so well the necessarily fragile nature of the perfected self in Shakespeare's conception of psychic unity: its inherent instability and its capacity for sudden transformation. The danger, too, has to be most apparent in men of abundant nature such as Shakespeare chooses for his major tragic heroes. In men so richly endowed, the fine point of balance is necessarily harder to achieve and sustain than in ordinary mortals. These men are great because they are extreme, and tragic because they are extremists: 'The middle of humanity thou never knewest, but the extremity of both ends' (*Tim.*, iv.iii.299–300). And it is surely incorrect to claim, as many have done, that they fall precisely because of their virtues; they fall rather because they are compelled to that point where their noble attributes are perverted and transformed into something quite different. The claim is valid only in the sense that it is their noble qualities which bring them to the boundary where things decline to their confounding contraries.

Marxist critics of Shakespeare, who begin with a firm commitment to the strictly environmentalist view of character and behaviour, argue that the contradictions which characterise Shakespeare's tragic heroes are not meaningfully related to the idea of an unchanging human nature, nor to the idea of unchanging laws encoded in universal nature. They maintain that the contradictions which Shakespeare's exploration of tragic experience discloses are a product of the socio-political conditions which prevailed in England during the sixteenth–seventeenth-century period, and can be properly explained only in terms of those conditions.[48] Such conditions unquestionably exercised a powerful influence on Shakespeare's sense of the contradictory; genetic concerns of this kind, however, must not obscure the textually demonstrable fact that Shakespeare consciously and systematically referred the contradictions which troubled him most to a transhistorical model of human and universal nature. Remarkably too, this procedure is conspicuously evident both at the beginning and the end of his career as a tragedian, and undergoes no fundamental change. This is a point I would like to demonstrate here by way of conclusion.

The hero of the first tragedy, *Titus Andronicus*, is Rome's supreme warrior; he is also a loving father and a peacemaker who mediates successfully in a political dispute which threatens to tear Rome apart. Yet this 'noble-minded' man (i.i.209; cf. lines 120, 158), honoured for his 'gentleness' (line 238), ruthlessly sacrifices a captive Goth as part of his son's funeral rites, deaf to pleadings for pity from the victim's mother; and in a fit of rage he kills another of his sons who challenges his right to dispose of his daughter in marriage exactly as he pleases. 'Thou art a Roman, be not barbarous' (line 378), he is told; but that is exactly what he becomes. His piety proves to be 'cruel, irreligious piety' (line 130), and his sword is turned 'unkindly' (line 86) not only against his family but also against Rome. Literally as well as spiritually, he becomes identified with the Goths, joining forces with them against the city of his birth (the 'violent'st contrariety' of *Coriolanus* (iv.vi.74) is anticipated already). Titus' transformation into his own opposite is clearly understood to be the consequence of his double nature: removed from the discipline of the battlefield, where it brings him great honour, the violence in his nature breaks loose and obliterates his loving kindness. The structure of this character portrait is eloquently simple and stark to the point of grotesquerie.[49]

'Kind Rome' (line 165) too has a dual nature and collapses in the same way into confounding contrariety. In all his Roman tragedies, Shakespeare imputes to this city a unique historical identity. Yet his lifelong attraction to it was arguably due to its association with certain qualities which seemed to him to make it a perfect archetype of the human community.[50] As he would have learned from Virgil, Ovid, and Lucretius (among others), Rome was a city dedicated to both Mars (father of Romulus) and Venus (mother of Aeneas) – to the arts of conquest and of peace. Rome conquered the barbarian world, but (or and) it was also the home of civility – of just law, eloquent pleading, and great poets. And in this conjunction of opposites, it seemed, lay both its singular greatness and its representative character. Rome's specific dedication to Mars and Venus reinforced its larger significance, since the famous but transient union of these two deities, and the birth therefrom of the goddess Harmony, was commonly interpreted as an allegory of universal nature's concordant discord.[51] (What the astrologers said about the conjunctions of the planets Mars and Venus reinforced this mythographical tradition.)[52] As Shakespeare makes abundantly clear in *Othello* and *Antony and Cleopatra*, he was very familiar with the cosmological interpretation of this myth.

In *Titus Andronicus*, the magnificent partnership of martial and civil virtue which constitutes the greatness of Rome collapses. As in all Shakespeare's Roman tragedies, Rome is at war with itself; the major enemy is within. The late emperor's two sons 'strive' ambitiously together 'For rule and empery' (1.i.19–20); the successful one marries Rome's conquered enemy, the Queen of the Goths, and this marriage is at once a symbol and a cause of the confusion which follows. Barbarism – in the form of injustice, cruelty, and contempt for the pleading hand and tongue – reigns in the city of Ovid and Cicero. The parallel between the metamorphosis of the city and of its noblest representative is striking, and one might well infer from it that Titus has simply internalised the contradictions of the state. That, however, does not seem to be Shakespeare's view. His elaborate use of the analogy between the state ('body politic') and the human body – sensationally focussed in the violation and mutilation of Lavinia by the Emperor's step-sons – has the effect of referring socio-political ills to human nature as to their major source. And his shift of the action into the fields and woods (during an imperial hunt) is designed to universalise the contradictions of both the individual and humankind by placing them in the context of general nature. Nature here presents a double face. On the one hand, 'The fields are fragrant, and the woods are green', 'The birds chant melody on every bush', and 'The green leaves quiver with the cooling wind' (II.ii.2; II.iii.12, 14). On the other hand, 'The forest walks' are 'Fitted by kind for rape and villainy' (II.i.116); they are 'ruthless, vast, and gloomy . . . By nature made for murders and for rapes' (IV.i.55, 59). There is 'a double hunt' (II.iii.19) afoot in this setting: one in which men and women enjoy a communal pastime, and one in which they are reduced to the status of helpless animals hunted by 'fell curs of bloody kind' (line 281): 'Single you thither then this dainty doe, / And strike her home by force if not by words' (II.i.117–18). Clearly, then, it is from single nature's double character that the frightful horrors of the tragedy emerge; indeed the young Shakespeare indicates that Tragedy itself finds its origin there: 'O, why should nature build so foul a den, / Unless the gods delight in tragedies?' (IV.i.60–1). In view of the emphasis I have placed on the Knight's Tale as a likely influence on Shakespearian (as well as Kydian and Marlovian) contrariety, it is important to note here that in Chaucer's poem *the wood and the hunt outside Athens* are made to serve an identical symbolic function. Chaucer's conception of the wood seems in turn to derive from Bernardus Silvestris' twelfth-century cosmological epic, the *Cosmographia*, where Silva (i.e. Wood), is the name given to elemental matter, the intractable and contrarious substance which resists being reduced to a stable and coherent form, and is responsible for the bleaker aspects of human history (see chapter 2).

Precisely the same movement of imaginative inquiry as is found in *Titus Andronicus* – a literal and philosophical shift outwards from the individual and the civilised community to the matrix of all things – can be seen in *Romeo and Juliet* and in *King Lear*. But it is perhaps in the flawed *Timon of Athens* that the purpose of such a strategy is most clearly rendered. Timon digs for roots in the woods outside Athens, but finds gold as well; and with this he bribes the discontented Alcibiades to destroy their native city. This could be read as an allegory on the evils of capitalism;[53] but if it is, it is one which traces those evils to basic human instincts, instincts not constructed by historically contingent social formations but intrinsic to universal nature. One long scene is devoted to Timon's contemplation of the fact that the earth, which is nature, is the mother both of nutrition and poison; brings men together in families and cities, divides them in greed and violence. On the one hand:

> Behold the earth hath roots;
> Within this mile break forth a hundred springs;

> The oaks bear mast, the briers scarlet hips;
> The bounteous housewife Nature on each bush
> Lays her full mess before you. (IV.iii.415–19)

On the other hand:

>   Come, damn'd earth,
> Thou common whore of mankind, that puts odds
> Among the rout of nations, I will make thee
> Do thy right nature [i.e. cause strife]. (lines 42–5)

When Timon retreats to the woods, finds himself 'To the conflict-ing elements expos'd' (line 232), and has to dig for roots, he is coming to understand reality, the nature of kind. The Latin for 'root', one might recall, is 'radix', giving us the word 'radical'. Shakespeare's tragedies are radical not just in the sense that they indirectly disclose the contradictions and tensions which affected English society at the end of the sixteenth and the beginning of the seventeenth century. They are radical above all in the sense that they contemplate directly the forces which, Shakespeare believed, sus-tain and confound the individual and society in every age: in ancient Greece, Rome, and Britain; in medieval England and Scotland; in Renaissance Italy and Denmark.[54]

A medieval approach:
Chaucer's tale of love and strife

I have said that the literary background to Shakespeare's use of the contrarious model of nature is entirely native: in *The Spanish Tragedy* and *Tamburlaine the Great*, the model was used by Kyd and Marlowe as a means of illuminating and universalising the contradictions and conflicts of the tragic world; in which practice they seem to have been inspired by the Knight's Tale. In this chapter I wish to approach Shakespeare's tragedies by way of Chaucer's tragi-comical romance and *A Midsummer Night's Dream*, the romantic comedy which overtly reveals Shakespeare's deep and creative engagement with Chaucer's tale at an early stage in his career. Given the essentially comic nature of both works, such a procedure may seem unduly oblique and paradoxical. But it will be remembered that *A Midsummer Night's Dream* continually reflects its author's awareness that the dividing line between comedy and tragedy is often as arbitrary in literature as it is uncertain in life. That kind of awareness is apparent in the Knight's Tale too; and in both works it is inseparable from a natural philosophy which habitually stresses the interdependence, interaction, and potential confusion of opposites. Texts which ground their interpretation of character and event on such a philosophy tend to see the tragic as a collapse in the harmonious union of opposites which is the achieved goal of comedy-and-romance, so that the two kinds can be mutually illuminating as well as provocatively close. It should not surprise us that the literary roots of Shakespeare's tragic contrariety can be traced in the other mode.

I

Critical discussion of the Knight's Tale has increasingly emphasised its elusive complexity. This aspect of the tale can be ascribed in large measure to its dualistic design: concept, emotion, character, and situation are all subject to a process of contrarious juxtaposition and exchange. Given such a design, it is understandable that most attempts nowadays to elucidate and even to characterise the poem seem to involve a running battle with critics who have arrived at diametrically opposite conclusions. Of course the poem itself moves ostentatiously towards a formal resolution of all its human and philosophical conflicts. But its meaning and character are determined by the sum of its parts and not solely by its ending; and one notable effect of the rest of the poem is to suggest that no resolution, agreement, or bond can lay any claim to permanence.

The major division among critics is between those who affirm and those who deny that the poem is essentially optimistic. Many hold that however tragic its implications it endorses a Boethian philosophy which accommodates the miseries of life to a system of divine providence which is rational and just. Others maintain that it radically undermines, or inartistically contradicts, this metaphysic by depicting a world in which men are the helpless playthings of arbitrary forces: 'As flies to wanton boys are we to th' gods . . .'[1]

The critic who cited Gloucester in her essentially tragic reading of the poem might also have quoted Kent's, 'No contraries hold more antipathy / Than I and such a knave', and noted that every affirmative statement or revelation in *King Lear* concerning the nature of humankind and the universe is promptly followed by one of contrary import (and vice versa). My point is that the affinity between the greatest of the *Canterbury Tales* and the greatest of Shakespeare's tragedies is at once more precise and more profound than their common emphasis on the cruel arbitrariness of life. It stems from the fact that each is manifestly the product of an intellectual environment where it was accepted that contrariety is an essential feature of the macrocosm and the microcosm and so of all our attempts to explicate them.

Thus the most fruitful of recent approaches to the dualities and contradictions of the Knight's Tale seems to me to be that indicated by Donald W. Rowe, who points out that the notion of the universe as a system of *concordia discors* was a familiar one in the Middle Ages and can be found not only in Boethius but also in two other authors whom Chaucer is known to have read, Bernardus Silvestris and Alanus de Insulis (Spenser's 'Alane': *Faerie Queene*, VII.vii.9). Rowe argues, further, that this conception had an informing effect on the whole thought and structure of the Knight's Tale. Part I begins and ends with a stark contrast between 'wele' and woe. Part II shows life pervasively conceived in terms of contraries, with the two friends-and-cousins, Palamon and Arcite, driven to despair and mutual hatred by their love of Emelye, and rejoicing when Theseus ordains that they will settle their dispute in the lists. In Part III, division and discord spread from the microcosm to the macrocosm, from the three lovers to the planetary gods. Part IV, presenting the funeral of Arcite followed in due time by the marriage of Palamon, indicates that the tragic cycle of things born to die is enclosed within a comic cycle, marriage being the archetypal image of *concordia discors*, a symbol of love's power to bind the contraries in a harmonious order. That order is Jove's order: although the harmonious conclusion was made possible by the intervention of the malignant Saturn, as well as by the good offices of Theseus, Jove is its prime mover. Saturn does not rule in the macrocosm, and he need not rule in the microcosm if man can let the spirit of mercy in him triumph over the spirit of vengeance and destruction.[2]

Rowe's brief account of the Knight's Tale in terms of discordant concord leaves much to be said on the subject; arguably, too, it requires correction. Although the marriages at the beginning and the end are strongly reminiscent of the discordant concord theme, they are probably insufficient in themselves to establish that universal nature (as distinct, say, from the goddess Fortune) is the ultimate model for the clashing oppositions and contradictions of Chaucer's fictive world. To establish that claim, we must investigate the poem's richly suggestive patterns of symbol, imagery, and wordplay. Chaucer's strikingly original conception of chivalry as a socio-political manifestation of nature's discordant concord must also be recognised. Moreover, Rowe's assumption that the use of *concordia discors* as a frame of reference necessarily entails an optimistic view of the human situation can, I believe, be challenged.

II

Although the main justification for such a challenge lies in the text, the question can profitably be approached by way of Boethius, Bernardus Silvestris, and Alanus de Insulis, the three authors who have most to tell us about the intellectual milieu of this, the most philosophical of Chaucer's Tales. Rowe observes that the notion of *concordia discors* is common to *The Consolation of Philosophy*, the *Cosmographia*, and *The Plaint of Nature*, and sees the three works as forming a kind of philosophical alliance. In fact, however, both Bernardus and Alanus differ considerably from Boethius in the use they make of the common cosmological theme. In *The Consolation of Philosophy*, it contributes to a transcendent vision of unity and justice, whereas in the *Cosmographia* (especially) and in *The Plaint of Nature* it sustains a narrowing concentration on life in time which is by no means comforting. Boethius writes rhapsodically about the way in which Love effects a 'stable feyth' and 'alliaunce perdurable' among the 'contrarious qualities of elemenz', bridling what would otherwise 'make batayle continuely, and striuen to fordo the fassoun of this world'. Briefly, and in effect parenthetically, he adds that mankind would be 'weleful' if it was governed by this same Love that rules the heavens.[3] What Boethius concedes parenthetically, however – that the impulse towards strife, division, and change is ineradicable in human nature – is of great importance for both Bernardus and Alanus. With them we are conscious of the fact that *concordia discors* and *discordia concors* were interchangeable terms from ancient times, and that the world model these terms defined was a singularly ambiguous one, allowing emphasis on either concord or discord, Love or Strife.

The pessimistic strain in Bernardus' cosmological epic is dramatised as a gloomy foreboding at the point where human history is about to begin. After the formation of the megacosm (i.e. macrocosm) out of the confused elements (here personified as Silva), Physis is called upon to create the microcosm out of the same material. From the first, however, the 'violent and teeming state of matter in its primordial confusion terrified the prospective artisan' and seemed quite inappropriate to the formation of a rational being: 'fire warred with moisture, and moisture with fire, and they adopted one another's roles'. Although Physis proceeded determinedly with her task, 'establishing laws and unbreakable bonds to ensure peace', she still found that 'the rough necessity of ever-flowing Silva', rendered doubly unstable by planetary influence, 'lurked close beneath the surface'. Indeed 'at the very point when she was disciplining the material for her destined task, what had flowed into her hands flowed away again, and the shape she had sought to fashion dissolved. Physis was appalled at this inconsistency which hindered her progress and cursed the unbridled lawlessness of her material.'[4] The history of humankind prophetically inscribed in the stars (this passage is echoed in the Knight's Tale) corroborates her misgivings: it is an incongruous mixture of spiritual achievement, violence, and crime.[5] It has to be said that Bernardus' vision of human destiny is formally and perhaps essentially affirmative; but as Winthrop Wetherbee has remarked, this affirmative stance 'rests in almost unresolved coexistence with a genuine pessimism about the obstacles to spiritual advancement presented by the nature and condition of man'.[6]

The pessimistic element in *The Plaint of Nature* is connected with contemporary history (the Iron Age of moral degeneracy and injustice prophesied in Bernardus is said to have come) and explained as a transformation in the nature and effects of love. Initially Love, or Venus, was sub-delegated by Nature to supervise the order of the universe. At first all went well; but in time Love allowed passion to eclipse reason and so began to operate outside the matrimonial, and even outside the heterosexual, bond. And so 'Love wars with Love': no longer a cause of concordant discord, unified plurality, and consenting disagreement, it generates strife, confusion, and incessant change.[7] Thus although there are oblique allusions to the Fall in both Bernardus and Alanus, their anthropological pessimism is spelt out in strictly cosmological terms: its justification lies in the doubleness of nature and its inherent potential for conflict and confusion. To this aspect of their thought Chaucer seems to have been deeply sympathetic when he wrote the Knight's Tale.

III

Chaucer's poem is above all else a tale of chivalry. The essential features of chivalry as they were generally understood stand out with brilliant clarity; yet they are projected in such a way as to suggest that the chivalric world reflects both the structure and the dynamics of the contrarious universe. Chivalry is represented as male prowess moderated and sublimated by love; as war turned into spectacle, game, and fellowship; as pride balanced by humility, the heroic self joined with others in a brotherhood of values. Above all, perhaps, it is a system of bonds – of promises, rules, and reciprocal obligations; more specifically, it is a system of bound opposites, a complex order made up of radically different and even mutually antagonistic impulses. Thus although Chaucer's chivalric world is a magnificently ordered one, the shadow of ambiguity, confusion, and impending transformation hovers continually about its most emphatic gestures and arrangements. It is a superb but temporary, almost illusory, imposition of pattern on process, stability on flux.

Chivalry finds its perfect embodiment in Theseus, the 'noble conquerour' and 'gentil duc'. In all he does, his intention is to establish limits and maintain distinctions, to moderate, mediate, and unite. At the beginning, he marries his defeated enemy, the Queen of the Amazons, and in doing so restores to the 'faire, hardy queene' her true identity, binding her in a relationship which is a union rather than a confusion of opposites: 'mighty Mars the rede' and 'verray wommanhede' (A 1748-9). At the end he arranges a marriage which joins the two warring cities of Thebes and Athens in an alliance that gives the superior partner its due 'obeisaunce' and a happy peace to both. In between these two parallel events his character is unfolded in a series of actions which are all ethically significant. His hatred of lawless will and the cruelty attendant on it is shown by his punishment of the tyrant Creon, by his anger at the secret duel of Palamon and Arcite in the wood, and by his formulation of strict rules for the tournament in which they have to settle their dispute. The compassionate and loving side of his nature is disclosed in his response to the appeals of the widows, of Perotheus, and of Ypolita and Emelye. It is evident also in his alteration of the rules for combat and in the festivities of the tournament – he would avoid 'destruction' of 'gentil blood', 'stynten alle rancour and envye', and make 'eyther side ylik as ootheres brother' (A 2539, 2732-4). Even the funeral rites accorded to Arcite reflect his moral character, showing not only his compassionate humanity but also his sense of balance and moderation, his genius for 'stinting' and harmonising opposite extremes. Just as he sought to temper the 'hoote fare' in the wood by dismissing it as absurd 'game' and 'jolitee' (A 1806-9), so here his 'wake-pleyes' soften the grim reality of the cremation. Like the tournament itself, these games – wrestling 'with oille enoynt', winning and losing 'in no disjoynt' (A 2960-2) – enact a harmony of strife and fellowship.

Theseus' character, however, is neither static nor unitary. Despite the exact parallels between the beginning and end of the poem, there are signs of an ameliorative change in his character, as if we were witnessing the last phase in an ethical evolution. Thus he rescinds the sentence of death on Palamon and Arcite, revises the rules for the tournament, and at the end formally accommodates his own will to that of Athens (ruling 'by oon general assent') and of the First Mover (who 'first made the faire cheyne of love'). All this indicates a movement from 'pride' (A 896) and forceful self-assertion to humble awareness of human interdependence and creaturely dependence. Being a composite of opposites, however, Theseus' character is occasionally confusing and unpredictable; indeed it is obvious that he could have followed a very different path from that which leads to peace and renewal. His war against Creon is prompted by pity and a hatred of tyranny, but his treatment of Creon's subjects is quite pitiless and takes no account of the fact that they were not responsible for the tyrant's actions. His blank refusal to consider a ransom for Palamon and Arcite puts a definitive touch to the conclusion of this chivalrous expedition: in the pages of Froissart, such a refusal would stand out as a tyrannous and unforgivable violation of the spirit of chivalry.[8] This other and terrible self momentarily re-emerges when his hunting expedition is disturbed by the duel of the two young knights: 'Ye shal be deed, by myghty Mars the rede!' (A 1747). It is this same self that will peremptorily send his son by the Amazon Queen to a violent and wholly unmerited death ('Hearing this, Theseus ordered that his son be killed', as one popular mythographer tersely put it.)[9] Chaucer did not have to remind his audience that the sense of an ending which his shapely tale of Theseus possesses is but a pause in the process of mythical history.

Like Theseus of the poem, Palamon and Arcite begin and end as models of chivalric unity. The poem's main concern, however, is with the way in which that unity is violently broken and painfully reconstituted. Between them, the two knights act out in large the paradox of Theseus' expedition against Creon: 'strif and rancour . . . / For love' (A 2784; cf. 1754, 2859). The bond which unites them as friends in arms in rendered trebly sacred by the fact that they are both cousins and blood brothers, each 'ybounden as a knyght' (A 1149) to further the other's interests. Arcite may be the more culpable of the two because he is the first to renounce the bond and because he so explicitly espouses the spirit of chaos: 'Ech man for hymself, ther is noon oother' (A 1149). But the question of relative culpability soon becomes irrelevant. Although the bond is just as binding on Palamon after his cousin rejects it as it had been before, Palamon quickly denies it without scruple. While still in prison he is already lamenting that 'man is bounden' to 'letten of his wille / Ther as a beest may al his lust fulfille' (A 1317–18); and when he overhears Arcite's declarations of love he instantly deems him his 'mortal foo' (displacing Theseus, their 'mortal enemy') (A 1590, 1553) and tries to kill him like a hunted beast (A 1654–9). The animal ferocity of this fight-in-the-wood is ironically underscored by the combatants' preliminary gestures to the knightly code of truth, courtesy, and brotherly affection.

The contradictions in knighthood as here exposed are not fully resolved by the order of the tournament. There is a new emphasis in the imagery on the taming of animality; but the overriding impression is of destructive animal energies barely restrained by the 'golden brydel' (A 2506) of rule and covenant. Palamon and Arcite, moreover, are quite unaffected by the spirit of comradeship and play promoted by Theseus among their followers: 'thise Thebanes two' are still deadly enemies, hungry as tiger and lion for each other's blood (A 2623–4).

Arcite's fatal accident (following his victory in the tournament) restores them to their gentle selves in a development which is at once tragic and comic, movingly beautiful and quite absurd. The 'fierse Arcite' is reconciled to 'his cosyn deere' (A 2676, 2763) and dies with the word 'mercy' on his lips – assuring Emelye, too, that no one is more worthy to be loved than 'Palamon, the gentilman'; describing him as the perfect model of chivalry (A 2788–808). Correspondingly, Palamon's grief for his dead friend Arcite, like his hatred for his mortal foe Arcite, threatens to exceed all bounds, and is 'stynted' only by the compassionate intervention of Theseus after 'certyn yeres' (A 2967–8). The persistent whisper of laughter in all of this does not negate its gravity. Rather, it serves to emphasise the perplexingly metamorphic quality of human nature and experience, and of our feelings about both.

IV

The principal characters in the poem are so dominated by their emotions, and their emotions are so closely linked to the dynamics of universal nature, that the action seems propelled less by individuals than by psycho-physical forces which course through the human and non-human spheres of existence. Here too the pattern is one of duality, conflict, metamorphosis, and confusion. All action results in either joy or woe. More significant, however, is the cause of action, which is to be found in the gentle and the ungentle emotions: in love, pity, and mercifulness on the one hand, and in jealousy, ire, and hatred on the other. There is an obvious distinction between rational and irrational conduct, but even this is subsumed by the central dichotomy. Rational action is inspired less by reasoning and principle than by pity, something which wells up instinctively in the 'gentil herte' (see especially A 1757–78).

Because it is the source of all emotion, and so of all motion and change, the heart is the key image in the poem (as it is, I shall argue, in *King Lear*: see pp. 175–83). It is referred to more than thirty times, most pointedly perhaps when Palamon overhears Arcite in the wood. Arcite laments that 'Love hath his firy dart so brennyngly / Ystiked thurgh my trewe, careful herte'; whereupon Palamon 'thoughte that thurgh his herte / He felte a coold swerd sodeynliche glyde, / For ire he quook' (A 1564–76). The significance of the parallel is twofold: first, the contrary impulses of the heart can by their violence become indistinguishable, creating a kind of chaos within; and second, violence within generates violence without – the idea of killing Arcite has entered Palamon's subconscious mind already. In the clash of swords and spears at the tournament, one of the cousins' followers 'feeleth thurgh the herte-spoon the prikke' (A 2606), and yet no one is killed in that way, Arcite's death being due to a fall from his horse under the influence of Saturn. But the semantic field which establishes the 'meaning' of Arcite's death is constituted of more than a chance fall and a malign planet. It involves every allusion to the heart and the various weapons aimed at it; it even includes, by way of pun, the description of Theseus, Diana's follower, as 'the grete hertes bane' ('al his joye and appetit' is to be so), and the passage on lustful Actaeon turned to 'an hert' by a vengeful Diana and torn apart by his hounds (A 2065–8). It is a semantic field which directs our attention to the detail and wording of the passage describing Arcite's departure from the lists, 'yborn out of the place / With herte soor', 'His brest tobrosten with his sadel bowe' (A 2691–5); it hints too at a link between his final moment, when 'the herte felte deeth' (A 2805), and the moment when he was 'wounded sore' by his first sight of Emelye, declaring: 'The fressche beautee sleeth me sodeynly ...' (A 1115–18). The *narrative* pattern of reconciliation and marriage rendered it desirable that Arcite should not be killed by Palamon; but it is counterpointed by a *poetic* pattern which reveals that Arcite's love, and Palamon's, begot ire, hatred, and death.

The passions of Chaucer's characters here are linked to universal nature not only by their assimilation to the cosmological dialectic of Love and Strife (Hate) but also by their continuous association with the basic constituents of the material world – the four elements, qualities, and humours. Allusion to this quadripartite system of contrariety and union is an outstanding feature of the poem, and strongly affects both its meaning and style. Within the frame of reference that it establishes, the death of Arcite loses even more of its arbitrariness, becoming part of a patterned process of which there is evidence everywhere. In fact, the Knight's diagnostic account of Arcite's last struggle (as elucidated by W.C. Curry) makes it a microcosmic image of that universal process (A 2742–58). As the poison from the wound gathers in his breast, the so-called 'expulsive virtues' seek to eliminate it; the 'retentive virtues' prevail, however, with the result that the hot and dry humours (choler and melancholy) overcome the cold and moist ones (phlegm and blood); the humoral balance is thus destroyed and the man dies.[10] It is significant that this fatal conflict of the qualities and humours in Arcite's body, like the wound to his heart, has been anticipated earlier. After his return to Thebes from prison, the ardour of frustrated love engendered in him an extreme melancholy, turning him from a vigorous young man into the image of a living corpse, 'lene . . . and drye as is a shaft . . . pale as asshen colde' (A 1362–4).

Theseus tells how the First Mover 'bond / The fyr, the eyr, the water and the lond / In certeyn boundes' by means of 'the faire cheyne of love'. The May morning (A 1491–6) when he goes hunting in the wood provides an image of that quadripartite unity gloriously at work.[11] But even there it is shown that perfect elemental unions, like Venus herself, are 'geery' (A 1536), unpredictable; the poem's chief emphasis is on the insistent urge of the elements to flee their bounds and (in Bernardus' phrase) to 'adopt one another's roles'. The most conspicuous elements are fire and water. Since it was held that everything was begotten from a combination of heat and moisture, and that fire is the most active of the elements, this is appropriate. But the main reason for their predominance is their close association with the emotions which govern the action: fire corresponds to passionate love, jealousy, wrath, and hate; water (as tears) to pity and sorrow. Although fire in the end is 'stinted' by water, its terrible power as an instrument of Heraclitean flux is registered throughout. The 'hoote fires' of amorous desire (A 2862; cf. 2320–40, 2383) turn easily into 'the fyr of jalousie' (A 1299), and that in turn leads to the 'eterne fire' (A 2413) of 'Mars the rede'. Before such fires the gentle 'drope of pitee' can vanish as quickly as 'the silver dropes hangynge on the leves' before the rays of 'firy Phebus' (A 920, 1493–6). And what remains then is cold and dry.

In the symbolism of the poem, wood and tree frequently do duty for fire. This is quite common in image patterns based on the four elements;[12] but peculiar to this poem's elemental imagery is its subtle punning on 'asshe'. Only once does Chaucer specify the ash tree, yet even when he uses the word in the other sense he is covertly alluding to the tree, as if hinting at the close affinity between flourishing life and total extinction. The pun is obvious enough in the lines describing Palamon as so altered by 'the fyr of jalousie' that he 'like was to biholde / The boxtree or the asshen dede and colde' (A 1299–1302), and in the description of the melancholy Arcite waxing 'drye as is a shaft; / His eyen holwe, and grisly to biholde, / His hewe falow and pale as asshen colde' (A 1362–4). It is detectable too (since the dead Arcite has just been described as wearing 'a coroune of laurer grene') in the reference to the black garb and 'asshy heeres' of the mourning Palamon (A 2875–83).

The last image is integral to the funeral rite; the other two anticipate it. This brings me to the point that the cremation ceremony – 'the fyr-makynge' (A 2914) – is one of the poem's most powerful symbols-in-action. It has been rehearsed at the start of the story in the burial of Creon's victims; and it is enmeshed in the symbolic texture of the poem by virtue of the fact that it takes place in, and is fuelled by, the same wood where Arcite and Palamon 'burned' with the hot 'fires' of love and aggression. Chaucer's description of the final cremation, the fire to which all other fires have led, brilliantly evokes the destructive and all-consuming nature of unbound passion as expressed in love and combat. This fire frights woodland divinities from the abode where they have lived 'in reste and pees'; it swallows up token tributes of green wood, spicery, cloth of gold, garlands hanging with many a flower, shield and spear and vestment. And it leaves the fierce Arcite 'brent to asshen colde'.

Given its poetic context, that final oxymoronic phrase is even more expressive perhaps than the famous lines,

> What is this world? what asketh men to have?
> Now with his love, nowe in his colde grave
> Allone, withouten any compaignye. (A 2777–80)

Yet it does not encapsulate the full meaning of the funeral rite, let alone of the poem. For 'the service and the fyr-makynge' are a work of sorrowing love and tender respect. The mourners who carry torches and feed the flames do so with 'infinite . . . teeres' (A 2827; cf. 2878, 2884, 2968). In fact their whole behaviour – like their 'eyen rede and wete' (A 2901) – images a return to natural harmony, with fire and water, the red and the white, in perfect agreement once more.[13] In that sense the funeral rite prepares for the marriage of Palamon and Emelye, and the alliance of Thebes and Athens. Arcite once lamented that not one of the four elements, nor any creature made from them, could do him comfort (A 1246–7). Yet the poem seems to say that there is comfort to be found in the knowledge that the most terrible changes in human life are all part of a universal system of 'dynamic permanence' where gain is loss and loss is gain.[14]

In line with a tradition which is as old as Aristotle, Bernardus Silvestris gave to primal matter the name of 'Wood' or 'Forest' (Latin, *Silva*) – hence his own nickname.[15] His attitude to Silva was ambivalent, for he saw her not only as lawless but also as packed with generative energy, fiercely resistant to form yet longing 'in her turbulence for a tempering power', for 'the shaping influence of number and the bonds of harmony'.[16] The wood in Chaucer's poem (as distinct from the trees) has a comparable importance and significance. It is where the lovers fight, where Theseus moderates his anger and builds the lists, where the cremation ceremony takes place. It is 'that selve grove, swoote and grene' (A 2860) where knights and ladies go maying and hunting; and it is one of those 'wodes wilde' (A 2309) where nature is red in tooth and claw and man and beast become undistinguishable. It is a comprehensive symbol of the elemental world in its twin dimensions.

In a significant departure from his source, Boccaccio's *Teseida*, Chaucer has Theseus build his lists in the wood. This has the effect of associating the 'art' (A 2791) of chivalry with that of nature. Building in the woods, Theseus follows the example of Noys or Providence, the craftsman who answered Wood's cry for form, number, and the bonds of harmony. First and foremost, the lists are a limit, bound, or boundary; the word had precisely that meaning before it was used to designate a palisade for tilting, and it continued to be used in that sense.[17] Thus in its context here, the creation of the lists corresponds precisely to the formation of cosmos out of chaos, these being synonymous in Pythagorean–Platonic tradition with limit and limitlessness.[18] In addition, the circular shape of the lists makes it an image of perfect form, suggestive both of the spherical universe and of the separated and harmonised 'Elements ... that in quaternion run / Perpetual circle'.[19] Its amphitheatrical design is indicative of an order based on hierarchy; but the placing of the two great gates at the eastern and western points of the circle, one for Venus and one for Mars, one white and the other presumably red, forcefully defines an order based on the binding of opposites. The temple of Diana at the northern point of the circle seems both right and wrong. It completes the structure in that the gods to whom Palamon, Arcite, and Emelye are devoted are all represented; but by postulating a missing fourth it suggests incompleteness. The missing deity for whom Theseus (a less than perfect Providence) has not prepared, and who subsequently commands an important place in the lists, is Saturn. Chaucer's choice of Saturn (not present in Boccaccio) as the fourth force was felicitous. For as every encyclopaedia (and of course every handbook on astrology and medicine) explained, the qualities of Mars are hot and dry, of Venus warm and moist, of Luna (Diana) cold and moist, and of Saturn cold and dry.[20] In other words, these four planets correspond exactly to the four elements and humours (Saturn was specifically identified with melancholy and Mars with choler).

More noticeable, however, is the simple fact that the number of the ruling gods creates a sense of balance and potential harmony. Perhaps too the four-part division of the poem, a division unique in the *Canterbury Tales*, was intended as an outer reflection of this inner symbolic design – the self-reflexive nature of the poem's structure and style has long been a subject for critical emphasis.[21] Silva's longing – in Bernardus' poem – for 'the shaping influence of number and the bonds of harmony' should be recalled at this point. It was a cosmological commonplace that number originally gave form and limit to primordial nature: 'Take number from all things and all things perish', as Isidore of Seville put it (summarising St Augustine).[22] And in ancient, medieval, and Renaissance numerology the number four held pride of place. The world, it was said, had to be formed out of *four* elements since (a) 'those bodies alone are closely held together which have a mean interposed between to create a strong bond'; (b) 'when that mean is doubled the extremes are bound not only firmly but even indissolubly'; and (c) 'the number four is the first of all numbers to have two means'. The mathematical principle of the mean is recapitulated in the structure of the four elements; each has two qualities which are shared by two of the other elements, so that 'each one of the elements appears to embrace the two elements bordering on each side of it by single qualities'; in this way the warring elements are 'bound . . . together with an unbreakable chain'.[23] Not just the elements, however, but the whole world in its every aspect was thought of as fourfold. The quaternary or tetrad was a schema to be found everywhere in the correspondent universe, functioning as source and sign of unity in multiplicity, harmony in discord, permanence in mutability, friendship in hate, justice in strife.[24]

If quadruple grouping is one way in which Chaucer altered Boccaccio so as to fit the gods more significantly into the life of his fictive universe, astrologising them is another. Since it was accepted that change in the sublunary world is brought about by the action of the planets on the elements, the planetary nature of the gods here has the effect of rooting them more firmly in the rhythms of universal nature. In Chaucer's treatment, however, the gods do not seem so much to determine what happens on the human plane as influence and above all mimic it.[25] Whenever we hear of their well-defined bad and good qualities, we have *already* seen these same qualities vividly at work in men and women, so that it is perfectly easy to imagine the action proceeding as it does without them. With rulers like Creon ('Fulfild of ire and of iniquitee') and Theseus ('he nolde no raunsoun'), and with friends like each other, Palamon and Arcite have no need to invoke the fickleness, cruelty, jealousy, and 'woodnes' of the gods as the cause of their miseries. Conversely, the pity of Ypolita and Theseus, and their own love for each other, would be enough to account for everything good in their lives. The poem's gods are not transcendent, omnipotent beings; they are immanent in nature, as much a part of it as are the elements and humankind. It is not to them but to the complex laws of nature itself (and beyond that, if at all, to the transcendent First Mover) that we must look for an explanation of what happens.

The cruel and violent aspects of the gods, it is often noted, are strongly emphasised. To seek to obscure this emphasis would be to give an unbalanced picture of the poem; yet we must not overlook the fact that the nature of each of the gods is shown to be contrarious.[26] This means that, like the elements, they have common qualities which enable them to come from time to time into peaceful and beneficent conjunctions. Diana is 'goddesse of clene chastitee' (A 2326) and ruthless with those (like Actaeon) who cannot control their sexuality; but she is also the goddess of childbirth and is agreeable from the start to the plan to marry Emelye to one of the cousins. As Venus' true servant, Palamon promises to 'holden werre alwey with chastitee' (A 2236), yet both he and Venus are pleased to accept that his happiness lies within the chaste bounds of marriage. And whereas the Venus depicted in the temple is an aggressive deity who brings misery and shame, the Venus whose 'heighe servyse' is integral to the rituals of chivalry (A 2487) is a noble figure who harmonises pleasure and restraint.

Unlike 'faire, yonge, fresshe Venus' (A 2386), Saturn is old, cold, pale and unloving; yet she is his 'deere doghter', so that although in one sense it is 'agayn his kynde' to 'stynten strif' between her and Mars (in the quarrel as to whose devotee should win in the lists), in another sense it is not. The fatal accident he visits upon the triumphant Arcite, Mars' devotee, proceeds from his benevolence rather than his notorious malevolence; and although from one point of view it is a cruel and meaningless catastrophe, from another it is not. It brings about a genuine reconciliation between the two friends, together with a full renewal of their nobility; and it allows for a marriage union unclouded by jealousy and regrets.

Then there is Mars the red, strife and division itself. Those who are of his 'divisioun' or company are all identified with severance: the barber, the butcher, the smith 'That forgeth sharpe swerdes', Conquest with a sharp sword hanging above him 'by a soutil twynes threed' (A 2023–30). Yet the pun on 'divisioun' is a reminder of the paradox that Mars can unite men as comrades under his banner; and it is not to his wrath but to his pity that his servant Arcite appeals (A 2378, 2392, 2418). He and Venus are 'noght of o compleccioun', a fact which 'causeth al day swich divisioun'; but as Saturn notes, 'ther moot be som tyme pees' between them (A 2474–6). The famous occasion when 'Mars, the stierne god armypotente' (A 2441) was discovered 'liggynge by' Vulcan's wife and 'haddest her in armes' at his will is remembered (A 2386–90). Again there is a pun – on the arms of love and of war – which is crucial. It has already occurred in much more overt form in Palamon's prayer to Venus (A 2247–8), and it has been lightly anticipated in the early picture of the 'Two yonge knyghtes liggynge by an by, / Both in oon armes, wroght ful richely' (A 1011–12). The same pun is conspicuously present in a key passage of Chaucer's *The Complaint of Mars*:

> And thus in joy and blisse I lete hem duelle.
> This worthi Mars, that is of knyghthood welle,
> The flour of feyrnesse lappeth in his armes,
> And Venus kysseth Mars, the god of armes. (lines 74–7)

Pointing to the possibility of concord between Love and Strife, the repeated puns on 'divisioun' and 'armes' underline the centrality of Mars and Venus in the mythological structure of the Knight's Tale.[27] The metamorphic identities and relationships of the forces they symbolise are the primary source of order and chaos and weal and woe in the imaginative world of the poem. Like other medieval poets, and like the favourite mythographers of the time, Chaucer seems not to have known the classical interpretation of the Mars–Venus–Harmonia myth as an allegory of nature's concordant discord, an interpretation which was to find much favour in the Renaissance.[28] Astrology, however, provided him with the comparable notion of these and other contrary gods coming into temporary and beneficent conjunctions and functioning as part of a larger harmony: 'Venus abatith the malice of Mars, as Ptholomeus saith'; 'Iubiter by his goodnes abatith the kynde malice of Saturnus'.[29] All four of the planetary gods in the Knight's Tale are brought into a relationship of concordant discord in its dénouement; but the device of Saturn – giving triumph in battle to Arcite and in love to Palamon – is such as to foreground what is already implicit in the marriage of Theseus and Ypolita, a union of Mars and Venus.

V

Besides functioning as symbols of natural processes, the planetary gods are associated with Fortune and Destiny and interpreted by Theseus in the Boethian manner as the irrational agents of a rational Providence.[30] A 'providential' explanation of events is certainly not inconsistent with the way in which the narrative of strife and reconciliation has been presented. But it does seem to operate on the periphery of the poem's emphases. Most of its authority as a clue to the meaning of events rests on Theseus' lengthy concluding speech; in general, too, its articulation is rhetorical rather than narrative and poetic. The truth is that almost all of Chaucer's imaginative resources have been expended on the functioning of a natural order whose sympathies, antipathies, and unchangeably dualistic design lend intelligibility to everything that happens. Rowe speaks of a comic, providential cycle enclosing the tragic cycle of human mortality, but the notion of enclosure seems to me to beg the question. The impression is rather of a relationship between the comic (the forces that make for unity) and the tragic (the forces that make for division and destruction) which is at once both cyclical and dialectical: each in turn encloses and is productive of the other, neither has ultimate sway. The narrator's 'concluding' comment on the lastingly gentle and unjealous union of Palamon and Emelye is obviously tinged with irony; and we are surely not meant to forget at the end either the sexual infidelities of Theseus (so disapprovingly recalled in Chaucer's Legend of Ariadne) or the tragic death of his son by the Amazonian Queen. In sum, this is a poem in which, as it were, the sublime assurances of Boethius do little to silence the complaints of Bernardus and Alanus concerning 'the crude necessity of ever-flowing Silva' and the war of 'Venus with Venus'.

In a properly providential treatment of the poem's chief tragic event, the death of Arcite,[31] much emphasis would rest on the immortality of the soul and the existence of an afterlife where joy is endless and justice perfect. But the narrator airily expresses complete ignorance as to where Arcite's soul may have gone; and, although Arcite is a pagan, Chaucer did not have to impute such an observation to the Knight – it is almost as if he is exploiting the story's pagan setting as a way of precluding any clear-cut commitment to providentialism.[32] Moreover, Theseus' subsequent reference to the way in which Jupiter 'converts' all things to their proper source is too abstract and generalised to counteract the negative effect of the Knight's remark. Again, if a providential view of the world were essential rather than peripheral to the poem's concerns, certain incidents would be powerfully stamped with the impression of a benign, transcendent deity intervening to direct the course of things. The *narrator* sees Theseus' arrival in time to separate Palamon and Arcite as just such an incident (A 1673); but the crucial redirection of events at this point may be regarded as due rather to the triumph of human compassion over human wrath. Like *King Lear*, the Knight's Tale advances but neither confirms nor rejects a providential view of the universe. Like *King Lear*, too, it suggests that if there is a divine providence at work in the world it will be detected, if anywhere, in the miracles of human love and forgiveness.

Whether the poem's metaphysics are providentialist or not is, however, a much less pressing question than whether its view of human existence is essentially optimistic or pessimistic (although the questions overlap, they are nonetheless distinguishable). Here a meticulously pluralist reading is desirable; or, rather, a recognition that the poem, being so completely impregnated by the notion of nature's concordant discord (or discordant concord), achieves a unity which embraces, not one which eschews, contradiction. It shows triumphs of pity, kindness, reason, and ceremonious order in human life; and, inextricably linked with all these, cruelty, fury, blind will, and anarchy. It shows change and catastrophe which make a mockery of human expectations and yet entail unforeseen effects of moral and material good. Convinced optimists and pessimists alike will find little difficulty in persuading themselves that, on balance, their own conception of the way things are is finally endorsed by the poem; but in reaching such a conclusion they will have contracted an astonishingly inclusive vision of life. Like Cleopatra's Antony ('painted one way a Gorgon, / The other way a Mars'), the image of life offered by this poem can profitably be compared to a perspective picture, one of those 'curious . . . Optick Prismes which seem to change shape and colours, according to the several stances from which the aspicient views them'.[33]

VI

The Knight's Tale is a poem of immense intellectual subtlety and formal sophistication, one which gives philosophic depth to chivalric romance by examining chivalry's conception of the noble self and the noble society in the context of a dialectical world view. Not surprisingly, it was the most popular of all the *Canterbury Tales* throughout the English Renaissance.[34] Moreover, its impact on creative endeavour in the period was greater than that of any other of Chaucer's poems, *Troilus and Criseyde* not excepted. Before Shakespeare turned to it in the writing of *A Midsummer Night's Dream*, (c.1596), it had been twice adapted for the stage (both plays are now lost). More important, and as has long been known, it was brilliantly adapted by Spenser in Cantos ii and iii of Book iv of *The Faerie Queene* (written c.1593, published 1596), and it seems indeed to have affected the whole conception and design of that book. Essentially, The Legend of Friendship is a completion of Chaucer's unfinished Squire's Tale along lines suggested by the Knight's Tale. Its theme is the disruption of friendship-and-love by strife and its eventual restoration through concord. The common theme too is placed in the context of nature's concordant discord – 'this worlds faire workmanship' (iv.i.30) – by explicit reference,[35] elemental imagery,[36] mythological allegory,[37] and, above all, by Pythagorean number symbolism. Book iv surpasses all the others in *The Faerie Queene* in the richness of its number symbolism,[38] and the dominant number is four: the number of the elements, of amity and concord, of opposites reconciled. In the Knight's Tale the death of Arcite means that the story ends neatly with two married couples; three of these individuals have been at war (Theseus with Palamon, Theseus with Ypolyta), and one of them (Palamon) is now married to his former enemy's sister-in-law: a grouping which reinforces the symbolic significance of the four planetary deities and the poem's quadripartite structure. Spenser's adaptation of Chaucer's plot in the second and third cantos is numerologically more complex and matches more exactly the pattern of nature's contrarious order. The tournament arranged to resolve 'unquiet strife' among 'warlike wooers' (IV.ii.37, 38) involves *four* knights, two of whom are killed. The two marriages which crown the ending occur simultaneously and both married knights have been involved in the tournament; moreover, each knight marries the other's sister, so that the reconciliation of binary opposites in the quadruple pattern is secured by two 'means'. Of course the story of Cambell, Triamond, Cambina, and Canacee constitutes only one episode in the narrative design of Book IV. However, quadruple grouping is the dominant structural principle in all of the other episodes: 'friendship is shown as occurring, not between pairs of characters, but among groups of four'; moreover, personal and interpersonal concord is seen to be dependent, like cosmic concord, on the completion of tetrads with double mean terms.[39] In addition, composition by units of four stanzas is a characteristic feature of the book as a whole.[40]

As we shall see, the way in which Spenser mediated the Chaucerian use of a contrarious world model seems to have had a considerable influence on *A Midsummer Night's Dream*. But even before the composition of Book IV of *The Faerie Queene* in 1593, two authors whose work was of enormous significance for the development of Renaissance tragedy appear to have found inspiration in the Knight's Tale and so served as another source of mediation. In Kyd's *The Spanish Tragedy* (c.1585–90) and Marlowe's *Tamburlaine the Great* (1587–8), elemental imagery, the Mars–Venus relationship (both mythological and astrological), and quadruple patterning are all combined in the service of an imaginative strategy which gives cosmic significance to the protagonist's experience of love and strife.[41] In this as in so many other respects, *The Spanish Tragedy* is by far the more important of the two plays. Its influence, both direct and indirect, stretches throughout the whole period.

In collaboration with John Fletcher, Shakespeare was to provide a full-scale dramatisation of the Knight's Tale in *The Two Noble Kinsmen* at the end of his career (c.1613). Any extended discussion of a work which was written some five or six years after the last of his tragedies would be unwarranted here. But it is worth stressing that Shakespeare's willingness to undertake this co-operative venture seems like a final and overt admission of his great indebtedness to that 'noble breeder', 'Chaucer, of all admired' (Prol., lines 10–13). And some note should be taken of the extent to which this play, for all its imaginative thinness, reiterates and elucidates themes from which so much of Shakespeare's work has been 'bred'. Both in characterisation and plot, the conflict, balance, and harmony of opposites is the informing principle; tragi-comedy finds its rationale in nature's *discordia concors*. Beginning with the sudden eclipse of matrimonial joy by funeral grief (Theseus' wedding is postponed until the end because of the widows' appeal), it concludes with a gentle modulation of funeral into marriage. Apart from the description of the souls of Emilia and Flavinia united in love 'like the elements / That know not why, yet do effect / Rare issues in their operance' (1.iii.61–3), there is a notable lack of any attempt to ground the central themes in the dynamics of nature by means of elemental and associated natural imagery. But the Mars–Venus myth is decisively foregrounded. The tournament which is designed to resolve the conflict within and between the two noble kinsmen is explicitly presented as an attempt to mediate between the rival claims of the two deities (v.iv.105–9). And its symbolic status is further enhanced by quadruple patterning – the contestants in this tournament are reduced to two groups of four, and a pyramid, emblematic of the number four and the emergent natural order (Plato, *Timaeus*, 55a), is placed beside them as the goal which the victor must touch (III.vi.292–6; v.iii.80). The relationship between Theseus and Hippolyta, and between the polar qualities of their noble characters, enacts the dialectic of the Mars–Venus myth in a manner which recalls Shakespeare's use of the same myth in *Antony and Cleopatra*, and creates echoes as well of *Othello* and *Macbeth*. By subduing both the force and the affection of the Amazon Queen, Theseus ('a deity equal with Mars' (1.iv.16)) prevents her from making the male sex her captive and shrinks her into the 'bound' – dictated by 'Nature' – that she was 'o'erflowing' (1.i.80–5). The ensuing marriage perfects their individual characters and generates balance and harmony. Hippolyta proves to be a 'soldieress / That equally canst poise sternness with pity' and 'make Mars spurn his drum' (lines 86–7, 182); Theseus' love for her is such that his harshness habitually succumbs to her womanly call for compassion. Thus – in perfect 'poise' – Hippolyta surrenders and conquers and Theseus conquers and surrenders. In its perfected form (as distinct from the gross state of confusion into which it had earlier degenerated (III.i.35–42)), the gentleness or nobility of the two noble kinsmen is defined in similar terms; and like the relationship of Theseus and Hippolyta, it forms a chiasmic order which reflects the containing structural pattern of 'marriage–funeral: funeral–marriage'. 'Arcite is gently visaged, yet his eye / Is like . . . a sharp weapon / In a soft sheath' (v.iii.41–3). Palamon has 'a most menacing aspect', but his 'sadness is a kind of mirth, / So mingled as if mirth did make him sad, / And sadness merry' (lines 44–53) – as Cleopatra said of Antony's temperament, 'O heavenly mingle!' (*Ant.*i.v.59). Here, unquestionably, are the psychology, ethics, and aesthetics of nature's concordant discord.

In terms of plot and character, Shakespeare's indebtedness to the Knight's Tale in *A Midsummer Night's Dream* was much less extensive than in *The Two Noble Kinsmen*: to it are owed 'the framing action of Theseus and Hippolyta, the setting in Athens and the nearby woods (in which the two rivals intend to fight over a girl), the hunting scenes, and the final wedding celebrations'.[42] In terms of theme, however, the debt was profound; for this is a comedy and a 'story of the night' whose extraordinary mingling of the light and the dark is rooted in the notion of nature's concordant discord:[43] Theseus' jesting query, 'How shall we find the concord of this discord?' is a major clue to what this most ingenious and ambitious of comic artefacts is all about. *A Midsummer Night's Dream* is alone among the comedies in having a comprehensive sense of nature's unstable, confusing, contrarious order. For that reason, no doubt, none of the other comedies (problem comedies included) has so many links with tragedy.

Some of the play's complex but controlled and significant patterning may be due to the way in which the Chaucerian legacy has been mediated by Spenser and stamped with his intense fondness for 'the numbers of creation'; but whether due to Spenser or not, this aspect of the play requires emphasis here, since it constitutes an element in Shakespeare's symbolic strategies that will be much more apparent in *Julius Caesar* and *Macbeth*. The Spenserian parallels are most conspicuous in the proliferation of quadruple units, clearly used as a collective symbolic reflection of 'this world's fair workmanship'. Although the duration of the action turns out to be no more than one full day, the play opens with Theseus and Hippolyta pronouncing – during the last quarter of the moon – that their marriage will not take place for four days: 'four happy days . . . Four days will quickly steep themselves in night; / Four nights will quickly dream away the time' (i.i.2, 7–8). If at the end one has the impression that four days have been magically encapsulated in one, that feeling would be entirely appropriate. For this remarkably heterogeneous but subtly integrated play is made up of four stories, fuses four worlds. Its central story, too, is about four characters whose lapse from love and friendship mirrors the strife and confusion which concurrently affects the relationship of the four elements and the four seasons: these break their bounds (bonds) and 'change their wonted liveries' so that it is impossible to tell 'which is which' (II.i.81–114). When the lovers' disordered relationships are about to be sorted out by Puck and Oberon, and 'gentle concord' (IV.i.140) restored, the numerical form both of discord (two men in love with one of the women and then with the other) and of concord is emphasised: 'Yet but three? Come one more, / Two of both kinds makes up four' (III.ii.437–8). As happy attendants at the court of Theseus in the last scene, the four lovers faintly echo the 'four Fairies' who attend on Bottom in a spirit of joyous partnership during his royal interlude with Titania (III.i.148, Qq.SD).

In this natural order, of course, unity is binary at root, two-in-one. There is in *A Midsummer Night's Dream* a combined emphasis on oneness and twoness which relies on the accepted meanings of the first two digits in Pythagorean numerology; this recalls Books I and II of *The Faerie Queene* and, more importantly (as we shall see later), it anticipates *Macbeth* and to a lesser degree *Othello*. One (the monad) was held to be no number at all but rather the origin of all number; it is therefore goodness itself, or God,[44] and is further identified with truth and light. Two (the dyad), is what breaks away from unity and limit; it is evil and is associated with the material world, and with rebellion, error, duplicity, confusion, darkness, and devilry. Says Plutarch:

Pythagoras affirmeth, that of the two first principles Unitie was God, and the sovereign good; which is the very nature of one, and is Understanding it selfe; but the indefinite binarie, is the divell and evill, about which is the multitude material, and the visible world.[45]

The dyad was especially associated with human nature, composed of and afflicted by, the 'tragic dualities' of soul and body, mind and flesh.[46] The dyad is good only when its components are distinguished and bound together in a concordant marriage; its characteristic tendency, however, is to transform unified duality into doubleness, duplicity, doubtfulness, excess. 'Double, double, toil and trouble'.

The symbolic significance of one and two would have been firmly imprinted on the minds of Elizabethan readers by Books I and II of

The Faerie Queene, where they give their names to the heroine, Una, and the villainess, Duessa: the first identified with truth and light, the second with falsehood, error, and darkness. Particularly instructive, however, was the allegorical portrait in Book IV of Ate, the Greek deity of strife and discord to whom Duessa there turns for assistance:

> Her face most fowle and filthy was to see,
> With squinted eyes contrarie wayes intended,
> And loathly mouth, unmeete a mouth to bee,
> That nought but gall and venim comprehended,
> And wicked wordes that god and man offended:
> Her lying tongue was in two parts diuided,
> And both the parts did speake, and both contended;
> And as her tongue, so was her hart discided [cut in two],
> That neuer thoght one thing, but doubly stil was guided.
>
> Als she double spake, so heard she double,
> With matchlesse eares deformed and distort,
> Fild with fals rumors and seditious trouble,
> Bred in assemblies of the vulgar sort,
> That still are led with euery light report.
> And as her eares, so eke her feet were odd,
> And much unlike, th'one long, the other short,
> And both misplast; that when th'one forward yode,
> The other back retired, and contrarie trode. (i.27–8)

Readers of this kind of literature would quickly have picked up the larger implications in Shakespeare's playing on oneness and twoness in *A Midsummer Night's Dream*, seeing it as intrinsic to his imaginative commentary on nature's ever-changing, quadripartite world. It occurs very conspicuously in Lysander's lyrical account of his love for Hermia and in Helena's even more lyrical version of her friendship with Hermia. Lysander tells Helena that because they have 'two bosoms interchained with an oath', 'two bosoms and a single troth', it follows that 'one turf' should 'serve as pillow for us both': 'One heart, one bed, two bosoms, and one troth' (II.ii.41–50). Two scenes later (III.ii.203–14), Helena reminds Hermia:

> We, Hermia, like two artificial gods,
> Have with our needles created both one flower,
> Both one sampler, sitting on one cushion,
> Both warbling of one song, both in one key,
> As if our hands, our sides, voices and minds,
> Had been incorporate. So we grew together,

> Like to a double cherry, seeming parted,
> But yet an union in partition,
> Two lovely berries moulded on one stem;
> So, with two seeming bodies, but one heart,
> Two of the first, like coats in heraldry,
> Due but to one, and crowned with one crest.

In the first situation, however, Hermia gently but firmly construes Lysander's protestation as sexual duplicity rather than earnest integrity. She detects a warning equivocation in his use of the word 'lie' and urges him to 'lie further off, in human modesty'; their oneness will last only if they maintain a due degree of 'separation' (II.ii.53–8). Here indeed, albeit in a lighthearted key, unified duality is presented as incipient doubleness and confusion. In the later situation, where all four lovers converge, dyadic confusion of a most painful kind (the painfulness counterbalanced by farce) prevails; and it is reinforced with suggestions of limits collapsing and darkness enveloping all. Helena recalls her 'ancient love' for Hermia only to accuse her of rending it asunder (III.ii.215): having wrongly interpreted the love declarations of Lysander and Demetrius as hate's derision, she wrongly interprets Hermia's friendly attitude as the hypocrisy of an *agent provocateur*: all these protestations of love and friendship add up, in her view, to a 'cunning ... devilish-holy fray' where 'truth kills truth'. And Hermia has similar problems. Coming upon the other three in the wood, she recognises Lysander first – by his voice:

> Dark night, that from the eye his function takes,
> The ear more quick of apprehension makes;
> Wherein it doth impair the seeing sense,
> It pays the hearing double recompense. (lines 177–80)

The word 'double' ironically signals her impending confusion: when her lover declares that he now hates her, she tells him, 'You speak not as you think' (line 191), and later declares that if he speaks in 'earnest' rather than in 'jest', then they cannot be the same people: 'Am not I Hermia? Are not you Lysander' (lines 273, 277, 280). What Helena says is equally baffling to her and leads to complete mutual misunderstanding: 'I am amazed at your passionate words; / I scorn you not; it seems that you scorn me' (lines 220–1). Yet Hermia descends to the same 'fierce vein' as the men, driven by their words and Helena's 'past the bound / Of maiden patience'. She loses her 'gentle tongue' (line 287) and furiously tells Demetrius: 'Hence-

forth be never number'd among men! ... with doubler tongue /
Than thine, thou serpent, never adder stung!' (lines 65–73).
And like the men, she passes from words of hatred to threats of
physical violence: she will tear out the eyes of her dearest friend (line
298). What we are shown then in this climactic scene is a farcical
model of chaos (strife and hate eclipsing love, violent transformation, lost identities, total confusion) in numbered form: a 'war' (line
408) of four following on the collapse of oneness into doubleness.

Hermia's metaphor for deadly duplicity recalls the nightmare in
which a 'crawling serpent' clung to her breast (an obvious reflection
of her fears about Lysander's 'lying' too close). The venomous,
double-tongued serpent is a major image in the play, its function
being to establish a correspondence between the duality of human
nature and of nature at large. The correspondence is echoed in the
language of the fairies. In their lullaby for the Queen, Titania's
attendants banish 'snakes with double tongue' and other offensive
creatures, and call instead for 'Philomel with melody' (II.ii.10–24).
This anticipates the end of the play, when all the fairies come to
bless the palace and its sleeping lovers. Here the fairies themselves
are beautifully birdlike: they dance 'trippingly', 'as light as bird
from briar', and give 'to each word a warbling note' (lines 383–5).
Yet the whole emphasis in their light tetrameter couplets is on the
menacing forces which encompass the sleeping lovers: the 'screech-
ing' (line 365) bird of death, the roaring lion, the howling wolf,
Nature's hand that blots nativity with mole, hare-lip, and scar. Even
when Puck steps out of character at the end to address the 'gentles'
in the audience, he expresses an actor's fear of 'the serpent's tongue'
among them (line 422).

Although the outdoor setting for the action is extended to become
'the world of nature itself',[47] so that we hear of mountains, rivers,
meads, and skyscapes, the focal point of this setting is undoubtedly
the wood. Shakespeare's wood carries essentially the same significance as Chaucer's; it is modified, however, so as to symbolise not
only the doubleness of nature but also its consequent capacity for
generating confusion. The wood is a place where gentle folk not only
become wild but also get hopelessly lost. It is a labyrinth, a 'maze'
(II.i.99), where 'every thing seems double' and therefore 'undistinguishable' (IV.i.184–7); where the 'mazed' wanderer 'knows not
which is which' (II.i.113–14). Chaucer's poem undoubtedly generates in the reader confusingly ambivalent feelings about human and
universal nature; here, however, those feelings are objectified in the

'amazement' to which the lovers – bewildered by the changes in each other – repeatedly give expression (III.ii.221, 344; IV.i.143).

It is apt that the fairies should be so conscious of the harshness as well as the beauty of nature since they themselves are embodiments of natural contrariety. They have superhuman powers, but they can make human mistakes. They love and are kindly, but they are capable of jealousy, derision, and fury. Their 'brawls' (II.i.87) may be dances (French bransles) or shindies, images of cosmos or chaos; and the 'debate' and 'dissension' between their King and Queen is such as to cause 'distemperature', sterility, and confusion in the macrocosm and the microcosm (lines 81–117). 'Spirits of another sort' than those 'Damned spirits' who have 'wilfully themselves exiled from light' (III.ii.382–8), they are folk forms of the so-called elemental spirits (of Platonic origin) who inhabit the four elements.[48] As such, they are Shakespeare's equivalent of Chaucer's planetary gods. Although supernatural and immortal, they are in a sense more natural – more passionately alive and contradictory – than mere mortals. They complicate and resolve the difficulties of the four lovers, but they are essentially an imaginative shorthand for those natural forces which have already united, divided, and confounded the lovers.

Set in decisive contrast to the wood and its permanent and transient inhabitants are Athens, home of law and civility, and Theseus and Hippolyta, a royal pair knit together in a marital union which reflects their own integrated and stable personalities. Theseus is introduced as a ruler conspicuously determined to distinguish between opposites and avoid confusion: he wooed Hippolyta with his sword, but he will wed her in another key; he dismisses Melancholy and its pale companions to funerals and will admit only the pert and nimble spirit of youth to his wedding celebrations. In the last scene, he begins by exhibiting the same determination: not for him an Athenian eunuch singing the battle of the Centaurs to a harp, nor 'some satire keen and critical, / Not sorting with a nuptial ceremony' (v.i.44–5, 54–5). His benign acceptance of the artisans' 'very tragical mirth' (line 57) would seem to reverse this attitude completely; in fact, however, it represents a logical progression beyond it to that higher plane of order where opposites are accepted, distinguished, and harmonised. Hippolyta has earlier recalled her delight in the 'musical confusion / Of hounds and echo in conjunction' when every region of the earth 'Seem'd all one mutual cry . . . so musical a discord, such sweet thunder' (IV.i.107–15). Applying this attitude to the social situation of courtly audience and hard-handed players, Theseus finds the answer to his own key question, 'How shall we find the concord of this discord?' (v.i.60), in the kindness and love of which all 'gentle' folk are capable:

> The kinder we, to give them thanks for nothing. (line 89)

> Love, therefore, and tongue-tied simplicity,
> In least speak most, to my capacity. (lines 104–5)

However, Theseus' status in the play as source and symbol of an ideal unity is arguably more provisional than it was even in the Knight's Tale; and this uncertain status is implicitly associated with the uncertain borderline between comedy and tragedy in life and on the stage. To anyone reasonably familiar with the Theseus legend and some of its major texts, the play seems a strange and wonderful interlude, quite at variance with, yet uncannily evocative of, a dark past and an even darker future. It is very pertinent here that whereas in Chaucer Theseus' wedding is the story's point of departure, with Shakespeare it is at once climax and containing framework. For here the emphasis is not on Theseus as an achieved embodiment of the martial and the venerean attributes, harsh valour and compassionate love (though it will be so in *The Two Noble Kinsmen*). It is on Theseus as the stable centre of society's matrimonial and familial order: that order which holds in check the passionate energies that threaten continuity and permanence in the human world. This emphasis is ultimately ironical; the irony is quiet and remote, but it is nonetheless an important element in the play's extraordinary resonances. Theseus' role as patron of marital and social order is called in question by Oberon's incidental but nonetheless arresting recollection that he ravished Perigouna and broke faith with Aegles, Ariadne, and Antiopa (II.i.78–80). Oberon cannot rightly be accused of jealous forgery here, for Theseus' reputation as a sexual adventurer and an utterly faithless lover and husband was as well established as was his reputation for conquest and rule; moreover, it was fresh in Shakespeare's mind while he wrote this play, for it was heavily emphasised by four of his source texts: Chaucer's *Legend of Good Women* and Ovid's *Metamorphoses* (both consulted for the Pyramus and Thisbe story), and Seneca's *Hippolytus* and Plutarch's *Life* of Theseus.[49] We must assume therefore that Theseus' self-presentation in the opening scene as the model of ordered relationships and marital love – promising an 'everlasting bond of fellowship' between himself and his new wife, and proposing (as he makes his exit) to 'school' Demetrius for having abandoned the lady he wooed and won with showers of oaths (lines 86, 116) – is to be viewed with some wonderment. Demetrius, the 'spotted and inconstant man' (line 110) who is to suffer a private rebuke, is his master's *alter ego*: change places and, handy dandy, which is which?[50]

Reverberations from the darker side of the Theseus myth can be heard elsewhere. The Fairy Queen's passion for *Bully* Bottom, half beast and half man ('O monstrous!' (III.i.99)), is the Cretan queen's passion for the sacrificial bull in another key.[51] Pasiphae's union with the bull begot the Minotaur, half bull and half man, and caused the labyrinth to be built (so as to conceal the hideous monster). Of that famous artefact there are insistent echoes in the punning motif of 'amazement'. Of course the story of the monstrous maze has general application in the play. Not only does it evoke Theseus' heroic destruction of the monster and his betrayal of Ariadne (who helped him conquer the maze, and whom he swore he loved and would marry). It also functions as a symbol for passionate love and its power to transform, degrade, and confuse its victims; as such, it has reference to all those in the play (foolish mortals and immortals alike) who are unable to reconcile love and reason.

At the end of the play, however, there are ironic reverberations from the myth which impinge mainly on Theseus. Delivering the matrimonial blessing, Oberon promises that 'all the couples three / [shall] Ever true in loving be' (v.i.393–4). But Theseus did not reform when he married the Amazon queen. In some versions of the myth, he is said to have killed her;[52] and whatever did become of her, her successor in the bridal bed, Phaedra, was embittered by his infidelities and partly driven by them into her fatal passion for Hippolytus, his son by Hippolyta.[53] Oberon's assurance that the issue of Theseus and Hippolyta 'ever shall be fortunate' (line 396) seems particularly strange, since Theseus (as already noted) caused the death of Hippolytus, having been roused to a fury by Phaedra's spiteful claim that the virtuous youth had raped her (when in fact she had tried to seduce him). This notorious blot on Theseus' record was uppermost in Plutarch's mind when, in the course of enumerating the great man's rapes, abductions, and adulteries, he remarked of the marriages: 'their beginnings had no great good honest ground, neither fell out their endes very fortunate'.[54]

To the very end, Shakespeare's comedy follows 'darkness like a dream'. The last part of Oberon's prayer refers to Theseus' palace: 'each several chamber bless / Through this palace with sweet peace; / And the owner of it blest / Ever shall in safety rest' (lines 406–9). In Seneca's sombre and heavily symbolic tragedy *Hippolytus*, Theseus returns from a sexual escapade to find that the palace in which he left Phaedra and Hippolytus is another labyrinth. It is dark with secrecy and riddling evasion, it requires all his legendary skill in threading a way through winding passages, and it largely defeats him: Hippolytus, conceived as yet another youthful victim of the Minotaur, is dead before Theseus properly identifies the 'monstrous' passion. Phaedra commits suicide, too, and the play ends with Theseus' command: 'Open wide my palace, gloomy and foul with slaughter.'[55]

Shakespeare's often hilarious comedy and Seneca's fuliginous tragedy are worlds apart and yet intimately connected. Harold Brooks has listed many passages in the comedy which Shakespeare borrowed from the *Hippolytus*.[56] He attaches no special significance to these connections and has overlooked the labyrinth–monster analogy used by both dramatists (and all that it signifies). But he makes the important point that 'Helena's abandonment in obsessive love owes a good deal to Phaedra's.'[57] Indeed his list of borrowings shows that the umbilical connection between Shakespeare's comic heroine and this famous victim of an overmastering tragic passion is apparent as early as the opening scene.[58] And the second scene shows just how conscious Shakespeare is of the fact that both his comedy and its characters are very close to tragedy; having transposed a tragic heroine into a comic one, he now presents a 'company' of artisans (i.ii.1) who are about to rehearse 'The most lamentable comedy and cruel death of Pyramus and Thisbe' (lines 11–12).

Seneca's *Hippolytus* is not the only genetic link between *A Midsummer Night's Dream* and formal tragedy. Borrowings from Seneca's *Medea* and *Oedipus* have also been found.[59] Shakespeare's use of the play-within-the-play, and of supernatural agents who are also stage spectators of the action, has often been attributed to the example of *The Spanish Tragedy*. But the kinship between *A Midsummer Night's Dream* and Kyd's tragedy goes much deeper than that. The main action of the earlier play is conceived as a comedy that suddenly and 'unnaturally' turns to tragedy. Moreover, the play-within-the-play at the end (like Bottom's play) is a tragedy where a comedy would have been appropriate (at a marriage celebration), and is censured as such; it also entails a violent confusion of illusion and reality and of marriage and funeral (Bottom's and Theseus' problems on a different level). These radical confusions, like the play's own mixing of high tragedy and comic jest, are intrinsic to Kyd's pioneering conception of tragedy as a process of violent contrariety akin to chaos.[60] Both *The Spanish Tragedy* and *A Midsummer Night's Dream* are intensely self-reflexive:[61] their form corresponds with their vision of a world in which the distinction between polar opposites – and particularly between 'comedy' and 'tragedy', happiness and misery – is a thoroughly unstable one.

It is hardly surprising that the intertextual process I have been describing was reversed in the early seventeenth century when *A Midsummer Night's Dream* was in turn digested by tragedy. As I have shown in detail elsewhere, Middleton and Rowley's *The Changeling* (1622) is much indebted to it.[62] This splendidly original and yet deeply traditional tragedy combines comedy with tragedy in a binary structure whose antithetical setting (Castle and Bedlam) carries the same symbolic significance as the palace/wood setting of *A Midsummer Night's Dream*. Its concern too is with the transforming power of love and the 'amazement' – the confusion and bewilderment – which the changes wrought by sexual passion generate. And its controlling philosophical idea is that of 'a contrariety in nature' (v.ii.13). Middleton and Rowley perceived with the utmost clarity the deliberateness with which Shakespeare skirted the borders of tragedy in *A Midsummer Night's Dream*, and, above all, they understood what he was implying when he did so. Other seventeenth-century dramatists echo Shakespeare's tragical comedy (and Seneca's tragedy) in their association of the tragic world with the monstrous maze of ancient myth.[63]

But of course the tragedy most intimately linked with this comedy is *Romeo and Juliet*, written at approximately the same time (whether immediately before or after, we do not know). As many have observed, they are in a sense the same play with different endings. The tragic tale of Pyramus and Thisbe, young lovers driven to suicide by parental opposition and mischance, a tale jocularly referred to by Mercutio in *Romeo and Juliet* (ii.iv.42), serves in the comedy as a pertinent reminder of an alternative ending and of the other play. Conversely, the characters of the Nurse and Mercutio make *Romeo and Juliet* the most exuberantly funny of Shakespeare's tragedies; indeed so close to comedy is the first half of this play that Shakespeare, it would seem, feels obliged to keep reminding us of a fatal consequence yet hanging in the stars. This bold combination, however, is consistent with the play's underlying conception of an oppositional world where 'all things change them to the contrary' (iv.v.90) and 'bright things come to confusion' (*MND*, i.i.149) with lightning speed. The oppositional dynamics of Shakespearian tragedy, and their grounding in a cosmology of Love and Strife, stand out more clearly in *Romeo and Juliet* than in any other of the early tragedies (or tragical histories). But we will best understand those dynamics, and *Romeo and Juliet* itself, if we have approached them by way of *A Midsummer Night's Dream* and the first of the *Canterbury Tales*.

3

Romeo and Juliet

I

Titus Andronicus (1593?), *Richard III* (1593?), and *Romeo and Juliet* (1595–6), Shakespeare's first attempts in the tragic medium, are strikingly different both from each other and from the tragedies of Shakespeare's maturity in many obvious respects. As I have already indicated, however, it is possible to detect in *Titus* certain shaping concepts which will prove to be essential in the mature tragedies; and these same concepts can be detected in the other two early tragedies as well. The three plays rest on a common substructure of ideas about the nature of the tragic experience and its relation to reality as a whole.

Titus, we have seen (pp. 21–3), is the tragedy of a civilised warrior in whom the stable partnership of martial valour and loving-kindness is shattered, so that the violence which had brought honour on the field to 'kind Rome', to his family, and to himself is turned against all three. This tragedy of lost oneness and identity is reflected in the condition of Rome, a city renowned for its combination of civility and martial virtue; its present degenerate state is summed up in the submissive marriage of its emperor to a ruthless barbarian queen. The tragedy of both Rome and its representative hero are in turn traced to the double nature of 'kind'.

Unlike Titus, Richard III is not a creature of double impulse. He is spiritually as well as physically 'deform'd, unfinish'd', sent by 'dissembling Nature' into the world 'scarce half made up' (i.i.19–21). His performances as an amiable friend and kinsman and as a 'jolly thriving wooer' (iv.iii.43) are fiendish dissembling: his doubleness is perfect duplicity. Wholly without 'tenderness of heart, / And gentle, kind, effeminate remorse' (iii.vii.210–11), he is 'kind in hatred' only (iv.iv.172 [F1]). The embodiment of domineering egoism ('I am myself alone'), and an agent of strife and division, he

56

identifies himself in his opening soliloquy with Mars ('grim visag'd war'), promising to wreck the peace and pastimes which his war-weary nation is preparing to enjoy under King Edward (i.i.9). Not for Richard the pursuits of Venus: lute, dance, my lady's chamber, love's majesty (lines 12–16). The tragedy is his only in the sense that he 'plots' it (line 32); in the other sense, it is England's tragedy, that of a nation at war with itself, torn between the rival claims of the House of Lancaster and the House of York.

In these plays, then, tragic experience is identified with strife, hate, disunity, and violent change and confusion, and traced to the contrarious order of nature. This underlying similarity is reinforced by the plays' conclusions. The natural longing for love, peace, and unity which Richard contemptuously acknowledges at the outset, and exploits in his treacherous hypocrisies, is answered at the end by Richmond, his conqueror. Lightly sketched though it is, Richmond's character is that of a man 'full made up'. He is a good warrior and a good friend, a conquering peacemaker. Through his marriage to Elizabeth he combines in himself the rival claims of the two houses; he is a reconciler who will 'unite the white rose and the red' in 'fair conjunction' (v.v.19–20). So too at the end of *Titus Andronicus*, the dead hero's brother addresses the people of Rome thus:

> You sad-fac'd men, people and sons of Rome,
> By uproars sever'd, as a flight of fowl
> Scatter'd by winds and high tempestuous gusts,
> O let me teach you how to knit again
> This scatter'd corn into one mutual sheaf,
> These broken limbs into one body. (v.iii.67–72)

Like all Shakespeare's tragedies, both plays postulate a contrarious natural order which is cyclical as well as dialectical. The impulse towards unity is expected to assert itself as inevitably as its opposite, and may even be dependent on it. However terrible the violence which has been unleashed, and however muted and qualified the hint of reintegration and renewal, these plays intimate that pure tragedy, like pure comedy, is an image of the world only half made up. As we shall see, that suggestion is more conspicuous in *Romeo and Juliet* than in any other of Shakespeare's tragedies.

Yet to link so exquisitely beautiful a play with *Titus* and *Richard III* might well seem a forced and fruitless exercise. Unlike theirs, its narrative lacks all potential for high tragedy. The story of two very young lovers who lead private lives, and who are driven to suicide by the pointless feuding of their families and the practice of arranged marriages, is potentially very moving; but it is not calculated to present a spectacle of evil and suffering that will stir us profoundly with questions about the human condition. Shakespeare, however, was obviously very conscious of the inherent limitation of the story as material for tragic drama, and addressed himself to the problem with quite remarkable thoroughness and subtlety. In consequence, to treat the play as uncertain, simple, or lacking in generality of implication, or as a tragedy of fate and passive suffering, is quite wrong. Increasing critical emphasis of late on its rare poise and complexity is fully justified.

Essentially, Shakespeare's solution to his problem was to generalise and complicate the tragedy by making the city in which it is set a microcosmic reflection of the great world. 'There is no world without Verona's walls' (III.iii.17), says Romeo, and he is at least right in assuming that Verona is a world in itself. And what matters to Shakespeare in the correspondent relationship between the little and the great world is not their hierarchical but their contrarious structure. Verona is made up of servants, citizens, gentry or nobility, and a princely ruler; but the social fact of prime importance in this hierarchical society is that it is split between two rival families whose mutual hatred erupts periodically into 'black strife' (III.i.175). This hatred has no causal or temporal beginning; it seems to have been always there, like a fact of nature. Its only justification lies in the honour code, with its demand that every slight to one's own or one's family's good name must be violently repudiated. But the honour code, as exemplified in the duelling Tybalt, is shown to be thoroughly irrational; it is male aggressiveness given a veneer of legitimacy, the militarism of chivalry broken loose from the claims of love and peace: '. . . talk of peace! I hate the word / As I hate hell, all Montagues, and thee' (I.i.68–9). A sixteenth-century Italian lawyer spoke of the duel as entirely natural, a manifestation of the hate which permeates the whole physical world;[1] and on the evidence of this play he was right. Shakespeare not only implies that the mutual hostility of the two families was always there (and therefore 'natural'), he also locates it very firmly in the dynamics of a world whose functioning turns on the interaction of Love and Strife (Hate). The tragedy of Romeo and Juliet, who reject hatred and division at the cost of their lives, and whose doomed marriage brings about the 'jointure' (v.iii.296) of their warring families, is fully implicated in the drama of the natural order. This connection is established by means of the play's rich pattern of elemental imagery[2], and, more overtly, by the Friar's famous set speech on the properties of plants:[3]

> The gray-ey'd morn smiles on the frowning night,
> Check'ring the eastern clouds with streaks of light;
> And fleckel'd darkness like a drunkard reels
> From forth day's path and Titan's fiery wheels.
> Now, ere the sun advance his burning eye,
> The day to cheer and night's dank dew to dry,
> I must up-fill this osier cage of ours
> With baleful weeds and precious-juiced flowers.
> The earth that's nature's mother is her tomb;
> What is her burying grave, that is her womb.
> And from her womb children of divers kind
> We sucking on her natural bosom find;
> Many for many virtues excellent,
> None but for some, and yet all different.
> O, mickle is the powerful grace that lies
> In plants, herbs, stones, and their true qualities;
> For nought so vile that on the earth doth live
> But to the earth some special good doth give;
> Nor aught so good but, strain'd from that fair use,
> Revolts from true birth, stumbling on abuse:
> Virtue itself turns vice, being misapplied.
> And vice sometime's by action dignified.
> Within the infant rind of this weak flower
> Poison hath residence, and medicine power;
> For this, being smelt, with that part cheers each part;
> Being tasted, slays all senses with the heart.
> Two such opposed kings encamp them still
> In man as well as herbs – grace and rude will;
> And where the worser is predominant,
> Full soon the canker death eats up that plant. (II.iii.1–30)

The Friar here envisages a spatio-temporal order of great dialectical complexity (that it is a temporal as well as a spatial order is an important point habitually missed in critical commentary). Thanks to the regular cycle of day and night, and of generation and decay, the elements of moisture, warmth, air and earth combine in a fruitful partnership from which human art can profit. Human art, however, requires a patient, discriminating awareness of nature's moving, changing, oppositional character. The fruitful earth yields both poisonous weeds and medicinal flowers. But the flowers may contain both poison and medicine; furthermore, poison can prove beneficial and medicine fatal. And in human nature the same laws apply. Each member in every opposition breaks down into a further opposition: contrarious structure and dynamics are inescapable. Here is a view of nature as at once comforting and treacherous, stable and ambiguous. It posits a world where opposites can change places all 'too soon', where confusion and grave error are perennial hazards, and where to 'mean well' (i.iv.48) is seldom enough. Of course the Friar makes no mention of the love–strife or love–hate antinomy; but Romeo, his 'only love sprung from' his 'only hate', enters just as (or just before) the speech ends, and the Friar is soon discussing the possibility of turning 'rancour to pure love' (line 92; i.v.136). It is clear both here and throughout that the play's rich (and much noted) cluster of polarities has nature's most basic opposition at its heart.

II

While it is necessary to observe the underlying affinities between *Romeo and Juliet* and the earlier (and later) tragedies, its unique character must be fully acknowledged. This can be ascribed mainly to its comic and its lyric dimensions. Yet to examine these is to perceive even more clearly the basic elements in Shakespeare's conception of the tragic: violent change and confounding contrariety reflecting a collapse in the tenuous balance and measured pace of nature's oppositional order.

The total effect of the play's richly comic dimension is to counter-act the heavily explicit indications of tragic inevitability by suggesting that the story could have ended quite differently.[4] The silliness of the servants and the two paterfamilias in the opening scene, the ludicrous affectations of Romeo in his role as Rosaline's unrequited lover, the ebullient mockeries of Mercutio, the sentimental babblings of old Capulet, and the enchanting garrulity of the Nurse: all these combine to make us feel throughout the first two acts (and in defiance of the Prologue) that the lovers' problem will resolve itself in the time-honoured fashion of comedy – constancy and skilful intrigue will overcome all obstacles, hard-nosed parents will be reconciled to a marriage of true love. Not until the entirely unexpected killing of the great jester in Act iii does the atmosphere become genuinely tragic. But even then there is more comedy to come: not just the absurd, nocturnal bustling of Father Capulet as he prepares for the wedding feast, but, more importantly, the entrance of the clown at the end of the funeral lamentations over the presumed-dead Juliet. At this point the comedy clearly becomes part of a general, self-reflexive strategy. When Peter asks the dejected musicians to play him some 'merry dump' (i.e. some merry sad song), and they retort, ''tis no time to play now' (IV.v.105–7), the original audience was to ask itself, 'How shall we find the concord of this discord?' What artistic justification can there be for disregarding so flagrantly the classical and neoclassical insistence on excluding all traces of comedy from tragic drama? The answer has in fact been prepared for in the proleptic ironies that occur in so many of the comic and satiric passages. To take but one example. Romeo's 'He [i.e. Mercutio] jests at scars that never felt a wound' (II.ii.1) anticipates the dying Mercutio's jest on his fatal wound ('No, 'tis not so deep as a well, nor so wide as a church door. But 'tis enough, 'twill serve. Ask for me tomorrow, and you shall find me a grave man') (III.i.93–5); and the link tells us that comedy and tragedy cannot be separated without adopting a static and monocular view of a world which is inescapably kinetic and duplex: each genre or mode is the tomb and womb of the other. Old Capulet's lament, however, prepares much more decisively than these early anticipations of generic exchange for the clown's untimely intrusion, and fully involves it in the imaginative design of the whole play:

> All things that we ordained festival
> Turn from their office to black funeral:
> Our instruments to melancholy bells,
> Our wedding cheer to a sad burial feast,
> Our solemn hymns to sullen dirges change;
> Our bridal flowers serve for a buried corse;
> And all things change them to the contrary. (IV.v.85–91)

Shakespeare implicitly acknowledges that popular demand for clowning in the midst of tragedy results in a 'Mis-shapen chaos of well-seeming forms' (I.ii.177). But he also presents himself as a successful Friar Lawrence, one whose art is effective in producing 'confusion's cure' (IV.v.65): that is, a complex, meaningful unity; a controlled *discordia concors* which holds the mirror up to nature in all its unpredictability.

As I have already remarked (p. 54), Shakespeare's metadramatic justification for the new mixed mode of tragedy was borrowed from

Kyd's *The Spanish Tragedy*, echoes of which are strongly felt throughout this play.[5] However, the audacity and invention with which Shakespeare incorporates the comic element are entirely his own. His use of lyric conventions in such a way as to reinforce the special emphases in this new kind of tragedy was also suggested by Kyd; but again what he accomplishes on the basis of Kydian precedent represents a huge leap in imaginative expressiveness.[6] There are three aspects of lyric convention which call for special attention here. The first and most obvious is the Petrarchan rhetoric of pun, antithesis, paradox, and oxymoron. This is a source of comedy in the posturings of Romeo in Act I; but thereafter it serves to articulate a pervasive sense of tragic duality, conflict, confusion, and swift contrarious change. The sonnet-prologue somewhat ostentatiously foretells this raid on Petrarchan idiom, and moulds it perfectly to the tragic conception. In 'the *two*-hours' traffic of our stage', the audience will see a tragedy set in one place and concerning '*Two* households, *both* alike in dignity'. 'Ancient grudge break[s] to new mutiny.' 'Civil blood [civil war] makes civil [peaceful] hands unclean.' 'From forth the fatal loins of these *two* / Foes, a *pair* of star-cross'd lovers take their life [are born/kill themselves].' Their 'death-mark'd love' (and that alone) serves to 'bury their parents' strife'. As Leonard Forster has remarked, the whole play is devoted to bringing the Petrarchan cliché of the 'dear enemy' to life.[7] By setting that cliché in so firmly dualistic a framework, by insinuating a conception of human nature as both gentle and violent, by postulating a repetitive cycle of peace and violence, by showing the paradoxical interdependence of fundamental opposites, and by repetition of the words 'love' and 'strife', the sonnet-prologue indicates just why the old cliché proves so attractive to the tragic dramatist. But it is not just in rhetorical figures such as paradox, oxymoron, pun, and antithesis that the principle of contrariety affects the expressive mode of the tragedy. It is manifest everywhere: in character contrasts and in opposed attitudes to love, in imagistic and symbolic patterning, and in scenic juxtaposition.[8]

The second inheritance from lyric tradition of special relevance here is the symbolic representation of love as a religion. The imagery of religion serves in the play to characterise love as the supreme value and the one source of redeeming grace; but it also points to the governing principles of contrarious unity and tragic doubleness. It comes into prominence when Romeo sets eyes on Juliet for the first time. A scene of exceptional lyric charm and wit, this is also a highly complex and illuminating microcosm of the given play-world; and religious symbolism is central to it. Romeo has spoken in a previous scene of 'the devout religion of mine eye' (I.iii.88), but this is where the trite Petrarchan phrase becomes meaningful. Indifferent to the dance, a silent watcher holding a candle, Romeo suddenly catches sight of Juliet. From that moment he is transformed, filled with a kind of reverent joy; and in words which evoke the birth of chivalry itself, he asks: 'What lady's that which doth enrich the hand / Of yonder knight?' (I.v.39–40). He feels that if his hand touches hers, a redeeming grace will pass into it: 'I'll watch her place of stand, and touching hers, make blessed my rude hand' (where 'rude' means 'uncivilised' and 'unregenerate', as in the Friar's phrase, 'rude will'). Of course the pair join words as well as hands, and most artfully. The first fourteen lines of their dialogue (line 91ff.) constitute a perfect sonnet in which Romeo has the first quatrain and Juliet the second; the sestet is broken up between them, and the concluding couplet is shared. It is obvious that the sonnet form and its complex rhyming scheme is designed to work in conjunction with the music and the dance to establish the idea of opposites harmonised: the concordant discord of a Montague and a Capulet.[9]

What is rather less obvious (or at least has not attracted critical attention) is that nine of the lines in this sonnet refer to the hand: to the profaning of hands, to the joining of hands, to praying hands, and to hands which impart a blessing. There is also a linking pun on 'palmer' (meaning 'pilgrim') and 'palm' which neatly reinforces the significance of the key image and connects it with the fact that Romeo, whose name is an Italian word for 'pilgrim' ('pellegrino che va a Roma'), has come to the masque in the disguise of a palmer (hence the candle). But what completes the significance of the hand image is the visible fact that Romeo, while praying and receiving grace in a perfect communion, is being watched by a very rude young man whose hand (I assume) flies instinctively to his hip in anger and frustration. 'Fetch me my rapier, boy', exclaims Tybalt to his servant (line 53), eager to fulfil the Prologue's prediction: 'civil blood makes civil hands unclean'. Temporarily restrained by Capulet, who cites Romeo's reputation as 'a virtuous and well govern'd youth' (line 66), Tybalt represents himself in soliloquy as the emergent alternative to the meeting of contraries we have just witnessed:

> Patience perforce with wilful choler meeting
> Makes my flesh tremble in their different greeting.

> I will withdraw; but this intrusion shall,
> Now seeming sweet, convert to bitterest gall. (lines 87–90)

Throughout the play attention is drawn repeatedly to the hand, so that we observe it at work revealing the twin possibilities of human nature. There is the gentle hand that prays, pleads, blesses, appeases, parts antagonists, unites lovers, forgives and makes friends: the hand of palmer, saint, helpless mortal, holy friar, peacemaker, reconciled enemy. And there is the violent hand that strikes, divides, and destroys – 'cut[s] ... youth in twain' (v.iii.99): the 'cursed hand' (iii.iii.104) not only of the indignant gentleman who would avenge a wrong or an insult ('*He draws*'), but also of the furious patriarch who feels like strangling his daughter when she pleads against his rude will: 'My fingers itch' (iii.v.164).[10]

The symbolism of the hand exactly pinpoints the tragedy of Romeo. When he comes married from the Friar's cell ('God join'd my heart and Romeo's, thou our hands' (iv.i.55)), he is insulted and challenged by 'the furious Tybalt' (iii.i.118); but he responds in conciliatory and even loving terms. However, the blessed hand of love (first extended, it would seem, from a kneeling posture) is scorned by the hand of Mars, and twice over:

> Romeo ... spoke him fair, and bid him bethink
> How nice the quarrel was, and urg'd withal
> Your high displeasure. All this, uttered
> With gentle breath, calm look, knees humbly bow'd,
> Could not take truce with the unruly spleen
> Of Tybalt, deaf to peace, but that he tilts
> With piercing steel at bold Mercutio's breast;
> Who, all as hot, turns deadly point to point,
> And, with martial scorn, with one hand beats
> Cold death aside, and with the other
> Sends it back to Tybalt, whose dexterity
> Retorts it. Romeo he cries aloud
> 'Hold, friends! friends, part!' and, swifter than his tongue,
> His agile arm beats down their fatal points,
> And twixt them rushes; underneath whose arms
> An envious thrust from Tybalt hit the life
> Of stout Mercutio ... (lines 150–66)

Tybalt's 'dexterity' is (by way of an etymological pun) his 'right hand' (Latin *dexter*); but the passage seems to suggest that the symbolic distinction between one hand (arm) and the other is quite lost here; and that confusion becomes Romeo's. With Mercutio's

death, he abruptly subscribes to the code of honour: momentarily
convinced that Juliet's love has 'soft'ned valour's steel' and made
him 'effeminate', he calls on 'fire-ey'd fury' to be his 'conduct now'
(lines 108–21). And so 'Tybalt is slain' – he 'whom Romeo's hand
did slay' (line 149; cf. III.ii.71; III.iii.104, 108). It is perhaps true
that 'we *want* him to show himself a man against the detestable
Tybalt';[11] but we must also perceive that the decision which proves
fatal to both Juliet and himself represents a regression from full
humanity as imaginatively defined by the play. It is only at the end,
when he kills Paris in self-defence (after having tried conciliation),
and then effects a moving atonement (at-one-ment) with his dead
rival, that Romeo achieves heroic integrity:

> O, give me thy hand,
> One writ with me in sour misfortune's book!
> I'll bury thee in a triumphant grave....
> O, what more favour can I do to thee
> Than with that hand that cut thy youth in twain
> To sunder his that was thine enemy?
> Forgive me, cousin. (v.iii.81–3, 98–101)

III

A third and much more important inheritance from lyric tradition which has been adapted and developed to fit the play's tragic
design is the theme of time and its associated imagery. In lyric and
sonnet, and especially in Shakespeare's own sonnets, Time is the
great enemy of both the poet-lover and the beloved. Capriciously,
Time retards his pace when the lovers are separated and acceler-
ates it when they are together. With his scythe and his frosts, he
destroys the flower of youth and withers the rose of beauty. The
poet's lines are in themselves an attempt to counteract his evil work:
they distil the perfume of the rose before it withers, win fame and
lasting memory for rare beauty and virtue. In the aubade or dawn
song, too, Time figures as the lovers' enemy: the rising sun cur-
tails their secret happiness and contradicts their sense of ecstatic
transcendence.

The extreme youth and immaturity of the doomed lovers in *Romeo
and Juliet* is the chief indication of time's cruel speed. According to
Capulet, his 'child is yet a stranger in the world' and has 'not seen
the change of fourteen years' (i.ii.8–9) (she is sixteen in Shakespeare's principal source, and eighteen in other versions of the

story). And when she is found as dead in her bridal clothes, Capulet speaks of death as lying upon her 'like an untimely frost / Upon the sweetest flower of all the field'; as 'a flower . . . deflower'd' by Death (iv.v.28–9, 37). Here, and in Capulet's earlier reference to Juliet as 'the hopeful lady of my earth' (i.ii.14), Shakespeare implicitly invokes the most poignant of all the myths of untimely death: that of Proserpina, daughter of Ceres (goddess of earth's plenty), who was seized while gathering flowers by Pluto, god of death and of funerals, and taken by him to live as his wife in his infernal kingdom. Among the most powerful images in the play are those of Death as Juliet's surrogate husband;[12] they are all echoes of this myth which embodies the idea of time's intrusion on a timeless, unchanging, paradisal world.[13]

Shakespeare will deploy this myth more overtly and extensively in relation to the love of Perdita and Florizel in *The Winter's Tale* (iv.iv.111–33). The allusion is pertinent here, since Romeo, like Florizel, is also identified with the flower of youth. There is even a significant play on his name which works in the same way as Florizel's: when the Nurse notes that 'rosemary and Romeo begin both with a letter', and implies that he is 'the flower of courtesy' (ii.iv.200, v.43), Shakespeare must be recalling that the Spanish word *romero* (= Ital. *romeo*) means both 'pilgrim' and 'rosemary'. But the flower image works comprehensively in the play, and in the final scene is superbly literalised to provide a vivid stage image of time's hostility to almost all Verona's youth. At the end, Benvolio is the only surviving representative of the younger generation: Mercutio and Tybalt are 'yet but green in earth' (iv.iii.42), the bodies of Romeo, Juliet, and Paris (described earlier as 'a very flower' (i.iii.78–80)) are before us, and lying about the stage are the flowers brought by Paris to the tomb and scattered everywhere in the violence of his fight with Romeo.

No less important in relation to the time theme than the floral imagery is the imagery of light (often fiery) and of darkness, amplified in numerous references to day and night, sun, moon, and stars. The function of this complex of images as expressing the transience as well as the splendour of the lovers' passion is strengthened by their own conviction that 'the garish sun' (iii.ii.25) is hostile to their secret love, whereas night is friendly, allowing it to shine in all its brilliance. The aubade theme of unwelcome daylight and reluctant parting is introduced after their only night together, and acquires an altogether new force in the circumstances of this particular relationship: if Romeo does not leave before sunrise, he will be killed.

As in *Julius Caesar* and *Othello*, two other tragedies in which time is of unusual significance, a narrative which originally extended over a much longer period is compressed into a very short time frame (here, four days) so as to give the impression of events unfolding with dangerous speed in a highly charged atmosphere.[14] Moreover, the familiar question as to whether or not this is a tragedy of mischance rather than of character arises mainly from the fact that so many of the actions which advance the tragedy are in some way mistimed: asynchrony is almost the determining principle of the action. If the wedding of Juliet to Paris had not been brought forward from Thursday to Wednesday; if Friar Lawrence's message had reached Romeo in time; if Romeo had reached the vault a minute later, or Juliet awakened a minute earlier; or if the Friar had not stumbled as he ran to the vault: if any one of these conditions had been met, then the tragedy would not have occurred. It does indeed seem as if a malignant outside force is responsible for destroying the lovers' happiness. Fortune and the stars are blamed from the start, but their malign influence is incorporate in the more palpable hostility of time: 'O lamentable day! O woeful time!' (IV.v.30); 'Ah, what an unkind hour / Is guilty of this lamentable chance!' (V.iii.145–6).

However, anyone coming to the play from a Renaissance epithalamium or marriage masque, or from Spenser's unconventional sonnet sequence, *Amoretti* (published, with his 'Epithalamion', in 1595), would quickly find evidence to suggest that the typical sonneteer's notion of time as the enemy of human happiness is only half-endorsed by Shakespeare's text. Such an intertextual approach is not at all necessary in order to perceive the wider implications of the time theme, but it certainly seems to have been presupposed by Shakespeare, and it does make one more fully responsive to the play's complex pattern of meaning. The *Amoretti* sequence is the record not of unrequited love but of a courtship which leads to the marriage day of 'Epithalamion'. The sonnet lover frequently complains against Time's cruel protractions and contractions (Sonnets XXV, XXXVI, LXXXVI), but his complaints are woven into the cycle of the seasons, to whose constraining order he painfully submits his passionate impatience. The same tension and reconciliation between time and desire is enacted in the extraordinary mimetic structure of 'Epithalamion', the poem which triumphantly celebrates the culmination of the twelve-months' courtship. The poem consists of twenty-four stanza units; the wedding takes place on midsummer day, and the bride arrives at the church (stanza 12) when the sun, whose progress from dawn to dusk is duly marked, is at its height. It ends with the prayer that 'a large posterity' will be the 'timely fruit of this same night' (lines 404, 417), and with the description of the poem itself as 'an endless monument' erected by the poet to his bride (line 433): permanence is achieved through accommodation to time's cyclical order, and through a poetic art structured on the numbers of time.[15] The poem is born of the assumption that harmony with the rhythm of time is the major pre-condition for enduring happiness in love and for fruitfulness in all undertakings. In his continuation of Marlowe's unfinished tragic narrative, *Hero and Leander*, George Chapman, who assuredly had read this poem as well as *Romeo and Juliet*, rendered Spenser's governing idea quite explicit when he wrote:

> Time's golden thigh
> Upholds the flowery body of the earth
> In sacred harmony, and every birth
> Of men and actions makes legitimate,
> Being us'd aright; *the use of time is fate.* (III.60–4)

Epithalamic tradition reinforces the comic dimension of *Romeo and Juliet* in that it points to the alternative ending, enhances the sense of waste and loss, and enables us to view the story from the widest possible perspective. The tradition is overtly invoked in Juliet's great soliloquy in III.ii ('Gallop apace') – often referred to as her epithalamium. The epithalamic norm of timeliness and ripeness is expressed on several occasions in the play, twice with specific relation to marriage. As befits a father, Capulet restrains the impatient suitor Paris, tying respect for time to a regard for interpersonal harmony and the ideal of 'multilateral consent' in marriage that was advocated by English moralists from about 1570 onwards:[16]

> Let two more summers wither in their pride
> Ere we may think her ripe to be a bride.

> But woo her, gentle Paris, get her heart;
> My will to her consent is but a part,
> And, she agreed, within her scope of choice
> Lies my consent and fair according voice. (I.ii.10–11, 16–19)

Juliet echoes her father's words when she restrains Romeo and expresses the hope that 'This bud of love, by summer's ripening breath, / May prove a beauteous flower when next we meet' (II.ii.121–3). And if the sun is scorned by the lovers it is referred to by others as 'the worshipp'd sun' (I.i.115) and 'the all-cheering sun' (line 133). Partnered by the moon, its presence is felt throughout, manifesting a dualistic temporal order which is not intrinsically capricious or malign; Juliet speaks of the 'variable' and 'inconstant moon, / That monthly changes in her circled orb' (I.ii.109–11), but her phrasing unintentionally acknowledges that the moon's changes are ordered. And the last image of the sun is as a kindly father grieving over the 'untimely death' (v.iii.233, 258) of the young: 'The sun for sorrow will not show his head' (line 305).

Of course references in *Romeo and Juliet* to the timely order which promises fruitfulness and permanence serve but to highlight the prevailing 'violence' – a key term which denotes both haste and destruction.[17] As its first word indicates, Juliet's 'Gallop apace' soliloquy is not so much an epithalamium as an epithalamium subverted.[18] Central to the meaning of the speech is Juliet's self-identification with Phaeton, the 'runaway' (III.ii.3, 6) son of Phoebus who sought to manage his father's fiery chariot, failed, and brought in 'cloudy night immediately' (line 4);[19] the speech is a superb manifestation of intense, erotic passion verging on willed self-extinction. Juliet herself had anticipated this perception when she warned the much more impulsive Romeo that their contract was 'Too like the lightning which doth cease to be / Ere one can say "It lightens"' (II.ii.119–20). It is in the scene which follows this ominous remark that the lyric image of the flower loses its simple significance (or innocence) by being projected into the contrarious order of all nature: 'Within the infant rind of this weak flower / Poison hath residence, and medicine power.'

However, it is important to avoid undue emphasis on the rashness of the lovers, for a fiery, passionate impatience animates and agitates the whole society into which they have been born. Capulet enjoins patience and concord on both Tybalt and Paris, but subsequently delights in the speed with which he sets up an enforced marriage; and he reacts with a frightening display of rude will and itching hands to the kneeling Juliet's plea for time. Mercutio 'make[s] haste' to take up the challenge rejected by Romeo: his bitter, 'I am sped', is a fitting epitaph (III.i.78, 88). And the effect of his death is that Tybalt and Romeo 'to't . . . go like lightning' (line 169). Paris proves to be as provocative and furious in quarrel (v.iii.63, 70) as he was impatient in love. Even the Prince contributes to the prevailing ethos. Distressed by the death of his kinsman Mercutio, he is 'deaf to pleading and excuses' and sentences Romeo to exile 'in haste' (III.i.189–92): patient consideration might have resulted in a more equitable judgement, and averted tragedy. And of course the Friar becomes deeply involved in the haste he deplored: his exclamation, 'Saint Francis be my speed! How oft tonight / Have my old feet stumbled at graves!' (v.iii.121–2), ironically echoes his advice: 'Wisely and slow. They stumble that run fast' (II.iii.94).

Shakespeare has thus created a hectic environment where fatal accidents brought about by unfortunate mistimings are in the end inevitable.[20] More important, it is presented as an environment in which haste is a poison that spreads to infect almost everyone: all references to poison, plague, infection, and pestilence combine to form a central symbol for Verona's passionate impatience and fatal speed. The Friar speaks of poison in the flower just before Romeo enters demanding to be married to his new love 'today' (II.iii.64). Mercutio's 'I am sped' is preceded *and* followed by the famous 'A plague a both your houses' (III.i.88, 97). Friar Lawrence's messenger is delayed because he is suspected of having been in 'a house where the infectious pestilence did reign' (v.iii.9–10) (the symbolic intent is evident from the fact that in Brooke's *Romeus and Juliet* the infected house is in Mantua, not Verona; and from the synonymity of 'infection' and 'rank poison' at I.ii.49–50). And Romeo, swiftly opting for suicide, obtains from the apothecary 'A dram of poison, such soon-speeding gear / As will disperse itself through all the veins . . . / As violently as hasty powder fir'd / Doth hurry from the fatal cannon's womb' (v.i.60–5). We may conclude that although the rashness of the lovers contributes to their tragedy, it is a pestilence caught from others. And we have to remember that there is a huge difference between the impetuosities of love and those of anger and hate – although they can work tragically towards the same end.

IV

It is apparent, then, that in *Romeo and Juliet* time is not a blind, external force hostile to youth and love but rather a complex ruling order which can be creative or destructive according as men and women are able to function within its inescapable limits. And in that sense the philosophy of the sonnets is heavily qualified. However, it seems to be in the nature of Shakespeare's tragic environment that time is already out of joint, so that the protagonists are compelled, as it were, to journey across a heavily mined battle-field. Furthermore, the greatness of the tragic hero and heroine, and especially of heroic lovers, lies precisely in their need to transcend limits; they can only be fully themselves if they 'soar above a common bound' (I.iv.18) and so court destruction. Around Capulet's house, 'the orchard walls are high and hard to climb; / And the place death' if Romeo is discovered; but he declares that he will 'o'erperch these walls' since 'stony limits cannot hold love out' (II.ii.64–7). Juliet's rejection of limit derives from her eloquently expressed awareness that love's bounty is 'boundless as the sea', 'infinite' (lines 131–5; see also II.vi.32–4).

No less important in the complex vision of this tragedy is the fact that although their own violence and that of their families makes the lovers the victims of time, they are, in the deepest sense, triumphant over time's destructive action.[21] It is this triumph which makes possible the reconciliation of their families; and although we may consider that to be a poor reward for the sacrifice of two such individuals, their resolute refusal to accept change and division when everything conspires to enforce it upon them is itself a thing of supreme value, something that endures like the statue of 'pure gold' which their parents erect in their memory – or like the legend of their loves. This triumph over change is all the more distinct in that it was not a foregone conclusion; somewhat awkwardly, but obviously enough, Shakespeare delineates in their characters and relationship a process of maturing, of fall and recovery, of constancy undermined and restored; and this in turn hints at the paradox that time's destructive action can be seen as part of a creative cycle.

In the orchard scene, Juliet expresses fears about Romeo's constancy, but her own constancy is clearly threatened after Tybalt's death. Her notorious oxymoronic outburst against Romeo ('O serpent heart, hid with a flow'ring face! ... Beautiful tyrant, fiend angelical' etc.) is intended to disclose a fierce struggle between hatred for the man who killed her cousin and love for her banished husband (III.iii.73–84). It is, however, an artificial crisis; not simply because of the overdone rhetoric, but also and mainly because Juliet's love for Tybalt is not an imagined nor even an imaginable reality – we have never once seen her with that thoroughly unlovable thug. Very different is the test to which she is put when she has to be buried alive in the family vault in order to remain 'an unstain'd wife to my sweet love' (iv.i.88). The horrors of death and putrefaction engulf her imagination, and the way in which she defeats them comes across very forcefully as a heroic act of love's constancy. It would be reasonable to say that the young girl clearly becomes a woman here. However, the text compliments her in a manner which few women today would deem agreeable, but which must be read in its historical context. The idea is that she transcends her sex, or rather the weakness traditionally ascribed to her sex; she is warned by Friar Lawrence that the whole plan to salvage her marriage will fail if any 'inconstant toy' or 'womanish fear' abates her 'valour' (iv.i.119–20). (We will encounter the same idea in the last act of *Antony and Cleopatra*.)

Characteristically, however, Shakespeare deconstructs the opposition of male constancy and female inconstancy in his delineation of the early Romeo. Romeo makes his debut with a carefully framed act of inconstancy, as ludicrous as anything to be found in the comedies; in the space of seconds, he transfers to Juliet his much publicised devotion to the frosty Rosaline: 'What a change is here!', exclaims the Friar (ii.iii.65). This change indicates a kind of maturing, a progress from fanciful to authentic passion. But its main purpose may be to highlight the issue of constancy and to hint at Romeo's potential unworthiness. His eagerness in the orchard scene to swear everlasting fidelity is what provokes Juliet's fear that he will prove 'variable' and 'inconstant', like the moon; and events show that she has good cause to be uneasy. As I have already noted, it is his lapse from love to male 'honour' that brings the world crashing about their heads. And it is finely ironical that he should decide there that her beauty has 'soften'd valour's steel' and made him 'effeminate'; because when he is told of his banishment, he falls weeping and screaming to the floor, and even attempts to commit suicide – thinking only of *his* loss and not of what Juliet will have to endure. The gravity of this moral fall – emblematised, as in a comparable scene in *Othello*, by his prostrate position – is spelt out by the Friar: he is not 'a man'; his 'tears are womanish'; his 'wild acts denote the unreasonable fury of a beast' (iii.iii.108–13).

In his recovery, Romeo's growth as a man and as a lover are coincident, interdependent. When the next piece of terrible news (that Juliet is dead) is brought to him, he has been buoyant with the expectation of good news; but now there is no wild ranting. Instantly he decides to die with Juliet, keeps the decision to himself, and gives an astonishing display of quiet stoicism in dealing with the servant who brought the news and must be made to serve his dark purpose. Moreover his dialogue with the wretched apothecary reveals in him a whole lifetime's understanding of human misery. And it is in the role of valiant and gentle manhood that he deals with Paris's insulting provocations: 'Good gentle youth, tempt not a desperate man'; 'Wilt provoke me? Then have at thee, boy!' (v.iii.59, 70). The union of the houses of Capulet and Montague follows logically from the constant oneness – the union of opposites – which the lovers achieve both individually and as a married pair. To consider the 'jointure' of the families in dissociation from that complex oneness is inevitably to devalue it, and, of course, to simplify the play's conclusion.

V

Perhaps the most discussed and problematic of the play's oppositions is that of character and fate. Some critics have taken extreme positions on this issue, either holding that everything in the action is determined by the initial stress on 'star-cross'd lovers', or insisting that the lovers are free agents whose uncontrolled passion brings upon them a morally just punishment. Others have speculated whether the two concepts coexist in a state of pure contradiction or whether they are reconciled.[22] The double perspective originates in Brooke's *Romeus and Juliet*, where the lovers are berated for their irresponsibility in the preface and sympathetically presented in the body of the poem as the victims of a malign fate ('the restles starres', 'the fatall sisters three, and Fortune full of chaunge'). Shakespeare has fully integrated this double view into the play, partly, perhaps, because the dualistic conception which governs the whole could so easily accommodate it.

There will always be disagreement on whether the issue of free will and pre-determination is a resolvable paradox or a pure contradiction we simply have to live with. This disagreement must inevitably be reflected in interpretations of a play which manipulates the question so conspicuously. But two points are worth making here. First, given the whole design of *Romeo and Juliet*, many in Shakespeare's audience would probably have reflected on the issue in the manner of Sir Kenelm Digby, who, in considering the problem of divine foreknowledge and human freedom, argued that liberty and a constrained necessity are mutually compatible and entirely consistent with the creation of a world whose order rests on the concord of contrarious and disagreeing qualities (see pp. 9, 261); they might reasonably have felt that in the end the play achieves a *discordia concors* of fatality and responsibility. Second, and as already implied here, insofar as the paradox is resolved within the play, the resolution is accomplished in terms of time, haste, and impatience. When the prince begins the inquiry intended to 'clear these ambiguities' (v.iii.216), his chief witness is the Friar, who tells a tale of untimely and mistimed actions. Lawrence does not practice astrology, but like Prospero (who does), he is a wise man who uses 'art' (v.iii.242) to control nature; and like Prospero he has the astrologer's awareness that timing – knowing the propitious and the unpropitious moment, and acting accordingly – is of the utmost importance in negotiating the changeful complexities of life ('ruling the stars'). His tale is one of sustained efforts to control a sequence of events whose problematical nature was temporal throughout. From the beginning of the play, we should recall, the hostility of external circumstance to the lovers is expressed in terms both of the stars and of time. Romeo fears that he and his friends will arrive at the Capulets 'too early', for his 'mind misgives / Some consequence yet hanging in the stars' that will lead to 'untimely death' (i.iv.106–11); and Juliet exclaims: 'My only love sprung from my only hate! / Too early seen, and known too late!' (i.v.135–6). Being what they are, however, they rush, and are driven by others, to actualise the fate which they see as prepared for them. For his part, the Friar accepts that he cannot stop Romeo's headlong commitment and accepts it as inevitable; but he also perceives the possibility of turning it to the good. However, when he agrees to the marriage, and yet again when he devises plans to cope with unexpected problems (Romeo's banishment and the Paris–Juliet marriage), he stresses that a happy outcome will depend entirely on exact timing (ii.iii.90–4; iii.iii.149–71; iv.i.69–117). Increasingly 'desperate' (line 69), his art, as we have seen, is defeated less by accident than by the passionate impatience with which the characters involved in the plot he is trying to control react to changing circumstance. In the end, he declares himself responsible for the tragedy and yet innocent: 'myself condemned and myself excus'd' (v.iii.226). Much the same, perhaps, can be said both of the stars (if literally understood) and of the lovers.

In subsequent tragedies, and especially in *Othello*, we will have the same sense of an inescapable doom working itself out through the choices, passions, and errors of men and women; the same sense, too, that 'the use of time is fate'. The limitation of this play as tragedy is that the compulsion to embrace a fatal destiny is too closely identified with mere haste, and too dependent on verbal and imagistic expression. In the later tragedies, by contrast, it is deeply embedded in character and linked to a capacity for violence and destruction which is truly frightening.

4

Julius Caesar

I

Students of Shakespeare's English histories are familiar with a remark made by Queen Elizabeth in 1601 apropos the performance of a play on Richard II which the followers of the Earl of Essex paid for on the night before their revolt. 'I am Richard II. Know ye not that?', she asked, meaning that if the revolt had succeeded she too would have been killed.[1] Whether she had any opinions about Shakespeare's *Julius Caesar*, written in 1599, we do not know; this is a pity, since in some respects it is much closer to contemporary politics than any play on Richard II could have been.

The year 1599 signalled a great ending, and it must have been accompanied by a sense of ominous foreboding rather than of confident renewal. The decade had been a period of acute distress, dislocation, and disorder.[2] Partly because of the bad harvests of previous years, and partly because of the enormous expenditure incurred by Essex's expedition to Ireland, the Elizabethan exchequer had, by 1599, reached its lowest point ever.[3] The country was governed by a monarch of sixty-six whose most trusted adviser was now a weary seventy-nine. The succession was in doubt, there were threats to the Queen's life, and continued fears of a Spanish invasion. The restless Essex, too, had gathered about him a group of discontented noblemen who shared his feeling of being slighted and marginalised by the Cecilian establishment of lawyers and social parvenus. Essex's enemies at court sensed that the army which Elizabeth placed at his disposal made him a serious threat to the realm, and before his departure for Ireland they were anxious enough to assemble their own army outside London to discourage undue ambition.

The Essex revolt which materialised two years later is of particular interest here for two reasons. It was led by a nobleman much loved by the monarch. And it was above all else an 'honour revolt'. It was in fact the last of a series of English revolts, stretching back to the late Middle Ages, in which the aristocratic code of honour was invoked to legitimise the politics of violence.[4] Kings were revered by the code, but the emphasis which it placed on individual will and moral autonomy, and the fact that the code was thought to be binding on kings and subjects alike, allowed for the possibility of resisting one's lord and even choosing another. The king might be thought to have failed the ruling class, but as a rule the rebellious nobility would claim to be acting in defence of the commonweal against the king's corrupt, upstart ministers and not against the king himself. Such rebels saw themselves as obedient to the claims of a noble lineage, and tied to one another by the indissoluble bonds of chivalric truth and friendship. With this historical paradigm (clearly articulated in John Hayward's *First Part of the Life and Reign of King Henry IV* (1599), one of the writings associated with Essex House), the Essexians were fully in accord; and no doubt that accord owed much to the extraordinary revival of the whole chivalric tradition in Elizabethan England.[5] Essex believed that his lineage and his office as Earl Marshall made him the natural leader of a community of honour against the regime of parvenus.[6] Thus although he hesitated at the end to move against the crown, he did so when his closest associates (among them Shakespeare's patron, the Earl of Southampton) urged that he could only redeem his honour by 'attempting something worthy of himself ... by delivering his friends from servitude, and the kingdom'.[7] Essex felt that the martial values of his class were devalued at court, and he and his followers deliberately cultivated the competitive and aggressive manner appropriate to the martial type. Among themselves, however, this tendency was contained by the claims of friendship, 'conceived in the powerful and passionate sense' of Cicero's treatise on the subject, the *De Amicitia*.[8] Thus Essex himself was to claim that no oath of secrecy or fidelity was needed to secure so strong a union of hearts as existed between him and his followers.[9]

From medieval times the way to honour was thought to have been shown by the ancients, and most notably the Romans;[10] thus in *Henry V* (Act v, Prologue, 23–35) Shakespeare connects Essex with Henry and both with Julius Caesar as major claimants to 'the name of honour' (*JC*, I.ii.89). It is not so surprising therefore as it might initially seem to find that in the Roman tragedy which Shakespeare wrote shortly after *Henry V* – when Essex's glory had begun to dim –

the concerns of the Roman ruling class seem to echo those of its Elizabethan counterpart. Here too is an ageing ruler whose greatness is but a memory, and an all-pervasive sense of ominous change. Here too is a disaffected group of noblemen led by the ruler's highborn 'angel', hankering after an ideal past, legitimising their cause by an appeal to the honour code, held together by the warmest ties of friendship, and convinced that they must deliver their country from base servitude. And here is a rebellious leader who fervently insists that no oath is necessary to bind noble spirits such as theirs to an honourable cause (II.i.114–40). For the likes of Southampton, the play must have provided a strange sense of the familiar in the remote.

II

Contemporary relevance, however, was only one small part of the achievement of *Julius Caesar*. This is a play in which Shakespeare's historical imagination is genuinely at work. Focussing on a singular and momentous crisis in Roman and European history, he presents us with a careful portrait of ancient Rome, its mores, its manners, its politics, and its greatness; and he writes in a style which evokes the Roman virtues of clarity, decorum, and restraint.[11] Perhaps, however, because of the claim implicit in the name and structure of the Globe playhouse (whose opening it may have been written to celebrate), Shakespeare made a remarkable effort to give this tragedy an omnitemporal and omnilocal dimension. The historical facts as recorded by Plutarch are treated on the whole with great respect, but they are systematically interpreted in the light of ideas about human nature and the world we live in that most of his contemporaries would have thought to have permanent validity. Before considering what I take to be the play's dominant concern, I should like to examine in some detail the complex symbolic means by which these universalising ideas are deployed.

Julius Caesar deals with an action of great magnitude, and presents in the character of Brutus a noble hero whose self-betrayal and self-division are imaginatively commensurate with the cataclysmic events in which he is involved; as such, it marks a decisive development in Shakespeare's tragic art. However, the play lacks much of the intensity and inwardness of the other great tragedies. This is partly because its titular hero vanishes in the middle of the action, but mainly because it is dominated by no fewer than 'four

fully developed characters of absorbing interest ... Caesar himself,
Brutus, Cassius, and Antony'.[12] It is important to note that when
Caesar is killed he is immediately replaced by 'another Caesar'
(v.i.54); for the number four is itself of great significance. In a play
which foregrounds the mixing and the conflict of the elements in the
macrocosm and the microcosm, and where Nature herself purportedly speaks to all the world (v.v.74–5), this number is clearly
symbolical: it is the number of natural unity, of opposites reconciled,
of love-and-friendship (see p. 37). Thoroughly individual though the
principal characters are, they are also representative figures. They
are 'the breed of noble bloods' (i.i.151), the natural leadership of
Rome; and the intimation is that Rome's tragedy (for this is not the
tragedy of any one man) is indistinguishable from their inability
to 'close / In terms of friendship' and 'stand fast together' (iii.i.87,
203–4).

The representative nature of these characters is underscored by
the fact that they are broadly identifiable with the four humoral
types which comprise humanity – Brutus is melancholic, Cassius
choleric, Caesar phlegmatic, and Antony sanguine ('blood'). It is
indicated moreover that the humours of the four leaders have
become 'ill-temper'd' (iv.iii.115) and excessive and so have contributed to the 'falling sickness' that afflicts the whole body politic.
Cassius' choleric urge to 'strike fire' in men like 'gentle Brutus' and
'dull Casca' begins a Roman fever. Brutus' black depression darkens
his reason and makes him 'suck up the humours' and 'unpurged air'
of the conspirators' night (ii.i.262–6). Caesar's insistence on being
always Caesar, always beyond change, motion, and emotion, merely
feeds his falling sickness (since 'security gives way to conspiracy').
And Antony's warm nature and consequent ability to 'stir men's
blood' (iii.ii.223) turns weeping citizens into barbarians. The
humoral conception of the four characters corresponds with their
actions and interactions in another way too. The wholly contrarious
nature of choler (hot and dry, corresponding to fire) and of phlegm
(cold and moist, corresponding to water) is reflected in the profound
mutual antipathy of Cassius and Caesar; and it is figured in Cassius'
fiery account of how he pulled Caesar ('a man of such feeble temper')
from a watery death (i.ii.99–114). The total contrariety of melancholy (cold and dry, like earth) and blood (warm and moist, like air)
is echoed in the oratorical styles of Brutus' and Antony's struggle for
the hearts of the citizens. The relatively frequent use of such terms as
'humour', 'complexion', 'temper' and 'element', overt references to

Cassius' choleric humour, and the tendency of the *dramatis personae* to set themselves up as shrewd psychologists would all have combined to prompt an Elizabethan audience to perceive this simple character pattern. So too would its familiarity with such pictorial illustrations of the four humoral types as are found, say, in *The Shepardes Kalender* or – on a wholly different plane – in Albrecht Dürer's 'The Four Apostles'.[13] All this, however, is not to suggest that the four leading characters are fully intelligible in terms of humoral psychology. My point is simply that each is given, especially at the outset, a general resemblance to one of the four 'complexions', and that this is done for more than psychological reasons. Shakespeare is relating the problems of Rome to those of the whole – or every – human community.[14]

Quadruple grouping is not confined to these characters. The bonds which 'incorporate and make us one' are exemplified in two structurally balanced and strongly contrasted marriages which are visibly affected by the divisiveness emanating from the 'bond' of 'secret Romans' (II.i.124–5, 273). The well-known passage in which Thomas Platter records his visit in 1599 to a performance of what was almost certainly Shakespeare's 'tragedy of the first Emperor Julius Caesar' is surely relevant here. After the performance, notes Platter, the actors 'danced ... most gracefully, two in men's clothing, two in women's clothing, wonderfully with one another'.[15] Although a concession to popular taste, this dance harmonised perfectly with the theme and method of the preceding tragedy, marriage and dance being familiar symbols for the concordant contrariety of the four elements and the natural order.

But there are other, more conspicuous, examples of quadruple grouping than the two marriages. We have been induced by modern productions (and critical commentary) to expect a crowd in the scene where Brutus and Antony contend for the hearts of the people. According to the text, however, the people are represented by the First, Second, Third, and Fourth Plebeian (presumably there were eight at the start of the scene, Brutus having instructed Cassius to 'part the numbers' and go with his half into 'the other street' (III.ii.3–4)). The text also makes clear that Cinna the poet meets his fate at the hands of four plebeians in the next scene: no doubt the same ones. Our naturalistic predilection for large numbers in these scenes has blinded us to their emblematic function.

The abrupt failure of the triumvirate ('The threefold world divided' (IV.i.14)) entails the reassertion of quadruple grouping among the Roman leaders and their various followers. This begins with two stage images of republican concord, pointedly placed just after the quarrel between Brutus and Cassius and before the acrimonious pre-battle parley. Both of these little tableaux are located in Brutus' tent; and since this was probably represented on Shakespeare's stage by means of a scaffold, if not by one of those structures known as 'mansions', their emblematic effect could have been quite pronounced.[16] In one, Messala and Titinius join the two reconciled friends and are warmly invited to sit 'close' with them around the candle-lit table (iv.iii.162). In the other, Lucius plays his sleepy tune, and he, Varro, Claudius, and Brutus – servant and master, sentries and general – seek 'good repose' in a spirit of affection and mutual respect in the one confined place. The significance of these two stage images, however, is that what harmony there is in the conspirators' party is of its very nature transient if not illusory – the light fails (iv.iii.273), the ghost of Caesar disturbs the sleepers' repose: 'The strings, my lord, are false' (line 290).

This idea is recapitulated in the more complex and expressive staging of v.i. The first part of the scene presents a stark image of division and incipient disintegration, with Brutus and Cassius at the head of one Roman army, and Antony and Octavius at the head of another, meeting symmetrically at the centre of the stage to parley together like stinging bees (lines 34–9). The conspicuous absence here of Lepidus the triumvir, the fact that Octavius is now addressed as 'Caesar' for the first time (the ghost of his namesake has just left the stage), and the suggestion of a pun in Antony's oddly phrased invitation to Octavius to step forward and complete the group ('Make forth' (line 25)) all combine to create a powerful reminder of the old quadruple structure that failed. In the second half of the scene, the symbolic impact of quadruple grouping is greatly sharpened by means of antithetical contrast and ironically disclosed analogy. After Antony and Octavius take their leave with words of bitter defiance, '*Lucilius and Messala stand forth*' immediately (Folio SD) to partner Brutus and Cassius. Hands are joined, the talk is mostly of love and friendship, and the scene ends with a ceremonious farewell. But this formal display of friendship serves to gloss over a serious flaw in the relationship between Brutus and Cassius (see lines 73–5), and it simultaneously bodes eternal division: 'this parting was well made' (lines 118, 121).

Indeed the play ends with a comment on Brutus' dream of republican unity which is fiercely ironic, if strangely consoling. A

brief but eloquently symbolic stage direction introduces us to the
fact that Brutus' surviving followers have been befriended by the
opposition and become part of a new Rome: '*Enter Antony, Octavius, Messala, Lucilius, and the army* (v.v.52; emphasis added).
And then Caesar rounds off Antony's panegyric on the man in
whom the elements were once well-mixed, and who 'made one' of
the factious for a time, by announcing that 'Within my tent his
bones tonight shall lie, / Most like a soldier, order'd honourably'
(lines 78–9). The waste is irreparable, yet out of strife comes unity.
This impression fully accords with historiographic traditions relating to the death of Caesar and the rise of Octavius. Plutarch,[17]
Appian,[18] Lucius Julius Florus,[19] John Carion,[20] and William
Fulbecke[21] all see the killing of Caesar as the logical culmination of
over one hundred years of internal strife and moral decline among
the Romans; but they also see it as the means by which Fortune co-
operated with divine providence to restore unity to Rome and to
bestow upon it and the world 'The time of universal peace'
(*Ant.*, iv.vi.4).

In this tragedy of friendship betrayed, lost, and tentatively
reconstituted, Shakespeare follows the example of Spenser's Book of
Friendship (Book iv) by extending fourfold patterning beyond
structure and characterisation to verbal design (see p. 43). Under-
standably, this remarkable experiment is located in the two rhetorical high points of the tragedy, the public orations of Brutus and
Antony, and in the comically terrible dialogue between the poet
Cinna and the same four citizens which follows as a kind of grotesque coda. Carefully balanced and deceptively coherent, Brutus'
speech justifies butchery by dividing the victim into four parts and
giving each its due:

(1) As Caesar lov'd me, I weep for him; (2) as he was fortunate, I rejoice at
it; (3) as he was valiant, I honour him; (4) but – as he was ambitious, I slew
him. (1) There is tears, for his love; (2) joy for his fortune; (3) honour for his
valour; (4) and death for his ambition. (iii.ii.24–8)

Antony's oration is fluid, unpredictable, passional. But there are
clear signs of Brutus' abstract, balanced order in the exordium; here
Antony pretends respect for Brutus and simultaneously begins the
process of demolition, sliding from imitation into something like
mocking parody: (1) 'The noble Brutus / Hath told you Caesar was
ambitious. / If it were so, it was a grievous fault ... (2) But Brutus
says he was ambitious, / And Brutus is an honourable man ... (3)

Yet Brutus says he was ambitious, / And Brutus is an honourable man ... (4) Yet Brutus says he was ambitious, / And sure Brutus is an honourable man' (lines 79–101).

Unity or wholeness is quadripartite: thus Cassius said to his friends that 'three parts' of Brutus were won over to the conspiracy and that 'the man entire / Upon the next encounter yields him ours' (I.iii.154–6). So too division or dismembering is a process of quartering: predicting that the butchery done on Caesar will lead to 'domestic fury and fierce civil strife', Antony declares that infants will soon be 'quarter'd with the hands of war' in 'all the parts of Italy' (III.i.264–9). His prophecy begins to be fulfilled in the short scene which follows his oration. Cinna the poet is the first Roman innocent to be quartered, and his dismembering is done in an exquisitely mocking, quadripartite style. In the third and fourth lines of his four-line opening speech, Cinna stumbles on a key pun: 'I have no will to wander forth today, / Yet something leads me forth' (III.iii.3–4). He is immediately confronted by the four plebeians from whom come, in rapid succession, four questions (name? destination? abode? marital status?) and four demands (answer directly, briefly, wisely, truly). Cinna then parodies this double-four catechism with an injudicious air of amusement, proceeds to answer each of the four questions in the manner demanded, and is finally rewarded for his humorous tribute to the tetrad by instant dismemberment: 'Tear him, tear him!' (lines 5–35).

The symbolic function of quadruple patterning is simultaneously exposed and reinforced by the use of elemental imagery, more conspicuous and pervasive here than in any previous play of Shakespeare's. The broad imaginative effect of this imagery is unmistakeable. In the joint speech of the tribunes (I.i.34–62), in Cassius' tirade against Caesar, in Casca's (symbolically central) description of the great storm, and in Antony's oration, the impression conveyed by elemental imagery is one of turbulent chaos wherein bounds and bonds are broken and transformation is the norm: water invades earth, wind 'incenses' water, and earth, water, and wind are subsumed in a river of blood-red fire. As in the Knight's Tale, and subsequently *Othello*, *King Lear*, and *Coriolanus*, the most important elements are water and fire, signifying the primary forces at work in nature: love and hate, pity (tears) and fury, gentleness and cruelty. The plebeian's image of Antony, 'his eyes red as fire with weeping' (III.ii.115) provides a perfect epitome of this symbolic dualism precisely as it functions in this particular play: love, friendship, pity, grief, is not only overcome by, but also is made to serve, and so quickly becomes one with, its opposite. When Antony observed 'beads of sorrow' in the eyes of Octavius' servant (seeing Caesar's body), his own eyes 'Began to water' and he reflected that 'Passion is catching' (III.i.284–6). In this he had found his demagogic cue: from his own genuine but manipulated tears come the 'gracious drops' (III.ii.194) of the plebeians, and from these comes a funeral pyre that threatens to engulf all Rome. Leaving the stage, the four chant in sequence: 'We'll burn his body in the holy place, / And with the brands fire the traitors' houses'; 'Go fetch fire'; 'Pluck down benches'; 'Pluck down forms, benches, windows, any thing'. The threat to Rome has its roots in human nature's unstable contrariety.

Another, and intimately related, symbolic dualism of great significance is that of hand and heart. For Shakespeare the harmonious relationship between these two parts of the body – the one that feels and the one that gestures and acts – is a major symbol of human integrity and a basic prerequisite for interpersonal at-one-ment. However, the reconciliation of Cassius ('Give me your hand') and Brutus ('Ay, and my heart too') (IV.iii.116–17) provides the only moment in the play where this symbolic harmony is made manifest: in a world of treachery, division, and psychic disunity, hand and heart are assimilated to the war of opposites. Of special note is the fact that the two components of this binary opposition are in turn split into opposites so that the whole becomes part of the process of quartering, total dismemberment. As in *Romeo and Juliet*, there is the gentle hand of love and the violent 'hand of war', the hand that unites and that divides. The first is seen in the repetitive ritual of hand-shaking and in that of hand-kissing. The second appears in the 'stubborn' and 'angry' hand which the brooding Brutus shows to his friend and wife (I.ii.35; II.i.246), in the hand of the common slave 'which did flame and burn / Like twenty torches join'd' (I.iii.17–18), and in the sword-clutching hands of the conspirators: 'Speak hands, for me!' (III.i.76). The two hands are horrifically confused when Antony solemnly shakes the bloody hand of each of the conspirators in false token of loving friendship.

Brutus assures Antony that although the conspirators' hands 'appear bloody and cruel' in 'strength of malice', their 'hearts . . . are pitiful' and are ready to receive him 'with all kind love' (lines 166–77). The heart is identified throughout with the claims of love and pity. The numerous uses of the image in this sense culminate in Antony's great rhetorical conceit that what killed Caesar was not so much the daggers as the sight of his 'well-beloved' Brutus: 'Then burst his mighty heart . . .' (III.ii.184–6). Antony has anticipated this conceit with his punning image of Caesar as a hart and his killers as crimsoned hunters (which in turn picks up the earlier image of the sacrificial 'beast without a heart'). Cassius replicates the conceit with histrionic grief in the quarrel scene, baring his breast to Brutus and bitterly inviting him to stab 'a heart / Dearer than Pluto's mine' (IV.iii.99–101). But if the heart is the source of all that is precious, and its hardening and piercing the essence of this tragedy, it is also the seat of those passions which beget conflict and destruction. Hand on heart, Antony discloses his awareness of this fact when in the process of turning the citizens' tears to fire: 'if I were dispos'd to stir / Your hearts and minds to mutiny and rage . . .' (III.ii.121–2).[22] So we hear also about men who are 'never at heart's ease / Whiles they behold a greater than themselves' (I.i.208–9), about 'hearts of controversy' (line 109), and about 'some that smile' but 'have in their hearts . . . / Millions of mischiefs' (IV.i.50–1). In Julius Caesar (as in King Lear: see chapter 7) the heart functions as a central symbol of human nature's radical contrariety.

III

Detailed attention to the symbolic patterns in Julius Caesar not only alerts us to the sophisticated nature of the play's poetic and dramatic art; it also serves to establish the framework within which to consider what I take to be the play's central concern: the conflict between love and honour.[23] To perceive the centrality of this conflict is to recognise that the relationship between Romeo and Juliet and Julius Caesar is by no means, as is often suggested, one of total discontinuity. Here, as in the earlier play, honour is an aristocratic ('noble') and male code rooted in the universal impulse towards self-assertion, strife, violence, and hatred. Love is the universal and characteristically female force dictating peace, reconciliation, and harmony.

Of course this is very much a political play about male relationships in which women play an entirely marginal part. But it is also a play about fellow Romans whose political relationships are characterised either by friendly or unfriendly feelings; and even when individuals have unfriendly relations they also have friends in common, so that friendship between them always seems a real possibility. Friendship too is not confined to members of the same class: the Roman servant here is his master's 'friend' (III.i.123), as is the citizen the statesman's: 'Friends, Romans, countrymen' are virtually synonymous terms. Friendship too is a warmly emotional relationship, so that these Romans repeatedly refer to their friendly feelings as 'love' and even (without homoerotic suggestion) to their friends as 'lovers'.

However, although love here is predominantly male, and the female characters contribute nothing whatever to the action, the women are of considerable significance. We think instantly of Portia and Calphurnia, but we should note first the 'three or four wenches' whom Casca refers to when reporting the scene of Caesar's fall. Recovering from his epileptic (or fainting) fit, Caesar apologised for having said or done anything amiss, asking the people to put it down to his 'infirmity'; whereupon the women 'cried, "Alas, good soul"', and forgave him with all their hearts'. Casca is contemptuous of these women, remarking that they would have done no less 'had Caesar stabb'd their mother' (I.ii.269–72). Obviously his antipathy to Caesar, like Cassius', has something to do with an inability to accept – or a fundamental lack of sympathy for – Caesar's non-political infirmities. Thus the contrasting reaction of the women to Caesar may have considerable relevance to the tragedy as a whole. In the quarrel scene, where he offers his heart and dagger to Brutus, Cassius passionately complains that 'A friend should bear his friend's infirmities', that 'A friendly eye could never see such faults' and (referring to his choleric temperament) should have 'love enough to bear with ... that rash humour which my mother gave me' (IV.iii.85, 89, 117–18). It is an appeal which Brutus himself will have to make to Lucius ('Bear with me, good boy' (line 254)) and which prompts reflection on attitudes to Caesar. We ourselves are won by Caesar's friendliness towards the conspirators at his home, and then repelled by his bombastic arrogance at the Capitol – to the extent that we may feel for the moment that his death is not unmerited. On the evidence, however, his arrogance does not denote a tyrannical disposition, since he has never divorced 'Remorse from power' (II.i.19); such arrogance may be just (to his friends) an irritating humour. One is left wondering how much mere intolerance of Caesar's physical and humoral infirmities contributed to his death.

Its crudity excepted, Casca's attitude to the women is to prove typical. Portia is loved by Brutus, and Calphurnia, it would seem, by Caesar; both are respected. What they stand for as women, however, is disregarded when the claims of male honour intervene. Caesar is prevailed on by Calphurnia not to go to the Capitol, but he must impute his decision to her apprehensive female 'humour' (ii.ii.56) rather than to any fearfulness on his own part; and when Decius arrives to play on his need to be 'always Caesar' ('I can give his humour the true bent' (ii.i.210)), 'foolish' Calphurnia is silenced forever (ii.ii.105). The defeat of Portia is more subtle and more poignant. Brutus agrees to confide in her, but only because she has achieved the male ideal of constancy by stabbing herself in the thigh – a symbolic violation of her sexual identity as well as a pre-echo of the assassination. Moreover, her tender reconciliation with Brutus is abruptly terminated ('Leave me with haste' (ii.i.309)) when Ligarius arrives to join the conspiracy – Ligarius, who fails to turn up at the Capitol.

Ligarius' name comes from the word *ligare*, which means literally to bind or to tie, and figuratively to bind together or to unite, as in a compact. His arrival completes the 'knot' (iii.i.118), or 'bond' of eight 'secret Romans' of which Brutus speaks so proudly.[24] This bond is set in clear contrast to 'the bond of marriage' which 'doth incorporate and make us one'. The marriage bond symbolises the union of opposites on which the stability of society depends; the nocturnal conspiracy is its dark parody, reminiscent of the demonic compact or marriage, and it is destined to produce 'domestic fury and fierce civil strife' rather than oneness and freedom (Othello's bond with Iago has the same spiritual and mythic status). The dark bond unquestionably involves love, the desire for oneness, but it also violates and perverts it. Brutus knows he can persuade Ligarius to join the conspiracy because 'he loves me well' (ii.i.219); and indeed Ligarius joins – 'to do I know not what' – without hearing any of Brutus' 'reasons' (ii.i.219, 333). Cassius plays heavily on their mutual love in order to get Brutus to join him; and sour Casca is eager to recruit Brutus because he 'sits high in all the people's hearts' (i.iii.157).

But of course what makes the secret bond so enormous a violation and perversion of love is that it involves the murder of Caesar by 'Caesar's angel'. The 'gentle Brutus' (i.ii.32, 70; ii.237, 279) accommodates himself to the brutal deed by 'fashioning' it not only as a political necessity but also as a holy act in which one friend is unselfishly sacrificed by another for the good of many friends (again, *Othello* is anticipated). Before coming to his decision, Brutus had been 'with himself at war' (i.ii.46). But when he tells Antony, 'I . . .

did love Caesar when I struck him', 'pity to the general wrong of Rome ... hath done this deed' (III.i.170, 182), he has vanished into a state of near-insane contradiction and moral chaos.[25] And from this he never really re-emerges: not even when he asks Volumnius ('Even for ... our love of old') to hold his sword so that he can run on to it, and the latter replies: 'That's not an office for a friend, my lord' (v.v.27, 29). In the violent delirium of gentle Brutus, where power is wholly disjoined from remorse, Shakespeare's conception of tragedy as a state of confounding contrariety, mirroring the state of primal chaos, reaches a new level of individualised intensity. Where Brutus' tragedy falls short of the standard set by his great successors in the canon is that the act which violates his better nature and moral identity causes him so little suffering, and leads to no increase in self-knowledge or general understanding.

IV

In the panegyric words of Antony and Octavius which close the play, we are left with a twofold picture of the noble Brutus: the gentle, harmonising Brutus, and the martial Brutus whose body must lie 'most like a soldier, ordered honourably'. For Plutarch, Brutus approximated to the ideal of balanced and complete nobility which he saw embodied in Pericles, who combined martial exploits with a good and gentle nature.[26] In Shakespeare the gentle, loving side of Brutus' nature is greatly emphasised; and it is refined too by secondary but quite potent stress on his bookish and reflective intellectualism. During the Renaissance the chivalric ideal of nobility as martial valour combined with love or loving-kindness was amplified under the influence of humanist thought and changing social conditions to include learning: join 'the ornament of letters with prowesse of armes', advised Castiglione, adding that Brutus was one of the 'many excellent captaines of old time' who did just that.[27] The new complete man excels in both 'arts and martial exercises' (*2 H4*, IV.v.74), and when he is a lover he has eloquence and wit; he will unite Mars with Mercury (god of eloquence and the arts) as well as with Venus. The Mars–Mercury paradigm, as R.M. Frye has shown,[28] is combined in Hamlet, with whom Brutus has long been compared; but both paradigms seem to converge in Brutus – no courtly lover to be sure, but certainly a loving husband and friend as well as a philosophical soldier.

Antony's claim that the opposites in Brutus' nature were well mixed accords with Plutarch's almost wholly admiring view of the man. It is quite at variance, however, with what we have seen of him in this play; it can only refer (magnanimously) to the Brutus who existed before 'passions of some difference' left him at war with himself. Although fully apparent, the two sides of his noble nature are thrown into total disjunction by the crisis with which he is confronted, so that in the mad suicide of Portia and the near-mad scene of Caesar's murder we behold the tragic overthrow of love and rationality by the demands of martial valour – or honour.

For Brutus valour is the essence of honour: 'as he was valiant, I honour him'. Nevertheless his attitude to honour accords with the highest formulations which that slippery concept was accorded in the Renaissance.[29] He wants to live up to the good name of his ancestors and like them is patriotically prepared to fight and lose his life for 'the general good' (I.ii.85). He is stirred to action by altruistic principle and not for reasons of personal gain or resentment; nor because of choleric vindictiveness; nor simply for the 'manly' pleasure of engaging in some 'enterprise / Of honourable-dangerous consequence' (I.iii.124–5). In these respects he differs from the other conspirators, although he does share with them the assumption that honour is incompatible with the acceptance of kingship. Shakespeare, however, probes with remarkable subtlety into human motivation in this play and finds a general tendency to confuse altruistic and egoistic motives, unselfish, patriotic endeavour and self-will. In this process Brutus' honour, and beyond that the republican ideal of an egalitarian nobility, is seriously questioned. What we are shown is a deep, competitive thrust towards personal dominance shared by all four major characters.

The great republican theme with which Cassius initiates the conspiracy is that no one man should be allowed to 'awe' and 'get the start of the majestic world', and so 'bear the palm alone' (I.ii. 123, 130–1); by implication, majesty and the honours of leadership are for everyone (or for all noblemen). Yet the whole burden of his illustrative anecdote is that he himself has a compulsive desire to take up every challenge, lead the way, and win the palm. Dared by Caesar (in friendly contest and 'with hearts of controversy') to swim the Tiber, 'Accoutred as I was, I plunged in / And bade him follow (lines 105–6); and he cannot forget that he was supremely the victor. A further irony is that he is now in effect a self-appointed leader: 'Into what dangers would you lead me, Cassius . . .?' (line 63).

Such ironies, however, might be said to matter only as anticipations of what we are to see in Brutus. Once in the conspiracy, he instinctively assumes the leadership and maintains it to the end; if ever a group was dominated (in Cassius' bitter phrase) by 'one man ... but one only man' (lines 153, 157), it is this. Cassius proposes that Antony should be killed, but Brutus overrules him. Cassius proposes an oath, but Brutus will not have it. Cassius, supported by Casca, Cinna, and Decius, proposes that Cicero be invited to join the conspiracy; Brutus vetoes the proposal, giving as his reason (this is fine) that Cicero 'will never follow any thing / That other men begin' (II.i.151–2). Metellus mentions Ligarius as a possible recruit, and Brutus gives an order: 'Send him but hither, and I'll fashion him' (II.i.220). At the Capitol he steadies the nerves of his jumpy followers, and after the murder decides that they should all face the public in a singularly impolitic manner. Cassius is awed by his steely authority, and so a great wheel comes full circle: in the opening scene, the tribunes rebuked the citizens for helping to 'grace' the chariot wheels of Caesar after his defeat of a fellow Roman; now Cassius lines up behind Brutus after the killing of Caesar: 'Brutus shall lead, and we will grace his heels ...' (III.i.121). Cassius' will is not wholly subdued, however. He opposes Brutus' decision to let Antony speak to the people, but is overruled; he opposes Brutus' plan to descend from the hills at Philippi to meet the enemy, but his 'good reasons', says Brutus, must give way to better. Of course it is not to Brutus' reason but to his 'will' (IV.iii.222) that he gives way: 'Against my will ... am I compelled to set / Upon one battle all our liberties' (v.i.73–5). He knows that if he had 'rul'd' (line 47) from the start, disaster would not be imminent.[30]

The same struggle of wills, the same impulse to lead, the same push towards one-man-rule (i.e. mon-archy) is apparent on the opposite side. Playing adroitly with Caesar's will, so that the citizenry become pure will ('The will, the will! We will hear Caesar's will'), Antony pretends to submit in order to lead: 'You will compel me to read the will? ... Shall I descend? and will you give me leave?' (III.ii.139, 159–62). His reward is: 'we'll follow him, we'll die with him' (line 210). In the triumvirate he quickly assumes leadership, proposing first that Lepidus be got rid of. Octavius reluctantly submits ('You may do your will; / But he's a tried and valiant soldier' (IV.i.27–8)), but accepts all his other confident proposals without demur. Almost at the last moment, however, Cassius' 'peevish schoolboy' abruptly resists, planting a seed of stubborn will from which will spring Rome's most famous monarchy. He will not take the left hand of the battle-field as instructed, but the right.[31] He offers no reason for crossing the astonished Antony 'in this exigent' ('I do not cross you, but I will do so') and begins to reverse roles: 'Come, Antony, away!' (v.i.21–2, 67). It is he who closes the play – and with a series of urbane commands.

Cassius and Brutus insist that submission to the will of one powerful man is base, a condition of bondage, total loss of freedom. Yet it is suggested that the desire to serve, the willingness to acknowledge and to follow the greater man, is an instinct as deeply implanted in human nature as the desire to rule. The citizens' decision to make Brutus king and then to follow Antony to death may illustrate fixed assumptions about their radical instability, but it also aligns them with their social superiors. Brutus is inferior to Cassius as a political and military leader, yet all the conspirators, including Cassius, bow to his moral authority; and they can follow him no less blindly than the citizens follow their leader of the moment:

> Set on your foot.
> And with a heart new-fir'd I follow you
> To do I know not what; but it sufficeth
> That Brutus leads me on. (ii.i.331–4)

Outside the group of eight, too, there are some who grant this kind of esteem to Cassius. For Titinius, he is 'the sun of Rome', and his death entails total darkness. The sun image has royal overtones: before committing suicide, Titinius places a garland on Cassius (would have had him bear the palm alone), and Cato exclaims: 'Brave Titinius! / Look where he have not crown'd dead Cassius' (lines 85, 96–7). Taken in a context where the willingness to honour and follow one man above all others is so conspicuous, the double irony of King Brutus and crowned Cassius seems to disqualify the republican objection to kingship, as if it involved no more than distaste for a name.[32]

A thoroughly Shakespearian suggestion (to be encountered in later tragedies) is that service, which can seem or become hateful, a state akin to bondage, may become entirely acceptable, indeed a condition superior to freedom, through love or friendship. It is love which make Cassius submit his imperious will to Brutus' faulty rule after the quarrel; which makes Lucius willing to harp in the night for his gentle master; and makes Pindarus prefer bondage with Cassius to freedom without him: 'So, I am free; yet would not so have been, /

Durst I have done my will. O Cassius!' (v.iii.47–8). Pindarus turns out to be the 'willing bondman' to whom Cassius contemptuously referred when he declared that he would commit suicide rather than live under a king (i.iii.86, 113). Striving will and loving acceptance are obviously reconcilable. In a world of clashing opposites, Pindarus is a resolved paradox.

Basic to both love and honour is constancy, a virtue much prized in the Renaissance but associated specifically with the Romans. Signifying unity in its root sense – 'standing with' or 'standing together' (*con-stare*) (cf. ii.i.142; iii.i.88) – constancy entails fidelity to self and to others, resoluteness and loyalty. Hamlet's Horatio ('more an antique Roman than a Dane') is the perfect exemplar of constancy, a man who cannot be tempted by Fortune to betray either himself or his friend; unchanging in a mutable world. It is apparent in *Julius Caesar* that the Roman self-image is based almost entirely on this virtue; but it is equally apparent that constancy is yet another focus for tragic contradiction and disunity. Brutus is manifestly the most constant of all the Romans. Nowhere is the nobility of his character more strongly felt than in his impassioned speech to the effect that no true Roman could possibly 'break the smallest particle / Of any promise that hath pass'd from him' (ii.i.139–40). As already noted, it is his constancy which holds the conspirators together and keeps them true to their purpose at the Capitol; and his suicide identifies him with the Stoic model of constancy in the face of shame and degradation. However, the gross contradiction inherent in his constancy – resolution in the murder of a trusting friend; truth to self and treachery to another – is underlined from the moment he joins the conspiracy. Roman constancy has become a mask, a dignified acting style, which hides a 'monstrous visage' (ii.i.77–85, 221–7).

V

Both Caesar and Brutus seek by their constancy to transcend change: Caesar would be with the stars and the gods, Brutus would join the statues of his ancestors. But despite their posthumous fame, in character and conduct they are shown to be wholly representative of a world in which swift contrarious change (imaged in Tiber's 'angry flood' bursting its banks) has become the norm. If the play could be said to have one all-embracing theme it is that of metamorphosis, transformation. Borrowings from Ovid's *Metamorphoses* have been detected in i.iii and ii.ii;[33] but Shakespeare's favourite poem seems to have exercised a powerful, subterranean influence throughout.

Apart from the great changes in Fortune, embodied with such dramatic power in the beautifully structured action,[34] change takes two forms: men change in time, and they change one another. The citizens who loved Pompey now love the man who conquered him (i.i.36–55). Brutus treats Cassius coldly and roughly instead of gently and lovingly, as of old (i.ii.33–6). To his wife he seems so ungentle that if he had changed as much in appearance as behaviour he would be physically unrecognisable (ii.i.237–55). He and Cassius change places as leader and lieutenant. Casca was quick mettle at school but is 'grown to be' a 'blunt fellow' (i.ii.294–5). Caesar 'is superstitious grown of late, / Quite from the main opinion he held once / Of fantasy, of dreams, and ceremonies' (ii.i.195–7).[35] He is deaf in one ear and claims unconvincingly to be the Caesar he always was; and nothing changes so swiftly as his pose of adamantine constancy at the Capitol. He falls because Brutus feared that being made king 'might change his nature' (ii.i.13). That fear is profoundly ironical, the great central change being that of the gentle, humane, and scholarly Brutus into the delirious assassin who kills his friend: Antony's phrase, 'O judgement thou art fled to brutish beasts, / And men have lost their reason' (iii.ii.104–5), links up with all the animal imagery (e.g. Casca the cur) to hint at the pun on Brutus' name which Hamlet will jocularly articulate.[36] After the great central revolution of Fortune's wheel, Antony changes from grieving follower to pitiless leader; and then Octavius the follower becomes leader. The conspirators keep changing too. Brutus sees 'change' in the conduct of Cassius towards him, 'A hot friend cooling' (iv.ii.7, 19); and certainly their joint attitude to political rectitude has altered. Brutus then changes his attitude to suicide, and Cassius (like Caesar) his attitude to omens. Cassius kills his own men when they desert him: 'Myself have to mine own turn'd enemy' (v.iii.2). 'It is but change, Titinius' (line 51), remarks Messala, referring to the exchanges of fortune on the field; but his words present themselves as an epigraph for the whole play.

The portentous upheavals which take place on the night of the conspiracy – when 'all things change from their ordinance, / Their natures, and pre-formed faculties / To monstrous state' (i.iii.66–8) – provide a vividly coloured backdrop to the human transformations which constitute the fabric of the drama. Casca professes himself profoundly 'mov'd' (i.iii.3) by this spectacular pageant of violent change, but in fact he is about to be moved himself in a more fundamental sense – changed by Cassius from a servile but disgruntled follower of Caesar into a deadly enemy. Moving or motion is an ancient philosophical synonym for change; moreover 'motion' (from which we get 'emotion') was a common Elizabethan term for passion; and the art of persuasion (rhetoric) was termed the art of moving – the orator seeks to change people, ideally by appealing to their reason, but too often solely to their will, through their feelings or emotions. This nexus of ideas is embedded in the thought patterns of *Julius Caesar*. The tragedy is deeply concerned both with the emotional side of human nature and with the way in which it makes people susceptible to change and vulnerable to the manipulative – especially the orally persuasive – skills, of others. Such concern is most apparent, of course, in Antony's brilliantly successful attempt to convert the plebeians to his side by catching their hearts and wills; nowhere in literature has there been a more powerful illustration of the might of the tongue and the dangers of demagoguery. Antony's triumph, however, is but the climax of a series of events in which men consciously set about re-fashioning others.

In the opening scene the tribunes effect an alchemic change in the plebeians, turning their jubilation at Caesar's triumph into 'tongue-tied ... guilt[gilt]iness': 'See where their basest mettle be not mov'd' (lines 62–3). Caesar wins the hearts of the women with his appeal for forgiveness, while Cassius simultaneously seeks to move Brutus against Caesar. In soliloquy he remarks that Brutus' 'honourable mettle may be wrought / From that it is dispos'd', and that anyone, however firm, may be 'seduced' (i.ii.307–11). The Plutarchan passage which prompted this soliloquy indicates that Cassius is thinking of the bad effect Caesar's company may have on Brutus' republican convictions.[37] In its dramatic context, however, the soliloquy works ironically to emphasise that Cassius himself is the means by which the noble Brutus, in an inversion of the alchemic process, will be seduced into base action. He has spoken feelingly to Brutus (already 'vex'd with passions of some difference') on the subjects of honour and Caesar; and although Brutus seems to have responded coolly ('I would not ... Be any further mov'd' (lines 166–71), he has in fact been projected into a realm of phantasma and hideous dream: 'since Cassius first did whet me against Caesar, / I have not slept ...' (ii.i.62–3). Once entered that world, too, Brutus becomes an even more remarkable agent of change than

Cassius. His first endeavour is to effect a mental transformation of Caesar's character: 'since the quarrel / Will bear no colour for the thing he is, / Fashion it thus ... Think him as ...' (II.i.28–32). Thereafter his function, as Casca foresaw, is to work 'like richest alchemy' so as 'to change to virtue and to worthiness' what would otherwise 'appear offence' (I.iii.159–60). Caesar is to be carved as a dish fit for the gods, not hewn as a carcass fit for hounds; 'This shall make our purpose necessary, and not envious'; 'so appearing to the common eyes, / We shall be call'd purgers, not murderers' (II.i.173–80).

VI

One of the inevitable consequences of living in so changeful an environment is deep uncertainty. A remarkable feature of *Julius Caesar*, therefore, is the extent to which it focusses on the act of interpretation: the puzzled question, 'What mean'st thou by that?' is a major element in the expository plan of the opening scene (line 17), and is echoed and re-echoed throughout the play.[38] Incidents of a conventionally ominous character occasion the most obvious instances of hermeneutic activity. But such are the dynamics of this play-world that mundane phenomena habitually assume an ominous character, so that actions, speeches, writings 'obscurely' penned (I.ii.318), and even manners, gestures, physiognomy, dress, shouts, distant scenes, and unexpected movements are all subject to interpretative inquiry.[39] Thus Shakespeare's method in this play could be termed metahistorical: that is, he dramatises the problems he himself is acutely conscious of in his attempts to make sense of historical events and to assess the reliability of his sources. In terms of chronicle and history play, this procedure constituted an artistic revolution in 1599; but what makes *Julius Caesar* so richly innovative – what in fact prepares the way for *Hamlet* – is that Shakespeare makes his audience unusually aware of its own involvement in interpretative problems. Undoubtedly we perceive more of the truth than do the *dramatis personae*. Unlike Cassius, for example, we all know in the end that the shouting horsemen who surrounded Titinius were jubilant friends and not triumphant enemies (v.iii. 10–71). But only the observant minority in an audience new to the play will penetrate the prejudice of Casca to perceive that the increasingly feeble manner in which Caesar 'put by' the coronet could be ascribed not just to reluctance but also (or solely) to the oncoming of an epileptic seizure (or fainting fit induced by the 'stinking' populace: we do not know which caused his fall). And we are left with important questions which cannot be answered: was the rumour that some senators 'mean to establish Caesar as a king' (i.iii.86) correct? did Caesar mean to accept the crown if offered it? and if he did accept it, would he have disjoined remorse from power? Or to move closer to the heart of the tragedy, did Brutus murder Caesar because he loved Rome, or because (or also because) he loved the idea of himself as Rome's lover?

What we do know is that Brutus, lost in melancholy fears about the future, argued confusedly from the evidence in deciding that Caesar's life must be terminated. We also know that Cassius (and the parallel is surely significant), his mind also affected by melancholy fears, 'misconstrued everything' and consequently ended his own life:

> Mistrust of good success hath done this deed.
> O hateful error, melancholy's child,
> Why dost thou show to the apt thoughts of men
> The things that are not? (v.iii.84, 66–9).

VII

Julius Caesar is about men who seek not only to read but also to anticipate and shape the future; to act as if it were already the present. In Shakespearian terms, they put the patterned rhythm of time 'out of joint'; and the chief sign of that disruption is the violent contraction of the individual's allotted life-span. This is an idea central to *Macbeth*; here it is intrinsic to a vision of the spatio-temporal order that is cunningly adapted to the nature of the historical subject and certain ideas closely associated with it.

Plutarch's view, we have seen, was that the rise to supreme power of one absolute ruler in republican Rome was providentially ordained. Although he thought Brutus a much nobler man than Caesar, he regarded the murder as a terrible crime. Yet he did not see it as frustrating the divine will: rather, it had the twofold effect of visiting retribution on Caesar for the defeat of Pompey and occasioning the rise of Octavius. The agents of Caesar's retribution are themselves punished in a reactive process which intimates that the violent revolutions of Fortune are (in this phase of Rome's history) part of a providential order.

In *Julius Caesar* the sole allusion to divine providence occurs when

Brutus defines his life-long attitude to suicide only to renounce it: he always held it cowardly and vile to 'prevent the time of life', and believed he should arm himself 'with patience / To stay the providence of some high powers / That govern us below' (v.i.103–7). The reference to time and patience is crucial; for in the play as a whole Plutarch's notion of a divine providence is replaced by time, the all-encompassing order to which the inhabitants of Shakespeare's tragic world, prone to error, impulse, and overmastering desire, find it so difficult to accommodate themselves. 'Be patient till the last'; 'Will you be patient? Will you stay a while?': the separate appeals of Brutus and Antony to the citizens (the latter entirely hypocritical) are dramatic ironies deeply embedded in the whole conception of the tragic action. Time it is which exacts retribution both on Caesar and the conspirators; but it is time too which brings forward the youth whose arrival in Rome is so opportune, and who so confidently assures Brutus before Philippi that he 'was not born to die on Brutus' sword' (v.i.58).

What gives the time design its special character and force is the fact that Julius Caesar and Octavius Augustus Caesar are historically identified with time's order, having given their names to the seventh and the eighth months of the year – Octavius not least because his first name means 'the eighth man' (*octavus*). For this reason, the symbolism of number is apparent in the delineation of the temporal as well as the spatial order of reality here: temporal number, denoting both chronology and frequency, occurs very often. The anachronistic use of the clock has been remarked often enough, but with ill-placed scorn or tolerance. We must recognise its symbolic function and note further that this is the only play in the canon where the *dramatis personae* – and so the audience – have actually to pause to count the clock. The two key numbers for time are the number four, the number of unity and completeness, and eight. Eight is the number of justice and regeneration:[40] the conspiracy consists of eight men who strike for justice's sake and in order to revive Rome's 'mortified' spirit, but it is Octavius alone who is destined to accomplish what that number signifies.[41]

Ideas of circular motion and of containing circularity are quite frequent in the play and strongly affect its imaginative colouring; they are reflected in the structure, in reported and enacted action, and, most significantly, in references to the sun and the clock. Their essential function as ironic reminders of human limitation and fatal inevitability could hardly be missed. However, an appreciation of their full significance requires some awareness that in Pythagorean–Platonic tradition the sphere – of which the Globe's name and structure were a lively reminder – expresses the perfection of the cosmic tetrad, its unified multeity and stable motion in both the four elements (described by La Primaudaye as 'a round daunce') and the four seasons of the circling year (*annus* or 'year' was said to derive from *annulus*, meaning 'ring'). Thus when Titinius is 'enclosed round about / With horsemen', and Cassius simultaneously concludes that he will end where he began, 'Time' having 'come round' (v.iii.23–8), we know we are in an intellectual environment where space and time are held to be correspondent cosmoi.

The first victim of time's retributive action is a leader who cut short the life of fellow Romans, and whose wisdom is now consumed with confidence: he refuses to believe that his time of danger has arrived and even claims to be beyond motion and so beyond time. The way in which Shakespeare alters Plutarch's chronology seems designed to suggest that Caesar's death, sudden and untimely though it is, is really an assertion of time's order: since the feast of the Lupercal fell on the fifteenth day of February, and the ides of March on the fifteenth day also, Caesar's fall at the base of Pompey's statue takes place exactly one month – four weeks to the day – after his entry 'in triumph over Pompey's blood' (i.i.51).[42]

Unlike Flavius and Marullus, the conspirators are not concerned with what Caesar did to Pompey, but with the crimes he might commit if given time. Although they refer to 'the time's abuse' (ii.i.115), and speak vaguely about redressing wrongs, the dramatic emphasis rests firmly on the fact that they deny Caesar the opportunity to prove their fears right or wrong; they 'prevent' his future, 'abridge' his 'time of fearing death' (ii.i.28; iii.i.106). Reference to the number of times Caesar was offered the crown delicately gives shape to this idea of an unnatural truncation. On the feast of the Lupercal, and yet again on the day of his death, it is reported with emphasis that he was 'thrice presented . . . a kingly crown, / Which he did thrice refuse' (iii.ii.96–7). The significance of the fact that the crown was offered three times (it was offered twice in Plutarch's *Life* of Caesar, and many times in his *Life* of Antony) relates to the rumour that it was to be offered again, and by the Senate, on the Ides of March (at the end of the fourth week). The rumour gives urgency to the conspirators' plot to kill Caesar: but they do not wait to see if it will materialise, or what Caesar will do if there is a fourth time.

The numerical pattern of the kingship offers is reinforced by a remarkable series of puns on the word 'forth' in the dialogue between Caesar and his wife and servant on the morning of the Ides. It is arguably not coincidental that there are eight puns and that the first of them occurs in the eighth line of the scene; for the clock strikes eight when the conspirators arrive (II.ii.115). And unless we are to indict Shakespeare of extreme insensitivity in the use of words, it seems certain that a continuous if covert pun on this adverb of motion is intended. The eight puns are all concentrated within the first fifty lines of the scene and are rhetorically signalled with obvious deliberation. Thus the scene opens with Caesar soliloquising to the effect that Calphurnia 'thrice' cried out in her sleep, 'Help, ho! they murder Caesar!' (lines 2–3), and within seconds she enters to ask: 'What mean you Caesar? Think you to walk forth?' (line 8). Again, when he twice assures her that 'Caesar shall forth' (lines 10, 28), and she warns him that the heavens 'blaze forth the deaths of princes' (line 31), he responds numerically: 'Cowards die many times before their deaths: / The valiant never taste of death but once' (lines 32–3). His response to the servant's message from the augurers – 'They would not have you to stir forth to-day. / Plucking the entrails of an offering forth, / They could not find a heart within the beast' (lines 38–40) – shows an even more conspicuous use of the same kind of cueing:

> No, Caesar shall not [stay at home]. Danger knows full well,
> That Caesar is more dangerous than he:
> We are two lions littered in one day,
> And I the elder and more terrible;
> And Caesar shall go forth. (lines 44–8; see also line 50)

Shakespeare's conception of the central deed as a violation of time's order is buttressed by the treatment accorded almost all the other actions of the conspirators. When Cassius first attempts to 'move' him against Caesar, Brutus gravely remarks on the need to move only as time, patience, and opportunity dictate (I.ii.162–71; cf. IV.iii.213–14). Almost immediately, however, he plunges with Casca and the others into the realm of phantasma – familiar, later, to Macbeth – where a hectic, confused present is engulfed by spectres of the future and ghosts of the past. Vile contagious Night (line 265) and 'Erebus [Hell] ... dim' (line 84) – the children of time-less Chaos – attend the birth of the 'monstrous' plot (cf. *Oth.*, I.iii.397–8) in a scene rich with temporal significance.[43] The scene opens with Brutus expressing uncertainty as to the time and calling Lucius from his sleep on the assumption that day is near. But he is uncertain also about the date, so before the boy can return to bed he has to consult the calendar and report to his master that 'March is wasted fifteen days' (line 59). Similar difficulties afflict some of the muffled men whom Lucius admits before he finally retires. Decius and Cinna presume day is near because they see a light in what they take to be the east; but Casca disagrees, and instructs them (erroneously) on the sun's position in relation to the seasons, the four cardinal points, and the months (lines 102–11).[44] The easy naturalism with which these two pieces of dialogue on time and place are managed, together with the dramatist's tactful refusal to over-direct his audience, has helped to conceal the irony they are designed to effect in context. The irony is that these men are planning to murder a leader whose greatest and most enduring achievement during his one year as 'dictator' was to reform the republican calendar – a calendar regularly interfered with for political reasons and hopelessly at variance with the solar revolutions. Plutarch seems to have felt that the solar or Julian calendar was the clearest sign that Caesar was 'the one only absolute governor' that factious Rome required.[45] Other historians, including Appian and Carion, also highlight the achievement of the calendar, Carion introducing it in such a way as to emphasise what he holds to be the criminal folly of the assassination.[46]

In striking at Caesar, then, the conspirators are by implication striking at the one representative, imperfect and ageing though he is, of time's rule. And time replies in kind. The great movement of ironic reversal which constitutes the second half of the play is initiated and brought to its conclusion by a series of untimely acts which time assimilates to its own economy: the untimely is rendered timely, and Fortune's wheel made one with the sun and the stars, the clock and the compass. Brutus begins the movement when he makes the characteristic mistake of speaking to the citizens before Antony ('I will myself into the pulpit first' (III.i.238)), and hastens it to its conclusion when he insists on 'coming down' from 'the upper regions' and giving the word of battle 'too early' (v.i.2–6; v.iii.5). Cassius' mistake is to conclude that the successful Brutus has been captured, order Pindarus to 'come down' from his observation post (line 33), and anticipate the end by suicide. His death, like Brutus', echoes the 'preventive' murder of Caesar, and it is made to seem like the fulfilment of time's design. For Cassius' deathday is also his birthday: 'Time is come round, / And where I did begin, there shall I end. / My life is run his compass' (lines 23–5).

In contrast to their uncertainties about where and when the sun would rise, the republicans in the final scenes watch his progress, know exactly when night will fall (v.iii.60–4, 109), and recognise that their 'hour is come' (v.v.20). This final resolution of the untimely into the timely is also one of violence into 'a glooming peace'. It is a peace which comes from the temporary reconciliation of opposites, the completion of a cycle, and the sense of a spatio-temporal order reasserting itself. The play embodies the cyclical theory of history current in the Renaissance (although the theory is here modified by the suggestion of progress in the concluding reminder of an Augustan future);[47] and, as was commonplace, the cyclical pattern of history (or time) is made co-extensive with the cyclical order of nature.[48] What is distinctive about Shakespeare's manipulation of the cyclical paradigm is its dialectical emphasis: the cycles are moved by the strife of the opposites.

But the adumbration of an order or pattern is secondary to the sense of tragic loss, especially of lost time, lost friendship, and lost peace. Remembering Cassius' parting words before battle,

> Now, most noble Brutus,
> The gods today stand friendly, that we may,
> Lovers in peace, lead on our days to age! (v.i.92–4),

and Brutus' sad promise to mourn his dead friend, 'I shall find time, Cassius, I shall find time' (v.v.103), one is struck both by the unfriendliness of 'the gods' and by the inability of the two friends to perceive the full meaning of those words uttered by Brutus in the dark garden: 'Peace! count the clock!' (ii.i.192). Intuited in this play is the experience of the doomed and withered Macbeth, denied what he now knows to be the true crown of life: ripe age, with honour, love, obedience, and troops of friends.

5

Hamlet

Hamlet is at once the most expansive and the most reticent of Shakespeare's tragedies: full of digression and contradiction, amplification and ellipsis. It offers 'too much', and much of what it offers is equivocal. It has, moreover a great 'hole in the middle', left by a major issue it could easily have articulated but refuses to do so.[1] And so of all the tragedies, it is, notoriously, the one which most persistently challenges the structural and semantic patterns we elicit from it.[2] Textual problems compound the difficulties of the interpreter, but must not be seen as one of their primary causes. It is necessary to bear in mind that questions about meaning ('Will 'a tell us what this show meant?') echo continually throughout the play itself.[3] It is also useful to recall that in *Julius Caesar*, which is clearly echoed at two points in *Hamlet*, the elusiveness of meaning, and the problem of interpretation, had been presented as natural concomitants to the experience of tragic chaos and confounding contrariety: Horatio's association of the ghost with the strange events which took place in Rome before the fall of Caesar significantly connects two attempts to construe ominous signs. In *Hamlet*, however, as in Kyd's *Spanish Tragedy*, the problem of meaning and interpretation is greatly intensified by the pervasive conception of life as a play – extemporally plotted, generically confused, and with characters miscast and acting strangely. All the *dramatis personae* are spectators as well as performers in the unfolding drama of their lives, and they are at one with us in the endeavour to determine the shape and significance of what is seen and heard.

Hamlet's jocular allusion to the civilised Roman whose 'brute part' (III.ii.102) was disclosed by the demands of honour offers yet another useful way into this most enigmatic of plays.[4] Hamlet's character, unlike Brutus', is multifacetted, but it too reveals a fundamental dualism which in turn is related to the structure and dynamics of contrarious nature. Like Brutus, Hamlet is called upon to perform a violent act which the code of honour represents as his sacred duty. Martial valour is no more alien to him than it was to Brutus, the scholarly soldier. Being the complete Renaissance man, he is skilled in both tongue and sword, the arts of peace and of war; at the end, he demonstrates his complete superiority with the sword to his much lauded rival.[5] The code of honour, however, with its characteristically exclusive identification of duty with violent action that takes no account of pity, human-kindness, and forgiveness, upsets the balance of his nature. And the disturbance in his nature is intensified by the fact that the violence to which he is driven by the honour code is accompanied by an intense personal hatred for his intended victim. Moreover, that hatred exists in a state of tortuous interaction with the instinct for love and compassion on which his character as a man of conscience and civility is based. Shakespeare learned from Kyd's *Spanish Tragedy*, and perhaps also from Kyd's (?) lost *Hamlet*, that revenge, which generates hatred from grief-stricken love, fire from tears, provides an apt vehicle for ideas about conflict in the self and about the metamorphous and paradoxical nature of human nature.[6] Hieronimo's explanation for the bloodbath he has brought to the court, 'The cause was love, whence grew this mortal hate', might be Hamlet's also.

Although not so conspicuous as in *King Lear*, the word 'nature' in its various forms occurs frequently in *Hamlet* (almost forty times) and is an obvious focus for much of the contradiction and confusion which lies at the heart of the play. It catches attention from the outset. Hamlet's stepfather tells him that his grief for his father is 'sweet and commendable in his nature' but that it is also 'a fault to nature, / To reason most absurd' (1.ii.87, 103–4). We might expect such contradictions from the incestuous and fratricidal usurper, but not from the ghost (if such it is) of Hamlet's natural father. However, the ghost condemns Claudius in the most bitter and self-righteous terms of '*murder most foul* and most *unnatural*', urges Hamlet, if he has '*nature*' in him, to revenge this murder, and yet at the same time reveals that he himself is suffering because of 'the *foul crimes* done in my days of *nature*' (1.v.12, 25, 81). The distinction between natural and unnatural conduct, and between right and wrong, is curiously blurred here; indeed, although the ghost insists that his brother's 'natural gifts were poor to those / Of mine', and that Gertrude went from a celestial bed to prey on garbage (lines 61–7), the distinction between the King and his unnatural brother is not quite so pronounced as both the ghost and the Prince (with his comparison of Hyperion to a satyr) would have us believe.

Laertes' moralising on the possibility of 'Contagious blastments' even in 'the morn and liquid dew of youth' (I.iii.42) reinforces these early suggestions of nature's uncertain doubleness. His use of the word 'contagious' is ironically proleptic of the 'contagion' with which he tips his foils in the final scene, and converges on the symbolic motif of poison and witchcraft. The motif has received abundant critical attention, but its dualistic implications have been ignored. Friar Lawrence's paradox, 'Within the infant rind of this weak flower, / Poison hath residence and medicine power', is most relevant to the tragedy of Laertes and Hamlet, although its articulation is much less explicit. Here too we are reminded that Nature yields not only rich medicines but also poisons so deadly that 'no cataplasm so rare, / Collected from all simples that have virtue / Under the moon', could cure the contagion they may cause (IV.vii.143–8; cf. v.ii.306). Whereas Laertes acquires his poison from a mountebank, Claudius mixes his own (line 320); he is analogous to the witchlike Lucianus, whose 'mixture rank, of midnight weeds collected, / With Hecate's ban thrice blasted', has a 'natural magic and dire property' that usurps 'On wholesome life ... immediately' (II.ii.238–42). Claudius' poisonous 'witchcraft' (I.v.43; IV.vii.84), however, is essentially a symbol for the cunning with which he uses his knowledge of human nature in order to seduce and corrupt others. It is particularly obvious in the way he turns Laertes from an angry antagonist into a willing accomplice by converting his love for Polonius and Ophelia, and particularly his pity for Ophelia, into a raging hatred for Hamlet: 'I must commune with your grief' (iv.vii.195); 'Was your father dear to you? ... [Did you] love your father'? (IV.vii.105, 108). However, the ghost uses the same technique when recruiting Hamlet for revenge against Claudius. 'Pity me not', he says, but his horrifying account of his sufferings inevitably excites the utmost compassion in the grieving son ('O thou poor ghost', 'Alas, poor ghost'); and his call for revenge is firmly based on filial affection: 'If thou didst ever thy dear father love ...' (I.iv.24).[7] Like Ophelia, 'young Hamlet' and 'young Laertes' are the flower of youth destroyed in 'primy nature' (I.iii.7) – the floral image is applied only to Ophelia, but Laertes' long speech on 'nature crescent' and blasted has the effect of generalising the metaphor. They are the victims of a 'witch' and a ghost who convert good impulses into a deadly venom; love and pity to hatred and fury. The point of essential significance, however, is that the materials for witch and spirit to work on are inherent in the infant rind itself.

One important effect of this thought pattern is that the dark supernatural (the realm of spirits and ghosts), like witchcraft, becomes a metaphor for the complexities of the natural; awe-inspiring though it is, the ghost is akin to Hecate, goddess of witches and of Lucianus; in effect, its power is based on 'natural magic'. This implicit identification (or at least intimate association) of the dark supernatural with the malignant and unpredictable forces in nature is crystallised in the beautiful passage referring to the state of peace which (according to a popular belief) prevails in the world before Christmas: 'no spirit dare stir abroad, / The nights are wholesome . . . no planets strike, / No fairy takes, nor witch hath power to charm' (I.i.161–3). More illuminatingly, perhaps, it is indicated in the parallel reference to extravagant and erring spirits who escape from their confine to hide 'in sea or fire, in earth or air' (lines 152–5).

Elemental imagery constitutes a major portion of the play's symbolism and provides clear evidence of the contrarious model of nature and its impact on characterisation and theme. The interaction between love and hate and pity and ruthlessness is figured from the outset in the imagery of fire and water. Horatio's description of the way in which, before Caesar's fall, 'stars with trains of fire' and 'disasters in the sun' caused an eclipse in 'the moist star' that rules the waters (I.i.117–20) anticipates the ghost's tale of subjection to 'sulph'rous and tormenting flames' (I.v.3), and the effect which that tale has on Hamlet. It makes Hamlet feel that he should 'drown the stage with tears' (II.ii.555) (a flood compared to his earlier 'fruitful river of the eye'); but it also renders him pitiless towards almost everyone except the ghost, its ultimate purpose being to make his blood burn and blaze (I.iii.116–17) and so thrust him into 'the fell incensed [i.e. fiery] pass / Of mighty opposites' (v.ii.62–3).

The symbolic interaction of fire and water is much more conspicuous in relation to two characters in whom Hamlet sees an *alter ego*, Pyrrhus and Laertes. 'Roasted in wrath and fire' amidst the flames of Troy, covered in blood which has been 'Bak'd and impasted with the parching streets' (II.ii.450–5), Pyrrhus the avenging son is a figure of nightmare proportions and all-consuming violence. His very name is descriptive of his nature, being simply the Greek word for 'flame-coloured' ($\pi\upsilon\rho\rho\acute{o}\varsigma$, from $\pi\hat{\upsilon}\rho$, 'fire'). Against the remorselessness of this 'Mars' incarnate (line 484), and the destruction which he epitomises, comes Hecuba, a female voice character-istically 'threatening the flames / With bisson rheum' or blinding tears. Her 'instant burst of clamour' as Pyrrhus prepares to butcher her husband 'would have made milch [moist] the burning eyes of heaven', but has no effect on Pyrrhus (lines 499–511). However, her woes reduce the First Player who recites them to tears and in-articulacy, so that he, by contrast, is unable to proceed. Greatly impressed, Hamlet feels that he should emulate the player and drown the stage with tears; but he feels too that his tears should make him as furious and merciless as the Greek avenger, so that he might fatten all the region kites with Denmark's 'kindless villain' (line 576).

Only in his mother's closet, and more by accident than intent, does Hamlet come near to imitating the man of fire. Lecturing Gertrude on the unnaturalness of burning passion in frosty middle age ('To flaming youth let virtue be as wax / And melt in her own fire' (iii.iv.84–5)), he works himself into such a fury that he can dispose of Polonius with as little remorse as Pyrrhus did 'old grandsire Priam'. With a nice dramatic irony which emphasises Hamlet's failure to understand himself, Shakespeare recalls that this transfor-mation of the Prince into a pitiless man of fire and blood has been vitally dependent on his compassionate and loving nature. 'Do not look upon me', he appeals to the ghost,

> Lest with this piteous action you convert
> My stern effects. Then what I have to do
> Will want true colour – tears perchance for blood. (lines 127–9)

The fire–water dialectic is forcefully expressed in the Claudius–Laertes exchanges in Act iv. Claudius uses all the 'witchcraft of his wits' (i.v.43) to fan 'the spark and fire' of Laertes' love for his father (iv.vii.110–13); but really it is the spectacle of his sister in madness ('O, heat dry up my brains, tears seven times salt / Burn out the sense and virtue of mine eye!' (iv.v.152–3)), and the news of her drowning, that 'incenses' Laertes beyond all bounds and makes him so compliant a tool for Claudius. Laertes weeps, and his tears momentarily inhibit but ultimately exacerbate his 'manly' rage: 'When these [tears] are gone, / The woman will be out ... I have a speech o' fire that fain would blaze / But that this folly douts it' (iv.vii.189–92).

Gertrude likens Hamlet's behaviour in the closet scene to 'the sea and winds when both contend / Which is the mightier' (iv.i.7–8);

and Laertes is later compared to 'The ocean, overpeering of his list' and eating 'the flats with ... impitious haste' (iv.iv.96–7). This extension in the pattern of elemental symbolism is characteristic of the last two acts, where the interaction of water and earth is introduced to give imaginative support to new emphases in characterisation and theme. Water is the element specifically associated with Ophelia, compassionate ('God a-mercy on his soul! / And of all Christian souls') as well as pitiable; chaste to the end despite the cynical forebodings of her father and brother; and yet tainted too by a world that seems to have soiled everything. In a decorative and lyrical set speech of a kind he will never attempt again in his tragedies, Shakespeare draws upon his reading of Ovid's *Metamorphoses* to turn Ophelia's death by drowning into an emblem of pathos and tainted purity: she becomes a 'nymph' (iii.i.89) who seems at first to dissolve through sorrow and tears into the translucent waters she haunts, but then (and here the Ovidian consolation is abandoned) sinks beneath 'the glassy stream' to 'muddy death' (iv.vii. 167–84). Set piece though it is, this speech has a poetic structure which firmly relates it to the rest of Acts iv and v. For despite the flare-up of 'incens'd' (v.ii.293) young men in the final scene, it is earth, wet, muddy, and decaying, and symbolic of corruption and death, that dominates the elemental imagery of the last two acts.

It is, of course, through the melancholy consciousness of Hamlet that most of the ideas about death and decay are mediated to us. Earth is the element correspondent to the melancholy humour, just as fire corresponds to choler. This is the tragedy of a hero who suffers from an 'o'ergrowth' of that 'complexion' or temperament (i.iv.27); one in whom 'the native hue of resolution' (i.e. blood-red, signifying the sanguine humour) is 'sicklied o'er with the pale cast of thought' (i.e. melancholy) (iii.i.84–5).[8] The prince of 'nighted colour' and 'vailed lids' who forever seeks his 'noble father in the dust' (i.ii.68–71), who meditates on the question of 'To be or not to be', who reduces the goodly frame of fire, earth, and air to a foul and pestilential congregation of vapours, and who sees man as the quintessence of dust, is also the quaint philosopher of the graveyard scene, brooding on 'the noble dust' of Alexander, on imperious Caesar 'turn'd to clay' (v.i.206), and on the base uses to which we all come in the end. He is also the hero who eventually, after much raging and self-laceration, goes to meet his death in a mood of pensive resignation.

And yet our final image is of Hamlet nobly on fire with just rage ('incens'd'), and then borne upwards, soul and body; more like Cleopatra's 'fire and air' than Caesar's clay. No one speaks on Nature's behalf to say that the elements were well mixed in him, although Ophelia recalled a time when he was harmony itself. Poetic symbolism, rather, has helped to stress that he was profoundly affected by the strife and confusion of nature's contraries, and all that that entails in terms of metamorphosis and mutability.

II

Hamlet himself is acutely conscious of the qualities and conditions that make for natural harmony and unity. He knows that the bond of opposites is also a bound or limit; things are properly distinguished, co-ordinated, and rendered 'fitting' when there is temperance, balance, restraint. Thus he explains to the players that they must find and sustain the fine point between excess and defect, and never 'o'erstep' the moderation of nature; and he praises Horatio for being one of those in whom passion and judgement are so well balanced that they remain constant – integrated and unchanging – in spite of Fortune's buffets. Constancy, or truth to self and to others, is crucial in his thinking and is widely reflected in the main concerns of the play. It relates in particular to the idea of contract or sworn faith, and so is connected on the one hand with law and on the other with marriage and friendship. Thus Horatio's exact description of the agreement made between Hamlet's father and the challenger Fortinbras ('a seal'd compact / Well ratified by law and heraldry' (i.i.86–7)) correlates with Hamlet's conception of true friendship as a 'seal'd' (iii.ii.63) choice, and his insistence that married love is a vow, a deed, part of the whole 'body of contraction' which holds the world together (iii.iv.45–7).[9]

What the tragedy shows, of course, is that the admirable world envisaged by Hamlet in which opposites are clearly distinguished, harmoniously related, and held together by firm and loving bonds, is violently 'blasted'. This word is used in the play in the sense of 'to burst or explode' as well as in the horticultural sense of 'to blight with a cold and violent gust of wind'. It is the first sense I would emphasise here, for among the thousand natural shocks that flesh is heir to, explosive military violence is one of the most conspicuous in the *Hamlet* world.[10] A literal fact, it is also a symbol for all the valiant striving and destructive strife which the action encompasses. The play begins with nervous soldiers and anxious talk about preparations for an impending war. The noise of cannon and kettledrum shatters the silence of the night in the third scene. In the final scene, drums, trumpets, and guns resound in the middle of the duel; Fortinbras makes his entry preceded by the 'warlike noise' of marching feet, drums, and guns; and the play ends as this conqueror dictates with 'a peal of ordnance shot off'. Fortinbras' threatened attack on Denmark at the start had been in clear defiance of a legal agreement. Bought off by means of his uncle's permission to attack Poland instead, he was allowed to march through Denmark on condition that he went 'with quiet pass' (II.ii.77; IV.iv.8). But when he returns 'with conquest from Poland', he lets off his 'warlike volley' for the benefit of the timid English (his future subjects, 'their cicatrice' still 'raw and red / After the Danish sword' (IV.iii.60–1)), then strides on to the battlefield of the Danish court, and blithely collects the spoils. He has broken the 'quiet pass' stipulation, but has not had to use his characteristic method of 'strong hand / And terms compulsatory' (I.i.102–3).

To this over-all impression of an explosive, daunting might, hidden at times behind the forms of right and the gestures of peace, and 'amazing' the eyes, ears, and minds of the beholder, the ghost makes a major contribution. He comes as a kind of spectral Mars (I.i.66), a 'dead corse ... in complete steel', 'bursting' out of his canonised cerements and the sepulchre wherein he was 'quietly interred' (I.iv.48–55); talking of sulphurous flames, making Hamlet 'burst in ignorance', and shaking his disposition with thoughts beyond the reaches of our souls. And demanding revenge. Even when he appears in his gown, his effect on Hamlet is that of an army descending by night on terrified, sleeping soldiers (III.iv.121–4). Hamlet remembers his father as the perfect, complete, integrated man, take him for all in all: imperious, with 'An eye like Mars, to threaten and command' (line 57), but 'so loving' to his wife 'That he might not beteem the winds of heaven / Visit her face too roughly' (I.ii.141–3). Yet there are hints that this perfect harmony, on which is built Hamlet's whole sense of the way things are and should be, is as subject to collapse, as open to doubt, as all such heroic integrity invariably is in a tragic world. Two tiny 'biographical' facts enclose large interpretative possibilities. First, on the day his wife was giving birth to their son, the king was off killing an 'emulate' rival who had issued a challenge to him (v.i.138–40). And second, during a parley (an established ritual, it should be recalled, in which an attempt is made to resolve disagreement by means of words rather than force), the King struck his Polack antagonist: angry, frowning, martial, violent (I.i.62–3).[11] The first of these details is tied into the fabric of the play by its location in the graveyard scene, where it contributes to a Lucretian sense of the interdependence of life and death. The second is anchored by means of its connection with the 'Pole' (Polonius) whom Hamlet's son strikes dead in a scene where he had promised to speak daggers rather than use them.

Hamlet's idealisation of his father is in part responsible for his instant acceptance of a call to revenge in which the only limit set is the curiously incongruous proviso that he should leave God and conscience to deal with his mother. It partly accounts too for his attraction to the likes of Pyrrhus, Laertes, and Fortinbras: the kind of men who believe that 'Revenge should have no bounds' (IV.vii.128), and who are prepared to send thousands to their graves like beds when honour's at the stake. In his lighter moments Hamlet can mock 'our outstretch'd heroes' (II.ii.263), much as Hal does the firebrand Hotspur. But the task he has undertaken is virtually impossible in the given circumstances to a man of his superior calibre, so that he becomes at times depressingly like those reckless and conscienceless heroes:[12] when, for example, he determines that Claudius should be killed in such a way as to ensure his damnation (is he being or trying to be the 'outstretched' revenger here?); when he jokes and sneers over the corpse of the man he has just killed (re-enacting Pyrrhus' 'malicious sport' with Priam's body (line 507)); when he anticipates with delight the sportive knavery of hoisting the enginer with his own petard; and when he sends Rosencrantz and Guildenstern to their deaths. Many critics have glossed over or even defended the savagery of this last action, but in terms of the standard Hamlet sets himself when he seeks to test the veracity of the ghost it is indefensible. The assumption that Rosencrantz and Guildenstern knew of and 'made love' to the plot to kill Hamlet has no apparent foundation; and even if they did know of it, their deaths were unnecessary. It is perhaps the 'changeling' letter – whose name I take to be punningly symbolic – that gives Hamlet away here; it is a perfect imitation of his enemy's style. As in the shuffled foils at the end, there is serious confusion at this point in the conflict of opposites.

Hamlet may disclaim all likeness to Hercules, but that he is possessed of heroic quality is beyond question. It is apparent in the fearlessness with which he confronts the ghost, in his willingness to taunt and oppose so cunning and powerful an enemy as Claudius, and in his boarding of the pirate ship. However, the heroic achievement which is proper to him ('rightly to be great') is one that unites resolution and restraint, valour and humanity (or conscience), sword and tongue. Whether he accomplishes that in the end is open to question; perhaps he comes as near to it as is possible for such a man in the disjointed and rotten state of Denmark. Before the end, however, Hamlet has been betrayed by the code of honour and martial violence to which the ghost and the memory of his father have called him.

III

As we have noted, it is the intricate relationship between love and the call to violence and hatred that characterises Hamlet's tragic situation. Polonius is ironically correct when he declares that the cause of Hamlet's distraction is love: a passion 'Whose violent property fordoes itself / And leads the will to desperate undertakings' (II.i.103–4). We think of Hamlet as an embittered intellectual, but he is perhaps above all a man of warm and loving nature. His praise of Horatio is not the eulogy of a cool and cerebral type but that of a friend whose stability of nature makes his friendship all the more true. And it is part of a movingly tender exchange whose tone is set by Horatio's, 'Here, sweet lord', and 'O my dear lord' (III.ii.51, 53). Ophelia speaks of Hamlet's 'noble and most sovereign reason' but for her that was manifest in the eloquence of his love: in the honey of his musicked vows, in the gifts with such sweet breath composed as made the gifts more dear. Rosencrantz and Guildenstern are welcomed as 'good friends' and conjured by 'the rights of fellowship' and 'the obligation of . . . ever-preserved love' to speak truthfully (II.ii.223, 283–5). The soldiers and players too are the recipients of his 'love and friending' (I.v.186). From such evidence we infer the depth of Hamlet's love for his father and mother, his delight in the love they showed for each other, and the shock to his sensibility caused by his father's death and all that followed.

Fratricide is a primal symbol of the shattering of human bonds. And however hard it may be for us today to regard the marriage of Claudius to his sister-in-law as incestuous, it is presented exactly as ordinary forms of incest are treated in Middleton's *Women Beware Women* (c.1621–5) and Ford's *'Tis Pity She's A Whore* (c.1633): as a reflection of primal chaos where human bonds and the order of society may be said to begin. The stamp of deep confusion is imprinted on this marriage at the outset (although thereafter it seems one of genuine affection). Claudius publicly refers to Gertrude as 'our sometime sister, now our queen', and repeatedly addresses Hamlet as 'cousin and . . . son' (I.ii.7, 64, 117). For his part, Hamlet cannot comprehend how his mother would fail to distinguish between two brothers who seem as different to him as Hyperion and satyr (line 140), sunlit mountain and dark 'moor' (III.iv.67). Even more than fratricide and incest, however, the shallowness and inconstancy of his mother's love for his father horrifies Hamlet, causing him to confuse all women with her. Thus the virginal Ophelia is rejected as another potential whore and breeder of sinners. The brutality of Hamlet's verbal attacks on his mother and (especially) on Ophelia mark the depth of his confusion: this is where the tongue becomes a dagger, leading to violent death, madness, and (perhaps) suicide. And yet it is not a question of simple transformation: for the verbal fury of the attack on Gertrude has a strongly moral component, and leads her to self-knowledge. And the obscene taunting of Ophelia is directly linked to wounded love: 'For look you how cheerfully my mother looks, and my father died within's two hours' (III.ii.121–3).

But if love drives Hamlet to the extreme point where opposites are deeply confused, it also seems to inhibit him there.[13] The great hole in the middle of this play is the unwritten soliloquy in which Hamlet weighs the rights and wrongs of private revenge and identifies the cause of his delay.[14] Hamlet's failure to do this testifies to the depth of his confusion. It has the added advantage of allowing Shakespeare to introduce a wide spectrum of moral and metaphysical questions as Hamlet's thoughts move round and about the predicament he does not understand.[15] It also allows Shakespeare to suggest the force of that instinct which prevents Hamlet from becoming another Pyrrhus or Laertes in the quest for revenge.[16]

Hamlet's state of confusion was signalled early on when he assured the ghost that he would sweep to his revenge 'with wings as swift / As meditation or the thoughts of love' (I.v.28–30): here he was proposing to confound with hatred and violence the two qualities which, in combination, distinguish him so clearly from the play's 'outstretch'd heroes'. But 'love' and 'meditation' themselves need distinguishing, for Hamlet's reflective capacity would not have saved him from the predicament into which the ghost and the unnatural brother have led him. In *Julius Caesar*, *King Lear*, and *Macbeth*, it is made clear that in times of great crisis the line between humanity and barbarism will be discerned, if at all, by 'the milk of human kindness', the capacity to 'see ... feelingly'. Shakespeare intimates that when reason operates as it should in human relationships, it is following that instinct; when it is not (and most often it is not in the tragedies), it usually functions in plain opposition to it. That instinct, I assume, is responsible for the delay which Hamlet's reason cannot account for.

Support for this interpretation can be found in Shakespeare's attitude to fear. Echoing the code of honour, Hamlet indicts himself of cowardice and assumes that fear frustrates not only his own revenge but also many other heroic enterprises of great moment (II.ii.565–72; III.i.83–8; IV.iv.43). He is right to accuse himself of fear but quite wrong in his understanding of it. As will become much more obvious in *Macbeth*, but is apparent also in *Troilus and Cressida*, Shakespeare sees fear as an important element in the rational humanity which keeps heroic endeavour from going beyond the pale; it is allied to pity and human kindness and it is at the very heart of what we call 'conscience'. In the council scene where Troilus equates reason with cowardice and dishonour, Hector contends that 'modest doubt' is 'the beacon of the wise', and explains that fear can be a form of sensitivity which begets rational speculation about the consequences in terms of human life of every martial undertaking (*Tro*.II.ii.11–15). So in *Hamlet* the 'pale cast of thought' – the fearful irresolution that is a conventional attribute of the melancholy man – is, by implication, doing what 'the pales and forts of reason' would normally be expected to do.

IV

Throughout *Hamlet* there are numerous echoes – sometimes no more than a word or a phrase – of how life should be ordered to satisfy our deepest needs. We hear of union, conjunction, and harmony; of things tempered, shaped, moulded, and differentiated; of fitness and form; of beauty, and truth, and constancy. For the most part, however, there is division, disjunction, imbalance, discord, contradiction, and deception; everything is unfitting, haphazard, roughhewn, in shreds and patches, in flux. The world as so presented is not only aesthetically and morally depressing: it is also, and in consequence, deeply perplexing, a site of endless semiotic disorder. The motif of the maze and 'amazement', which we encountered in *A Midsummer Night's Dream*, and was much favoured by other trage-

dians of the period, is conspicuous.[17] When Polonius proclaims that
he will find out where truth is hid though it is hid within the centre,
his words signal that he, like everyone else, is moving through a
labyrinth: 'What should this mean? ... Can you devise me? ... I am
lost in it' (IV.vii.47–53). It may well be that many of the interpretative 'blind alleys' (as Graham Bradshaw argues) into which the
critic of *Hamlet* continually runs are the consequence of Shakespeare's impossibly difficult attempt to graft 'an unprecedentedly inward, intellectual prince' on to a crude old revenge play.[18] I would
contend, however, that if Shakespeare experienced any such difficulty he has turned it to his own advantage by making disjunction,
contradiction, and consequent bafflement an integral part of the
play's meaning.

In the beginning, the text suggests, is the word: the word as bond
or solemn commitment between one person and another: above all,
the declaration of enduring love. Gertrude's betrayal of her husband, in Hamlet's view (III.iv.44–8), turns all contractual agreement, of which the marriage contract is the type, into a body without
soul, 'a rhapsody of words' – a 'rhapsody' meaning 'a mingle
mangle', 'a confused and meaningless heap'.[19] The disjunction of
words and deeds, and so the essential futility of all words ('words,
words, words'), is perhaps the primary symptom in the play of a
world 'disjoint and out of frame' (I.ii.20), and subject, like most of its
inhabitants, to the law of flux and confusion. Hamlet is tortured by
the presence of this disjunction not only in his mother and throughout the hypocritical court but in himself too: his life has become
a shamefully unfulfilled promise ('now to my word ... I have
sworn't').

The failure to match words and deeds, with its inevitable corol-
lary in the failure or refusal to fit words to thoughts, gives rise to the
phenomenon of uncertain identity. Who here recks his own rede?
Who is true to himself? Who is 'I, Hamlet the Dane'? Although the
assembly of qualities that make up the character of Hamlet is
unique, in mind and conduct he is or has become a tissue of contradictions; intelligible up to a point, but not reducible to a coherent
portrait; and so, endlessly fascinating. He responds with awe and
reverence to the ghost, and then treats him as a jokey devil ('old
mole' etc.). Having conversed with a supernatural traveller, he
denies the existence of such. He rules out self-slaughter because it is
condemned by divine law but ignores the biblical '"Revenge is
mine", saith the Lord.' He characterises Fortinbras' expedition as a

moral ulcer but praises it as an expression of divine ambition. He
tells the players not to mock Polonius, and Polonius that one should
treat all men according to one's own honour and dignity; his own
treatment of Polonius by no means concurs with these injunctions.
He asks for a passionate speech which, he claims, is written in a
wholesome, unaffected style; it is pure bombast (at its Shakespearian best). He urges the players to practise temperance, not to lose
control of voice or gesture, and in general to suit the word to the
action, the action to the word; after which he is extremely violent in
word and deed. He warns his mother to confess herself freely and not
to excuse herself on the ground that he is truly mad rather than
mad in craft, and at the same time he promises to 'answer well' the
death he 'gave' Polonius (III.iv.180); but when the time comes he
asks and answers: 'Was't Hamlet wrong'd Laertes? Never Hamlet
... Who does it then? His madness' (v.ii.218–29). And enveloping
all these contradictions between precept and practice, or purpose
and action, is the extreme variability of his moods, culminating in
the mysterious 'sea change' which he undergoes on his return from
England. We have, of course, to remember that minor inconsistencies are never noticed in the theatre. But these inconsistencies are
too palpable and too well accented by irony and verbal reminisc-
ence to be anything but intentional. Next to denying their existence
or significance, the great mistake is to assume that they can be made
fully intelligible. Hamlet communicates the illusion of life-likeness as
no other character does precisely because he cannot be arrested
in a unified image of 'Hamlet'.

Apart from its disjunction from fitting action, language itself
is flawed by doubleness in two senses of the word: excess and
ambiguity. The anonymous captain's reply to Hamlet's query about
Fortinbras' expedition against the Poles, 'Truly to speak, and with
no addition ...' (IV.iv.17), exemplifies a lost ideal. Pointers to the
dangers of 'too much' are to be found everywhere, from Hamlet's
early meditations on the 'habit that too much o'erleavens / The form
of plausive manners' (I.iv.29–30), to Claudius' acute play on the
word 'pleurisy' (Latin, *plus/plura*, 'more'): 'For goodness, growing to
a pleurisy, / Dies in his own too much' (IV.vii.117–18).[20] Reflecting
the destructive overflow of noble qualities in characters such as
Hamlet and Laertes, eloquence, the sign of a civilised society in
Renaissance thinking, is constantly slipping over the line between
splendour and decay. The theatrically problematic length of *Hamlet*
arises from the fact that most of the principal characters are, in

accordance with Shakespeare's design, addicted to the use of two words or speeches where one would do. In his vanity, Polonius assumes that 'a double blessing is a double grace' and launches into a second farewell speech to his loquacious son. And passionate disillusion with the world's duplicity drives Hamlet along the same path. In the nunnery scene he bids farewell to Ophelia, comes back to resume his harangue, bids farewell a second time, and returns yet again to condemn female two-facedness (the parallelism is neat): 'God hath given you one face, and you make yourselves another' (III.i.143–4). This o'erleavening of moral indignation reaches its climax in the closet scene. Four times Gertrude cries out, 'O Hamlet, speak no more' (III.iv.88, 94, 96, 101), after which the ghost intervenes. But even then Hamlet returns to his theme; as his imaginings become increasingly unwholesome, three 'goodnights' punctuate his compulsive returns for much more than 'One word more, good mother' (line 180).

However, the principal form of excess in speech is artful inflation. This is at its most conspicuous in the affected eloquence of Polonius and Osric and the bombast of Laertes and Hamlet. But it is Claudius, master of the 'double varnish' (IV.vii.132), who inaugurates and sets the seal of approval on the inflated style: his glossy and repetitive public manner functions to conceal a rottenness which spreads out from himself to affect the whole court. In his opening speeches he exhibits one verbal trick in particular which is picked up by almost everyone else – the doublet: 'sweet and commendable', 'simple and unschool'd', 'loving and . . . fair', 'cheer and comfort', 'gentle and unforc'd'. Hendiadys (etymologically, 'one from two') is a special form of doublet which occurs frequently in the play; it consists of two substantives linked by a conjunction in the expression of one idea (as in 'cheer and comfort'). It has been argued that the purpose of this figure is to suggest confusion or contradiction where the speaker intends complementarity and essential oneness of idea.[21] Although it would fit nicely with my own analysis, I am not convinced by this claim. It appears to me that the great majority of doublets in *Hamlet* function with other forms of amplification as symptoms of verbal superfluity hovering on the edge of nullity: 'What was I about to say? By the mass, / I was about to say something. / Where did I leave?' (II.i.50–2).

Hamlet twice speaks disapprovingly of ambiguous and equivocal speech, but is himself prolific in it. His puns and quibbles show that equivocation is the only linguistic instrument left for the man of truth in a court so corrupt as that of Claudius. They are also indicative of his great mental acuteness: his very first utterances in the play are equivocations which concisely expose the twin diseases of excess and confusion generated by his father's presumptive double: 'A little more than kin, and less than kind', 'Not so, my lord; I am too much in the sun' (I.ii.65, 67). Nevertheless, some of the language in Hamlet's deliberations might be placed in the same category as that of the common people, who are 'muddied, / Thick and unwholesome in their thoughts and whispers' (IV.v.78–9), and of Ophelia, who

> Spurns enviously at straws, speaks things in doubt,
> That carry but half sense. Her speech is nothing,
> Yet the unshaped use of it doth move
> The hearers to collection; they yawn at it,
> And botch the words up fit to their own thoughts. (lines 6–10)

This unusually exact description of incoherent speech and interpretative difficulties comes immediately after Hamlet's most tangled and contradictory soliloquy, where he moves unconsciously from condemnation to (envious) praise of Fortinbras' quarrelling over a straw, and proffers a most tortuous definition of true greatness. Some editors have tried heroically to extract a coherent structure of thought from this soliloquy, but the attempt is misguided.[22] The account of Ophelia's speech which follows the soliloquy characterises it very accurately, and constitutes, moreover, a timely pointer to the play's self-reflexive method. It is in effect an expanded version of Cicero's dry comment on interpretative over-confidence: 'Indeed ... / But men may construe things after their fashion, / Clean from the purpose of the things themselves' (*JC*,I.iii.33–5).

All this excess, dislocation, and confusion in language is likened to the state of primal chaos: the word and the world are one. The messenger reporting the return of Laertes at the head of a rabble who 'call him lord' and 'king' speaks not only of the ocean 'over-peering' the land (its 'list' or limit), but also of 'antiquity and custom', the 'ratifiers and props of every word', being 'forgot or not known'. Thus it seems to this messenger 'as [if] the world were now but to begin' (IV.v.96–103).

Ritual and play, the large and complex forms of expression by which society is united, suffer in much the same way as speech.[23] In ritual form, defect or truncation ('come tardy off') rather than excess ('o'erdone') is the primary source of disorder. Claudius sent his brother to his death without the last rites, 'unhous'led ... un-anel'd', and attempts to do the same to Hamlet; who in turn ensures that Rosencrantz and Guildenstern are executed 'not shriving-time allow'd'. The mourning period for the king is disgracefully brief by Elizabethan standards,[24] and this disgrace is grossly compounded by the hasty re-marriage of his widow. Claudius seeks in his open-ing speech to gloss over this strident clash of ritual opposites, but his syntactical and figurative tricks merely serve to emphasise it. Polonius' burial is 'obscure' and calls for explanation (IV.v.209–13), and Ophelia's is obscure and puzzling in a different way. Her 'maimed rites' would normally 'betoken' suicide (v.i.213), but since there are two versions of how she drowned, 'her death was doubtful' (line 221); the harshly simple ritual form chosen by the churlish priest is at best misleading. This rite, moreover, is an inverted version of the disorder which opens the play, being a funeral where there should be a marriage (lines 237–40). But of course what reduces the ritual to a singularly horrifying image of chaos is the wrestling match in the grave between the prospective bride's beloved and her brother. We are so familar with *Hamlet* that it is no longer possible for us to experience the full *frisson* of this audaciously theatrical and richly meaningful event.

The train of ritual disorders set in motion by Claudius continues to the very end. Horatio's exquisite requiem for the dead prince, calling on flights of angels to sing him to his rest, is harshly ter-minated by the sound of kettledrum and the tramp of soldiers' feet. And if the soldier's burial – 'the rite of war' (v.ii.391) – is appro-priate in the sense that Hamlet has at last killed his mighty opposite, and died nobly, it is inappropriate in other ways. For 'the soldier's music' of kettledrum and cannon functions as oxymoron (like 'mirth in funeral and ... dirge in marriage') in relation to a prince who hated noise and died with the word 'silence' on his lips. As of sound, too, so of sight: 'Such a sight as this / Becomes the field, but here shows much amiss' (lines 393–4).

Any consideration of social form as play in *Hamlet* has to take account of the extraordinary range and degree of informal play to be found in the tragedy, most of it focussed on the protagonist. There is Hamlet the entertaining courtier, master of the merry quip; Hamlet the sardonic satirist of courtly pretence and hidden corruption; Hamlet the melancholic whose inappropriate jocularity is a classic symptom of his emotional condition;[25] Hamlet the cunning revenger whose assumption of an antic disposition is more effective as an outlet for his bitterness than as a device for coping with his enemy; Hamlet the theatrical producer and amateur playwright who introduces and concludes his tragic show, 'The Murder of Gonzago', in a spirit of high glee ('For if the king likes not the comedy . . .'). And in addition to the jesting, antic tragic hero there is the Chief Councillor–Fool and the Gravedigger–Clown.

Although as late as 1612 John Webster felt it necessary to apologise for bending to popular taste and mixing comedy with tragedy in defiance of classical precedent and neoclassical precept, by 1600 most of the judicious must have been reconciled to the fact that the new mode had come to stay. Nevertheless Shakespeare seems to draw attention to the mixture when Polonius distinguishes between 'the law of writ and of liberty' (presumably 'plays composed according to the rules and plays written in complete freedom from them');[26] and he follows Kyd in using the mixed mode reflexively as a metaphor for the confusions of a tragic world. Custom may enable the sexton to sing in a grave without inhibition, but the 'daintier sense' of Hamlet, the detached observer, recoils at such conduct (v.i.59–60). And yet that same self-indulgent, melancholy observer soon perceives that 'the antic' Death mocks and grins at all human gravity ($R2$,III.ii.162–3), and whimsically imitates him; more important, his earlier response to the gravedigger's blunted sense of propriety reflects ironically on his own behaviour when he discovers who is being buried and feels 'outfac'd' by Laertes in grief. Shakespeare would seem to be implying that if one is to hold the mirror up to contrarious, metamorphic Nature in its tragic mood it is impossible to ignore the interplay of opposites as demanded by neoclassical precept.

The two 'plays' in *Hamlet* (that term is carefully applied to the game of foils) function according to the convention established by Kyd in that each is used by a revenger as a covert means to achieve his end; each is poison in jest, play in deadly earnest. There is, however, a distinction of great importance between them. Hamlet's device is not designed to kill; its purpose is to establish whether the King is guilty or not, and if he is, to make him 'speak' his malefactions (II.ii.589). This is Hamlet of the 'courtier's . . . tongue' at work.[27] Hamlet's role as object of revenge in the King's play enables Shakespeare to present him in a sympathetic light, generous and free from all contriving in choosing his weapon, magnanimous in forgiving the repentant Laertes; correspondingly, it allows all the emphasis at the end to fall on Claudius' responsibility for what has happened. As with the play performed in the last scene of *The Spanish Tragedy*, this 'play's' function as an image in large of confounding contrariety is emphasised by means of an elaborate opening ceremony of reconciliation. Prompted perhaps by the Queen's request that he 'use some gentle entertainment to Laertes' before they 'fall to play' (v.ii.197–9), Hamlet apologises to Laertes for the death of Polonius. Although disingenuous in part, Hamlet's speech is sincere in its gesture of brotherly love; a gesture which Laertes hypocritically reciprocates: 'I do receive your offered love like love, / And will not wrong it' (lines 243–4). Claudius' protestations of bias in favour of Hamlet, and the showy gesture of the 'union' in the poisoned cup, completes the symbolism of an entertainment, which, in its confusion of love and hate, play and violence, and unity and division perfectly reflects the nature of Claudius' reign.

V

The final exhibition of 'purposes mistook / Fall'n on th' inventors' heads' (lines 376–7) – Claudius and Laertes undone by their own poison – introduces a sense of order, a cyclic pattern whereby the whirligig of time brings in its revenges. Insofar as there is in the world of *Hamlet* an objective order counterbalancing or encompassing the baffling confusion it so richly depicts, that order, as in the other tragedies, is nature in its temporal dimension. Here, however, the divine providence with which Brutus tentatively associated time emerges in the last act – or, more exactly, in Hamlet's consciousness before the duel – as the ultimate regulator of human affairs which time subserves. Whether the text sufficiently persuades us that Hamlet is right in this belief, or that his attitude is anything more than fatalistic resignation to the course of events, may be open to question.[28] There can be no doubt, however, that time as the order of nature in its dynamic perspective is fully integrated to the play's structure of meanings.

Horatio's insistence in his last speech that he must explain to the nobility without delay what has happened, 'lest more mischance / On plots and errors happen' (lines 386–7), returns us to the beginning of the tragedy, where he and the other sentries show a conspicuous awareness that doing the right thing – that which is 'fitting our duty' (I.i.173) – entails vigilant attunement to time (lines 6, 13, 27). Indeed what binds these men together in friendship and mutual dependence is their regard for time. And since they are guarding the nation against an impending attack, timeliness is by implication the basis of socio-political as well as interpersonal order. In fact this is made fully explicit in the account of how Fortinbras' threat has affected the nation. 'Eruption to our state' (line 69) is a condition of 'sweaty haste' in which the distinction between night and day, and between work-day and rest-day, has been wholly obliterated (lines 70–8). Moreover the order of nature at large and even of supernature are in turn identified with time's order. Bernardo's leisurely and euphonious specification of the time when the ghost last appeared –

> Last night of all,
> When yond same star that's westward from the pole
> Had made his course t'illume that part of heaven
> Where now it burns, Marcellus and myself,
> The bell then beating one – (lines 35–9)

– identifies human time with the measured and harmonious motion of the heavenly bodies. The ghost's arrival truncates Bernardo's verbal mimesis of time's order, and this negative impression of its nature is reinforced by Horatio's charge that it 'usurps' the time of night (line 46). On the other hand, the ghost explains, and its behaviour shows, that its activities (whether we construe them as good or bad or a mixture of both) are subject to a strict limit of time, one which accords with time's most basic distinction, that between night and day. The ghost responds to cockcrow and 'the god of day' as if to 'a fearful summons' (line 149), since (as it explains later to Hamlet), it is 'doom'd for a certain term to walk the night, / And for the day confin'd to fast in fires' until the crimes done in its 'days of nature' are purged away (I.v.10–13). So the retributive and containing order to which it is subject, is, or manifests itself through, the cyclic order of time. To complete this imaginative elucidation of time's order, the opening scene ends with an unforgettable hint of that order's beneficent and peaceful aspect, imaged in the metaphoric fusion of dawn and peasant worker: 'But look, the morn in russet mantle clad / Walks o'er the dew on yon high eastward hill' (lines 166–7).[29]

One purpose, then, of the exposition is to establish that time is the limiting order to which everything must conform. Accordingly, the text offers a more-or-less continuous interpretation of action in terms of its fitness or unfitness to time. This is best considered, perhaps, in relation to the crimes of Claudius and the anguish, errors, and eventual triumph of Hamlet as instrument of justice. Like all Shakespeare's great villains, Claudius is acutely conscious of time and of the need to seize and master it. As he addresses his court and expands in confidence, playing the part of the sun-king, he seems to see himself as lord of time: 'Take thy fair hour, Laertes; time be thine ... spend it at thy will!' (I.ii.62–3). His most obvious characteristic, however, is to act with great speed so as to steal time, which is life, from others, and in the process to generate in human affairs the equivalent of a spring 'blasting' or a solar eclipse. Death descends upon his brother in his 'secure hour', and he is 'cut off' in the 'blossoms' of his sins without benefit of shrift (I.v.61, 76). And of course the incestuous marriage follows with such sweaty haste that wedding cheer and funeral dirges and baked meats are all one for his 'imperial jointress'.

If the speed with which Claudius acts initially establishes him as a source of chaos, thereafter it shows him to be an efficient defender of his position: a dangerous enemy as well as a striking contrast – a mighty opposite – to Hamlet.[30] Hamlet's sulky insinuations in I.ii are followed by the 'hasty sending' for Rosencrantz and Guildenstern (II.i.4) and the spying operation. After the nunnery scene, which shows that amorous love and madness are not Hamlet's problem, comes the 'quick determination' that he 'shall with speed to England' to collect neglected tribute (III.i.169). 'The Murder of Gonzago' and the killing of Polonius ('It had been so with us had we been there') give this determination a new and remorseless urgency: the two sponges must 'haste' them on their 'speedy voyage' with 'fiery quickness' and there must be no return journey for Hamlet (III.iii.24; IV.iii.43, 54–7). When Hamlet does return, Claudius acts with the same decisiveness, this time showing his opportunistic appreciation of what the moment offers: here, the grief of Laertes. Having persuaded Laertes that he must act promptly if his love is not to prove subject to time's corrosive effect, he quickly decides 'what convenience both of time and means / May fit us to our shape' (IV.vii.149–50).

This pattern of consistently swift and decisive action finely counterpoints Hamlet's wavering between delay and fatal rashness. For Hamlet, everything takes on the dimension of time, and the time is out of joint; and his inability to re-shape it becomes for him a problem of when to act. He is troubled by memory, which keeps consciousness in time, and is a prerequisite for truth to self and to others – for resolution and constancy.[31] The bestial oblivion of his mother and the court appals him ('a great man's memory' gone in two hours (III.ii.122–8)), so that he surrenders himself totally to the ghost's parting appeal to remember its command (I.v.91). But this surrender, as he understands it, entails the deliberate forgetting of every other commandment written in the book and volume of his brain (I.v.91, 102–3). And that, it would seem, is a major cause of his subsequent disorientation: a mind obsessed by one thing to the exclusion of all else, and a nature partly and instinctively at odds with what that mind dictates.

After several months' delay, the chance arrival of the players prompts action, and suddenly it seems that the opportune moment has come: ''Tis now the very witching time of night . . . Now could I drink hot blood' (III.ii.378–80), 'Now might I do it pat' (III.iii.73). The reason Hamlet gives for not doing it now is that the time is not right; he needs 'a more horrid hent' (opportunity, occasion), one when Claudius is not praying but 'fit and season'd for his passage' to Hell fire. The villains of Renaissance tragedy always show a perverted sense of the appropriate moment, and Hamlet's explanation for his delay here is the ultimate form of such a perversion. But apart from the puzzle as to whether Hamlet means this or not, it is ironically misplaced, since Claudius is not at all in the repentant state which his kneeling posture suggests. And it casts a strange light on what follows in the closet scene. Hamlet kills the man he takes to be Claudius without thought of the 'more horrid hent'; and although he has thus whetted his sword he describes himself as a 'tardy son' and accepts the ghost's charge that his purpose has become 'blunted' (III.iv.106–11). Here indeed is deep confusion.

The 'rash and bloody deed' of Polonius' killing is the fatal act into which the ghost's command and the disjointed time have compelled Hamlet. It is followed by a relapse into passivity and then by the determination, inspired by Fortinbras' mindless derring-do, to think nothing but bloody thoughts. This may account for the sudden burst of activity on board the ship to England, when rashness takes on a strange complexity. Before he can 'make a prologue' to his 'brains', Hamlet arranges a double murder which is no more necessary or just than that of Polonius. Moreover he takes an ignoble delight in emulating, in this rash act, what is most shocking in his mighty opposite: 'without debatement more or less, / He should those bearers put to sudden death, / Not shriving-time allow'd' (V.ii. 45–7). On the other hand, Hamlet construes his impulsive desire to open his companions' packets, and his consequent discovery of the plot in which they are wittingly or unwittingly involved, as a sign that divine providence is now directing him, shaping his rough-hewn ends (lines 6–11, 48); and he concludes that in these circumstances rashness is praiseworthy. This conviction might find justification in standard Christian teaching to the effect that divine providence makes use of both chance and evil in its ultimately rational ordering of human affairs. Together with the chance encounter with the pirates, the accidental exchange of the foils, and Gertrude's impulsive drinking from the cup, Hamlet's opening of the packets contributes to a concatenation of cause and effect which ensures that the usurper is both exposed and punished.

Hamlet's new-found sense of creatural security 'in the great hand of God' does not effect a complete spiritual regeneration in his character. Apart from delighting in the adroitness with which he disposed of his former friends, he protests (rather too much perhaps) that they are not near his conscience. He is to remain the sullied and problematic hero of a corrupting and impossibly problematic world. The chief effect of his sense of providential involvement in events is that he alters his attitude to time: it is not for him to create or even to identify the opportune moment for action: it will come to him, and 'the readiness is all' (line 215). When it does come – the perfect 'now' of open and manifest justice rather than the 'horrid hent' of a secretive revenge – Hamlet accepts it unhesitantly, assuring the King's messenger that he will not 'take longer time' in responding to the challenge: 'if his fitness speaks, mine is ready now – or whensoever, provided I be so able as now' (lines 192–5).

VI

The degree of satisfaction which audiences and readers derive from the resolution of Hamlet's problems and the restoration of order which follows will vary considerably from one individual to another. Nigel Alexander, whose view of the play is in one respect similar to my own, says that the survival of Horatio, representing friendship, and the crowning of Fortinbras, representing war, symbolises the concordant discord of Mars and Venus,[32] a state of ideal harmony. It seems to me, however, that the reconciliation of opposites and the re-affirmation of unity and integrity are to be found only in Hamlet and Laertes, who exchange a noble forgiveness and find friendship in death; the importance of this ritual being emphasised by contrast with the evasive and dishonest reconciliation they performed earlier. To say that Fortinbras is reconciled to Horatio and the nation he was out to attack at the start of the play is true, but raises unsettling questions about the nature of that reconciliation and the order which is to follow. Fortinbras, as his name and activities indicate, represents might without right. He blandly claims that he has 'some rights of memory in this kingdom' (line 381), but our memory of what Horatio said about him in the opening scene informs us that he has no rights whatsoever. He happens to be on the spot with a conquering army when a political vacuum has arisen, and opportunistically embraces his fortune and claims his vantage; and with just a trace of Claudius, he purports to do it 'with sorrow' (lines 380–2). It is remarkable that Shakespeare should have created this character as Denmark's reward for Hamlet's efforts; he could so easily have given the new ruler a different name, made him a cousin of Hamlet, and endowed him with the attributes of a Hal, an Edgar, or a Malcolm; but with obvious deliberation he did not. It is even more strange that Hamlet should add his 'voice' to Fortinbras' 'election' (lines 347–8), since the problem of judicious choice or 'election' has been associated with Hamlet throughout. He has been enraged by his mother's failure to discriminate between the two brothers: even madness would reserve 'some quantity of choice / To serve in such a difference' (III.iv.73–6). He has picked honest Horatio out of ten thousand: 'Since my dear soul was mistress of her choice / And could of men distinguish her election, / Sh'hath seal'd thee for herself' (III.ii.61–3). He has known all along that 'on his choice depends / The safety and health of this whole state' (I.iii.20–1). And yet his last act, so carefully chosen by Shakespeare, is to choose Fortinbras. This choice satisfies our desire for the immediate restoration of some kind of order, but, on reflection, it does not fit; it makes the present and the future seem incongruent with the past.

Kaleidoscopic and elusive though it is, *Hamlet* evinces the outlines of a coherent and meaningful pattern which has its roots in Shakespeare's conception of the contrarious cosmos and double nature. Fratricide and incest have initiated a state of psychological and social chaos in which the opposites of love and hate, pity and fury, friendship and war, marriage and funeral, workday and holyday, and day and night are wholly confused. But the hero, working at last in conjunction with time, and beyond that with a timeless order of justice, puts an end to the confusion which his mighty opposite has created. Or does so in part; for the playworld of *Hamlet* retains its perplexing character to the last, where we are left with more words and deeds which we must botch up fit to our own thoughts.

6

Othello, the Moor of Venice

I

A tragedy of unparalleled intensity and strange beauty, *Othello* is without doubt one of Shakespeare's major achievements. By general consent, however, it lacks some of the grandeur and the breadth of implication which belong to the other great tragedies. This limitation is inherent in the nature of the subject, that of a marriage destroyed by slander, jealousy, and murder. To this subject Shakespeare gives an appropriately domestic, even claustrophobic, character. The action begins in the context of imperial warfare, with the Turks launching yet another attack on Christendom, and the hero called upon to save one of its key outposts, the island of Cyprus. But with the reported destruction of the Turkish fleet by a storm in Act II, the larger context provided by history ceases to concern the *dramatis personae*. The focus then turns inward, so that at the end we are looking fixedly at the marital bed and its tragic loading. Thus although the Turco-Christian conflict contributes indirectly to the fate of Othello and Desdemona, their personal tragedy would seem to have no political repercussions and no political significance whatever.[1]

Comparable to this lack of political emphasis is the want of a continuous imaginative connection between the human drama and the world of external nature.[2] There are allusions to the elements that clip us round, to the ever-burning lights above, and to the animal kingdom below; but by comparison with *Julius Caesar, King Lear*, and *Macbeth* they are slight. This particular aspect of the play's style prompted Helen Gardner to remark that those who like to interpret Shakespearian tragedy with reference to Elizabethan ideas on world order have an impossible task on their hands in dealing with *Othello*. There are no signs here of the great chain of being, she observes drily, nothing whatever about 'degree, priority, and place';

in this respect the play's affinities are with the comedies and not the tragedies.[3]

II

Although it has undoubted validity, critical emphasis on the play's lack of magnitude and resonance (relative to the other major tragedies) has, I believe, been excessive. Consider first the question of historical setting. In 1603, one year before the presumed date of *Othello*, Richard Knolles published his *Historie of the Turkes*, a monumental and absorbing work which Shakespeare almost certainly read. Shakespeare would have learned from it (if he did not already know) that when the Turks decided to seize the rich and beautiful island of Cyprus they did so at their first attempt (in 1570), without mishap of any kind, and with characteristic savagery. Despite their defeat at the battle of Lepanto in the following year, the Turks retained Cyprus, multiplied their conquests, and by 1603 were dubbed by Knolles and everyone else 'the present terrour of the world'.[4] Shakespeare would also have noticed that Knolles lent all his authority to one of the great commonplaces of the time, namely, that the success of the Turks in seizing one Christian country after another was not due to their military invincibility but to the mutual envies and treacheries of the Christians: Knolles's major – and admonitory – theme is Christian disunity, the enemy within.[5] Concerning Cyprus in particular, Knolles viewed its 'bloudie tragedie'[6] as a paradigmatic chapter in the unfinished conflict between Christian and Turk in that the island fell because of dissentious rivalries between the commanders of the fleet sent to defend it and because of inadequate leadership on the island itself.[7]

In the original novella (published 1566) on which *Othello* is based the setting is contemporary and there is no mention of war or of any immediate threat to Cyprus. Shakespeare, however, brought the action forward in time to a precise historical moment: that is, when the Turks set out from Constantinople with 'a most mighty preparation' of two hundred galleys to seize Cyprus (I.iii.4, 219).[8] One critic has argued that the purpose of the historical context thus provided is simply to establish, in the opening scenes, the superior worth of the Moor and the depth of Desdemona's love (prepared as she is to follow him to war); thereafter it is forgotten as the play spirals inward from 'state affairs' to 'house affairs' and what men 'privately determine' (I.iii.190, 147, 275).[9] I would suggest, however, that this limitation on the imaginative effects of the historical frame presupposes too much suspension of historical consciousness on the part of Shakespeare's original audience, and that in fact the Turco-Christian conflict is exploited as a largely silent but eloquent presence throughout the play. One purpose of the historical frame is to intensify the prevailing atmosphere of ominous and ironic foreboding – a fearful preoccupation with what 'succeeds in unknown fate' (ii.i.191). Thus in the third scene it projects the mind forward with a keen sense of tragic potentiality ('There are many events in the womb of time which will be delivered' (i.iii.363–4)), making the lovers' serene confidence in their future appear pitiable, and Desdemona's decision to go to Cyprus a choice of awesome magnitude. From this point, it seems as if their fate is sealed. Similarly when it is reported at Cyprus that the entire Turkish fleet has perished in the storm, and the jubilant cry is raised, 'Your wars are done ... our wars are done' (ii.i.20, 200), either Shakespeare was guilty of an extraordinary historical faux-pas or his audience was to infer that the new Governor and his people are gravely in error: blind to the existence of a treacherous enemy who waits like rocks 'ensteep'd to enclog the guiltless keel' (line 70).[10] Another function of the historical context is to underscore the theme of the enemy within. A Jacobean audience's expectation that the hero and heroine would perish on the doomed island is fulfilled in a quite unexpected manner; that is properly dramatic, but it is also an ironic pointer to the fact that not all Turks are turbaned. That jubilant cry goes up in the very scene where Iago grimly promises in aside and soliloquy to destroy the Governor's happiness and peace of mind. A 'most heathenish' (v.ii.316) Christian, Iago is the spiritual ally of intending invaders ('it is true, or else I am a Turk' (ii.i.114)) and is endowed with the vicious qualities habitually ascribed to them in the sixteenth century – ruthlessness, Satanic deceit and treachery, contempt for 'the ordinaunce of matrimony' and the bonds of society.[11] Indeed what he does to Othello must be seen as preparing the way for the Turks in a very literal and practical sense. This has an obvious bearing on the claim that the fall of Othello has no political repercussions or implications.

For modern audiences and readers the crucial fact about the condition of Cyprus at the end of the play is that order has been restored and Cassio installed as Othello's successor: the (second) storm is over. However, Othello has been presented as the only man capable of holding the island against the Turks, whereas his gentlemanly lieutenant is manifestly a lightweight character. To this we must add Jacobean awareness that Cyprus will be savaged by the Turk in a very short time, and that the immediate cause of its collapse will not be inadequate fortifications but the quality of its leadership: 'captaines fitter for pleasure than for warre', albeit 'gentlemen ... most courteous'.[12] It seems probable then that the play was intended to leave its audience of 1604 with the thought that what Iago, Roderigo, and Othello 'privately determine' in their envies and jealousies, *or rather something very like it*, was responsible for the calamity that awaited Cyprus 'in unknown fate'. Some such thought as this was posited from the start: 'For if such actions may have passage free, / Bondsmen and pagans shall our statesmen be' (I.ii.97–8; cf. II.ii.160–210). Additional warrant for such an interpretation can be found in another play about love and war written at approximately the same time as *Othello*. *Troilus and Cressida* also dramatises an 'extant moment' in a larger history where 'what's past and what's to come is strew'd with husks / And formless ruin of oblivion' (IV.v.166–8); and it has a comparable ending. Troy (Ilium), like Cyprus, still stands, and young Troilus, like Cassio, has taken the great warrior's place; but 'Hector is dead' and 'there is no more to say' – except 'So, Ilion, fall thou next!' (V.viii.11; V.x.22).[13] What I am suggesting then is that the fictive history of Othello has been located within the tragic history of modern Christendom – as read by Renaissance observers – in such a way that it functions as a microcosm of that ongoing catastrophe, and even (by a kind of imaginative sleight-of-hand, which confuses fiction and history) as an important turning point in its development. In its relation to history, and from a Jacobean perspective, *Othello* may have seemed a hauntingly reverberant tragedy.

III

Other reverberations stem from the fact that the Turco-Christian conflict, being an especially fierce part of the long struggle between Christendom and Islam, was steeped in myth and symbol. Thus in *Othello* it functions as a modern equivalent for the Roman–Goth conflict which served in *Titus Andronicus* as a symbolic vehicle for investigating the theme of civilisation and barbarism and the double nature of the noble protagonist (see p.22). As in the earlier tragedy, this anthropological dualism is explored in dialectical fashion, the relationship between the opposites being disclosed as extremely unstable: here, it would seem, the most civilised individuals can 'turn Turk' (ii.ii.162), while the most noble and eloquent voice heard in Venice is that of an 'erring barbarian' (i.ii.354). But the religious aspect of the Turco-Christian polarity is no less potent than the anthropological in extending the imaginative scope of *Othello*. A steady stream of religious allusions serves to spiritualise the play, edging it with wonder and mystery, turning it into a tragedy of the soul (something precious, violable, and easily lost), and providing it with fit metaphors for its extreme conceptions of good and evil and joy and suffering.

No Jacobean would have been surprised to find that the imaginative matrix of the play's anthropological and religious antinomies is the structure of the natural order itself: not the stable order of 'degree, priority, and place' (a false trail) but the insecure order of 'harmonious contrarietie' or 'concordant discord'. A comparable structure of parallelism is to be found, for example, in Sir Thomas Browne, who links warfare in the self to that between Christian and Turk, and both of these to the battle of opposites in the world of nature at large:

I find there are many pieces in this one fabrick of man; this frame is raised upon a mass of Antipathies. I am one methinks, but as the World; wherein notwithstanding there are a swarm of distinct essences, and in them another World of contrarieties; we carry private and domestick enemies within, publick and more hostile adversaries without ... Let me be nothing, if within the compass of my self I do not find the battle of Lepanto, Passion against Reason, Reason against Faith, Faith against the Devil, and my Conscience against all.[14]

Although sparse by comparison with the other major tragedies, allusions in *Othello* to nature's 'World of contrarieties' serve – in their context of multiple oppositions – as very precise signals to the cosmological paradigm on which the whole design rests. I would refer in particular to the descriptions of the storm in ii.i (a protracted and violent battle between lightning, wind, water, and land); to Cassio's prayer for the safety of Othello: 'O let the heavens/ Give him defence against the elements' (ii.i.44–5); and, finally, to Othello's despairing vision of Hell as a vast region where the lost soul is buffetted eternally by molten rock and scorching winds, a vision which horribly fulfils his tender exclamation: 'Perdition catch my soul, / But I do love thee; and when I love thee not / Chaos is come again' (iii.iii.91–3).

Various critics have observed that Shakespeare gave tragic weight and dignity to Cinthio's sordid tale of jealousy and revenge by turning it into a drama of the universal emotions of love and hate. To this one must add that for Shakespeare and his audience these emotions had a degree of universality far beyond what we ourselves impute to them. A further point to be made is that love–hate and love–strife are aspects of the same dualism, and that in the latter formulation it is not synonymous with good and evil. In certain conditions and within certain limits, strife is a positive force: as Othello recalls, there are the big wars – fought in defence of a civilised community – that make ambition virtue (line 354).[15]

A very conspicuous feature of the play which obviates the need for an abundance of natural images as pointers to its underlying philosophy of nature is the beautifully apt manipulation of the myth of Mars and Venus, the deities from whose union was born the goddess Harmony. There were two well-known interpretations of this myth.[16] In the first, the goddess Harmony is ignored and the myth is interpreted moralistically as a warning to the man of action about the dangers of amorous sensuality. This interpretation is evoked in the first act of *Othello* as part of a complex of dramatic ironies when the hero assures the Senate that if Desdemona goes with him to Cyprus he will not permit 'light-wing'd toys of feather'd Cupid' to interfere with his military duties (i.iii.266–74). In the other interpretation, the goddess Harmony is all-important and the myth is treated as an allegory of the natural order itself, the fruitful union of opposites in a system of concordant discord. The myth in this sense is evoked in ii.i when 'the warlike Moor' and 'the divine Desdemona', having survived the 'foul and violent tempest' that threatened to separate them forever (lines 27, 73, 34), reunite ecstatically at Cyprus and are enthusiastically welcomed ashore by the islanders. This is the supreme moment in the relationship of the two lovers, and Shakespeare chose that it should be so with great deliberation. For Venus (as Richard Knolles recalled) was said to have risen from the sea near Cyprus, her cult flourished on that island, and so she was commonly referred to by poets as 'the Cyprian queen'.[17] Through the gracious welcoming speeches of Cassio, epithalamic tradition is deployed in conjunction with the myth to reinforce the status of the scene as a dramatic symbol of universal amity. What is suggested here is a generative concord that encompasses the married lovers, the human community to which they belong, and the 'fruitful ... elements' (ii.iii.330–1).

The play's religious polarities (angel and demon, heaven and hell, salvation and perdition, redemption and bondage) are blended with its natural ones to give the impression that the whole of imaginable reality is subject to a dualistic principle. The fluent economy with which Christian motifs are assimilated to the essentially naturalistic structure of thought and expression is remarkable. In the figure of Desdemona, Christian (or Christ-like) charity – at once compassionate, forgiving, and redeeming – is coincident with the love that in nature resolves conflicts and binds opposites. In the figure of Iago, Satan's pride, envy, and total commitment to undoing the work of the Creator (beginning with the happiness of a man and a woman) is one with the universal hate-and-strife which threatens to undo bonds and reduce cosmos to chaos. Othello's colour (to be compared with that of Aaron, the 'barbarous, misbelieving Moor' in *Titus Andronicus*) is at once a reminder of the unregenerate state from which he has been redeemed by baptism, and the basis of a striking, visual dualism – the union of white and black – that focusses all the oppositions, paradoxes, and ambiguities which are traced to the natural order of interacting opposites as to their one identifiable source.

Perhaps the most intricate fusion of natural and supernatural symbolism occurs in the motif of the bond, a figure on which numerous verbal and imagistic variations are played. This is a central motif in most Shakespearian tragedy, but it is more conspicuous and pervasive here than in any earlier play in the canon; in this respect *Othello* comes closer to *Macbeth* and *King Lear* than to *Hamlet*. As a symbol of human relationships, the bond signifies both affection and commitment, 'love and duty' (or 'love and service'), fulfilment and constraint. In its ideal form it represents a harmony of opposites, as when Othello explains that he has gladly put his unhoused and free condition into circumscription and confine because of his love for the gentle Desdemona (1.ii.25–7). Precisely because it is a union of opposites, however, the human bond is presented here as fertile ground for conflict and tragic change. This is firmly intimated in the opening scenes. Iago discussing his position as the Moor's ancient, Desdemona explaining her roles as daughter and wife, and Othello referring to his future as both military commander and newly-wed husband, all focus our attention on the ways in which love and duty (or service) can become disjoined and mutually hostile.

A remark made by Brabantio locates the first point of connection between the natural and the supernatural conceptions of the bond. His claim that if he had other daughters besides Desdemona her escape would teach him to hang clogs on them (I.iii.197–8), shows how, with the rejection of limit and restraint by either or both partners, bonds can become or seem mere bondage, a form of tyranny. This conceptual pattern overlaps in the play with a very basic set of theological ideas and symbols: that in which the soul's relationship with God is seen as both a legal covenant and a marriage, sin as a breaking of this bond which entails bondage to, or adultery with, the spirit of evil, and divine love or grace as the power that redeems the enslaved soul from its captivity. What requires emphasis is that the many allusions in *Othello* to 'all seals and symbols of redeemed [and unredeemed] sin' (II.iii.332) have special imaginative force because of their singular fitness to the play's historical context. The religious symbolism of bonds and bondage originates in the Old Testament, where the Babylonian captivity of the chosen people is ascribed to their 'adulterous' lapse into polytheism and concomitant breaking of the covenant. However, the Turco-Christian conflict, in which many Christians 'turned Turk', countless more were enslaved, and some ransomed, was understood to be a continuation of the conflict between Satanic heathenism and true faith as recorded in the Old Testament.[18] Thus some of the most fundamental symbols for the soul's relation with good and evil have a literal as well as a figurative value in the context of Turco-Christian warfare, and are reinforced accordingly. And *Othello*, as the tragedy of a Moor who was rescued from darkness by baptism, captured and sold to slavery by 'the insolent foe', redeemed hence (lines 137–8), then married to the divine Desdemona, and finally 'married' to and ensnared by the demi-devil Iago on a Christian island which itself is doomed to a state of bondage: as such, *Othello* is a tragedy resonant with large meanings.[19]

In mythical terms, however, Othello's adversary is the incarnation not only of Satan but also of Vulcan, the crafty and deformed god who was quite out of place in Heaven, and who put an abrupt end to the union of Mars and Venus by ensnaring them together in his net. It is the fusion of Christian with classical myth, and of religious themes with natural philosophy, that gives to *Othello* its special range of suggestion. Symbolically speaking, however, Cyprus is less important as the small-scale model of a world where Christian and heathen, true faith and false, wrestle for supremacy, than as the place where the union of Mars and Venus is sealed and ruptured.

IV

Despite its singularity, then, and its apparent lack of general meaning, *Othello* does evince a pattern of ideas and symbols which expands its imaginative horizons and links it with other Shakespearian tragedies. This becomes even more apparent when we consider the nature and interrelationships of its characters in some detail. One must begin such a consideration, however, by acknowledging that Othello is unquestionably the most singular of Shakespeare's heroes; the singularity of the play as a whole is very much a reflection of his character. Difference and alienation are written into his composition from the start. His colour, his undisclosed origins, his life of wandering and adventure, his sonorously opulent speech, his massive self-assurance, and his acknowledged pre-eminence as a military leader: these attributes combine to assure us that Othello is not like the rest of men. Nevertheless, he is presented within a pattern of characterisation which implies affinities with other men and women. As roving warrior he is the very antithesis of the gentle, housebound Desdemona; but they have something in common which binds them together in a relationship of complementary opposition: her 'downright violence' in loving (line 249), and his 'constant, loving ... nature' (II.ii.283). It is Desdemona and Iago who are perfect opposites with nothing in common. Othello stands between these two characters as between two poles of his nature.[20] When the force represented by Iago eclipses that represented by Desdemona, Othello disintegrates; he ceases to be the noble Moor of Venice and becomes simply the Moor, an erring barbarian. This schematic pattern of likeness and difference is part of a wider, less pronounced pattern which links Othello with the outraged, superstitious, and irrational Brabantio, who misconstrues the Moor's 'magic', and whose 'particular grief' so 'engluts and swallows all other sorrows' that he is indifferent to 'the general care' (I.iii.54–7); with the jealous Bianca, who miscontrues the handkerchief; and with Montano and Cassio, Othello's predecessor and successor as governor of the island, each of whom is transformed under the influence of Iago from an eminently civilised servant of the state into a night-brawler – 'turn'd Turk' (II.ii.158–88).[21]

Othello's names and titles too have the effect of generalising his identity. The name 'Othello' is itself unique, but it has been suggested that it was formed to carry a faint suggestion of 'Ottoman', i.e. 'Turk'.[22] Given the paradoxical nature of the play's full title, given too the fact that in Elizabethan times 'no clear distinction was made between Turks and Moors',[23] this suggestion seems right. But the name or title I would like to emphasise is that of 'General'. Othello is addressed as 'General' for the first time in the third scene of Act I (lines 36, 55), and in the ensuing scene this title becomes part of an antithesis which is destabilised by wordplay. Brabantio distinguishes between 'the general care' (i.e. the impending attack on Cyprus) and his own 'particular grief' (I.iii.54–5), and the Duke, addressing Othello not as 'General' (as one might expect) but as 'valiant Othello', proceeds in the same sentence to refer to 'the general enemy Ottoman' (lines 47–8). The antithesis and its attendant wordplay (to be found in more overt form in *Troilus and Cressida* I.iii.341–2; II.i.2–4) serve a triple purpose. They suggest from the outset that the private tragedy of the General and the Senator's daughter has implications which extend far beyond particular griefs; that this most singular of heroes is in some sense a generic figure, like Troilus of Troy (*Tro.*, IV.iv.31); and that opposites, however much we might try to distinguish them, have an inbuilt tendency to become indistinguishable.

Strange and exotic though he is, then, Othello is no extra-terrestrial visitor, but rather an exalted, simplified, and magnificent representative of general human nature.[24] And it can reasonably be said that he is so mainly because the attributes of valour and love, martial fire and tender regard, striving and fellowship, self-assertion and humility, are developed in his character to a unique degree and held together in the bonds of a magical concordance. This union of contrary attributes is not something that occurs for the first time when he falls in love with Desdemona; it originates in the depths of his nature and has been developed by experience. His soldiership is 'an alacrity ... in hardness' (I.iii.232–3) placed at the disposal of society and obedient to military discipline. Before his fall begins, the 'fire and brimstone' (IV.i.228) of his martial wrath is hinted at as a great force held in abeyance:

> Hold your hands,
> Both you of my inclining and the rest.
> Were it my cue to fight, I should have known it

Without a prompter. (I.iii.81–4)
He that stirs next to carve for his own rage
Holds his soul light: he dies upon his motion. (II.iii.165–6)

These are potent hints, but most of the emphasis in the first two acts is on the 'constant, loving' side of his nature. Despite his martial background, it is clear that he has always moved in an ambience of reciprocal love. Brabantio 'lov'd' him (I.iii.128), and so did the officers on Cyprus who had served under him. Cassio finds his loss of office unendurable because it means he is no longer 'a member' of Othello's 'love' and so has ceased to 'exist' (III.iv.113): for him, Chaos is come again when the bond between him and his 'dear General' (V.ii.302) is broken. Since much emphasis has been placed by some critics on an element of egoism in Othello's love for Desdemona, one must stress that he gives and returns affection as easily as he receives it. The meeting with his subordinates on Cyprus is a reunion of old friends whose 'great love' he now treasures all the more because he can share it with Desdemona (II.i.202–3). Despite all the excitement of the occasion, he remembers to have the captain of his vessel fetched from the port and made much of (lines 207–9). And on the following morning (after the riot), he sends to Cassio, through Emilia, an assurance that he will consider reinstating him when it is prudent to do so, and the even more important assurance: 'he protests he loves you, / And needs no other suitor but his likings / To . . . bring you in again' (III.i.47–50). Clearly, the bond of duty which unites the General and his officers is also – in Cassio's telling phrase – an 'office' (i.e. 'duty') of 'the heart' (III.iv.114). So that when 'the warlike Moor' (II.i.26) marries 'the gentle Desdemona' (I.ii.25), he does not enter an entirely new world; rather, he reaches the goal of his life's pilgrimage and consummates his faith in the value of love. Furthermore, the curtailment of his freedom dictated by his marriage is not an essentially new experience for him; as the ensnaring Iago knows so well, he always has been, and needs to be, bound to others. A stranger in Venice he undoubtedly is, but to see him as essentially solitary, 'without ties of nature or natural duties', presenting to the world 'a vision of man free', is to misread him seriously.[25] What we must see in the unfallen Othello is the resolved paradox of 'free duty' (I.iii.41) and the heart's office; a union of Mars and Venus, where Venus represents not just sexual love but love in its fullest sense as the binding and harmonising force in nature.

Othello harmonises the opposites in his nature – is 'well tun'd now' (II.i.197) – because he recognises that valour and love alike are subject to limit and rule. Despite his affection for Cassio, he refuses to be 'partially affin'd' (II.iii.210) when he finds him guilty of betraying his office: 'Cassio, I love thee;/ But never more be officer of mine' (lines 240–1). As I have already noted, too, he recognises that his love for Desdemona must not be allowed to interfere with his military–political duties, conjuring up, with an appropriate sense of the grotesque, the satiric version of the Mars–Venus myth. This awareness of the need for limit and constraint is expressed primarily in terms of respect for time. Although the call to arms against the Turk comes before he has consummated his marriage, he responds with 'prompt alacrity', telling Desdemona gently, 'We must obey the time' (I.iii.232, 300). And when he assures the dismissed Cassio of his love, he also explains that he will reinstate him only when he caȟ 'take the safest occasion by the front' to do so (III.i.49).[26] But it is on the day of his arrival at Cyprus that his respect for time as a limit governing both love and soldiership, and keeping each within its proper bounds, is most forcefully revealed. In the proclamation read on his behalf concerning the celebration of his nuptials, his men are told: 'All offices are open, and there is full liberty of feasting *from this present hour till the bell hath told eleven*' (II.ii.7–9; emphasis added). Even as he retires to bed with Desdemona he reminds Cassio to join him at the earliest in the morning, when the island's fortifications are to be inspected. And on that fatal morrow, when Desdemona presents herself as Cassio's impatient solicitor, he responds gently, 'Not now, sweet Desdemona; some other time' (III.iii.56).

From the perspective of the second half of the tragedy, 'That's he that was Othello' (V.ii.287): integrated, finely balanced, contained, all-in-all sufficient; at one with himself, with others, and with the fundamental norms of nature's spatio-temporal order. His fall from greatness is swift and complete, a spiritual transformation more shocking than any other in Shakespeare. His deeply trusting nature becomes eaten up with jealousy, his love turns to hatred, his gentleness to a singular cruelty. He succumbs to a consuming, fiery impatience and rushes headlong into a 'contriv'd murder' (I.ii.3) that disgraces both his soldiership and his humanity. As a theatrical event, this metamorphosis is spectacularly effective. As a tragic fact, it is bewildering, terrible, and – except for critics such as Thomas Rymer, T.S. Eliot, and F.R. Leavis – most pitiable.

The near-incredible nature of Othello's transformation is explicitly registered within the play itself:

> My lord, this would not be believ'd in Venice,
> Though I did swear I saw't (IV.i.238–9)

> Is this the noble Moor whom our full senate
> Call all-in-all sufficient? Is this the nature
> Whom passion could not shake? (lines 253–5)

Such comments are at once a challenge, a deliberate underlining of a terrible fact, and a device for neutralising scepticism by anticipating it. Plausibility, of course, is achieved by other more persuasive means. The sheer power of Othello's passionate language commands our imaginative assent as we watch him on stage. The ingenious use of the double time scheme intimates on the one hand that events happened too quickly for Iago to trip up in his machinations, and on the other hand that there was enough time for an adulterous affair to take place and for Iago's poison to infect Othello. Moreover Othello is so presented that it is possible to explain his transformation on the basis of his own unusual character and personal history. His barbaric instincts, it can be argued, lie close to the surface of the civilised persona he has acquired from his Venetian employers. His colour and age undermine his confidence in his ability to hold Desdemona's love when men like the suave Cassio are cited as rivals. His ignorance of Venetian society and of women leaves him unable to challenge Iago's generalisations about the loose morals of Venetian wives. He has not had enough time to get to know and therefore to trust Desdemona; perhaps indeed he is not in love with the real Desdemona at all, but rather with an etherial product of his own egotistical imagination. Then too he is a man of action pure and simple: splendid when decisive action is called for on the battlefield, but in the sphere of civic and domestic relations blundering, gullible, and indeed quite stupid ('Open your eyes, you black fool!', as the old lady expostulated during a performance).

This kind of analysis and explanation can be carried on at book-length and comes easily from an anti-heroic and Freudian culture. But although it demonstrates the rich potentialities of the text it appears to me to be fallacious at several points and ultimately to move in the wrong direction. For example, nine months may not have been enough time for Othello and Desdemona to get to know each other (Shakespeare seems to allow that much: see I.iii.84). But Iago and Emilia seem to have 'known' each other for as many years, and yet with all their shrewdness they view each other's conduct at the end with total incredulity. Furthermore, the play opens with a father so obstinately incapable of accepting what his retiring and obedient daughter has done that he puts it down to drugs and magic. Or take the question of Othello's gullibility. If Othello is stupid in being taken in by Iago, then so is everyone else; the bluff ensign has convinced everyone that he is basically 'a good sort' and, above all, that he is absolutely honest.[27] Except from Iago's viewpoint, 'gullibility' in this context does not signify deficient intelligence. On the one hand, it points to the fact that there is no art to find the mind's construction in the face, there being always a slumbering second self. On the other hand, it predicates a form of decency which is characteristic of 'free and noble' natures and makes them more vulnerable than others to human wickedness. The complete trust which both Desdemona and Othello have in Iago is indicative more of spiritual excellence than of social immaturity.

The trouble with finding an explanation for Othello's fall solely in terms of his own exotic and displaced character is that it fixes us in attitudes of moral and cultural superiority which the text (in the manner of *Titus Andronicus* and, to a lesser extent, *The Merchant of Venice*) is intent on subverting; it thus diminishes the tragic effect of the play by dispelling the emotions of wonder, fear, and pity. Exaggerating the General's uniqueness, oddness, or abnormality, this kind of explanation evades the terrible truth that although his greatness is his own his tragedy has its roots in our common humanity:

> In men, as in a rough-grown grove, remain
> Cave-keeping evils that obscurely sleep. (*Luc.*, lines 1249–50)

The incredible story of what Othello does to his wife, his friend, himself, and the island he was sent to defend is a drastically heightened and accelerated version, such as is legitimate in the non-naturalistic medium of poetic drama, of a spiritual biography which happily lies dormant and unrealised in everyone.

To be more specific, Othello succumbs to Iago's evil influence not only because of his own unusual make-up and situation but also, and more significantly, because of the unstable balance of forces in general human nature. Iago moralises pertinently on the way in which reason should counterbalance '*our* raging motions' and 'the blood and baseness of *our* nature' (i.iii.327–30; emphasis added); and Othello himself warns that passion is likely to darken his reason and provoke him to violence (ii.iii.197–9). It is possible to read the tragedy as a straightforward battle between reason and passion, with passion perverting reason in Iago and overthrowing it in Othello;[28] but in fact this dualism is assimilated to the more complex and – given the nature of the story and the characters involved – more appropriate dualism of love and strife. The essential meaning of the tragedy is encapsulated in Iago's cunning reply to Othello's angry demand for an explanation of the riot in which his civilised officers turned Turk. Provocatively, Iago connects the sudden confusion of friendship and violence with the pleasurable strife of the bridal bed, as if conscious that the traditional war metaphors of sexual love can easily be literalised; the speech provides a perfect image of the instability of all relationships and identities in a contrarious world order:

> I do not know. Friends all but now, even now,
> In quarter, and in terms, like bride and groom
> Divesting them for bed; and then, but now,
> As if some planet had unwitted men,
> Swords out, and tilting one at other's breast
> In opposition bloody. I cannot speak
> Any beginning to this peevish odds. (II.iii.171–7)

At root, Othello's jealousy is the explosion of an elemental force seeking to overwhelm the force which contains and moderates it (to Emilia he says, 'She was false as water', and she retorts, 'Thou art rash as fire to say that she was false' (v.ii.137–81)). His jealousy is red Mars rampant in the home, madly contracting the battlefield to a bridal bed and that to a strawberry-spotted handkerchief. In the temptation scene, Othello is driven by a variety of emotions, including bewilderment and despair; but the chief emotional constituents of the scene are fury, hatred, and a terrible fiery impatience. He will not count the changes of the moon or the minutes of the clock but must destroy 'within these three days' the two loved ones who have become his enemies (III.iii.182, 476). The specification of a temporal limit (to be echoed precisely in Desdemona's kindly impatience) is an ironic accentuation of the fact that all true constraint has been shattered.

V

Yet the transformation of Othello is never absolute nor entirely stable; vestiges of his noble self remain, lending plausibility both to the transformation process and to the recovery which takes place in the last scene. Even when he commits himself solemnly to 'black vengeance' and 'tyrannous hate' (lines 451–3), his emotional state is complicated by the need to believe that Iago is his loving friend, 'bound to' him 'forever' (lines 123, 217, 483). Indeed in the very scene where he will humiliate and strike Desdemona in public he is at first tossed agonisingly between hatred and love as the memory of her sweetness returns to him; it is clear that even at this point he would relent in his murderous resolve were it not for the fact that Hatred stands beside him in person. In the prose of this extraordinary dialogue, the drama of contraries is enacted with rare psychological intensity and naturalism; and yet behind it lies the timeless appeal of womanly gentleness to male hardness and cruelty – the appeal of Zenocrate to Tamburlaine, of Ypolita and Emelye to Theseus, of Venus to Mars:[29]

OTH. I would have him nine years a-killing. A fine woman! a fair woman! a sweet woman!
IAGO. Nay, you must forget that.
OTH. Ay, let her rot, and perish, and be damn'd to-night; for she shall not live. No, my heart is turn'd to stone; I strike it and it hurts my hand. O, the world hath not a sweeter creature; she might lie by an emperor's side and command him tasks.
IAGO. Nay, that's not your way.
OTH. Hang her! I do but say what she is: so delicate with her needle, an admirable musician – O, she will sing the savageness out of a bear! – of so high and plenteous wit and invention.
IAGO. She's the worse for all this.
OTH. O, a thousand, a thousand times – and then of so gentle a condition.
IAGO. Ay, too gentle.
OTH. Nay, that's certain. But yet the pity of it Iago! O, Iago, the pity of it, Iago!
IAGO. If you be so fond over her iniquity, give her patent to offend; for, if it touch not you, it comes near nobody.
OTH. I will chop her into messes. Cuckold me! (iv.i.174–96)

What is important about the triumph of hatred here is the way in which it is transposed to the key to bitterness, for that quality is a notable and significant feature of the changed Othello. Even in its most terrible form – as when later in this scene he subjects Desdemona to physical and verbal abuse – his bitterness is an emotion which keeps reminding us that he himself is suffering intensely and that his furious hatred is being fed by the memory of a 'sweet' love.

That epithet is the one applied most often to Desdemona; it is almost part of her name. When Iago can convince him that her sweetness is corrupt and fraudulent, the 'sweet Othello' (IV.i.235) whom she has always elicited is no more. It was not without design that Emilia should speak of men's palate for both sweet and sour (IV.iii.93), or that Brabantio, Othello's strange counterpart in several ways, should lament: 'Gone she is; / And what's to come of my despised time / Is nought but bitterness' (I.i.161–3).

The other vestiges of Othello's noble self recall his great self-control and his Christian faith; but they are essentially spurious, products of his need to hide from others his murderous intentions, or to hide from himself the reality of what he is doing. At Iago's behest, he practises patience – the 'most cunning' and perverted patience of the Machiavel (IV.i.90). Very briefly, he plays the gracious host and obedient servant of the state with the messengers from Venice. And he subjects Emilia and Desdemona to a laborious parody of judicial interrogation. Serving to exaggerate by contrast the 'savage madness' (IV.i.55) which smoulders immediately behind them, these semblances of the controlled Othello find their most elaborate expression in the murder scene. He sees himself here as the perfect Christian justicer, suppressing his own emotions, concerned to protect others from the corrupting influence of the condemned sinner, and anxious that her once 'sweet soul' (V.ii.53) should be saved from damnation – redeemed – by prayer and repentance. The Othello whom Desdemona sees, however, is also an erring barbarian whose eyes roll, who gnaws his lips, and whose very frame shakes with passion (lines 41, 46–7). And what finally kills her is nothing like the unmoved determination of the patient justicer but a sudden torrent of rage and impatience that cuts short all time for prayer: 'Out, strumpet! Weep'st thou for him to my face? ... It is too late' (lines 81–6). Although he has done a deed that is as remote from justice as any imaginable, Othello remains convinced for a while that he proceeded upon just cause and acted in a manner befitting his noble self. This delusion helps to make the deed terrible rather than horrible and to show that Othello is both victim and source of evil.

Since the 'deed of shame' occurs so very late in the play, the process of restoring Othello to something like his former nobility has to begin immediately and calls for special emphasis and delicacy.[30] What Shakespeare aims at is an impression of atonement, in both senses of the word: the hero is to be redeemed from the effects of what he has done by the intensity of his sufferings and by his readiness to acknowledge and accept the implications of the deed; in this way he achieves oneness with others and with his lost self.

Given the nature of the deed and its freshness in the memory, and given too its larger consequences in unknown fate, it is entirely appropriate that the Moor's spiritual recovery should be less than perfect. However, those who attribute Othello's fall primarily to his own eccentric psychology have exaggerated and multiplied its imperfections to the point where it is made to seem an entirely sham recovery. The one obvious flaw is his description of himself as 'an honourable murderer' who did 'naught . . . in hate, but all in honour'. The disclaimer of hatred is palpably untrue, and the appeal to honour can remind us only of a brutal, wounded pride. At the same time, it should be noted that this half-justification (he does call himself a murderer), given as an answer to Lodovico's question, 'What shall be said to thee?', is advanced with a certain ironic percipience, as if he did not expect to be believed: 'Why, anything: / An honourable murderer, if you will' etc. (lines 296–8). His subsequent claim that he is not easily jealous has met with scepticism and even ridicule from some; but it is surely a just claim. Objections to it ignore the testimony of Iago, who has told us that Othello's nature is free and open and disposed to trust everyone (i.iii.393–6); and they are based on naturalistic expectations – inappropriate in relation to a poetic drama – about the pace at which change of character should be registered. A potentially more serious criticism is that Othello fails to perceive that even if Desdemona and Cassio had been guilty of adultery, the murder and the attempted murder would still have been outrageous. This is perfectly valid if we step outside the imaginative parameters of the play; but there is no hint of it whatever in the text, either direct or oblique; indeed Shakespeare seems to have gone out of his way to prevent it from entering the minds of his audience. Such an attitude would be eminently just and natural in Cassio, yet his only complaint is that Othello could possibly have suspected him of treachery: 'Dear General, I never gave you cause' (line 302); and when Othello instantly asks Cassio's forgiveness, he clearly receives it.

Indeed it is a striking fact that in the second half of this long and brilliantly sustained scene all feelings of censure and revulsion are deflected away from Othello in the direction of Iago:

> O, Spartan dog,
> More fell than anguish, hunger, or the sea!
> Look on the tragic loading of this bed.
> This is thy work. (lines 364–7)

Lodovico, functioning as the voice of the community here, knows that Othello must answer to the state for what he has done, but the nearest he comes to a moral judgement is to describe Othello as 'this rash and most unfortunate man' (line 286). In fact he rises above judgement to express a truly tragic response, seeing something inexpressibly terrible and pitiful in what Othello has done:

> O, thou Othello, that was once so good,
> Fall'n in the practice of a damned slave,
> What shall be said to thee? (lines 294–6)

The only one to criticise Othello in the final scene (apart from himself) is Emilia. Her fearless and ferocious condemnation is a heartwarming revelation of selfless love and loyalty to Desdemona. But it occurs in the first half of the scene, where it is calculated both to vent and to dispose of our feelings of moral outrage. Moreover its sheer extravagance ('O gull! O dolt! / As ignorant as dirt!' (lines 166–7)), makes the desire for categorical judgement seem out of place. After Emilia's blistering assertions, Lodovico's deeply moving question seems to say everything by concluding nothing.

Othello's recovery begins even before the breath has left Desdemona's body. He perceives that her death, far from giving him any satisfaction, has reduced his life to meaninglessness; his sense of loss and disintegration is of cosmic proportions:

> My wife! my wife! what wife? I have no wife.
> O insupportable! O heavy hour!
> Methinks it should be now a huge eclipse
> Of sun and moon, and that th'affrighted globe
> Did yawn at alteration. (lines 100–4)

Although he clings desperately to the belief that she was false, a part of him clearly longs to reinstate her as a being of incomparable worth (richer than 'pure and perfect chrysolite'); and that part acknowledges that if she were true, damnation – 'beneath all depth in hell' – would be the only punishment commensurate with his crime (lines 140, 148). This feeling takes complete possession of him when Iago has been unmasked. It is expressed in language of sublime force which suggests that Othello is already suffering the anguish of the damned and that his suffering is contingent on the greatness of his heart and the power of his moral imagination:

> Whip me, ye devils,
> From the possession of this heavenly sight.
> Blow me about in winds, roast me in sulphur,
> Wash me in steep-down gulfs of liquid fire. (lines 280–3)

The way in which Othello threatens to 'come forth' with his sword of Spain against all impediments and stops, only to withdraw the threat as a 'vain boast' (lines 255–68), is another important step towards final recovery. Indeed with its subtle blend of heroic assertion and ironic humility it prepares for the great valedictory speech. Justifiable pride and necessary humility conjoin in the first sentence of this speech: he has done the state *some* service (litotes instead of hyperbole), but will say no more of that, for he has to acknowledge in himself the base Indian (who threw away a priceless pearl) and the malignant Turk (who wronged Venice and a Venetian). But then humility and pride are reconciled, and boasting becomes an honour (I.ii.20): for a noble deed of long ago is not only recalled but re-enacted, deed matching word as the Spanish sword – just such a sword as drove the Moors out of Europe – is turned in punishment against himself.

Emilia dies 'in music', both literally (singing Desdemona's song) and metaphorically (speaking as she thinks) (v.ii.250–4). Othello also dies in music, concordantly. His valedictory speech-act is intensely felt but controlled and sonorous. It asks for and aims at truth, neither more nor less. By means of it, he sorts out the confusion in himself between the champion and the enemy of civilised values, expelling one and reinstating the other. And he dies on a kiss, on the bridal bed he has so bitterly maligned. He thus reconstitutes the bond of duty and love and recovers his lost unity. T.S. Eliot has claimed, and F.R. Leavis vigorously reaffirmed, that in his final speech Othello is simply cheering himself up and escaping from morality by adopting an aesthetic attitude.[31] I would argue, however, that the moral and the aesthetic are one in this tragic valediction, aspects of a restored harmony in the self and its relation to society. And the touch of theatricality is appropriate to what in the conventions of Renaissance tragedy is always something of a ritual, the Noble Death.[32]

VI

Although it simplifies the tragedy to impute Othello's transformation chiefly to the wickedness of Iago, there can be no doubt that Shakespeare relies heavily on the exceptional malice and cunning of the villain both to give plausibility to his hero's fall from the heights of nobility and to make his regeneration at once credible and acceptable. The depth of Iago's malice is such that we might be inclined to accept his own hypocritical protestation, 'Fie, there is no such man; it is impossible' (iv.ii.135); yet every good stage performance convinces us of his intense reality. What strains credulity most in a *reading* of the play is not that so malignant a creature can exist but that he could pass for decent and affable among all those who are familiar with him. Yet if we recall what we learn from our news media about serial murderers and former war criminals who have passed for years among family and acquaintances as likeable and normal individuals, we cannot but wonder at the combination of insight and audacity in Shakespeare's portrait of Iago.

But there is considerable truth in the claim that 'even when a critic sets out, as A.C. Bradley does, to study Iago's character as if he were an actual living man, what seems to emerge most clearly is the dominance of the man by a certain force or spirit'.[33] As I have suggested, he is both a vividly realised individual and a representative of the enemy within, the element of native barbarism which threatens civilised society far more than its legendary enemies.[34] He is also an embodiment of the spirit of Strife, who despises love and peace, breaks the bonds of unity, and generates confusion and terrible change. Nowhere perhaps is the larger significance of his character more apparent than in the reunion scene of ii.i. Initially and implicitly he is identified with the elemental fury of the 'foul', 'violent', and 'ruffian' storm that 'parted' Othello from Cassio and Desdemona and shook the battlements of Cyprus (lines 6–7, 33–4, 93). Later he is the alien figure who stands visibly and menacingly outside the civilising circle of love and community:

He takes her by the palm. Ay, well said, whisper. With as little a web as this will I ensnare as great a fly as Cassio. Ay, smile on her, do; I will gyve thee in thine own courtship. (lines 166–8)

> O, you are well tun'd now!
> But I'll set down the pegs that make this music,
> As honest as I am. (lines 197–9)

Although Iago's distinctive personality (jocular, cynical, contemptuous, and gross) is strongly impressed on this scene, so too is his
role as a vehicle for the force in nature which undoes the precious
harmony of opposites. The scene has distinguished prototypes
which serve to justify this interpretation. There is the ball scene in
Romeo and Juliet, where 'the fiery Tybalt' watches in fury ('Fetch
me my rapier, boy') while Romeo joins hands with Juliet ('Palm
to palm is holy palmer's kiss'), kisses her on the lips, and unites
a Montague with a Capulet in the elaborate *discordia concors* of music,
dance, and shared sonnet (see p.63). And there are the twin bower
scenes in *The Spanish Tragedy* (ii.ii, iv). Kyd's lovers playfully enact
their mythological duet ('If I be Venus, must thou needs be Mars')
to the sound of the nightingale, with ceremonious touching of hands
and lips, and in rhymed stychomythic dialogue (*discordia concors*
versified). But they are watched by the eavesdropping Machiavel
Lorenzo and the foppish, disappointed suitor Balthasar (exact
counterparts of both Iago and Roderigo) who match every expression of love and union with grim assurances of hatred and
division, and finally rush in to 'disjoin' the lovers forever.[35]

Iago's impulse to disjoin and destroy is closely linked to his self-
love or pride. The General has a touch of this and Iago recognises
and plays on it; but whereas Othello can speak sincerely of 'humble
love' (iii.iii.462), Iago does homage only to himself, keeps his heart
attending on himself, and loves nothing but 'his own pride and
purposes' (i.i.12, 51, 54). Iagoism is egoism or I-ism, the spirit of a
man who habitually caresses in his speech the first-person singular:

> Were I the Moor, I would not be Iago . . .
> In following him I follow but myself . . .
>
> Heaven is my judge, not I for love and duty,
> But seeming so, for my peculiar end . . .

The happiness which others can find in the humbling bonds of love
and duty is an offence to Iago's outlook; thus his pride converts
by way of resentment and jealousy to hatred; and both pride and
hatred find an outlet in cunning, vindictive action.

Iago's pride is reflected in his conception of himself as a man of
'gain'd knowledge', (i.iii.378), a 'learn'd spirit' (as Othello puts it)
who knows 'all qualities . . . Of human dealing' (iii.iii.263–4). It is
an illuminating conception, closely connected to the play's underlying structure of ideas as well as to Iago's delight in manipulating
others. It first comes to the fore in his response to Roderigo's comi-

cal display of suicidal despair in Act I. Iago projects himself here as the all-wise moral physician who can place his patient's malady in the context of general nature and recommend the appropriate cure. What he advises is a restoration of emotional equilibrium through a willed tempering of passion by reason; and he justifies and illustrates his therapy by means of a horticultural analogy (I.iii.318–31). Such analogies were commonplace in discussions on the relationship between art (science, education, culture) and nature, but Iago chooses his figure with notable discrimination: the gardener plants nettles and lettuces together because these, having the qualities of dryness and moisture respectively, aid each other's growth; he plants hyssop and thyme together for precisely the same reason, and weeds out thyme when it grows to excess.[36] Reinforced with a meticulously balanced sentence structure, this figure would seem to place Iago in the same category as Friar Lawrence, who knew all about the opposites in nature (heat and moisture, baleful weeds and precious flowers, poison and medicine) and about the need to balance and temper them carefully (*Rom.*, II.iii.1–33). However, since Iago is sedulously nurturing Roderigo's sickness here, his true counterpart is not Romeo's benevolent Friar, but his dark apothecary. Like him, Iago specialises in administering 'distempering draughts' (*Oth.*, I.i.100), whether in the form of alcohol or of verbal 'poisons' which, 'with a little act upon the blood, Burn like the mines of sulphur' (III.iii.332–3). He (and not Othello) is 'a practiser / Of arts inhibited and out of warrant' (I.iii.78–9), all his knowledge of nature being used to release its destructive potential. Thus his clinic with Roderigo at the end of Act I is followed immediately by the ruffian storm and Cassio's prayer for Othello: 'O let the heavens/ Give him defence against the elements' (II.i.44–5).

If Iago's black art is defined poetically as a calculated disturbance of elemental harmony, dramatically it is shown as an adroit manipulation of time. When it suits him, he can both preach and practise patience. But the success of his plotting depends almost entirely on the extreme swiftness with which he and his victims react to events: his pun on 'speed', equating haste and success, is crucial (IV.i.108). He is above all else an opportunist, a 'slipper and subtle knave; a finder-out of occasion' (II.i.239–40; cf. lines 262–6). Yet despite his superb sense of timing, he is a *mere* opportunist who has no true understanding of time at all.[37] He thinks and acts only in terms of immediate solutions and satisfactions and has no thought for the long-term consequences of his plotting: the idea that Othello would want to kill Desdemona, that Roderigo would seriously threaten to ask Desdemona for his jewels, that Cassio would have to be killed, or that Emilia would turn against him, never crosses his mind. It has always been observed that his unusual oath at the start of the play, 'By Janus' (i.ii.33), is eminently appropriate, Janus being the two-faced god. But this oath has a much deeper significance than as a pointer to Iago's duplicity, for Janus himself was no double-dealer but rather a god who prudently looked both backward and forward, like 'the sun [who] alwaies looketh round about him, both before and behind in ech part and corner of the world'. Janus was thus the god of time and patron of all those who,

besides that by their wise counsels they doe act politikely and discreetly, instantly, and for the time present, carrie likewise in themselues a fore-prouiding prescience to preuent, and thereby to remedie succeeding mis-cheefs, and ensuing daungers; for that with the one face before, and the other behind, they continually behold and view round about them, record-ing things past, and premeditating those likely to follow.[38]

Thus like his hypocritical praise of patience and ripeness (iii.i.358–65), and his knowing reference to the 'many events in the womb of time which will be delivered' (i.iii.366–7), the oath 'By Janus' serves as an ironic index of Iago's status as time's enemy and, ulti-mately, time's fool. Coming at the start of the tragedy, however, the oath operates with singular force to encompass other characters and to magnify the ironic sense of an unforeseen calamity. Moreover those members of Shakespeare's audience who recalled what time actually did deliver in 1570 would have attended to the oath with special care and been acutely responsive to the assumption of both Desdemona and Roderigo that happiness is be found on the island of Cyprus.

   Iago's plot to keep Roderigo compliant and poison the happiness of Othello develops as a series of extemporal devices whose success depends on both his intuitive sense of the opportune moment and his genius for fuelling and exploiting the impatience of others. Bra-bantio is informed that 'Even now, now, very now' his daughter is being tupped, and that if he acts quickly he might avert disaster (i.iii.89–93). Roderigo is filled with fatuous hopes and so with an ever-mounting impatience that ultimately has to be relieved by the killing of Cassio: 'Quick, quick, fear nothing; I'll be at thy elbow' (v.i.3). Cassio is provoked at the precise moment when his miscon-duct is likely to dishonour him (on guard duty) and to infuriate his General (in or 'divesting' for the bridal bed). Once dismissed, he is persuaded to 'importune' (II.iii.307; III.iv.109) Desdemona to have him reinstated immediately, and Emilia is 'set on' (line 272) to facilitate this device by drawing Othello out of the way.[39] Cassio's boundless impatience ('I would not be delay'd (III.iv.115)) communicates to Desdemona, who impulsively commits herself to securing a speedy end to his misery. Her light-hearted promise is laden with ironic premonition of 'Chaos ... come again' (the phrase occurs thirty lines later):

> If I do vow a friendship, I'll perform it
> To the last article. My lord shall never rest,
> I'll watch him tame, and talk him out of patience;
> His bed shall seem a school, his board a shrift;
> I'll intermingle everything he does
> With Cassio's suit. (III.iii.21–6)

Within seconds, the loving Desdemona importunes Othello, and just when he is preoccupied with his military 'duties to the senate' and the grave matter of the island's fortification (III.ii, 2, 5). Although he tries to postpone a decision on Cassio ('Not now ... some other time'), she sets a limit to the postponement: 'let it not / Exceed three days' (III.iii.55, 62–3). Even when she has provoked his first furious outburst, she decides to renew her efforts and pursue the lieutenant's case to the 'uttermost' (III.iv.168). Desdemona's error here is genuinely tragic. Her refusal to accept the limits determined by time and 'the time' – to 'take the safest occasion by the front' – proceeds from her abundant loving-kindness. This is something which of its very nature flies from limit and measurement (*Rom.*, II.ii.133–4; *Ant.*, I.ii.15–17), but which in the circumstances comes close to exemplifying Friar Lawrence's harshly paradoxical formula: 'Virtue itself turns vice, being misapplied'.[40] Her reference to nocturnal pestering (recalling the activities of Iago in I.i and II.iii) indicates that this is where love, by its very overflowing, has lent itself to the work of hatred and violence. The final irony will come when her own 'balmy slumbers' are 'wak'd with strife' (II.iii.250) once more.

Desdemona's persistent pleadings are essential to Iago's attempt to talk Othello out of all patience. His first tactic in this endeavour is to use vague hints that grate on the Moor's hatred of uncertainty and quicken the pulse of his imagination: 'By heaven, I'll know thy thoughts' (III.iii.163). Another tactic is to talk in general terms about the unbearable state of uncertainty in which the suspicious cuckold lives, counting the 'damned minutes' of every day (line 173). But his masterstroke is the advice to practise patience and 'leave it to time'. When this advice is first offered, it serves to establish his credentials as a figure of peace and order (line 249). On the second occasion, however, it is timed just for the moment when Othello is so transfixed with rage at what he thinks has been done to him that the very thought of delay provokes the terrible vow of a 'violent' and 'swift' revenge – to be accomplished 'within these three days' (lines 456–77).

With the expulsion of patience, the 'young and rose-lipp'd cherubin' (IV.ii.64), darkness descends and the light is put out. Darkness has been pressing in on the *Othello* world from the beginning. As Robert Heilman has observed, this is predominantly a night play: 'at least half the action takes place during the hours of darkness' and 'references to daylight are so few and casual as hardly to be noticeable'.[41] The predominance of darkness, in which Iago's activities flourish, signifies not only error and evil but also disharmony with time's order, in fact Chaos: as I recalled earlier, Chaos was thought of as a state of universal night when there was no sun, moon, or other planets, and consequently no time. In promising to bring a monstrous birth to the world's light, Iago appropriately identifies himself with Hell and Night (I.iii.397–8), these being in classical mythology the children of Chaos (see p.16).[42] And when he puts out the light, Othello with equal propriety utters a cry of anguish in which the perception of chaos is a perception of time destroyed (Shakespeare seems to have remembered here that the word 'chaos' was formed from the Greek word 'yawn' or 'gape'):

> O insupportable! O heavy hour!
> Methinks it should be now a huge eclipse
> Of sun and moon, and that th'affrighted globe
> Did yawn at alteration. (V.ii.101–4)

This significant interrelation of the night–darkness symbolism, the time theme, and the general speed and violence of the action is evidence of the coherence and scope which Shakespeare's model of the natural order helps to give to the tragedy. But of course it is only a subordinate part of a much larger fabric of meaning derived from that grand frame of reference.

VII

The chief instrument in Iago's black art is the tongue, as he himself well knows: 'I had rather have this tongue cut from my mouth / Than it should do offence ...' (II.iii.213–4).[43] His hypocrisies, his lies, his parleys to provocation (line 21), and his habitual attempt to debase what is noble and begrime what is beautiful are poison poured in at the ear (line 345; II.iii.329–33; IV.i.44–6). The play as a whole exemplifies the classical and Renaissance axiom that speech is the greatest instrument for evil as well as for good known to man.[44] Speech is the bond which unites human beings, 'the Instrument of *Societie*';[45] but Iago uses it to create division and chaos. Speech too is what distinguishes man from beast, but Iago renders others incapable of it. Shakespeare is here building on an association of villainy with the corruption of speech which goes back to the coarse-mouthed, hypocritical, and equivocating Vice of the morality plays; even the way in which Othello's speech changes under the influence of Iago has its precedent in the relationship between such characters as the eponymous hero of *Mankind* and the devil Titivillus. In *Othello*, however, the corruption of speech is integral to a conception of tragedy as the undoing of a bonded unity in the self and society whose basis is the 'harmonious contrarietie' of the natural order. Thus Iago's most illuminating forebear may be the traitor Sinon as depicted in the passage on the Fall of Troy in *The Rape of Lucrece*. Sinon it was who persuaded the Trojan King to admit the Greek 'horse' within the city walls; what he did to Troy, Iago does to Othello. 'His words', we are told, 'like wildfire, burnt the shining glory / Of rich-built Ilion' (lines 1523–4); but they were kindly, tearful words, a form of chaos in the self that begets chaos on a huge scale:

> 'Look, look, how list'ning Priam wets his eyes,
> To see those borrowed tears that Sinon sheds.
> Priam, why art thou old, and yet not wise?
> For every tear he falls a Troyan bleeds;
> His eye drops fire, no water thence proceeds;
> Those round clear pearls of his that move thy pity
> Are balls of quenchless fire to burn thy city.
>
> 'Such devils steal effect from lightless hell;
> For Sinon in his fire doth quake with cold,
> And in that cold hot burning fire doth dwell;
> These contraries such unity do hold,

Only to flatter fools, and make them bold;
  So Priam's trust false Sinon's tears doth flatter
  That he finds means to burn Troy with his water'. (lines 1548–61)

The most spectacular achievement of Iago's corrupt tongue is the transformation of the eloquent and controlled Othello into the incoherent, subhuman creature who foams at the lips and hungers to tear the human form ('That cunning'st pattern of excelling nature') into pieces ('Noses, ears, and lips' (IV.i.43, 196)). Behind this, however, lies Iago's essential achievement, the undoing of all the words, vows ('a frail vow betwixt an erring barbarian and a super-subtle Venetian' (I.iii.354–5)), tokens (a strawberry-spotted handkerchief) and gestures (shaking or kissing the hand) that constitute the fabric of human relations. Under his influence, every sign becomes meaningless or, what is worse, acquires a second and contrary sense. But in the process of creating misinterpretation and confusion, Iago also relies on the simpler device of preventing people from talking to one another: Roderigo must not be allowed to talk to Desdemona, nor Cassio to Othello, nor Emilia to anyone ('Go to, charm your tongue' (line 186)). Thus Iago's final utterance summarises the meaning of his career, just as Othello's valediction does his: it is a terse refusal to match question with answer, indeed a total renunciation of speech: 'Demand me nothing . . . From this time forth I never will speak word' (lines 306–7).

The chief verbal symptom of Iago's corrosive effect on others is a breakdown in the unitary relation between sign and signified (ambiguity, equivocation) and a larger breakdown in the relation between questions and answers. Attention is drawn to these two sources of disharmony in the opening scenes when Brabantio indignantly tells Roderigo and Othello that they will have to 'answer' for their actions (I.i.120; I.ii.87), and later, when all questions have been answered, remarks with ironic ineptness on the inability of words, 'equivocal' ('strong on both sides') or otherwise, to affect the bruised heart (I.iii.218–19). The two disorders may appear independently, as in Iago's grimly prophetic pun, 'The Moor! I know his trumpet' (II.i.176), or in conjunction, as when Iago and Othello are communing about Desdemona's purported strumpetry. Most of Iago's answers to Othello's urgent questions – 'What dost thou think?' (III.iii.108), 'What dost thou mean?' (line 158) – are not answers at all but hints and evasions, sustained equivocations. And they are reinforced with sharply ambiguous words and phrases which work with extraordinary effect in such a context to awaken in Othello's imagination the hideous image of the double-backed beast. Cassio should really be allowed to 'have his place, / For sure he fills it up with great ability' (line 250); he said he did 'Lie ... with her, on her [i.e. 'belie her'], what you will' (IV.i.34). Provoking Othello's decline into gibberish ('It is not words that shake me thus'! (line 40)), and anticipated by the dull clown's evasive response to Desdemona's questioning about where Cassio lies ('I dare not say he lies anywhere' (III.iv.2)), the pun on 'lie' is the key equivo-. cation in the play. In both contexts it is closely associated with the handkerchief, that errant token of love which is being turned into the one certain sign of betrayal.

The breakdown in the relationship between Desdemona and Othello is at once signalled and accelerated by their own equivocations. Othello's are deliberate, an aspect of the evasiveness and duplicity he has acquired from Iago. For example, when Desdemona asks why he speaks so faintly, instead of communicating his fears of cuckoldry, he expresses them only for himself, speaking of 'a pain upon my forehead here' (III.iii.286). The effect of this equivocation is singularly damaging: when Desdemona proffers to bind his head, he knocks her handkerchief aside and it falls to the ground – to be discovered by Emilia and given an entirely new meaning by Iago. Language, symbol, theme, action, and plot are all one in this dramatically eloquent incident. In his next encounter with Desdemona (III.iv.33–44), Othello presumes to interpret her hand as signifying both virtue and vice, and reflects on the divorce between hand and heart (he is about to question her on the handkerchief: the status of hands and handkerchief as linked and exemplary signs, subject to misreading, is now obvious).[46] Baffled by his enigmatic ramblings, Desdemona changes the subject – or thinks she does – and proceeds to intensify his suspicions: 'I cannot speak of this ... I have sent to bid Cassio come speak with you' (III.iv.33–48).

Frightened by his new mood, Desdemona lies in answer to Othello's question about the handkerchief. Her equivocations, however, are quite unintentional, words which in any other context would be innocuous but which in the world of Iago and the changed Othello it is easy to 'construe ... quite in the wrong' (IV.i.101–3). When she tells Lodovico about the 'unkind breach' and 'division' between Othello and Cassio, and adds, 'I would do much / T'atone them, for the love I bear to Cassio' (IV.i.220–7), her words – and especially the word 'bear' – simultaneously exemplify and contribute to the loss of oneness which she laments: reminding Othello of the two-backed beast, they unleash in public the 'Fire and brimstone' (line 228) of his violent nature and prompt his bitter equivocations on 'obedient' (lines 252–3). In the interrogation of the 'brothel' scene ('Why, what art thou?' (iv.ii.34)), she herself asks a question: 'What ignorant sin have I committed?' (line 71). But she receives no answer, for Othello is reminded of a second sense which that verb had in the seventeenth century – 'to commit adultery' – and so is provoked to another fiery outburst that widens the breach between them:

> Committed!
> Committed! O thou public commoner!
> I should make very forges of my cheeks
> That would to cinders burn up modesty,
> Did I but speak thy deeds. What committed! (iv.ii.73–7)

Understanding a fury in his words, but not the words (lines 32–3), Desdemona from now until the end has almost no 'answers but [what] should go by water' (line 102), just as he has almost none but what go by fire. So the surge of rage which he seems to need to kill her is sparked by an ambiguous, tearful response to his assertion that Cassio cannot now be questioned because 'his mouth is stopp'd':

DES. Alas, he is betray'd, and I undone!
OTH. Out, strumpet! Weep'st thou for him to my face? (v.ii.80–1)

A rhetorical question, of course, but Desdemona is too bewildered and terrified to deal with it anyhow, and so is murdered.

If Othello's fall is caused by a divorce between words and thoughts fostered by Iago (verbal doubleness), his recovery is due in large measure to Emilia's determination to reunite them by telling all she knows. Having lied in answer to Desdemona's question about the lost handkerchief (*her* contribution to the tragedy), she now sees that she is 'bound to speak' (line 187) on her mistress's behalf and to defy her husband's command of silence, even at the price of her life: 'So come my soul to bliss, as I speak true; / So speaking as I think, alas, I die' (lines 253–4). Reuniting duty (what one is 'bound' to do) and love as well as thought and word, her death is true atonement and at-onement.[47] And so, for the same reason, and on a much loftier plane, is Othello's.

It should come as no surprise that the bond of speech is integral to the play's cosmological vision. Those who praised the arts of language in the Renaissance said that the universe itself is eloquent, a harmonious expression of the divine reason.[48] Of course music was the major symbol for the order of the universe in Pythagorean–Platonic cosmology, but eloquence and music were intimately associated. Indeed Orpheus was regarded as the god of both arts. He was revered as the patron of those who use the harmonious power of words to create peace among men, bringing them out of savagery and the wilderness into cities, senates, and parliaments:[49] we are offered powerful realisations of this conception in Act I when Othello casts his spell on Brabantio and his armed band, and later in the Senate. Like Kyd's *The Spanish Tragedy*, *Othello* is to a very large extent the tragedy of Orphic man.[50] It involves the corruption of a verbal concord that is analogous to the harmony of the 'elements that clip us round about' (III.iii.468) and, beyond that, of the changeless heavens. As Lawrence J. Ross has shown, the General's purported preference for the music that is not heard (III.i.15; cf. *MV*, v.i.65) is an ironic allusion on the Clown's part to the music of the spheres.[51]

As I have been intimating, too, the Pythagorean identification of the number one with good (with limit, cosmos, divinity, light) and the number two with evil (with the unlimited, chaos, darkness, and devilry), although not signalled by means of overt number symbolism as in *The Faerie Queene* and *A Midsummer Night's Dream* (see above, pp. 46–50), is wholly embedded in the imaginative patterning of *Othello*. Iago's lies and equivocations ally him with the two-tongued Ate, Spenser's allegorical embodiment of cosmic Strife; more immediately, they link him with the double-tongued serpent which is Shakespeare's symbol in *A Midsummer Night's Dream* for the natural force that undermines the 'union in partition' (or unified duality, or concordant discord) achieved by lovers and friends. His treacherous duplicity, in short, is intrinsic to a cosmological perspective on good and evil.

VIII

Great writers, claims Lucien Goldmann, are able to crystallise world views in a lucid and coherent form.[52] Shakespeare demonstrates this capacity in *Othello* with singular ease and tact. He concentrates with rare clarity on person, place, and time, and yet quietly and continually invests circumstantial particulars with hints of the general, the universal, the omnitemporal. In dramatising a 'private and domestic quarrel' (II.ii.207) of love and hate, he illuminates the nature of man and woman, the unfinished history of human conflict, and the forces which perennially unite, divide, and confound us. And in respect of this paradox, his play is self-reflexive. Accepting that he too 'must be circumstanc'd' (III.iv.102), and confining most of his action to one place and time (obeying 'the *unities*'), Shakespeare finds in limit and restraint the grounds for expressive freedom. Bound in the nutshell of a domestic tale, his imagination encompasses infinite possibilities. But as he will remind us in the Epilogue of that other self-reflexive, island-world play, *The Tempest*, the achievement of his bound and liberal art depends for much of its efficacy on the generous exercise of *our* imagination. And it depends, too (need one add?), on our knowledge of the discursive practice which is his medium of interpretation and expression.

7

King Lear

I

In Act IV, scene vi, the blinded Earl of Gloucester meets his king in the fields near Dover. Once the epitome of power and majesty, Lear has now been reduced to the level of a lunatic vagabond; yet Gloucester instinctively kisses the hand of the master he loved and reverenced, and asks: 'Dost thou know me?' (line 135). It is a most poignant question, since Gloucester must be wondering whether Lear will ever appreciate that it was because of kindness and loyalty to his king that his eyes were gouged. Nevertheless, Gloucester rises above the intensity of personal feeling to engage in impersonal and generalised reflection. Appalled by Lear's mad ramblings, he exclaims: 'O ruin'd piece of nature! This great world / Shall so wear out to nought' (lines 133–4).

In *King Lear*, Shakespeare's tragic art reaches its maximum of intensity and comprehensiveness, and this incident can be taken as exemplifying its characteristic procedures. Gloucester's response to Lear is rooted in feelings engendered by the immediate situation, and by a keen sense of the human person and human relationships; yet Lear's mad incoherence makes him think instantly of universal nature, the end of the world, and the return to primordial confusion. Moreover, one very simple word which Gloucester uses serves both to involve the whole experience of the play in the present moment and to underpin its cosmic perspective. Plato coined the term τὸ πᾶν as a synonym for the word 'cosmos'; it means literally 'all', 'everything', so that the word 'nothing' or 'nought' became another word for 'chaos'.[1] Counterpointed continually by the word 'all' ('Of all these bounds, even from this line to this', 'I gave you all', etc.), the word 'nothing' echoes throughout the play, beginning with Cordelia's famous answer in the first scene. And its use here by Gloucester suggests that the action of the play, although it begins in what Goneril calls 'domestic and particular broils' (v.i.30),[2] was contextualised from the start in relation to the ultimate poles of natural experience.[3]

An amalgam of emotional force and sharp realistic detail, the intense particularity of *King Lear* undoubtedly owes something to the play's embeddedness in contemporary English history. The disintegration of feudalism, the emergence of a capitalist society, the plight of the poor and the homeless in such a society, the Christian communism soon to be advocated by the Levellers;[4] the transfer of lands from the old aristocracy to the new entrepreneurs;[5] the problems of self-definition experienced by the aristocracy in a socio-political order which had greatly reduced its wealth and influence;[6] sixteenth- and seventeenth-century disagreements over what constitutes the sacred in political and religious authority:[7] strong echoes of all this have been justifiably detected in the play's dramatisation of a legendary British past. But however much it was nourished by contemporary experience, *King Lear* is considerably more than an oblique encounter with the socio-political contingencies of its own time. It proceeds on the assumption that the problems of human nature and society which it explores are problems for all time and all places. In its dialectic and cyclic view of history, it balances an urgent search for constructive change in the present with a terrible awareness that all solutions to human problems, and all resolutions of human conflict, are temporary; given the nature of human nature, and of the world we inhabit, the same problems will recur endlessly in different forms. No other text of Shakespeare's seems so bent on penetrating the actualities of observed experience to confront what it holds to be the unchanging complexities of human nature and the natural world.

Not only individual incidents and scenes, but the whole design of the play, both structure and style, reveals an imaginative procedure which habitually seeks to disclose the universal in the particular without ever blunting the latter's particularity: 'Thou hast seen a farmer's dog bark at a beggar? ... And the creature run from the cur? There thou might'st behold the great image of authority' (IV.vi.154–8). And what ultimately prompts such a procedure is the notion of a universe structured throughout on correspondences; in no other Shakespearian tragedy, as Theodore Spencer observed,[8] are the parallels between the individual, the state, and the natural world so abundant. But it would be wrong to infer that correspondence is the primary informing idea in the tragedy, since the effect of all the correspondences is to show that everywhere, at every level of reality, there is duality and opposition.[9] Plain-speaking Kent's furious description of his relation to the oily Oswald sums up the structural dynamics of the tragedy: 'No contraries hold more antipathy / Than I and such a knave' (II.iii.82–3). What is figured here is not so much a stable, hierarchical order thrown into convulsion as a fiercely contrarious and changeful world where a mere word – like the word 'Nothing' – might precipitate chaos, and a few more words – like 'No cause, no cause' – might miraculously renew all. And like those Renaissance pessimists who foresaw the imminent disintegration of the whole natural order (Gloucester with his speech on 'These late eclipses' has often been linked with them), the play assumes that a violent acceleration in the strife of nature's contraries is what will bring about the promised end.[10]

II

Perhaps the most obvious means by which Shakespeare extends the significance of his 'domestic and particular broils' is the structural device of the secondary plot. The story of Gloucester's family not only interacts with that of Lear's but parallels it exactly in terms of action, character, and theme; one has the impression that what is happening at the top of society is happening all the way down the ladder of degree. However, the outstanding common feature of the two families is violent conflict arising out of stark contrariety in character and temperament. In the subplot there are Edgar and Edmund, two half-brothers whose very names suggest both affinity and difference. Edgar is a loyal, loving, trusting, and morally serious son, whereas Edmund is treacherous, pitiless, cunning, and flippant. And these two brothers reflect two sides of their father, who jests about Edmund's adulterous begetting, turns ruthlessly against Edgar, and yet risks his own life out of compassionate love for the outcast King. When at the end Edgar, as Edmund's 'unknown opposite' (V.iii.153), challenges and defeats his younger brother (now improperly titled 'Earl of Gloucester'), he is resolving an opposition and dispelling a confusion that originates in their father's make-up.

The pattern of duality and opposition in the royal family is more elaborate and more exactly reminiscent of the structure of universal nature. This is a family of four, and the play ends with the extraordinary spectacle of all four lying dead on the stage, a natural unit destroyed by its own oppositional dynamics.[11] The play began with the father's decision to divide the kingdom between his three daughters so 'that future strife / May be prevented now' (I.i.43–4); it moves to its end with a battle between the forces of Goneril and Regan on the one hand and of Cordelia and Lear on the other, 'the opposites of this day's strife' (v.iii.44). Again, violent conflict began in temperamental opposition, in inherent nature. Cordelia is loving, compassionate, truthful and reticent; Goneril and Regan are selfish, cruel, hypocritical, and (when it profits them) verbose. These extremes meet and struggle for supremacy in Lear. The King is a warm and generous man who has no doubt that loving-kindness is a supreme value; but he is also egocentric, choleric, cruelly unjust, hyperbolical, and quite incapable of appreciating the value of reticence. The oppositions in the two fathers and the two families are reflected in the *dramatis personae* as a whole; Lear, Gloucester, and Albany apart, the characters fall into two distinct groups, one characterised by 'unselfish and devoted love' and the other by 'hard self-seeking'. I quote from A.C. Bradley, who intriguingly reflects in passing that this design is reminiscent of the Empedoclean conception of a world governed by the contrary forces of Love and Hate. Bradley's commitment to the Hegelian version of a contrarious world order prevented him from pursuing this thought any further and so recognising the presence in the play of a model of nature that was intrinsic to the discursive practice of Shakespeare's audience.[12]

An obvious but profoundly significant aspect of the play's thought and design which greatly emphasises its oppositional character is that of extremity. When the bond of opposites which constitutes natural order is broken, things by definition revolt against limit and fly to extremes. This idea is fundamental to the old cosmology and is manifest in all Shakespeare's tragedies: even in *Romeo and Juliet* 'everything [is] in extremity' (I.iii.103). *Lear*, however, is a play which consciously seeks to 'top extremity' (v.iii.207) in every respect. This emphasis was inspired by the source play, *King Leir*, where the nouns 'extreme' and 'extremity' are used in basically two senses – (a) inordinate intensity of feeling, violent measures; (b) the utmost point of adversity or suffering – in such a way as to connect the character and fate of the protagonist. The terrible degradation and misery into which Leir is plunged ('Ah my dear Lord, how doth my heart lament, / To see you brought to this extremity') springs from the wicked daughters' perception that since 'he . . . is always in extremes' they can easily 'convert his love [for Cordella] to hate'.[13]

What is an interesting moralistic trope in the old play becomes an informing idea which penetrates every aspect of Shakespeare's tragedy: not only characterisation but theme, emotional tone, symbolism, and style are all affected by it.[14] Although ubiquitous, however, the idea of extremes still seems to emanate mainly from the character and fate of Lear. Here is a man whose love for his favourite daughter and most loyal counsellor turns in a 'trice of time' to 'hate' (I.i.175, 210, 216); who in the space of two weeks is flung from the arrogant splendour of absolute power to impotence and destitution; who learns that Pomp must 'shake the superflux' of its wealth to the naked and houseless poor and create a more balanced and equitable society (III.iv.35; IV.i.68); who oscillates between rage and patience, violence and gentleness, pride and humility, thundering grandiloquence and quiet simplicity; who endures the utmost anguish in advanced old age, and then, at 'th' extreme verge' (IV.vi.26) of life, is suddenly subjected to wholly unbearable – because contrary – extremes of passion; whose fate (even more than Gloucester's) gives rise to the question: Are there any limits at all to the cruelties which life can inflict on us?, and to the uncompromising answer: 'the worst is not / So long as we can say "This is the worst"' (IV.i.28–9). Here is a king whose epitaph is: 'we that are young / Shall never see so much nor live so long' (V.iii.325–6); and whose tragedy as a whole suggests 'the promis'd end' (line 263), the return of *all* to *nought*.

Even the setting of the play is distinctly oppositional. The effect of this opposition is one of complexity, instability, and confusion rather than of conflict and extremes. Court and castle prove inhospitable and cruel, whereas communal values flourish in the open country. But the open country itself is dichotomised. There is the nocturnal, storm-ridden, barren heath near Gloucester's castle, and there are the sunlit, sustaining cornfields near Dover. The sustaining fields in turn are choked by those idle weeds with which Lear – figuring in the Gloucester encounter as a 'ruin'd piece of nature' – has crowned himself. And this particular reminder of the ease with which double nature can confound itself is complicated by the fact that the weeds which choke the corn (rank fumiter, hemlock, cuckoo flowers, and darnel) were prized for their medicinal properties. Among them are plants used to induce sleep ('close the eye of anguish') and cure diseases of the brain: just such 'simples operative' as Cordelia's doctor would use to 'Cure this great breach' in Lear's 'abused nature' (IV.iv.1–15; IV.vii.15).[15] Nothing in nature, it seems, is simple, least of all simples; extreme opposites are involved in everything, and each term in every antithesis breaks down into a further opposition. It was along these lines, of course, that Friar Lawrence was thinking when Romeo interrupted his pastoral meditations (see above p.59).

The scenes at Dover include a vision of natural harmony restored: 'sunshine and rain at once', ripeness (IV.iii.15–21), the 'untun'd and jarring senses' wound up and 'in temper' (IV.vii.16, 24; I.v.43), father and daughter reconciled, love eclipsing strife. Conjunct with this vision, however (and anticipating the violent change in his fortunes in the last act), is the memory of Lear exposed to the fury of the warring elements on the barren heath, like a lone, lightly armed sentry engulfed by a marauding army:

> Was this the face
> To be oppos'd against the warring winds?
> To stand against the deep dread-bolted thunder?
> In the most terrible and nimble stroke
> Of quick, cross lightning? to watch – poor perdu! –
> With this thin helm? (IV.vii.31–6)

More than anything else, it is the paradigmatic strife of the elements that focuses attention on the oppositional principle at the heart of the play. Much like the storms in *A Midsummer Night's Dream, Julius Caesar*, and *Othello*, the tempest in *Lear* figures literally as conflict among the four elements, and symbolically as an omen of primordial chaos casting an apocalyptic shadow on the 'debate' and 'dissension' that confounds 'human mortals' (*MND*, II.i.101, 116). But nowhere in the canon is the violence of the warring elements and the sense of chaos projected with such imaginative force as in the heath scenes of *King Lear*. Personified, apostrophised, and energised by association with Lear's mighty passions, the elements become as participants in the drama. Their introduction precedes the actual storm, and it is Lear who, in his terrible curses on Goneril, opens the door to them:

> You nimble lightnings, dart your blinding flames
> Into her scornful eyes! Infect her beauty,
> You fen-suck'd fogs, drawn by the pow'rful sun,
> To fall and blast her pride. (II.iv.163–6; cf.I.iv.299)

On the heath, Lear enters imaginatively into a phantasmagoric battle played out in the heavens between lightning, wind, and rain. He 'strives . . . to outstorm' the elements (III.i.10–11), urges them to

'Strike flat the thick rotundity o' th' world' and to 'crack nature's moulds' (iii.ii.1–8). He sees them as faithful agents of his wrath ('I tax not you, you elements, with unkindness', line 16), and then as treacherous servants who join forces with the wicked daughters to turn their 'high-engender'd battles' against him (lines 21–5).

Lear's counterpart on the heath, Poor Tom the Bedlam beggar, is equally familiar with the elements; but he is a passive rather than a defiant and questioning victim. Tom has had to endure the persecutions of the sky (ii.iii.12), has shivered in the wind that blows through the sharp hawthorn, and has been led by 'the foul fiend through fire and through flame, through ford and whirlpool, o'er bog and quagmire' (iii.iv.46–51). Yet in the case of Tom as well as Lear the savagery of nature, insofar as it is associated with punishment for sin, carries with it the suggestion of a potentially remedial function, like nature's medicinal poisons. Reading *King Lear* in the light of pastoral tradition, Rosalie Colie construed it as an example of 'hard pastoral' – meaning pastoral where nature is seen as wholly harsh but morally educative.[16] This reading overlooks the dichotomous structure of the country setting in the play and the binary conception of nature which coincides with it; but it is not inconsistent with the delineation of nature in the heath scenes. Depending on the suffering individual's response, the warring elements here (to cite Shakespeare's first pastoral play) can become counsellors that feelingly persuade men what they are, so that out of the experience of chaos might come some kind of renewal.

Yet the heath scenes function above all as a central and horrific image of a world 'come to great confusion' (iii.ii.92). The words are those of the Fool, who simultaneously proclaims and exemplifies the advent of chaos. He exemplifies it simply by his presence in the midst of high tragedy. Never has the classical and humanist demand for the separation of tragedy and comedy and of kings and clowns been so thoroughly flouted as in *King Lear*. Thomas Kyd's brilliant conception of tragedy as a mirror of confounding opposites in which the element of play and jest demanded by the Elizabethan groundlings becomes formally justified as a metadramatic metaphor, part of a meaningful *discordia concors*, is taken here, like everything else, to vertiginous extremes.[17] For the educated members of Shakespeare's monarchically conditioned audience, the grandeur of Lear's character and the eloquent intensity of his feelings could not but have called up the Senecan and neo-Senecan ideal of tragedy as a form in which the misdeeds and the sufferings of the great are thoroughly

insulated against every trace of the low and the ludicrous. The
Fool's impudent and obscene mockings of the King's folly in the first
two acts, and his shrill and pathetic attempts to 'out-jest / His heart-
struck injuries' (III.i.16–17) in the third, must have hit them with a
discordant force which we can now only guess at. There was, of
course, the tradition of the licensed fool; but this is an 'all-licens'd
fool' (I.iv.199) who has stepped far beyond the boundaries which
define his social function. There was too the tradition of saturnalian
game – and the play is filled with vivid echoes of it – where the
lowest on the social scale is installed as the highest and vice versa,
and role-change and indecorum become the order of the day. But
this play shows misrule unconfined, the inversion of hierarchical
opposites normalised, riotous play in deadly earnest. 'All with me's
meet that I can fashion fit' (I.ii.175), says the jocular villain whom
Lear's abrupt renunciation of authority almost leads to the throne;
this philosophy is not peculiar to Edmund but underlies everything
that the censorious Goneril and Regan have to say to their father on
what befits his age and position. The Fool is a wise fool because he is
acutely aware that everything in the realm of Albion is handy-
dandy. It is his major theme, and Lear comprehends it only when he
has lost his wits. The King then takes the place of the Fool (who
'goes to bed at noon') and becomes the jesting and obscene voice of
unpalatable truths about the mad confusion of the world.[18] This
development in the character of a royal, tragic hero out-tops all
extremity in the process of introducing comedy to tragedy.

The sense of the grotesque engendered by the cruel and bitter
comedy of *King Lear* (on which G. Wilson Knight has written so
well)[19] is intrinsic to a larger perception of the abnormal that springs
from the contemplation of human degradation, both physical and
moral. Human beings treat their fellow humans as no better than
animals: the beggar shunned by society and exposed to the extremity of the skies appears to be indistinguishable from a poor, bare
forked animal, a worm. But in their lack of all restraint – in their
fury, their cruelty, and their lust – human beings become truly
bestial. Man and beast in the perspective of this play are not just
closely related species on the scale of creation (as Montaigne
suggested). They are seen as hierarchical opposites whose distinction should be maintained at all costs – in the play's imagery there
are no attractive, intelligent animals (like the sportive dolphin and
the wily serpent in *Antony and Cleopatra*) which would encourage us to
assume that no essential distinction need be made between the two

species. Thus the key emphasis is not on bestiality but on monstrosity, a sickening or horrifying mixture of naturally distinct kinds – exemplified by the centaur (IV.vi.125). Comparing Albany unfavourably with Edmund, Goneril reflects bitterly on 'the difference of man and man' (IV.ii.25); but the relevant difference at that point, as elsewhere, is between man and monster: between human beings who retain their identity as such and those who, like Edmund and Goneril, exhibit 'fierce quality' and 'lusty stealth' in the relentless pursuit of their desires (I.ii.11–12) while appearing at the same time as reasonable and civilised beings. Albany articulates the distinction clearly enough when Goneril's contemptuous sneers bring home to him the full extent of her inhumanity. His moral outrage is such that he is tempted to do more than becomes a man, and so to cease being one; but he remains 'border'd certain' (IV.ii.33) within the limits defined by his humanity:

> Thou changed and self-cover'd thing, for shame,
> Bemonster not thy feature. Were't my fitness
> To let these hands obey my blood,
> They are apt enough to dislocate and tear
> Thy flesh and bones. (lines 62–6)

Cordelia is the first against whom the charge of monstrosity is directed: to be stripped of her father's favour so utterly and so quickly, her crime must surely have been 'monstrous' (I.i.217), suggests France. But of course France is incredulous, and the charge is really directed against Lear. Indeed in the violence of his reaction to Cordelia's 'nothing', Lear explicitly identifies himself with the anthropophagi and the dragon. It is *his* loss of self-control that lets loose the monsters.

III

Lear's association of himself with those who make their generation messes to gorge their appetite is a powerful symbol for breaking the natural bond. It is that breach more than anything else that is responsible for chaos – for the loss of human and personal identity, the disintegration of society, violent extremes of strife and misery, and the disappearance of differences and distinctions. All Shakespearian – indeed all Renaissance – tragedy turns on the violation of human bonds, these being conceived as a reflection of the bonds which unite the warring opposites in nature.[20] But as countless critics have felt, the idea of the bond is more deeply and pervasively embedded in the imaginative life of *King Lear* than in that of any other play of the period.[21] Like *Othello*, it ends with a violent sundering ('he that parts us shall bring a brand from heaven' (v.iii.22)) which makes life unendurable for the protagonist; but it begins with sudden and violent division too, and it is concerned throughout with the shattering, the sustaining, the reconstituting, and the shattering again of intimate personal relationships. As in *Othello*, the villain of the play is a devil of division; unlike Iago, however, and with an anarchic indifference that is alien to Claudius, this villain is involved in a wholesale breach of familial bonds – parental, filial, sibling, and matrimonial – that undermines the very structure of society. Edgar's comment on the effect of his father's adultery – 'The dark and vicious place where thee he got / Cost him his eyes' (v.iii.172–3) – is usually interpreted nowadays as an unacceptably harsh piece of moralising which the drama itself does not endorse; but that, I think, is to ignore its philosophic status as part of a continuing emphasis on fidelity as the only alternative to social chaos. Fidelity to wife, child, parent, and master, and indeed to every personal commitment, are all one in the ethic of this play: 'obey thy parents; keep thy words justly ... commit not with man's sworn spouse', says Edgar in his role as Lear's philosopher (iii.iv.80–1). Gloucester's begetting of a son whom he can acknowledge only by blushing or brazenness, and who inevitably becomes an aggrieved, autonomous creature convinced that he owes everything to himself and nothing to others, cannot be detached from the chain of tragic causality which engulfs both families.

The bond motif is wholly bound up with such major concerns as the relationship between justice and love and the nature of personal identity. In interpersonal and social as well as in cosmological terms, the bond involves both love and justice; it comprehends natural affection and the duties which that dictates, so that in its ideal form it predicates a glad and spontaneous performance of 'offices' (ii.iv.177) and responsibilities. Thus when Lear renounces his paternal bond with Cordelia, he strips her – in a most pregnant phrase – of her 'dear rights' (iv.iii.44), that which she is owed as a loving and a beloved daughter; and when she herself returns to invade England with a foreign army we know that she has been prompted to do so neither by 'ambition' (which she explicitly rules out) nor by a reluctant sense of what ought to be done, but rather by 'love, dear love, and our ag'd father's right' (iv.iv.28). Cordelia's loving performance of 'a childlike office' (II.i.106) in support of what is just stands in significant contrast to her behaviour in the first scene. In declaring that she loves her father 'According to my bond: no more nor less', and that when she marries she will have to subtract fifty-per-cent of her care and duty (I.i.91–101), she reduces the bond to *mere* duty, a coldly legalistic contract subject to the mechanics of calculation; her words here, unlike her actions later, reflect no awareness that 'there's beggary in the love that can be reckon'd'. She has, however, been driven into this position by her father's crass display of materialism and coercion. Even before he gets down to dividing his family and kingdom, Lear shatters the whole concept of the bond as a harmonious union of love and duty by making the first the slave of the second. Beginning with Lear's tyrannic treatment of both Cordelia and Kent, the play offers a comprehensive and devastating satire on what passes for justice in organised society. But however comprehensive its satiric scope, the play also indicates that the main source of all injustice in society is a loss of human-kindness and imaginative sympathy – of love in the larger sense. Love and love alone begets and sustains a true awareness of the other person as an individual with feelings and rights of her or his own. This corresponds with the interchangeable emphases in cosmological tradition – one associated mainly with Plato, the other with Aristotle – on either love or just law as the binding and conserving force in nature; the compatibility of the two emphases rested on the notion that love of its very nature begets law.[22]

Personal identity as well as justice is dependent on the bond. The desire to be recognised and acknowledged – a desire closely connected with a belief in the importance of gratitude for kindness and loyalty – is one of the most urgent and poignant feelings registered in the play. Edmund's pathological hardness would seem to owe something to the fact that he has been acknowledged only with blushes, brazenness, and lewd jocularity; that of Goneril and Regan to the way in which they are habitually acknowledged as second best in their father's affections. Gloucester's eloquently simple, 'Dost thou know me?' reveals a deep yearning for recognition. And Kent's impending death is a kind of desperate journey in quest of his master's recognition: his pathetically emphatic words, 'I am the very man ... That from your first of difference and decay, / Have follow'd your sad steps' (v.iii.286–8), have meant nothing to the distracted Lear. But of course the anguish of not being acknowledged is pre-eminently Lear's; and from the moment he begins to doubt himself the dependence of personal identity on the bond becomes apparent. For those whose attitude towards him was determined by his conception of the bond as a matter of material give-and-take, Lear rapidly becomes, when divested of property and power, a mere nobody, neither king nor father. But for those whose bond entailed both love and duty, he remains the person he was, and is given all the respect due to a king, a father, and old age. In his new humility he describes himself to Cordelia as 'a very foolish, fond old man'; but she addresses him tenderly as 'your Highness', 'my royal Lord', 'your majesty' (IV.vii.44–84). Kent, Gloucester, and the anonymous gentleman who brings Lear to Cordelia use the same idiom of loving respect. This is a play which powerfully endorses the sentiment uttered by Florizel in *A Winter's Tale*: 'I cannot be / Mine own, nor anything to any, if / I be not thine' (IV.iv.43–5). Outside the bond, no one is known or knows himself.

By a familiar Shakespearian logic, the bond of speech reflects the prevailing disorders in interpersonal and socio-political relationships. Linguistic confusion properly begins with Lear's renunciation of royal responsibilities. This act undermines his claim to the name of king and also sets in motion a chain of events which allows the illegitimate Edmund to assume his father's title and to come within a hair's-breadth of Lear's. In consonance with this misplacement of titles and names, the Edmund–Goneril party develops a language of its own characterised by antonymic nominalism (as I have elsewhere defined this phenomenon):[23] everything is re-named from an opposite point of view and the gulf between the two parties is fiercely accentuated. Goneril's speeches rebuking her father show the emergence of this new language. Alluding to possible penalties for his misbehaviour, she explains that 'necessity will call discreet proceeding' what in other circumstances would be deemed 'shameful' (I.iv.210–12); she explains that 'All's not offence that indiscretion finds, / And dotage terms so' (II.iv.195–6). But it is in relation to Edmund, the first person to be honoured by the new party, that the alternative language becomes conspicuous. Addressing Cornwall, Edmund refers to his father's loyalty to the old King as 'treason' and his own betrayal of his father as 'loyalty'; at which point Cornwall gives him his father's title ('It hath made thee Earl of Gloucester') and invites him to call *him* 'father' instead (III.v.11–23). The linguistic split is horrifically apparent in the first judicial proceeding of the new regime, the punishment of Gloucester: he addresses his guests as 'Your graces' and 'good my friends' and in return is named 'filthy traitor', 'villain', and 'ingrateful fox' (III.vii.27–34). In the next appearance of the new party, the split is explicitly foregrounded in Oswald's almost comical report to Goneril (with Edmund by her side) on his encounter with Albany, a man 'so chang'd':

> I told him of the army that was landed;
> He smil'd at it. I told him you were coming;
> His answer was 'The worse'. Of Gloucester's treachery,
> And of the loyal service of his son,
> When I inform'd him, then he call'd me sot,
> And told me I had turn'd the wrong side out.
> What most he should dislike seems pleasant to him;
> What like, offensive. (IV.ii.4–11)

This report prepares for Albany's alliance with Edgar in the last act; it is an alliance which not only prevents a further degeneration in language but restores the proper relationship between sign and referent for the foreseeable future. Scornfully dismissing Regan's claim that Edmund can rightfully 'call' him 'brother' (on the grounds that she herself will call Edmund her 'lord and master') (V.iii.62–79), Albany dubs Edmund a 'half-blooded fellow', arrests him on capital treason, and delivers Edgar's challenge. Appearing in the lists as the knight without a name, Edgar denounces Edmund's base and treacherous character in appropriate terms and recovers his own noble name. And since to Albany his 'gait did prophesy / A royal nobleness' (lines 175–6), we must presume that the King's displaced title will also be his: the fact that he is Lear's 'godson' ('He whom my father named', said Regan (II.i.91–2)) is undoubtedly meant to emphasise the fitness of such a development. This reconstitution of social, moral, and linguistic order in the figure of Edgar is a consolatory fact to be set against the unspeakable horror of Cordelia's hanging.

IV

Debasing what is noble and ennobling what is base, the contrary language of *King Lear* is a kind of continuous paradox. Of course paradox proper is an outstanding feature of thought and expression in the play. Its general effect is to throw into bold relief not only the clash of opposites in nature and experience but also their sinuous and unstable relationship. A simple distinction can be made between negative and positive paradox. Prominent in the language of the evil party, negative paradox signifies moral or social topsy-turvydom, an undoing of the desired order of things: as when Regan claims that Edmund 'is too good to pity' his blinded father (III.vii.89), and Goneril accuses Albany of 'harmful mildness' (I.iv.353; cf. IV.ii.58). Negative paradox also occurs in grotesque, imagistic form in the Fool's allusions to the folly of Lear, who makes his daughters his mothers and keeps his brains in his heels. Positive paradox signifies some kind of renewal through destruction, discovery through loss: it accords with the belief that there is 'some soul of goodness in things evil, / Would men observingly distil it out' (*H5*,IV.i.4–5). Rosalie Colie points out that although all Lear's troubles come from Cordelia's firm 'Nothing, my lord' (which shows the unwisdom of his 'Nothing will come of nothing'), his undoing nevertheless is his re-creation as a man; so too Edgar is a better person for having been Poor Tom ('Edgar I nothing am').[24] Actually, the all–nothing paradox is never explicitly formulated in *King Lear* (as it is in *Timon of Athens*: 'nothing brings me all things' (v.i.186)); but it is variously expressed in other terms throughout the play. Furthermore, maximum emphasis is given to it at the start, as if it were being established as a central idea. Stripped of her dowry and dowered with her father's curse, Cordelia suddenly becomes in the eyes of her prospective husband an 'unprized precious maid'; she is 'most rich, being poor; / Most choice, forsaken; and most lov'd, despis'd' (lines 253–9; cf. line 230). Shakespeare intensifies the paradoxical effect here by openly concurring with the rhetorician's definition of paradox as the figure of wonder or strangeness: 'Gods, gods!', adds France, ''tis strange that from their cold'st neglect / My love should kindle to inflam'd respect' (I.i.250–9; cf. I.ii.110–11).[25] But this expression of wonder is deserving of attention for another reason: through the imagistic antithesis of 'cold'st' and 'inflam'd', it quietly associates the proliferation of paradox with the oppositional dynamics of nature, where there is a continual metamorphosis of the elements, one into the other.[26] The implication of *King Lear* is that *in every respect* the world we inhabit is 'full of changes' (I.i.287) and 'strange mutations' (IV.i.21) that can make us hate and love and love and hate it.

Of course the metamorphosis of deprivation into riches and of hate into love which is focussed on France and Cordelia in the opening scene is essentially a pointer to the personal tragedies of Lear and Gloucester. Lear will discover (among many other things) that 'the art of our necessities is strange / That can make vile things precious' (III.ii.70–1); and Gloucester will find that 'our means secure us, and our mere defects / Prove our commodities' (IV.i. 21–2). The idea of discovery and understanding – of and through contrariety – gives rise in turn to the great twin paradoxes of reason in madness and vision in blindness.

Although there is far less verbal ambiguity in *Lear* than in the other major tragedies, there is some unobtrusive play on certain key words which shows in yet another way how language reflects the contrariety and mutability of all things natural. Terence Hawkes has pointed out that there is a homonymic pun on the verb 'love' in the opening scene which brings together two almost opposite meanings, the familiar sense and the sense of 'to appraise, estimate or state the price or value of' (from the Old English *lofian*, 'to praise'). The use of the word 'love' in this second, material sense he rightly imputes to Goneril and Regan; but he is incorrect, I believe, in claiming that Cordelia's 'I love your majesty / According to my bond: no more nor less' constitutes a rejection of the material in favour of the spiritual conception of love.[27] As I have suggested above, Cordelia's justifiable resentment has driven her into a momentary and fatal identification with her father's materialistic approach to human relationships, so that her use of the word 'bond', like the word 'love', functions as an oxymoronic pun, and helps to convince her father that she is (paradoxically) 'so young and so untender' (line 105). I would add, moreover, that in this same scene the words 'tender' (line 195) and 'dear' (lines 55, 75, 182, 196) function in precisely the same way. Thus in the opening scene there is a set of puns which collectively signal a confusion about the nature of love that is to prove catastrophic; just as there is a set of paradoxes that pinpoints the potential benefits of catastrophe.

A more comprehensive form of confusion is localised in play on the words 'kind' and 'natural'. This must be read as part of Shakespeare's predictable reaction to the univocal and piously orthodox conception of nature which is invoked throughout *King Leir*. The word 'kind' in its various forms ('kindness', 'unkind' etc.) is the key word in the old play: it occurs about forty times, and it is used – in place of the word 'love' – in the fatal test: 'Which of you three to me would prove most kind' (line 233). There is a more or less continuous quibble in the old play on two meanings of the word which projects the author's unqualified assumption that to be natural is to be kind (loving, compassionate), and to be unkind is to be unnatural.[28] Shakespeare's response in *King Lear* to this assumption is in a sense what his play is all about and so is manifest everywhere in the text. It can be pinpointed, for example, in the Fool's reaction to Lear's claim that Regan is a 'kind and comfortable' daughter who will both treat him lovingly and 'flay' her unnatural sister's 'wolvish visage' (I.iv.307–8). Says the Fool: 'Shalt see thy other daughter will use thee kindly' – i.e. according to her (wolvish) nature or kind (I.v.13). Gloucester's wholly mistaken estimate of Edmund as a 'Loyal and natural boy' (II.i.84) involves a similar but more intriguing pun. Since Gloucester immediately commits himself to ensuring that Edmund's illegitimacy will not prevent him from inheriting the earldom ('I'll work the means / To make thee capable'), we must presume the presence of a pun on 'natural', and one which would have had much more force in Shakespeare's time than it does now. For centuries, a natural child meant a legitimate one; but it would seem that in the sixteenth century fathers and sons who wished to gloss over the fact of illegitimacy began to use the word 'natural' as an attractive synonym for 'illegitimate' (on the basis of an older sense: 'related by blood rather than adoptive'). Hardly as authoritative as Burke's *Peerage*, but no less fastidious, (Sir John) Ferne's *Blazon of Gentrie* (1586) commented sardonically on this strange mutation in the meaning of the word among the upper classes: 'he hath smoothed vp the matter with a fine terme, in calling him a sonne naturall, a prety word'.[29]

The word 'nature' is used in at least seven senses in *King Lear*.[30] This reflects Shakespeare's awareness of the extreme slipperiness of the concept and helps to draw attention to the fact that a number of the characters in the play are motivated by antithetical notions of what nature dictates. It has long been argued that in *Lear* Shakespeare dramatises a philosophical conflict about the nature of nature that was becoming urgent in his own day: between on the one hand the so-called doctrine of Natural Law which held that nature is essentially moral, dictating altruism, community, limit, and reason; and on the other hand the new Machiavellian–Hobbesian view that nature is an amoral system which encourages egoism and the unscrupulous use of force and cunning to achieve one's desires.[31] It is certainly possible to find echoes of this debate in the play. However I would contend that Shakespeare, in responding to the old play's uncomplicated endorsement of the benignant nature championed by theologians, was not simply intent on testing it by reference to the malignant nature of the new philosphers; rather, he was appealing to, and endorsing, a unitary theory of nature which embraces both perceptions. In that theory, of course, all nature is animated by sympathies and antipathies, love and strife; at its best, it is a fragile system of concordant discord, 'sunshine and rain at once'; at its worst it is absolute discord – in Lear's words, 'kill, kill, kill, kill, kill, kill' (iv.vi.188). The major problem is not that human beings have to choose between two moral philosophies but rather that human and universal nature is intransigently double. As we have seen, this problem is dramatised in the central character and his contrasting offspring. When Lear says 'I will forget my nature: so kind a father' (i.v.32), he is referring to a self which is partly actual and certainly potential. And when in his fury he tells Kent that opposition to his decree is something 'Which nor our nature nor our place can bear' (i.i.171), he is referring to another and manifestly existent self. Yet we cannot treat this other 'self' as the merely malignant side of his nature, for it is that which has made him every inch a king, a man who in his old age can kill the murderer of his daughter. The two Lears are polarised in his daughters, whose behaviour prompts Kent to wonder how 'one self mate and make could ... beget / Such different issues' (iv.iii.34–5). And it is possible to detect within each of these offspring hints of a further polarisation – in the cold-hearted pair who fall wildly in love with Edmund; in the daughter who publicly rebuffs her father, then risks her life to save him, and grimly asks: 'Shall we not see these daughters and these sisters?' (v.iii.7). What is defective then in the 'two natures' approach to *King Lear* is that it obscures both its philosophic unity and its dialectical and psychological subtlety. These aspects of the play should become even more apparent in what follows, where I shall examine what seems to me to be the play's defining peculiarity, that which marks it off most from the other tragedies both in character and achievement.

V

How do we account for the consensus view that *Lear* is pre-eminent among Shakespeare's – perhaps among all – tragedies? In what consists its singular greatness? Most answers to this question rightly focus on its enormous scope as an inquiry into the nature of humankind and the whole framework of reality within which it operates.[32] Yet this is to acknowledge only the philosophic dimension of *Lear* and to leave out of account the extraordinary power with which it fixes all our attention on its vision of the human predicament. My short and simple explanation for its pre-eminence, therefore, is that it appeals more profoundly both to the heart and the mind than does any other play. Of course every work of literary art appeals to the understanding through the sensibilities; but *King Lear* is a tragedy of the heart in a unique sense. Its searing effect on the whole self is an extension of its self-conscious engagement at every point with the human heart as the beginning and the end, the source and the explanation, of almost all our concerns. Referred to about sixty times in the play, the heart is arguably its major image. To follow a selection of the principal passages in which it occurs is to come very close to an understanding of what the play is all about and why it affects us so deeply. And by no means is it to digress from the subject of this book.

What sets the tragedy in motion is Lear's outrageous demand for a public protestation of love, Cordelia's inability to 'heave' her 'heart' into her mouth (1.i.90–1), and her fatal ability to articulate the hurtful idea that she loves her father according to her bond, no more nor less – and what that entails in terms of subsequent subtraction. Lear's criterion for truth and sincerity is simple: 'But goes thy heart with this?' (line 104), he asks. When she indicates that it does, his love turns by way of humiliation and rage to hatred, and so the bond is undone. His terrible execration concludes: 'as a stranger to my heart and me / I hold thee from this for ever' (lines 114–15); an idea which he reiterates to the protesting Kent: 'So be my grave my peace, as here I give / Her father's heart from her!' (lines 125–6). Kent's angry speech takes up the heart motif, beginning with an image of his own heart pierced by Lear's arrow, and ending with a comparison between Cordelia's love and that of her 'empty-hearted' sisters (lines 142–53). The first of these images is by far the more important of the two, for this is a play in which the heart is moved and assaulted from beginning to end: 'stirred', 'overwhelmed', 'invaded', 'struck' (2), 'shook in pieces', 'broken' (6), 'cracked' (2), 'flawed' (2), 'ripped', 'burst' (2). The assault is vividly literalised in the last scene when there is displayed a bloody knife, hot and smoking, which 'came even from the heart of – O! she's dead' (lines 222–5). The assault affects all the good characters (including the Fool, who 'pines away' after Cordelia's departure), and in the end extends even to Edmund ('This tale of yours hath mov'd me') as well as Goneril; but its chief victim, of course, is Lear. The assault on his feelings begins in the first scene, where his angry and cruel injustice is prompted by a wounded heart – by the sudden conviction that the beloved daughter on whose 'kind nursery' he had thought to set his rest (lines 122–3) is 'so young and so untender'.

After Cordelia has left for France, Lear begins to regret what he has done and to wonder how it all happened: 'O most small fault, / How ugly didst thou in Cordelia show! . . . drew from my heart all love / And added to the gall' (I.iv.266–70). To intensify his regret there is the horrified discovery that Goneril and Regan, on whose kind nursery he is now dependent, are not only empty-hearted but 'marble-hearted' (line 259). Complaining to Regan about Goneril's unkindness, he represents himself as another Prometheus; but whereas Prometheus' torment was to have his liver continuously torn by a vulture, with Lear the lacerated organ is the heart. Appealing to Regan's 'tender-hefted nature', and pointing vigorously no doubt at the object of pain, he cries: 'O Regan, she hath tied / Sharp-tooth'd unkindness, like a vulture, here . . . struck me with her tongue, / Most serpent-like, upon the very heart' (II.iv.132–3, 158–9, 170). But Regan joins forces with Goneril, and together they proceed to strip him of all his dignity as a king, a father, and even as a man, reducing him from 'noble anger' (line 275) to tears. It is at this point that the first signs of a mental crack-up appear; but it is to be observed that the cracking of the mind is figured in terms of the heart; and that because 'Storm and tempest' (Folio SD) are heard at this precise moment for the first time, the cracking of Lear's heart seems to echo through heaven's vault:

> You think I'll weep.
> No, I'll not weep. [*Storm and tempest*]
> I have full cause of weeping; but this heart
> Shall break into a hundred thousand flaws
> Or ere I'll weep. O fool, I shall go mad! (lines 281–5)

At which point he rushes out into the storm.

For the first time it would seem, Lear now begins to inquire into the fundamentals of life; and where should the inquiry lead him? 'Let them anatomise Regan; see what breeds about her heart. Is there any cause in nature that makes these hard hearts?' (III.vi. 75–6). The progress of this inquiry is inseparable from, indeed dependent on, the intensity of his own feelings. 'Wilt break my heart?', he asks Kent (III.iv.4), and then explains that the tempest in his mind takes all feeling from his senses 'Save what beats *there*': that is, in the 'frank heart' which 'gave all' (lines 12–14, 20; emphasis added). He is possessed in turn by a sense of boundless ingratitude;

by self-pity; by the old rage and its attendant desire for a fiery revenge ('red burning spits'); by shame; by compassion for both the Fool ('I have one part in my heart / That's sorry yet for thee' (iii.ii.72–3)) and the world's poor naked wretches. The compassionate Gloucester refers to him simply as a 'poor old heart' (iii.vii.61). The phrase is doubly apt, being paradoxical: Lear's heart is great and it is coming to full life in old age; and in the life of the heart lies the discovery of true riches.

Lear's Shakespearian prototype, Titus Andronicus (an aged hero subjected to the extremities of fortune and feeling), refers to his daughter as 'the cordial of mine age to glad my heart' (i.i.165–6). There is an etymological pun on the word 'cordial', since it derives from the Latin *cor* (declined *cordis, cordem*), which means both 'heart' and 'feeling'. This pun is very relevant to both *King Leir* and *King Lear*. We are not in a position to say whether *Titus Andronicus* was written before *King Leir* or vice versa; but if it was written before, then Shakespeare, in turning to *King Leir* in 1606, would have noticed that its author took several hints from *Titus*; if it was written after *Leir* (as I suspect may have been the case), then it would seem that the Lear story as handled by the anonymous playwright had made a deep impression on Shakespeare at the very outset of his career. For the hero of the old play talks much about his 'throbbing' and 'panting' heart; and in addition there is a heavily overt pun on 'cordial' linked with a similar play on the name of Cordella: 'Ah deare Cordella, cordiall to my heart' (line 709); 'And thou, poor soul [i.e. the weeping Cordella], kind-hearted as thou art' (line 2236). In *Lear*, there is nothing as overt as this, but there can be no doubt that Cordelia's name is meant to be descriptive of her nature and her dramatic role, and that a kind of silent pun animates her name throughout – in fact from the moment she protests her inability to heave her heart into her mouth.

When Cordelia returns from France in Act iv, scenic juxtaposition is used to effect a powerful dramatic contrast between her tender nature and the hardness of the 'dog-hearted daughters' (iv.iii.46): Goneril in iv.ii ('Fools do those villains pity who are punish'd / Ere they have done their mischief', lines 54–5), and Regan in iv.v ('It was great ignorance, Gloucester's eyes being out, / To let him live; where he arrives, he moves / All hearts against us', iv.v.9–11). Cordelia's return is anticipated by the messenger's report in iv.ii of how Cornwall's servant, 'thrill'd with remorse' (i.e. 'pierced [ME P*irlian*] with pity'), rushed to the defence of Gloucester at the cost of his life (line 73). And it is announced by a gentleman who reports to Kent how his letters 'pierce[d]' her to a 'demonstration of grief' (iv.iii.10) in which she said almost nothing but expressed a great deal. This moving and authentic self-revelation recalls and contrasts with the opening scene where, in her determination to be 'true-hearted' (i.ii.110), she effectively belied her heart:

> KENT.   Made she no verbal question?
> GENT. Faith, once or twice she heav'd the name of father
> Pantingly forth, as if it press'd her heart;
> Cried 'Sisters! sisters! Shame of ladies! Sisters!
> Kent! father! sisters! What i' th' storm? i' th' night?
> Let not pity be believ'd!' There she shook
> The holy water from her heavenly eyes,
> And clamour moisten'd; then away she started
> To deal with grief alone. (iv.iii.24–32)

Proceeding from and summoning the restorative powers of nature ('All you unpublish'd virtues of the earth, / Spring with my tears', iv.iv.16–17), these same tears restore Lear to his sanity. When he awakes from his long sleep, she is yet again unable to heave her heart into her mouth; but her tears tell him everything he needs to know ('Be your tears wet? Yes, faith'); and they give an astonishing eloquence to her two famous monosyllables: 'No cause, no cause' (iv.vii.71, 75).

So Cordelia's presence – her 'kind nursery' – cures Lear's 'heart-struck injuries' (iii.i.17). But so too her violent death cracks his sanity and ends his life. Indeed he dies quite simply of a broken heart; this last terrible scene is all about the piercing and cracking of the heart. Before Lear comes on stage carrying the body of Cordelia, Edgar has been telling Albany about Kent's 'piteous tale' of how he cared for Lear in his miseries; and he has also been telling them how he himself cared for his father. Kent had broken down in telling his tale and suffered something like a minor stroke: 'which in recounting, / His grief grew puissant, and the strings of life / Began to crack ... I left him tranc'd' (v.iii.215–18). In the old anatomy, the strings of life (i.e. the heart strings) had a literal existence. So when Kent later sees Lear die, says to himself, 'Break, heart; I prithee break' (line 312), and indicates immediately afterwards that he has not long to live, we must assume that he dies literally of a broken heart. Edgar too is emotionally afflicted in telling *his* piteous tale ('O that my heart would burst!'); but that detail merely points to the climax of his story, the death of his father. Gloucester's 'flaw'd heart – /

Alack, too weak the conflict to support! – / 'Twixt two extremes of passion, joy and grief, / Burst smilingly' (lines 182, 196–9). This in turn anticipates explicitly and narratorially what is implicitly dramatised in the death of Lear. Because of his sudden conviction that Cordelia lives, Lear's old heart is struck in swift succession by an ecstasy of grief and an ecstasy of joy and breaks at last into 'a hundred thousand flaws'.

King Lear encompasses so much that to give it anything like a descriptive label is inevitably to diminish it. Yet it seems legitimate to claim that it is, among other things, and to an extent that distinguishes it from all other tragedies, a tragedy of the heart. The phrase calls immediate attention to a number of the play's outstanding features. In the first place, *King Lear* exhibits a range and intensity of feeling that is unique in the canon. Apart from extreme physical anguish and all the distress of exposure to the elements, there is hatred, contempt, rage, vindictive cruelty; ambition and lust; shame and remorse; pity, compassionate love, and great joy; disillusion, grief, and despair; shock, horror, and bewilderment fanning out into a sense of dread incomprehension before the mysteries of our planetary existence. But the play is also deeply preoccupied with the role of feeling, or the lack of it, in the life of men and women. We may believe that ideas, or socio-economic forces, or power are the primary determinants of what people say and do; but Shakespeare seems to imply here that the clue to thought and action and ultimately to social change and human history lies in the heart. A naïve suggestion, it may seem, but consider the text. 'I know his heart', says Goneril contemptuously of her father (I.iv.331), meaning: 'I know exactly how he will behave; how he thinks and acts is how he feels.' So too when Edgar tears open Goneril's murderous love-letter to Edmund, he declares: 'To know our enemies' minds we rip their hearts' (IV.vii.261; Folio). On occasion 'mind' and 'heart' become interchangeable terms or are used as doublets ('proud in heart and mind', III.iv.84); but the preferred term is 'heart'. It would seem that the systems of belief and value by which we live, the ideologies which we use to rationalise our behaviour and our preferred social practices, derive ultimately from the heart and not the head.

Interpreting the play from a Marxist perspective, Jonathan Dollimore has claimed that in *King Lear* we are shown 'the woeful inadequacy of what passes for kindness' in the context of a society where injustice flourishes; justice, he adds, is shown to be 'too important to be trusted' to 'empathy' and 'pity'.[33] In my view, however (as in that of countless others), feeling as unselfish, compassionate love emerges as the supreme value in this play. And by no means does it signify a socio-political dead-end. It is the first prerequisite for understanding: those who are responsible for injustice will not see because they do not feel (IV.i.69–70), and when they begin to see they 'see it feelingly' (IV.vi.149). Pity also leads to remedial action, both interpersonal and social, medical and political. The partnership between Cordelia with her tears (from which spring all the blest secrets of the earth), and the wise and gentle doctor with his simples, is a partnership which reminds us that medicine originates in human compassion. The political value of pity is first shown in the revolt of Cornwall's servant who, 'thrill'd with remorse, / Oppos'd against the act, bending his sword / To his great master' (IV.ii.73–5). Of course he loses his life and fails to save Gloucester's other eye. Nevertheless, the death of Cornwall seriously weakens the evil alliance. Moreover the report of this act of heroism has a strong effect on Albany, whose horror at the pitiless treatment of Lear is already preparing the ground for his shift of allegiance to the opposition and his firm stand against Edmund (IV.ii.29–80). No doubt too it was this servant's reaction which alerted marble-hearted Regan to the political value of pity: it was stupid (she perceives) not to kill off the blinded Gloucester, because 'where he arrives, he moves / All hearts against us'. But it is in Edgar that the socio-political potential of pity is fully realised. Not only does he 'nurse' his father through his 'miseries' (v.iii.180–1), saving him both from the demon of despair and from the sword of Oswald; he also saves Albion from the nightmare future in which it was to be ruled by King Edmund and Queen Goneril. Edmund tells the ambitious captain whom he appoints to kill Lear and Cordelia that 'to be tender-minded / Does not become a sword' (v.iii.32–3). Edgar disproves this triumphantly. Beginning as an amiable dupe, he emerges in the end as a figure in whom the contrary traits of human nature are perfectly harmonised. Mightier than Edmund with the sword, he is yet 'pregnant to good pity' and enriched with 'the art of known and feeling sorrows' (IV.vi.224–5). It is entirely fitting that he should succeed to the throne; he will not become the kind of ruler who 'disjoins / Remorse from power' (*JC*,II.i.18–19). Largely because of his self-protective role-playing (four alien roles in all), the impact which he makes on us as an individual character is not commensurate with the fact that he is given more lines in the play than anyone else except Lear. He is, however, a figure of great importance in the play's pattern of meaning.

The assault on the heart and the value of compassionate feeling have an important bearing on the role of the audience too. When Edgar is recounting his piteous tale to Albany and Edmund, he hesitates to complete it because he senses that to do so would be to 'amplify too much ... And top extremity' (v.iii.206–7): as if his listeners could bear no more. This is a metadramatic moment when Shakespeare simultaneously speaks to the audience about his fictional work and involves them as participants in its reality. At this point in the action, he still has the hanging of Cordelia to spring on us, and he is obviously thinking about what it will do to our feelings. Throughout the play, he has been asking how much misery life can inflict on human beings, and how much they can endure. Now he is wondering how far a tragedy can go, and how much an audience will take. And of course he was right to wonder. When Dr Johnson came to edit the play, he confessed he had been unable to read it for many years because he found the death of Cordelia unbearable; he thus condoned Nahum Tate's softened version of the tragedy, in which Cordelia survives – the version that was played throughout the eighteenth century. But despite that oblique apology through Edgar, his surrogate self, Shakespeare resolutely brings us to the edge of the abyss and beyond. Implicitly, he declares that tragic art has a moral function: 'Expose thyself to feel' – if only by imagination – 'what wretches feel' (III.iv.34), and perhaps the armour of detachment and indifference will crack. We must reply with Edmund: 'This tale of yours hath mov'd me, / And shall perchance do good' (v.iii.199–200).

And yet Shakespeare's attitude to the heart and its capacity for feeling is ambivalent; or, more correctly, he shows the heart's contrary potentialities. Just as the play tends to deconstruct the traditional hierarchy in which the head is privileged at the expense of the heart (for reason and discretion here have been appropriated and perverted by the wicked), so too, by a characteristic procedure, the hierarchical opposition of heart and head is complicated by means of a further dichotomy. Many have cited with approval Edgar's concluding injunction in which the heart is clearly privileged at the expense of the head: 'speak what we feel, not what we ought to say' (v.iii.324). But this, surely, is an ironic reminder of the dangers of both feeling and speech. 'True-hearted' Cordelia was driven by a love of plainness, and by irritation with 'the glib and oily art' of those who 'speak and purpose not' (I.i.225–6), to tell a hurtful untruth, and with fatal consequence. On a wholly different plane of responsibility, Lear was licensed by power to speak what he felt, and before he knew what happened he had cursed and done hideous injustice to the two people who loved him most. 'Honest-hearted' (I.iv.19) Kent, who deemed it his 'occupation to be plain', was licensed (he thought) by anger to revile Oswald and insult the Duke of Cornwall ('anger hath a privilege' (II.ii.65, 87)); yet this performance accelerated his master's tragedy. Poor Tom reminds us that a number of vices are bred in the heart (III.iv.53, 82, 94), but he refers to the most important vice in the action of this play when he mentions 'the fury' of the 'heart, when the foul fiend rages' (lines 128–9). Containing both love and gall (I.iv.269–70), the heart can generate rage or pity, fire or tears (an imagistic antithesis which is strongly felt); these opposites too can be dangerously close, since wounded love or grief can turn quickly to fury and hatred. Next therefore to compassionate love in the scale of values, in fact complementing it, is patience: that is, self-government in feeling and suffering. This is exemplified in the Cordelia of Act IV. When she heard how cruelly her father had been treated 'she was mov'd', reports a gentleman, but 'Not to a rage'; 'she was a queen / Over her passion, who, most rebel-like, / Sought to be king o'er her'; thus 'patience and sorrow strove / Who should express her goodliest' (IV.iii.13–17). This psychic and ethical ideal is implicitly compared to the fruitful harmony of the elemental order, 'sunshine and rain at once' (line 18).

The greater the human being, the greater the heart; but keeping the heart whole, balancing and harmonising its diverse impulses, can require miracles of natural art and great good fortune. As I have been implying, the heart is the central microcosm in the correspondent and contrarious universe of *King Lear*. 'Heaven's vault should crack' (V.iii.259); 'Crack nature's moulds' (III.ii.7); 'Blow winds, and crack your cheeks; rage, blow' (line 1); 'the bond crack'd 'twixt son and father' (I.ii.94); 'my old heart is crack'd, it's crack'd' (II.i.90): it all comes down to that. In the heart is dramatised the great problem of double nature with all its potential for disunity, confusion, and anarchy. At root, one might say, the problem is one of kindness, which Lear, like most of us, associates with the heart. He assumes that it is natural to be kind, especially towards one's own kind, and unnatural to be selfish and cruel. He describes himself as a kind father whose frank heart gave all; but in fact his kindness was a thoroughly selfish arrangement. He thinks that when Regan hears how Goneril's unkindness struck him on the very heart she will show herself to be truly his daughter and not a 'degenerate bastard' (i.iv.253; ii.iv.129); but she has inherited her nature from the man who pitilessly rejected Cordelia and Kent, so that in truth she does use him 'kindly' (i.iv.306, 170). Coming to terms with nature, learning the difference of kind and kind, seeing what breeds about the heart: this is Lear's tragic experience. It bewilders, it tortures, it destroys, and it ennobles him.

VI

An important component in the oppositional design of the play is the traditional antithesis of nature and art, where art is understood as everything that constitutes civilisation – the conscious ordering of life by reason; laws and institutions; technology and the arts; learning and education. Symbolically embodied in the twin setting of 'grac'd palace' and open country, this dualism is an intrinsic part of the play's inquiry into the nature of humankind. Side by side with Lear's question, 'Is there any cause in nature that makes these hard hearts?', there is throughout the contrary albeit implicit suggestion that human 'art' is the cause of almost all our miseries. A favourite topic for philosophical discussion in the Renaissance, both in its aesthetic and its anthropological and ethical dimensions, the question of nature and art found a special place in pastoral poetry and drama.[34] Thus Shakespeare had confronted it in *As You Like It* and was to deal with it more intensively in *The Winter's Tale* and *The Tempest*. It is undoubtedly helpful to have these plays in mind when engaging with this aspect of *Lear*.

The tragedy offers abundant support for the primitivistic argument (associated in the Renaissance mainly with Montaigne) that the arts of civilised societies are corrupting. The 'glib and oily art' of those who 'speak and purpose not' (i.i.224–5) is the key to success at Lear's court, whereas simple truth and honesty – or plain naturalness – proves disastrous. The ceremonial opening scene suggests a conception of ordered society as little more than institutionalised deception, hypocrisy, and injustice. Crucial to the elaboration of this notion is the imagery of dress, which in the context of the art–nature debate had great resonance. Primitivists like Montaigne were deeply impressed by the fact that the inhabitants of the New World 'weare no kinde of breeches nor hosen'. The nakedness of these peoples was taken as a sign that they were well 'contented with what nature affoordeth them', and also as the symbol of a natural innocence uncorrupted by the 'lying, falsehood, treason, dissimulations, covetousness', the 'fashions ... pompe, and the forme' of civilised societies.[35] In such discourse, dress inevitably becomes a symbol of concealed corruption. Plain-speaking Cordelia appropriately makes use of the symbol in this sense in her caustic farewell to her glib sisters in the opening scene (line 280). But the most striking instances of the symbol occur in Lear's bitter vision of a world where the sins of Authority are hidden behind robes and furred gowns, and the tattered attire of the poor exposes their small vices to the savagery of dogs in office. Lear's imitation of Poor Tom's nakedness ('Off, off you lendings!' (iii.iv.107)) is the clearest expression of his new-found conviction that society wholly obscures the truth about human nature.[36] This gesture is echoed when he enters '*fantastically dressed with weeds*' and declares: 'I am the King himself ... Nature's above art in that respect' (iv.vi.84–6). Here however the argument changes dramatically: Lear's physical appearance and mental condition – 'O ruin'd piece of nature!' – suggests that without art – without society and all that it signifies – he cannot remain 'the thing itself', either as human being or as king; the complex meaning of the wild flower symbolism, soon to be adumbrated, reinforces this suggestion. In quite a different manner, Kent's quarrel with Cornwall weakens the hierarchical distinction between nature and art. Kent's insolent parody of flattering courtly eloquence does not invalidate Cornwall's trenchant point that the bluntness of those who make it their occupation to be plain is itself a style and one which frequently 'constrains the garb / Quite from his nature' (ii.ii.97–8). Cornwall is wrong to doubt the sincerity of Kent's furious diatribe against Oswald ('nature disclaims in thee: a tailor made thee', ii.ii.51), but he has drawn our attention to the fact that Kent in his rage has fallen into a self-indulgent parody of his own 'naturalness' which in effect harms his master. It seems obvious that being natural in the best sense is itself an art (since it requires judgement and discrimination) and that the relevant distinction is not between (falsifying) art and (truthful) naturalness but between good and bad art.

Dress symbolism has in fact a positive as well as a negative meaning throughout.[37] At the simplest level, 'raiment' is inseparable from 'bed, and food' and 'shelter' as the indispensable means for humanity's survival in the natural world (ii.iv.154; i.i.182); it

belongs to 'the art of our necessities' (III.ii.70). Furthermore, dress
is related to medicine (nursing, healing) as an aspect of dutiful or
humane care for others ('half my care and duty', 'all my paternal
care', 'I have ta'en too little care of this'). Such care is unquestionably an art, but the point which is imaginatively stressed throughout
the play is that it is an art whose source and power lie in nature; it
springs from compassion and it relies on 'man's wisdom' (IV.iv.8)
in the blest secrets of the visible world – 'the wisdom of nature'
(I.ii.100). The art of caring is perceptible in Kent's observation that
unless Lear's 'oppressed nature' and 'broken sinews' are given the
balm of sleep (and at that point they are suddenly denied it) they
will 'stand in hard cure' (III.vi.97–100); and then again at the close
of the next scene when the Third Servant runs to fetch some flax and
white of eggs to apply to Gloucester's bleeding face (III.vii.105).
These two passages are important as anticipating the twin roles
of Edgar and Cordelia as the play's great exponents of a caring,
natural art.

Since the most famous manifestation of Edgar's art is often
isolated and interpreted as futile illusion rather than a positive and
important element in the complex vision of the tragedy, it is necessary to note the studied parallelism between his art and the combined art of Cordelia and the Doctor. Most of Act IV consists of an
interweaving of scenes dealing with the care of the two rejected
children for their father. This structural parallelism is reinforced
verbally: the Doctor, for example, assures Cordelia that opiates will
close Lear's 'eye of anguish' (IV.iv.14) and Edgar tells his father that
his 'eye's anguish' has weakened his other senses (IV.vi.6). On both
sides the closeness of the art of nursing and healing to nature-
kindness is conspicuously emphasised. Thus Cordelia prays that the
'aidant and remediate' plants of the earth will 'spring' with her tears
(the pun is perfect) and speaks of the 'medicine' on her lips as she
kisses the sleeping Lear (IV.iv.15–18; IV.vii.26–7). To the father
whose despair he has sought to 'cure' (IV.vi.34), Edgar identifies
himself as a man who, 'by the art of known and feeling sorrows', is
'pregnant to good pity' (lines 223–5) – for Edgar, compassionate
nature and remedial art are wholly one. Edgar's art, however, is of a
much more comprehensive kind than Cordelia's. It extends well
beyond the care and cure of his father to effect both his own survival
and a complete change in the unfolding 'plot' (IV.vi.272) of the
nation's history. It is associated more with drama than with medicine, its constituent elements being disguise, role play, plotting, and

– in the cliff scene – a stunning eloquence.[38] Like drama itself (as understood by most Renaissance playwrights), it is an art whose feigning is ultimately instrumental in disclosing truth (the villainy of Goneril and Edmund; Edgar's own nobility). It should be compared with the art of Camillo and Paulina in *The Winter's Tale* and, especially, with that of Prospero in *The Tempest*, all of whom engage in deception and manipulation in order to achieve unity and harmony. Unlike them, of course, and like the hapless Friar Lawrence, Edgar cannot avert tragedy; yet he does put an end to a monstrous regime and offers some promise of renewal.

In a brief but influential study of *King Lear*, Nicholas Brooke treats Edgar's description of the cliff and Gloucester's mock suicide as an elaborate make-believe used by Edgar to justify the notion of a providentially ordered universe ('Think that the clearest gods . . . have preserv'd thee', iv.vi.73–4). Brooke has made this scene central to his interpretation of the play as one which offers no final consolation whatever, no hint of regeneration; a black and comfortless tragedy where the illusion of Edgar's moral allegory is harshly contradicted by the facts of natural experience.[39] I would question this interpretation for two closely connected reasons. First, it fails to place Edgar's illusion in the wider context of compassionate art. And second, it assumes that Edgar's only or primary purpose in deluding his father is theological rather than humane – to inspire him with faith in benevolent gods rather than to save him from the demon of suicidal despair.[40] In his determination to refute a theological interpretation of the play, and in the apparent assumption that that alone would accommodate an element of hope, Brooke ignores the fact that a metaphysic of regeneration is not necessarily dependent on belief in divine providence but may be founded on a conception of (artful) nature itself. The weakness of the whole argument can be pinpointed in Brooke's interpretation of the structure of iv.vi, where the entry of Lear 'fantastically dressed' in the second half is construed as experience contradicting the cosy morality of Edgar's exercise in make-believe presented in the first half.[41] I would contend that the connection between the two halves of the scene is one of similarity and not of difference. The connection is indicated – quite overtly – in the first words uttered by Lear as he comes on stage here: 'I am the King himself . . . Nature's above art in that respect' (v.vi.84–6). Clearly, the King is by no means 'above art'; he is a ruined piece of nature whose recovery depends, as Gloucester's has done, on compassionate art. That recovery has been anticipated in IV.iv ('What can man's wisdom / In the restoring of his bereaved sense?', lines 8–9), and it will be accomplished in the next scene. Of course the curing of each man is temporary, but it is not a morally and metaphysically insignificant interlude, as Brooke believes. It is part of an extensive web of meaning which connects nature, art, and morality. In Lear's case, too, the cure is a necessary preliminary to what matters most to him: full, conscious reconciliation with his wronged child; reconstitution of the bond.

Whenever in his plays he touches on the perennial debate on the relationship between art (nurture, culture) and nature, Shakespeare as a rule neither privileges one of the opposed concepts at the expense of the other, nor deems them to be radically incompatible; rather, he appeals to the notion of interdependence and essential oneness. This is a position which can be traced back through Cicero to Aristotle and Plato.[42] More to the point here, perhaps, it enjoyed axiomatic status throughout the Middle Ages and the Renaissance because of the medical teachings of Galen, who gave primary emphasis to the curative power of nature (*vis medicatrix naturae*), spoke of it habitually as a craftsman, and saw the physician's function as essentially that of co-operating with it.[43] In *Romeo and Juliet*, the notion of the interdependence of art and nature is localised in a pun on the second-person singular of the verb to be ('thou art');[44] in *King Lear* it is encapsulated in phrases such as 'kind nursery' and 'our foster nurse of nature' (IV.vi.12) (where the root connection between 'nurse' and 'nurture' is to be noted). The notion cannot be said to originate in, but it undoubtedly gained strength from, the idea of nature as a system of 'harmonious contrarietie'. It finds its place in *King Lear* as part of the process of shattered unity and polar extremes. In the *Lear* world, there are the overdressed and the naked; flattery and plainness; extreme cunning and gullible naïveté. And although the bonding of art and nature is shown to be a realisable ideal, the tragedy focuses mainly on the incapacity of 'man's wisdom' to contain the worst effects of a particular and terrible eruption in nature. In this sense, the relationship of art and nature belongs to the war of opposites.

VII

Edgar's much-discussed apophthegm (or 'sententia'), 'Ripeness is all', is indicative of his belief that the art of living entails fruitful accommodation to nature, nature in this formulation being nature-as-time. The negative attitude which many have adopted towards the apophthegm (as towards Edgar's imaginary cliff) is due in large measure to a failure to place it in its wider conceptual and dramatic context.[45] *King Lear* is characteristic of its age in being a tragedy of terrible violence; and as in so many other tragedies of the period (and the plays already examined here), violence as untimeliness (rashness, importunity, impatience) and violence as destruction are intimately connected, both practically and philosophically. Nothing is more natural to impassioned clay than a sudden desire to accelerate the normal course of things; but nothing – in the world view that lies behind this play – is more likely to undo the balance of natural order.

The whole order of Lear's life and kingdom explodes in the first scene as a result of his 'hideous rashness' (line 150; cf. lines 294, 299). In 'a trice of time' (line 216), he renounces all his royal responsibilities, disinherits and disowns his beloved daughter, and banishes his best counsellor. He also reaches for his sword to strike at Kent ('strike' is one of his favourite verbs), and is barely restrained by his horrified sons-in-law; his gesture emblematically signals the impending release of a pitiless violence that will culminate in the sudden hanging of Cordelia by a captain who is identified simply as 'a sword'. Gloucester's tragedy begins similarly in the next scene. He laments Lear's rashness (i.ii.25–6), but when he has heard Edmund's tale and seen his sword and bleeding arm, 'the heat of his displeasure' and 'the speed of his rage' are such that he must 'violently proceed' against Edgar 'without any further delay' (lines 79, 88, 153, 158). Gloucester's fatal impetuosity is in character – like Lear's ('The best . . . of his time hath been but rash' (i.i.294)). Indeed Gloucester's characteristic impulsiveness is first established by reference to an event which is the original cause of his terrible injustice to Edgar and a contributory cause of his own blinding: that is, the begetting of Edmund, whose mother 'had a son for her cradle ere she had a husband for her bed' (i.i.14).

Lear's furious precipitancy gives the new regime its cue. The opening scene ends with Goneril's decision to 'do something, and i' th' heat'; so that within a fortnight, and 'at a clap' (i.iv.294), half of Lear's retainers are dismissed. The rest of the plot to reduce him to nothing gallops at the same pace: 'Stew'd in haste, half breathless, panting' (ii.iv.31), Oswald arrives at Regan's place with news of Lear's impending arrival and instructions for her to leave promptly; thus Regan and Cornwall arrive at Gloucester's castle 'i' th' night, i' th' haste' 'out of season', announcing 'businesses / Which craves the instant use' (II.i.24, 119, 127–8). That business culminates with Lear's ejection into the 'wild night' (II.iv.307). It also leads to the punishment of Gloucester, which in turn foregrounds the familiar conceptual nexus between justice and time, injustice and haste. The first judicial act of the new party is motivated simply by rage and revenge, and the approach to it is accordingly 'most festinate', 'speedy', 'swift'. 'Hang him instantly', cries Regan; and although Goneril's instant alternative, 'Pluck out his eyes', is the punishment chosen, we will subsequently have reason to recall that demand for instant hanging (III.vii.1–10). But the past is also involved in this scene, for the blinding of Gloucester on a charge of treachery is a hideous version of what happened in the opening scene. In the new as in the old regime, 'power' does 'a court'sy to . . . wrath' and is wholly contemptuous of 'the form of justice' (lines 24–5).

Calculated swiftness, however, is much more characteristic of the evil party than is choleric haste. And in this swiftness we encounter the Machiavel's familiar perversion of 'maturity' or 'ripeness' – that is, of the capacity to wait patiently for the appropriate moment ('opportunity', 'occasion') and to grasp it firmly when it comes. Reminiscent in this of Claudius and Iago, Edmund steers Gloucester into violent action precisely by simulating the utmost respect for this kind of judicious behaviour (I.ii.76–82, 151–8). Goneril appeals to the same twin ideal of vigilance and promptness in her letter urging Edmund to murder Albany and 'supply his place'; she is very concise, but her phrasing neatly underscores the fact that her conception of timeliness is a horrible perversion of an ethic rooted in nature: 'You have many opportunities to cut him off; if your will want not, time and place will be fruitfully offer'd' (IV.vi.264–6). Goneril's richly suggestive euphemism for murder sticks in the mind, not only because of its paradoxical conjunction with 'fruitfully' but also because it has been used already by Regan in one of her iciest sentences: 'If you do chance to hear of that blind traitor, / Preferment falls on him that cuts him off' (IV.v.37–8). Whether as murder or as suicide, the blight of untimely death – violent curtailment and separation ('slivering' and 'disbranching') – now hangs over the nation and its two principal families. It is articulated as a theme at the deaths of Cornwall ('I bleed apace. / Untimely comes this hurt' (III.vii.96–7)) and of Oswald ('O, untimely death! / Death!' (IV.vii.252–3)). It is also set against nature's norm – immediately after the wounding of Cornwall – by the Third Servant:

'If she live long, / And in the end meet the old course of death . . .'
(III.vii.99–100). That old course, one might add, is what Lear had in
mind when he spoke of ending his days in Cordelia's kind nursery.
What I am suggesting, then, is that the terrible ending is part of a
context which gives it substantial meaning and a degree of inevitability. Edmund's instructions to hang Cordelia – 'Mark – I say
instantly' (v.iii.37) – are carried out with a speed that his own
repentance cannot undo: 'Quickly send . . . Nay, send in time. Run,
run, O, run! (lines 244–7). The sense of unripeness when the old
King enters to nurse the corpse of his daughter is absolute.

In their attempts to resist violence and to remedy its ill effects, the
good characters conspicuously ally themselves with Time. Having
intercepted Goneril's 'fruitful offer' to Edmund, Edgar decides to
show it to Albany 'in the mature time' (IV.vi.275). Two scenes later,
he prepares for a much more active involvement in events, but again
his concern is to act only 'When time shall serve' (v.i.48). This
association of timeliness with active commitment to life informs even
the famous piece of proverbial wisdom which he offers his father.
Returning to find Gloucester under the tree, 'in ill thoughts again'
and preparing to 'rot even here' (the stage image reverses a familiar
Renaissance emblem of ripely-wise old age),[46] he declares:

> Men must endure
> Their going hence, even as their coming hither:
> Ripeness is all. Come on. (v.ii.9–11)

Edgar's energetic 'Come on' is addressed almost as much to himself
as to his father; it signifies his refusal to despair in the face of
Cordelia's defeat and his determination to face up to the challenge of
the moment in the way he has planned.

Like Edgar's, Kent's sense of the mature time first manifests itself
in the fourth act. Despite Cordelia's return, he will not undisguise
himself 'till time' and he 'think meet' – to do so would be to 'shorten'
his 'made intent' (IV.vii.9–11). As it happens, the right time for
revealing himself to his master never arrives; that is his personal
(and singularly poignant) tragedy. But his attitude here combines
with that of Edgar (who found the letter in the previous scene), and
of Cordelia and the Doctor in this same scene, to set up a powerful
contrast to Goneril's idea of the ripe moment. The scene begins on a
quiet note of intense anticipation and measured restraint. In seeking
to 'repair those violent harms' that her father has suffered at the
hands of his daughters, and under 'the most terrible and nimble

stroke / Of quick cross lightning' (lines 28, 34–5), Cordelia patiently
submits herself to the wisdom of the Doctor. Lear is wakened only
when he has slept long; and although it is found that 'the great rage'
is killed in him, the Doctor judges it dangerous to let him dwell on
'the time he has lost', so that after the reconciliation takes place he
is left 'till further settling' (lines 78–82). Lear's consciousness of
waking to 'fair daylight', and the figurative (lines 15–17, 52) and
literal involvement of music, crown the scene with a sense of perfect
timing and restored harmony.

Cordelia (the devotee of truth) prophesied that time would unfold,
what plighted cunning hides (i.i.280). This prophesy calls up the
proverbial association of time, truth, and justice; and it is fulfilled.[47]
Deceit and treachery are unmasked, and wickedness meets with
retribution. Addressing the man who has emerged as the agent of
time and justice, Edmund calls attention at the end to this process,
and in doing so seems to identify the wheel of Fortune with the
action of Time.

> What you have charg'd me with, that I have done.
> And more, much more; the time will bring it out.
> 'Tis past, and so am I. (v.iii.162–4)

> Th' hast spoken right, 'tis true;
> The wheel is come full circle; I am here. (lines 173–4)

Possibly too there are reminders of Lear's partial responsibility
for the last and by far the most terrible reaction of Time against
the prevailing violence. When Edmund dispatches Edgar to save
Cordelia and Lear ('Quickly ... Run, run O, run'), and gives him
his sword as a token of reprieve, we might well recall that the first
person in the play to reach for the sword was Lear himself, and that
he did so in order to silence the man who sought to *protect* both him
and his daughter. If we do recall this, then we are more likely to
see the death of Cordelia not only as an instance of cruel, senseless
fortune but also as the final bitter, fruit of the disordered time which
Lear initiated. We might be encouraged to think thus by the fact
that the violent Lear, always quick to strike when offended or
opposed ('strike her young bones, you taking airs', 'strike flat the
thick rotundity o' th' world'), erupts at the end, heroic, terrible, and
proud. Heart-struck, and misled by appearances (as in the beginning), he rages against the silence of his appalled followers: 'Howl,
howl, howl, howl! O you are men of stones! / Had I your tongues
and eyes, I'd use them so / That heaven's vault should crack'

(v.iii.257–60). He remembers and praises his servant Caius, not as the man who 'did him service / Improper for a slave', but as the fellow who would 'strike, and quickly too' (lines 220–1, 285). And having killed the captain who hanged Cordelia, he boasts of the days when, with his good biting falchion, he would make men skip (lines 275–7).

I would reject, then, the claim of Wylie Sypher that time yields no meaningful pattern in the play but rather reinforces the general effect of a meaningless and absurd universe.[48] Partly for the same reason, I cannot accept the claim that nature and morality pattern, experience and ethics, are wholly at odds here.[49] The many allusions to 'instant' action and reaction serve at appropriate moments as stage directions demanding a quickened tempo. But their function is not simply dramaturgical. They interrelate both with one another and with other ethico-psychological ideas within a broad guiding philosophy of nature. The pattern of time is reinforced too by the emergence of a new ruler whose timely challenge in the ritual of chivalric law frustrates the institution of violent injustice under Edmund and Goneril – the law of 'Hang him [her] *instantly*'. Wise before he is old, Lear's godson is a reflective man of action who, like Hal and Malcolm, waits for the morally and pragmatically appropriate time for action, and then acts decisively. He is a man equipped to redeem the time.[50]

What I have said about the metaphysic of time and the role of Edgar is not presented as determining the final impression of the tragedy; it is simply an attempt to draw attention (no doubt by overemphasis) to a frequently disregarded but textually demonstrable element in the play's complex vision of natural experience. That it should be disregarded is fully understandable. The significance of the good child who survives the disjointed time, and of the timely justice which he embodies, is all but obliterated from consciousness by the death of the good child who is hanged and by the emotional devastation of her father. As I have mentioned before, the untimeliness of tragic death – the idea of a natural cycle shattered, and of reasonable hopes pitilessly denied – is a characteristic feature of Shakespeare's tragedies (had it something to do with the death of his son Hamnet in 1596, aged eleven?). But nowhere else does Shakespeare attempt, as he does here, to capture the full anguish of that experience. The suddenness with which Cordelia is wrenched from Lear after their great reunion ('Have I caught thee? (v.iii.21)) communicates a sense of incomprehensible rupture, of unbearable finality, and of time rendered personally meaningless, such as is found in no other piece of tragic literature: 'Thou'lt come no more, / Never, never, never, never, never' (lines 307–8). In its final impression, this is above all else a tragedy of the pierced, gored, and broken heart.

VIII

Although gods and demons are referred to more often and more emphatically in *King Lear* than in any other of the tragedies, it is by far the most naturalistic of these plays. The contradiction is merely apparent, however, for the supernatural beings to whom reference is made are demonstrably embodiments of natural forces and qualities.[51] It may be that Shakespeare was making a Christian commentary on pagan belief such as the theologically-minded King James would have approved; more likely, however, he was either imagining a world without God (in which tragedy is wrought to the uttermost) or implying that that is the kind of world we have. However, although the supernatural (as understood by the *dramatis personae*) is shown in reality to be not supernatural at all, it is by no means devoid of imaginative force in the play. The habitual conviction of the characters (mainly the good ones) that gods and fiends are actively involved in their lives reflects the intensity and bewilderment of their responses to the forces of nature which are unleashed within and around them.

Very few pagan gods are actually named, and these are all noticeably identifiable with nature – Apollo–Phoebus (i.i.108, 158), or the sun; Hecate (i.e. Diana), or the moon (i.i.109); Jupiter–Jove, or 'the Thunder-bearer' (ii.iv.226–7);[52] 'blind Cupid', or sexual desire (iv.vi.138); and Nature herself. Nature is beyond question the major deity. She is named only three times (i.i.212; i.ii.1; i.iv.275), but is invoked on all three occasions with special deliberation; and the frequent use of the abstract noun 'nature' in its various senses helps to make her a felt presence throughout. This assimilation of the divine to the natural is evident in the variable significance of the word 'Heavens', which sometimes refers to the gods and sometimes to 'the wrathful skies' (iii.iv.42). The assimilation is even more apparent in the vividly concrete imaging of the elemental phenomena which purportedly release all of the stored vengeances of Heaven – the taking airs, blinding flames, nimble lightnings, oak-cleaving thunderbolts, spouting cataracts, and fensucked fogs.

The naturalism of the supernatural is reflected also in its contrarious structure. The sharp Christian dichotomy of otherworld beings into the divine and the demonic is utilized; but the gods themselves are contradictory. The play's first supernatural reference (in Lear's oath disowning Cordelia) alludes simultaneously to gods of light and mysterious gods of the dark (I.i.108–9). Subsequently we discover that the gods in general are 'kind' and cruel, 'ever-gentle' and violent; and that the 'dear goddess' Nature has two characters. Lear's Nature is patroness of the family and of loving-kindness; Edmund's stands up for bastards and encourages both lusty stealth and fierce quality. Yet Lear's Nature is double, too, a deity to be invoked in curses as well as in prayers; she is the vindictive agent of sickness, deformity, and sterility as well as the dispenser of earth's blest and health-giving secrets (I.iv.276–85).

Above all else, it is the humanity – or rather the humanity and the inhumanity – of supernatural beings that identifies them with nature. The failure of the gods to grant the protection or reward that is asked of them is shown with conspicuous irony on two occasions. A much more frequent source of irony, however, is the way in which the characters attribute to both gods and demons what is immediately and palpably of human origin. Immediately after his three guests have plucked out his eyes, Gloucester accuses the gods of wanton cruelty. Lear calls upon Pomp to '*show* the heavens more just' (III.iv.36), and both his phrasing and the context (one of homelessness and beggary) indicate that the justice and the injustice of the heavens alike are man-made. Gloucester is told to 'think that the clearest gods . . . have preserv'd' him (IV.vi.73–4), and he does just that; but what has preserved him is the miracle of his son's love, to whose lips blessings spring as readily as curses do to Lear's. The fiend that stood beside Gloucester on the cliff ('I took it for a man') was Gloucester's 'worser spirit', his weak, despairing self (lines 78–9, 220), and the 'ever-gentle gods' (line 219) who will continue to protect him from that spirit are his son. The 'brand from heaven' (v.iii.21) that parts Cordelia from Lear is sent by Edmund ('to be tender-minded does not become a sword'). Humans are half-god and half-devil (IV.vi.126–8); or, in extreme, either heavenly spirits (IV.iv.30; IV.vii.49) or fiends (IV.ii.67). The sacred radiance of Apollo is the 'sunshine and rain at once' in the tearful smiles of forgiveness, the 'fair daylight' of mutual understanding and love. The 'darkness' inhabited by devils (I.iv.251; IV.vi.129) and underworld deities is 'the lake of darkness' (III.vi.7) in men's souls; it is 'the dark and vicious place' where they commit 'the act of darkness' (v.iii.172; iii.iv.86). Shakespeare took due note of Samuel Harsnet's claim in the *Declaration of Egregious Popishe Impostures* (1603) that the demons expelled by Catholic exorcists were simply human thoughts and sins; but he extended this demythologising process to all demons and beyond them to all gods.

Systematic rationalism of this kind was approved Christian practice in dealing with pagan mythology. But although *King Lear* may well have passed the censor with no objections being raised, it must at least have evoked for most Christians the dark night of the soul when faith seems groundless even to the most devout believer. The text does not actually subvert the doctrine of divine providence, for that doctrine firmly acknowledges that the good need not expect justice in this life, that God seldom intervenes directly in human affairs, and that his providential plan is worked out, not through miracles, but through the good and bad deeds of men and women and the operations of nature. On the other hand, there is an arresting absence of any kind of imaginative support in the play for the idea of an omnipotent and benevolent deity. And there is no firm hint of an afterlife where flights of angels sing the afflicted to their rest, or where the wicked meet with a punishment commensurate with the evil they have done. Human beings here are left utterly alone with nature, their own and the world's. Their assumption that gods and fiends are somehow responsible for what they themselves do and experience is just one form of the confusion in which they live.

It does not necessarily follow, however, that this is an essentially pessimistic play about a chaotic and meaningless universe. It could plausibly be argued that it is unshakeably optimistic. Contrary to what Edmund claims, not all men and women are 'as the time is' (v.ii.32); in the most adverse circumstances imaginable, the loyalty of some proves constant, their generosity of spirit measureless. They grow in wisdom and goodness through suffering; they repent, forgive, and reconstitute natural bonds. They discover many variations on the paradox that there is some soul of goodness in things evil: in the midst of chaos, vile things become precious, the blind see, the insensitive feel, the binding force of loving-kindness reasserts itself (it is a striking fact that nihilistic readings of the play ignore – have to ignore – its paradoxicality). It is equally true, however, that this tragedy communicates a profound pessimism: it exposes the extreme fragility of all social order, human bonds, and personal identity; the limitlessness of suffering and evil; the brutal injustice of life as it affects the innocent and the virtuous. In truth, neither perspective alone will accommodate the richness of the play's vision. In keeping with its underlying conception of the natural order, the play resists all univocal description in terms either of pessimism or optimism; it encompasses both.[53]

It has been suggested that a useful way to see the total design and outlook of the tragedy is to view the subplot as a moral romance or tragi-comic fable whose comfortable optimism is subverted by the tragic mainplot.[54] However I would argue that, insofar as they differ, the two plots are complementary opposites functioning together as parts of a complex artistic whole whose image of the natural order is at once dialectical and cyclical. The analogous divisions in both families interact, and out of the interaction comes mutual destruction; yet there emerges from the destructive process a ruler who, although lacking the heroic proportions of his godfather, is endowed with most of 'the king-becoming graces'. That this positive aspect of the play's underlying philosophy is very much in the background at the end is obvious; all the emphasis is on the horror of violent and eternal separation and the consequent shattering of the heart. Yet even that has a positive dimension, since there is joy as well as grief in Lear's end. The joy (for that is how I read 'Look there, look there!')[55] *may* be based on an illusion, but it echoes the very real joy of reunion and reconciliation ('We two alone . . .') and seems designed to show that Lear's 'flaw'd heart', like Gloucester's, 'burst smilingly', ''Twixt two extremes of passion'. It is not the illusion as such that should command our interest, but rather the symbolic drama of the human heart which the illusion facilitates. And the drama of the human heart is the drama of the natural world.[56] True or false, Lear's belief that Cordelia's lips have moved is a faint, ambiguous echo – following on Nature's immense cruelty – of Nature's kindness.

8

Macbeth

I

Even though the text overtly invites us to do so, nothing might seem more reductive than to consider *Macbeth* as a tragedy of ambition. The meaning of Macbeth's ambition, however, is complex, being deeply enmeshed in Shakespeare's conception of microcosmic and macrocosmic nature, so that it reaches out to engage in a significant relationship with everything else in the play. In this respect Shakespeare is developing a conception of ambition which was systematically and explicitly articulated in Marlowe's *Tamburlaine the Great*, where the hero, a 'fiery thirster after sovereignty' (Part I,II.vi.31), justifies his ambition and its attendant violence by an appeal to the dynamics of Nature:

> Nature, that fram'd us of four elements,
> Warring within our breasts for regiment
> Doth teach us all to have aspiring minds. (Part I,II.vii.18–20)[1]

Thus 'martial' Tamburlaine is identified throughout with the element of fire, at once the 'noblest' and most 'aspiring' as well as the most destructive of the elements (see p.5). Zenocrate is the Venus whose tears moderate his violence, his marriage to her being analogous to the concordant discord of Nature herself. Her death unleashes all the destructiveness in his nature, so that he ends his career with the burning of Babylon and dies as the victim of a fiery fever.[2]

The character of Macbeth and the whole atmosphere in which he moves set Shakespeare's tragedy at a vast remove from Marlowe's. But in addition to the common subject of an ambitious usurper, and the shared Renaissance sense that ambition can be a noble virtue or a deadly vice, the two plays have an underlying philosophical affinity that must have been readily perceptible to Renaissance audiences.

Macbeth's ambition is a desire not so much for power and wealth as for 'greatness'. It proceeds from a restless striving which he himself scarcely understands and which compels him to 'o'erleap' all obstacles of person, time, and place so as to win, as tokens of his transcendent worth, golden opinions and the golden round. It is a form of desire made manifest not only in martial valour but also in a powerful imagination which obliterates the achievements and satisfactions of the present with its bewitching delineations of future deeds. It makes him yearn always for 'more' (I.iii.70), drives him to 'do and ... do and ... do' (line 10), makes him vault beyond great and greater to 'the greatest' (line 117). But counterbalancing this compulsion towards striving and strife is Macbeth's 'milk of human kindness' (I.v.14), signifying the impulse which binds him to others in affectionate partnership; thus before his tragic transformation he is a man loved (I.vi.29; IV.iii.13) as well as admired by all. Emblematised as he stands shoulder to shoulder with Banquo in defence of a just social order, this union of contrary impulses is already on the point of collapse at the beginning of the play; and its collapse is Macbeth's and his country's tragedy. Critics have rightly pointed out that although *Macbeth* is the shortest of Shakespeare's tragedies, it has some claim to being 'the most complex and subtle in its statement'.³ Many, too, have pointed out that the characterisation of its criminal hero has a strange ambivalence which is reflected in a ubiquitous sense of doubleness. That the play's subtle complexities are generated by its dualistic outlook is generally acknowledged; what remains to be emphasised is that its dualistic character emanates from a particular construction of reality which Shakespeare absorbed from his own culture.

Perhaps more than any of the other tragedies, *Macbeth* dramatises a struggle between the forces of unity and disunity. Without opening up the debated question as to what extent it is a tragedy tailored to please King James, one can reasonably detect in this emphasis a discreet nod in the direction of James's title – in which he himself took pride – as the prince of peace and union. The emphasis can be seen in the characterisation of Duncan as a conscientious ruler who leaves fighting to those of his nobility who relish it, rewards them generously for their endeavours, and seeks to bind them all to him and to each other in a gracious and fruitful mutuality.⁴ Although the order which Duncan represents is a feudal order, Shakespeare naturalises, validates, and interprets it not by the discourse of hierarchy but by that of contrarious unity. Some three years before

Macbeth, Middleton and Dekker celebrated James's coronation and progress through the city of London with an 'entertainment' which actually personifies the Four Elements and shows them joining hands in a renunciation of their 'natural desire/ To combat each with other' – symbolising an end to the dissensions which afflicted English society at the close of Elizabeth's reign.[5] So too Shakespeare delineates the essential significance of Duncan's character in the superb passage where he and Banquo evoke an image of nature's opposites, both elemental and sexual, joyfully united in a procreant harmony (I.vi.1–10). To argue that *Macbeth* deploys the 'naive', 'geriatric', unequivocal discourse of a metaphysically sanctioned absolutism, and that this hierarchical discourse is mischievously negated at every point by a double-vision discourse that reflects the deconstructive energies and indeterminacies of language (a subversive process which Shakespeare himself was by implication unaware of) is entirely unacceptable.[6] As even this purportedly 'naive' and 'geriatric' passage suggests, the double vision of the play is manifestly the product of its controlling discourse: the harmonious order jointly imagined by Duncan and Banquo accommodates hierarchy, but it is essentially a loving partnership of nature's opposites; and the poetry no less than the dramatic context makes clear that this contrarious, 'pendent' order is as fragile and vulnerable as it is fruitful.

Evil is regularly referred to in the most orthodox manner in *Macbeth* as unnatural, on the assumption that whatsoever is natural is good. But this simple conception of nature is assimilated to a more comprehensive view which acknowledges 'nature's mischief' (I.v.50) no less than its bounty (III.i.97), compunction (I.v.4), and love. The fate of Macduff's nest and its abandoned 'birds', pitilessly destroyed 'At one fell swoop' by Macbeth's 'Hell-kite' (IV.iii.216–19), stands in diptychal relation to the Duncan–Banquo passage on the temple-haunting martlet and correlates with numerous imagistic echoes of nature's dark ferocity. This natural ferocity is intimately associated with demonic evil and with the attempt of the fallen angels (IV.iii.22) to undo the work of the Creator; many in Shakespeare's audience would no doubt have recalled standard Christian doctrine to the effect that the strife of the elements in the world and in humankind was a consequence of the Adamic fall.[7] But the demonic supernaturalism of the play functions more as intensification than as explanation: it adds horror, mystery, and awe to the extraordinary spectacle of cruel violence erupting in the 'gentle weal' and its most 'worthy gentleman'. The most important insight furnished by the play is that the equivocating witches and the malignant spirits that tend on mortal thoughts are potent precisely because they are in tune with the bewildering doubleness of the natural order.

II

One of the most remarkable features of this tragedy is the way in which number symbolism co-operates with nature symbolism in the process of signalling key ideas relating to the tragic theme of disunity and chaos. This may be largely due to the fact that here, as in *Julius Caesar*, Shakespeare the tragedian shows a more than usual interest in time, the movement of the heavenly bodies, and history. The tradition of numerical symbolism and the temporal sensibility were closely related in literature since there was a natural connection between the time sense, astronomy, and the art of exact measurement according to number.[8]

It has long been recognised that *Macbeth* abounds in trinities and that this accords with the traditional association of the number three with the rituals of witchcraft.[9] But threes and twos, trebling and doubling, are closely linked throughout the play;[10] and this relationship, I would add, is extended to include the idea of endless multiplication – 'terrible numbers', 'multitudinous seas', 'the multiplying villainies of nature', 'confineless harms'. What this pattern does – or would have done for a Renaissance audience attuned to cosmological discourse – is to evoke in large the Pythagorean concept of cosmos as limit and measure and of chaos as the unlimited, the innumerable (see p.36). In its totality, therefore, the number pattern corresponds with Macbeth's grim calls for the frame of things to disjoint (III.ii.16) and the united elements to 'Confound and swallow ... up' all natural and human order (IV.i.52–60) if his desires are not fulfilled. More particularly, this symbolic pattern focuses sharply on the idea that 'doubleness' is the root cause of tragic change and confusion, so that the witches' refrain, 'Double, double, toil and trouble;/ Fire burn, and cauldron bubble' (IV.i.10–11, 19–20, 35–6) might be taken as the play's epigraph.

We have seen that in *A Midsummer Night's Dream* and (less obviously) *Othello* Shakespeare exploited the traditional association of 'the indefinite binarie' with the undoing of unity and limit, and with error, rebellion, duplicity, confusion, darkness, and devilry.

More obviously relevant to the concerns of *Macbeth*, this symbol is thoroughly integrated to the tragedy and semantically modified to support its special pattern of meaning. On the one hand, the symbol signifies excess, transgression of limit, the beginning of multiplication (doubling). It relates thus to Macbeth's fondness for the word 'more' ('Tell me more!') and his contempt for 'enough' ('And damn'd be him that first cries, "Hold, enough!"'). It relates also to Banquo's prayer for restraint (ii.i.8), to his warning that unlawful augmentation may mean loss (lines 26–7), and his perception that Duncan, who retires to bed 'shut up / In measureless content' (lines 16–17), has discovered the great paradox that self-fulfilment entails self-containment. But doubleness also signifies duality-without-unity, contradiction, duplicity, and so, too, confusion and doubt (there is covert play throughout on the aural link between 'double' and 'doubt': 'I . . . begin / To doubt th' equivocation of the fiend' etc.). The most frequent manifestations of doubleness are specifically stylistic and are to be found in the extensive use of antithesis, paradox, oxymoron, pun, equivocation, and dramatic irony (a form of continuous and unintentional pun or equivocation.)[11] But doubleness as a numerical phenomenon is heavily stressed throughout, and at the start it is projected in such a way as to illuminate the whole nature of the impending tragedy. In scene ii (after the three witches have chanted their confusingly dualistic sing-song – 'the battle's lost and won', 'Fair is foul and foul is fair'), the Captain reports on the progress of the battle against the rebels, and in doing so depicts a fierce struggle between two almost undistinguishable opponents (in this context even the names of the two men add to the sense of near-identical opposites). The battle, reports the Captain, stood 'doubtful', like 'two spent swimmers that do cling together / And choke their art (i.ii.7–10). Then 'brave Macbeth' 'carv'd out' a passage through the rebels until he confronted 'the merciless Macdonwald' (on whom 'the multiplying villainies of nature / Do swarm') and quickly sliced him in two, having first 'unseam'd him from the nave to th' chops' (lines 7–23). The next part of the Captain's report focuses on the heroic partnership of Macbeth and Banquo, and here the emphasis is on the way uncurbed valour might prove self-destructive: undo the unity of the self, make the hero his own enemy. The two men were 'As cannons overcharg'd with double cracks' (where 'crack' signifies both 'split' and 'explosion'). Undaunted by the increased numbers on the opposite side, they 'Doubly redoubled strokes upon the foe' and seemed as if they would 'memorise another Golgotha' (lines 37–41). The impression of doubleness, doubt, and confusion which emanates from these two passages – Duncan's 'worthy gentleman' is also a 'butcher' (v.vii.69) in the making; the two honourable captains threaten to emulate the soldiers who crucified Christ – is reinforced in Rosse's account of the battle and causally associated once more with the idea of excess: Macbeth stood firm against Norway's 'terrible numbers' and confronted the rebellious Thane of Cawdor 'with self-comparisons, / Point against point, rebellious arm 'gainst arm, / Curbing his lavish spirit' (lines 53–8). The hint of contrarious transformation arising from the syntactic displacement of the word 'rebellious', which should qualify the second 'arm', is resoundingly accented at the end of this scene by the King's declaration that Macbeth is to be rewarded with Cawdor's title.

In the third scene Macbeth meets the witches for the first time, and their equivocal prophecies begin the process of fissuring his unstable identity. Because they tell him 'Two truths' (that he is both Glamis and Cawdor), and also revive old thoughts about murdering Duncan (as is usually inferred from his guilty 'start' at line 51), Macbeth judges that their 'soliciting / Cannot be ill; cannot be good'. Banquo resolves this paradox by recourse to standard Christian doctrine, remarking that the instruments of darkness tell us trifling truths 'to betray's / In deepest consequence'. But Macbeth seems not to hear his 'partner', for he drifts off immediately into the 'Two truths' soliloquy and reveals that his 'single state of man' is so shaken that nothing is but what is not: in imagination, he is already murdering the King whom he serves so valiantly (i.iii.122–44).

Initially, Lady Macbeth's influence is more important than that of the witches in undoing Macbeth's single state. She is fully conscious of how doubtful he stands ('Art not without ambition, but without / The illness should attend it ... wouldst not play false, / And yet wouldst wrongly win' (i.v.16–19)). She is also possessed of an instinct for doubling, and a contempt for unity, singleness, and limit, that will overwhelm him. In her hypocritical welcoming of Duncan, she protests that all her service, 'In every point twice done, and then done double, / Were poor and single service' when matched against his generosity (i.vi.14–18). This prepares for her assault on Macbeth. His 'better part of man' claims that to do more than becomes a man is to be none; but she retorts with consuming conviction that on the contrary he would be 'so much more the man' if he were to murder Duncan (i.vii.46–51). And before this vision of being 'so much more' the man he is – with his courage 'screw'd to the sticking place' – Macbeth collapses in awe: 'Bring forth men children only!'

One of Shakespeare's favourite symbols for the binary nature of human beings, the hand (our two-handedness), is incorporated in the pattern of symbolic doubleness and developed into one of the most imaginatively potent verbal and visual motifs in the play. In *Romeo and Juliet* and *Julius Caesar*, there was the hand of love and the hand of hate, the hand that unites and the hand that violently divides. Here that symbolic dichotomy remains, but the eye joins the gentle hand in opposition to its violent counterpart. This complication of the manual symbol allows it to mesh with the light–darkness dualism and at the same time to serve as an index of the psychophysical disorder which Macbeth and his wife bring upon themselves – and ultimately on the whole of Scotland – when they commit themselves to the path of murder. In i.iv and i.v, each of them independently identifies the hand with action that is not only violent but also wilfully blind: carried out so swiftly as to escape the restraining censorship of the eye, symbolising (as the most sensitive of the bodily organs) that side of human nature which recoils in pain from the perception of physical cruelty. Macbeth's,

> Stars, hide your fires!
> Let not light see my dark and deep desires!
> The eye wink at the hand; yet let that be,
> Which the eye fears, when it is done, to see. (i.iv.50–3)

is echoed in his wife's

> Come, thick night,
> And pall thee in the dunnest smoke of Hell,
> That my keen knife see not the wound it makes,
> Nor Heaven peep through the blanket of the dark
> To cry, 'Hold, hold!' (i.v.47–51).

That the eye has largely displaced the gentle hand as the violent hand's opposite (moving the emphasis away from simple contrast to the idea of an intense and traumatic revulsion) is most clearly shown when Macbeth steels himself for the killing of Banquo:

> Come, seeling night,
> Scarf up the tender eye of pitiful day,
> And with thy bloody and invisible hand

Cancel and tear to pieces that great bond
Which keeps me pale. Light thickens . . . (iii.ii.46–50)

The most memorable uses of the hand–eye opposition are both visual and verbal. The dagger which marshals Macbeth towards Duncan's chamber is a false creation of the heat-oppressed brain which makes fools of his eyes as it moves invitingly before him, 'the handle toward my hand' (ii.i.33–44). The play on 'hand' and 'handle' simultaneously identifies the hand with the dagger and hints at its alienation from the body. This hint is confirmed after the murder with Macbeth's horrified cry: 'What hands are here? Ha! they pluck out mine eyes' (line 59). Lady Macbeth's remark that a little water will clear the blood from his hands is, of course, echoed by her obsessive hand-washing in the final act. But what I wish to stress about that delirium is the way in which it restores the original symbolic antithesis. For she is now in imagination the sympathetic and loving wife whose hand is tenderly extended to comfort her distraught husband: 'Come, come, come, come, give me your hand. What's done cannot be undone. To bed, to bed, to bed' (v.i.48–63). This image of what might have been is undercut in the last scene with Malcolm's news that Macbeth's fiend-like queen took off her life 'by self and violent hands' (v.ix.36–7). The double-hand symbol occurs also in the contrasting allusions to the 'hand accurs'd' (iii.vi.49) which rules Scotland and that of the gracious king whose 'touch' cures those afflicted with ulcerous diseases 'pitiful to the eye' – 'such sanctity hath / Heaven given his hand' (iv.iii.144–52). This is clearly the antithesis which encloses the hand–eye opposition, since gracious Edward's hand is visually paralleled in the first half of the play by that of gracious Duncan: 'Give me your hand. Conduct me to mine host: we love him highly' (i.vi.28–30).

The equivocating, duplicitous witches are initially instrumental in destroying Macbeth's single state of man by playing on his two-fold nature, ensnaring him in doubleness, and projecting him unrestrained into a realm of multiplying villainy. Their identification with threeness, however, is no less emphatic than that with doubleness; it functions as a continuous reminder that Macbeth is undone by his desire for more, his belief that the titles of Glamis and Cawdor are not enough.

Why the number three should be associated with witchcraft in Christian tradition might seem puzzling. The Christian deity after all is a Holy Trinity; indeed in many cultures, three is a symbol of fullness, power, and divinity. The explanation, of course, lies in the fact that witchcraft, like devilry, is a rival system which parodies what is seeks to overthrow.[12]

The witches' threeness, like their doubleness, is encoded in the play at every level of expression. The resources of language (as well as the structure of the human body) are such that it was much easier for Shakespeare to give continuous and unobtrusive expression to the idea of an ensnaring duality; and he had already had abundant practice in doing so. But he addressed the problem of encoding threeness in an astonishingly thorough and inventive manner. Character grouping at a secondary level, and also emblematic imagery, provide periodic echoes of Act I's opening emphasis on 'we three'. The Porter admits three imaginary sinners into Hell, the first an equivocator (II.iii.4–17). Macbeth hires three murderers to kill Banquo and Fleance, the third apparently an afterthought to 'make assurance double sure' (IV.i.83). And in Macbeth's final meeting with the witches, his demand for 'more' (line 103) of their 'more . . . than mortal knowledge' (I.v.2) is answered by three equivocal apparitions and then by 'a show of eight kings . . . Banquo following' – a group of nine, the witches' favourite multiple of three. This procession reflects the ironic process of retributive reaction against Macbeth's lust for more that is now well under way in the tragedy. Thus it seems to him as if the line of kings descending from Banquo 'will . . . stretch out to th' crack of doom'; and he cries in rage, 'I'll see no more' (IV.i.117–18). The 'twofold balls and treble sceptres' (line 121) carried by some of the kings bring together the two fatal numbers in a manner which connects contemporary history (in the person of King James, supposed descendant of Banquo) with the retributive process. The twofold balls are usually taken to refer to the double coronation of James at Scone and Westminster; the treble sceptres were the two used for investment in the English coronation, and the one used in the Scottish coronation.[13] This two–three emblem would seem to signify both unified duality and authentic fullness or supremacy (i.e. divinely sanctioned kingship).

Threeness is mirrored also in action and time. The witches make three appearances in all (if we follow the general view that III.v. is not Shakespearian). Duncan, it would seem, is murdered at 3 a.m., and the Porter and his friends carouse until the same hour.[14] Macbeth commits three major crimes: the murders of Duncan, Banquo, and Macduff's family; and one of the most striking – and generally unnoticed – facts about the first crime is that it involves two additional and entirely unplanned murders: little did Lady Macbeth think when she sent the terrified Macbeth back with the daggers that he would spontaneously kill the two grooms.[15] The Macbeths appear as king and queen for the first time at the beginning of the third act ('Thou hast it now, King, Cawdor, Glamis, all', line 1); and Lady Macbeth's sleep-walking is seen by the Doctor only on the third night (v.i.1).

It is language itself, however, that the number three most conspicuously informs; and this is always effected in such a way as to accent the motifs of doubleness and excess. The chant which opens the play begins with a couplet followed by a triplet: five lines in which the witches proclaim their threeness and at the same time identify themselves with confounding opposites and storm-chaos:

> 1 *Witch*. When shall we three meet again?
> In thunder, lightning, or in rain?
> 2 *Witch*. When the hurly-burly's done,
> When the battle's lost and won.
> 3 *Witch*. That shall be ere set of sun.

Each of them departs at the behest of a familiar, two of which are named. The name of the Third Witch's familiar is withheld; it will be added on the third appearance of the witches – in the third line of the scene (iv.i.3). In fact the addition of a tantalising third is the principle which structures the witches' greeting – a kind of mock investiture (i.iii.48–50) in which each line is itself a structure of three threes:[16]

> 1. *Witch*. All hail, Macbeth! hail to thee, Thane of Glamis!
> 2. *Witch*. All hail, Macbeth! hail to thee, Thane of Cawdor!
> 3. *Witch*. All hail, Macbeth, that shalt be King hereafter!

Banquo picks up this triple pattern in his interrogation of the witches: 'My noble partner / You greet with *present grace*, and great prediction / Of *noble having* and of *royal hope*' (lines 54–6). Anticipating the royal entry of Act III, scene i, Macbeth translates the triple promise into a royal drama which will reach its desired climax after the second act: 'Two truths are told, / As happy prologues to the swelling act / Of the imperial theme' (lines 127–9; cf. lines 116–17). Two scenes later Lady Macbeth appropriates the triple greeting and grimly determines that its third component will materialise: 'Glamis thou art, and Cawdor; and shalt be / What thou art promis'd' (i.v.13–14).

Other manifestations of the witches' addiction to the number three occur in I.iii just before Macbeth's arrival, and are notable for the exactness with which they are enwoven in the play's unfolding pattern of meaning. Macbeth's entry is immediately preceded by the following chant, which the witches recite in unison:

> The Weird Sisters hand in hand,
> Posters of the sea and land,
> Thus do go about, about;
> Thrice to thine, and thrice to mine,
> And thrice again to make up nine.
> Peace! The charm's wound up. (lines 32–7)

In the first lines here we have doubleness, adroitly linked in the third line to the idea of ambition by means of an etymological pun: the Latin *ambire* means 'to go about', and *ambitio* means 'going about in order to win popularity and power'. More important, however, ambitious doubleness leads to threeness and thence to multiplication.

The First Witch's promise of vindictive action against the captain of the *Tiger* isolates the play's key word, 'do/deed', and anticipates, and numerically emphasises, the tragic pattern whereby Macbeth's 'horrid deed' traps him in a hell of torturing, sterile, restless, and endless activity:

> I'll do, I'll do, and I'll do

> I'll drain him dry as hay:
> Sleep shall neither night nor day
> Hang upon his penthouse lid;
> He shall live a man forbid.
> Weary sev'n-nights nine times nine,
> Shall he dwindle, peak, and pine ... (lines 10, 18–23)

The word 'do' or 'deed' echoes insistently throughout the play, but on several occasions, beginning with Macbeth's, 'If it were done, when 'tis done, then 'twere well / It were done quickly' (I.vii.1–2), it repeats the First Witch's triple iteration (cf. lines 46–8; III.ii.43–4).

Before the final appearance of the witches, verbal threeness is heard in the ghostly voice which tells Macbeth that he will sleep 'no more' (II.ii.41–3), in the outcry after Duncan's body is discovered ('O horror! horror! horror!', II.iii.62), and in the Porter scene. The Porter, however, delights in conjoining threes and twos. He mimics the knocking on the door with a 'Knock, knock, knock', followed shortly by 'Knock, knock', a pattern which he repeats a few sentences later. He tells the two men who enter that he was 'carousing till the second cock' (i.e. 3 a.m.), and that drink 'is a great provoker of three things'. Its provocations, he explains, are equivocal and duplicitous (II.iii.1–37).

The triadic principle affects language most conspicuously in the third and last appearance of the witches. And here too its partnership with both doubleness and limitlessness is strongly emphasised. A double 'Thrice' opens the scene (IV.i.1–2) and the couplet refrain, 'Double, double, toil and trouble;/ Fire burn and cauldron bubble' is chanted three times (lines 10–11, 20–1, 35–6). The 'secret, black, and midnight hags' (line 47) pour into their cauldron the blood of a sow that has eaten her nine farrow (line 65). Both the first and second apparitions address Macbeth as 'Macbeth! Macbeth! Macbeth!' (lines 71, 77), and he answers, 'Had I three ears, I'd hear thee' (line 78). Although they warn him to beware Macduff, they tell him equivocally to

> Be bloody, bold, and resolute: laugh to scorn
> The power of man ... (lines 79–80)

> Be lion-mettled, proud, and take no care
> Who chafes, who frets, or where conspirers are. (lines 90–1)

In accordance with this fierce insistence on diabolical threeness, the scene ends with Macbeth's terrible determination that from now on he will set no limits – either of number ('*all* unfortunate souls / That trace him in his line') or time ('be it thought and done') – to his killing.

The last expressions of threeness are given to the two Macbeths, and they function clearly as elements in the pattern of condign punishment which characterises the latter part of the play.[17] Lady Macbeth's final words are, 'To bed, to bed, to bed' (V.i.64); and her sleepless husband sees himself condemned to a near-interminable succession of days and nights: 'Tomorrow, and tomorrow, and tomorrow ...'

III

It will be apparent, I hope, that the number symbolism which I have outlined above simply could not be a critical invention. Conventional canons of taste might wish to exclude consideration of such material from any account of *Macbeth* as a major Shakespearian tragedy, and relegate it instead to the pages of some learned, minor journal for the benefit of those who take pleasure in such arcane matters. To ignore it, however, would be to disregard something which clearly meant a great deal to Shakespeare; which makes *Macbeth* (like *Julius Caesar*) a far more intricate and artful play than has customarily been thought; and which provides us moreover with firm clues as to its meanings. Its special relevance in this context lies, of course, in the fact that number symbolism is part of the language of cosmology; its presence helps to support my general approach to the tragedy.

At the heart of the play lies the great cosmological theme of love and strife, articulated in Macbeth's (no longer valid) description of himself as a man with 'a heart to love, and in that heart / Courage, to make's love known' (II.iii.116–17). His tragedy is that of a valiant soldier whose courage overspills into a violent cruelty, and whose capacity for love and pity gives way to a destructive hatred that finally embraces life itself. The union of woman and man (and especially martial man) being symbolic of the union of opposites in all nature, Macbeth's marriage, like Othello's, is crucial to an understanding of his character and destiny. Lady Macbeth may be totally unlike Desdemona, but this play too should be read as the tragedy of a marriage as well as of a great man. Macbeth and his wife had, it would seem, a true bond. His deep love for her is economically but firmly indicated. We infer it from the way he writes instantly to share his success with her; from the terms of endearment which spring easily to his lips;[18] from his admiration for her powerful will and his need for her respect; and from his desire to protect her from the knowledge of Banquo's impending murder. Given the vicious role she has to play, her love for her partner, and her affectionate disposition, are much less apparent than his, especially at the beginning. But they are real nonetheless. It is true that she scorns 'the milk of human kindness' and renounces her woman's milk for gall, but it is also true that she admits to having tenderly loved the babe that milked her (I.v.17; I.vii.54–5). Her tenderness manifests itself after Duncan's murder when her own misery responds to Macbeth's and she seeks to comfort him with gentle words. In her, 'Gentle my lord, sleek o'er your rugged looks ...' (III.ii.28), the emotional rather than the social sense of the word 'gentle' is primary, and it has reference to both wife and husband: at once kindly and fierce. Her tenderness shows yet again after the departure of the guests on the night of Banquo's murder ('You lack the season of all natures, sleep', III.iv.141); and, of course, in the sleep-walking scene. The tender love-and-pity shown in these glimpses of her womanly nature is what should have predominated in her relationship with Macbeth. According to the chivalric model, and the mythic one which underpins it, her gentleness should have moderated his martial fire and in so doing have helped him to achieve and maintain heroic integrity. What happens instead is that Lady Macbeth, in her desire to help her husband realise his ambition, effects a willed but temporary suppression of her 'feminine' qualities, allows the 'masculine' element in her nature to predominate, and at the same time brings about a complete suppression of those 'feminine' elements in her husband's nature which are essential to full humanity.

In *King Lear* we saw that 'to be tender-minded' and 'pregnant to good pity' does indeed 'become a sword'. Here, however, the element of humane feeling which keeps a brave defender of 'the gentle weal' (III.iv.76) from becoming a merciless rebel is expanded to include fear as well as love-and-pity (a complication anticipated in *Hamlet*). Macbeth has a capacity for fear which is wholly at variance with an accepted notion of manliness.[19] But the accepted notion, which Lady Macbeth uses as a scornful whip to drive him to murder, is largely invalidated here. Initially, Macbeth's fear and compassion are almost synonymous. The mere thought of murdering Duncan becomes for him a horrid image that unfixes his hair and makes his heart knock at his ribs; it also overwhelms him with the image of Pity as a naked newborn babe exposed to the elements, its plight assaulting every eye and drowning the wind with tears (I.iii.135–8; I.vii.19–25). And there is pity as well as fear (the eye's pity) in his refusal to return to the scene of his crime: 'Look on't again I dare not' (II.ii.50–1).

The rest of Macbeth's career becomes a continual and never fully successful attempt to overcome fear (the fear now of guilt and insecurity) by means of reckless violence. In this development, the decision to kill Banquo is finely significant. When he calls upon Night's bloody and invisible hand to tear to pieces the great bond that keeps him pale, the word 'pale' signifies not only fear but also a defensive limit: it is the palisade which protects the gentle weal from wolf, bear, and shag-eared villain. In rejecting the moral instinct of fear ('honest [i.e. honourable] fear' it is called in *The Rape of Lucrece*, line 173), Macbeth goes beyond the pale of humanity to become a figure of terror, obsessively fighting 'pale-hearted fear' (IV.i.85) in himself and his reluctant followers: 'Hang those that talk of fear (v.iii.36; cf. lines 10–17). In the last act, he himself records, and then manifests with haunting eloquence, the results of his war on fear. Hearing the cry of women, he asks flatly, 'What is that noise?', and recalls that his senses would once have cooled to hear a night-shriek: direness, familiar to his slaughterous thoughts, cannot once start him (v.v.7–14). The situation pointedly echoes the night when he 'heard a voice cry, "Macbeth doth murder Sleep, – the innocent Sleep"', and asked his wife in terror, 'Didst thou not hear a noise?' (ii.ii.14, 35; cf. line 58). What Macbeth has succeeded in destroying is the fear that is entwined with his feeling for others, the fear of the tender eye. The implications of that success are disclosed when the cause of the women's fearful cry is announced. His response to the news of his wife's death is one of total insentience: he has no time to mourn for her now, and even if he had, there would be no point: life is meaningless, and so is death (lines 17–28). This from a man once full of the milk of human-kindness, who dearly loved the woman who has died: a wife whose last, mad, tender words were, 'To bed, to bed, to bed'. Shakespeare's sense of tragic change and loss is nowhere more acute than here.

Macbeth's response to his wife's death, as has often been noted, is significantly contrasted with Macduff's reaction to the news that his family has been slaughtered. Macduff stands in paralysed silence for a while, and when urged to convert his grief to rage and 'dispute it like a man', he replies:

> I shall do so;
> But I must also feel it as a man.
> I cannot but remember such things were,
> That were most precious to me. (iv.iii.220–3)

Macduff has been accused by his wife of being deficient in both love and courage. But these terse, expressive lines show him to be the complete man, and provide a final comment on the ideal of man-liness as heartless daring presented by Lady Macbeth and internal-ised by her husband. Critical comments on this final contrast, however, tend to imply that Macduff is the full man Macbeth never managed to become, the model which discloses his intrinsic insuf-ficiency. This, I believe, is a serious misreading of the text, and one which weakens its tragic impact. Macduff is merely a diminished version of what Macbeth once was. Indeed one of the most remark-able features of Macbeth's disintegration is that he remains in

turné

some sense a man of humane feeling even when his sensibility is in ruins. The ever increasing coarseness and brutality which he exhibits in his address to others is counterpointed by sudden soliloquising or quasi-soliloquising revelations of a self that hates what it has become. After his furious berating of the hapless Seyton, comes:

> I have liv'd long enough. My way of life
> Is fall'n in the sere, the yellow leaf;
> And that which should accompany old age,
> As honour, love, obedience, troops of friends,
> I must not look to have; but, in their stead,
> Curses not loud but deep, mouth-honour, breath,
> Which the poor heart would fain deny, and dare not. (v.iii.22–8)

After the order to 'Hang those that talk of fear', comes: 'Canst thou not minister to a mind diseased . . . Cleanse the stuff'd bosom of that perilous stuff / Which weighs upon the heart?' (lines 40, 44–5). And after the contemptuous killing of Young Siward comes the wholly unexpected confession to Macduff: 'my soul is too much charg'd / With blood of thine already' (v.viii.5–6).

Whether the image of the nobly courageous soldier is restored in Macbeth's final 'bear-like' (v.vii.2) stand – whether the first Cawdor's epitaph, 'Nothing in his life / Became him like the leaving it' (i.iv.7–8), and Young Siward's, 'like a man he died' (v.viii.43), function as analogy or contrast – is a question which has generated much disagreement. Having already considered the matter elsewhere, I shall merely draw attention to something which seems never to be remarked on, and which has special relevance in the context of this interpretation. Macbeth's last words are: 'And damn'd be him that first cries, "Hold, enough!"' (v.viii.34). These words are the epitaph Macbeth gives himself, and with an economy that is characteristic of Shakespeare's most mature art, each of them reaches deep into the imaginative roots of the play. In the doctrine of contraries, as we have seen, the idea of limit is crucial. The bond which unites opposites is also a bound or boundary which separates and distinguishes them; things decline to their confounding contraries when the limit is transgressed. The great man stretches himself to the utmost point of endeavour; beyond it he becomes his own opposite, ceases to be. Once the brightest of angels (iv.iii.22) and loved by all, Macbeth in the end is hated as the blackest of devils (lines 52–6), his soul given over to 'the common enemy of man'

(III.i.68). In fact Macbeth, the great defender, has become the common enemy.

IV

The idea of limit is implicit in that of the deed, one of the most complex and significant image-concepts in the play.[20] The term incorporates a pun which was not peculiar to Shakespeare but can be found as early as the fifteenth-century morality play, *Everyman*: it is implied there that every deed or action is a deed in two senses of the word: it is a bond with inescapable, binding consequences and can never be relegated to the past as a thing over-and-done-with. Marlowe tied the pun to the myth of the devil compact in *Doctor Faustus*, setting up an ironic relationship between the deed or 'deed of gift' which Faustus makes with Lucifer and his covenant with God, represented by Jerome's Bible – the Old and New Testament or Covenant. The essence of Faustus' tragedy is that in seeking by his covenant with Lucifer to escape from the limitations imposed upon him by the divine covenant he sacrifices a condition of limited freedom ('the freedom of the sons of God') for what turns out to be a state of degrading servitude; the deed of gift, and every one of his 'proud audacious deeds', make him the terrified and obedient servant of 'proud Lucifer'.[21]

In *Macbeth*, the broken covenant is constituted primarily of the 'strong knots' (IV.iii.27) by which human beings seek to 'bind' (I.iv.43) themselves to one another in love, kindness, and gratitude: the knots which Macbeth acknowledges to be 'strong . . . against the deed' (I.vii.14). The archetype of this kind of bond is not the soul's covenant with God but the bond which reconciles and joins the warring opposites in nature. The divine bond is secondary; it is suggested by the grace of 'gracious Duncan' and 'holy Edward', generous- and gentle-handed men who personify the qualities which unite whole communities as well as individuals. The divine bond's opposite is the 'bond of fate' (IV.i.83) into which the Macbeths enter when, in pursuit of more and more, and in their willingness to cancel and tear to pieces every bond that keeps them pale, they call for aid upon Night, the spirits, and the witches.

The whole tragedy might be read as an exploration of the 'deed' pun. Once Macbeth has done 'the horrid deed', he is committed by the logic of consequences to more and more of the same, so that his guilt becomes inescapably obvious and resistance to him inevitable.

Instead of being strong as the rock and free as the air, he finds himself 'cabin'd, cribb'd, confin'd, bound in / To saucy doubts and fears' (iii.iv.20–4). Lady Macbeth's assurance that 'A little water clears us of this deed' and its 'filthy witness' (ii.ii.66, 46) is answered in the sleep-walking scene by her discovery that the bloody deed is indelible, a past act that is eternally present: 'What's done cannot be undone' (v.ii.65). But the terrible folly of her assumption is underscored throughout by continual play on 'do-deed-done-undone', by the whole design of the play, with its emphasis on ironic reversal and condign punishment, and above all by the delineation of Macbeth's tortured psychological state. The bloody deed ruptures his inner being ('To know my deed, 'twere best not know myself' (ii.ii.72)), isolates him entirely from his kind (even from his 'dearest partner of greatness') and prompts him in the end to wish that 'th' estate o' th' world were now undone' (v.v.50). Macbeth knows he has surrendered his soul to the devil, but whereas Faustus is tortured by the thought of an eternity in Hell, Macbeth never once reflects on the pains of the afterlife. In effect, damnation is just a metaphor for the suffering he has brought upon himself in this world by sinning against kindness and humankind.

V

The theme of the deed in turn is incorporate in that of time.[22] The connection can be inferred from the use of legal terminology which identifies the allotted span of life as a lease (iv.i.99), copyhold (iii.ii.38), or bond (line 49) granted to the individual by Nature as Time. The connection is disclosed in dramatic form through Macbeth's initial realisation that if the deed is to be done then it must be 'done quickly', and by his subsequent commitment to violent, unreflecting action: 'This deed I'll do before the purpose cool' (iv.ii.154). Furthermore, the meaning of the deed is that time is an organic unity or natural order in which the relationship between past, present, and future cannot be severed. In *Doctor Faustus*, the clock whose chimes mark the end of the hero's rebellion and the beginning of retribution suggests that time is an arm of divine justice. In *Macbeth*, time itself is the ultimate arbiter of justice, and comprehends in itself all the binding laws against which the hero rebels.

In no other tragedy of Shakespeare is time so comprehensive in its significance or so continuously implicated in what is said and done.

The term itself spreads out in every direction so that it signifies all humans and the world in general ('To beguile the time, / Look like the time'), history ('the volume of . . . time', 'recorded time'), and a natural order which is also a corrective order: 'Time thou anticipat'st my dread exploits' (iv.i.144). Perhaps what most distinguishes the treatment of time here is the insistent emphasis on its function as part of a spatio-temporal order, an order of time-and-place. This idea is foregrounded at the outset in the witches' questions (summarising the whole purpose of their first dialogue): 'When shall we three meet again?'; 'Where the place?' The same idea is localised in the conception of Macbeth's usurpation as 'Th' untimely emptying of the happy throne' (iv.iii.68), and its untimely occupation. Such indeed is the emphasis on the necessary relationship between time and place that all references to time alone effectively signify the entire 'frame of things' (iii.ii.16).

The importance of time in this tragedy seems to arise naturally out of Shakespeare's exploration of the psychology of ambition, especially as it manifests itself in Macbeth's singular temperament. Ambition is a perpetual dream of the future; and in a highly imaginative man like Macbeth it is an obsession with what *might be* so intense that it makes *what is* almost unreal, and certainly worthless, by comparison. For such a man, prophecy is fatally attractive; it plays on his habitual tendency to become 'rapt' – spiritually transported to other times and places. So Macbeth's destiny is fully disclosed in the third scene when the witches encapsulate his whole life – past, present, and future – in three titles. Wishing desperately that they had told him 'more', Macbeth breaks away from the quartet of friendship which he has formed with Banquo, Rosse, and Angus, and drifts into the 'Two truths' soliloquy where he sees the image of himself as Duncan's murderer and finds that nothing is but what is not. Banquo's remark, 'Look how our partner's rapt' (i.iii.143) anticipates the tragedy of isolation and disintegration which is to follow. This little emblematic drama repeats itself when Macbeth leaves the chamber where Duncan is being entertained to soliloquise about if and when it were done; and yet again when he leaves the table to talk to the murderer of Banquo, his chief guest – after which he is 'rapt' as never before.

If the witches are fatally in harmony with Macbeth's obsession with the future, so too is his wife. His letters about 'the coming on of time', she tells him, have 'transported me beyond / This ignorant present, and I feel now / The future in the instant' (i.v.56–8). In

getting Macbeth to actualise the future which seems so immediate
to her, she echoes the witches' opening dialogue by constructing
an argument in which she perverts the notion not only of what
becomes a man but also of what befits time and place. What better
than to kill the king when he comes 'here to-night' to shower more
honours on us? Never did 'time, nor place ... adhere' as they do
now (I.v.28, vii.51–2; cf.II.i.59–60). This claim heralds a state of
chaos in which nothing ever seems to fit time or place, so that
Duncan's murder is very aptly termed 'Confusion['s] ... masterpiece' (II.iii.67). The first sign of such 'disjointing' in the frame of
things is very pertinent to Lady Macbeth's own tragedy. While
Macbeth trumpets his false grief, Malcolm and Donalbain perceive
that this is neither the time nor the place to grieve for their father:

> What should be spoken
> Here, where our fate, hid in an augur hole,
> May rush, and seize us? Let's away.
> Our tears are not yet brewed. (lines 119–22).

Just so, Lady Macbeth's death is announced to her husband in a
besieged castle when the tenderness she scorned has been drained
out of him: 'She should have died hereafter ...'

More noticeable, however, is the way in which the Macbeths set
themselves up as masters of time and place. The midnight bell is
delayed until three o'clock so that it becomes a signal for murder
rather than 'good repose' (II.i.29). The frantic scene in which the
news of Duncan's death is announced ends with Macbeth's authoritative words, 'Let's briefly put on manly readiness, / And meet in
the hall together' (II.iv.132–3). In the next scene we hear that 'he is
already ... gone to Scone / To be invested' (II.iv.31–3), Duncan's
body having been placed in the storehouse of his predecessors; and
in the two scenes following – the appropriately hectic tempo of the
play is now established[23] – he is sitting on Duncan's throne,
appointing times and places for his subjects. Banquo is to ride
swiftly on his business so as to appear tonight as chief guest at the
banquet (III.i.15, 37). Banquo thinks he is 'master of his time' (line
40), but Macbeth is preparing to 'take tomorrow' (and tomorrow
and tomorrow) from him (line 22) by means of a plan which is
most exact in its ordering of time and place:

> Within this hour, at most,
> I will advise you where to plant yourselves,
> Acquaint you with the perfect spy o' th' time,

The moment on't; for't must be done to-night,
And something from the palace. (lines 127-31)

The feast itself begins as an elaborate parody of fitness in time and place (iii.iv.1–6). This serves only to emphasise the violent exclusion of the chief guest, and the abrupt manner in which the other guests are 'displac'd' (line 108) and dismissed ('go at once', line 117). More generally, it emphasises the feast's function as a symbol of the confusion which characterises Scotland in the new regime.

A striking peculiarity of the play is the emphatic manner in which Macbeth's appropriation of time and place is reflected in nature at large and represented as a violation of Nature's organic unity and creative cycle. When Duncan is murdered the darkness and tempest associated initially with the witches take control of all nature, so that the perception of chaos is intense. Most notably, the moon and stars are invisible during the night (an answer to the Macbeths' demonic prayers), and the sun fails to rise when 'by th' clock 'tis day' (ii.i.115; ii.iv.6). As a creature of the night who uses the midnight bell to signal violence rather than 'good repose', Macbeth attacks sleep, which is 'the season of all natures': not just a restful division between one day and the next, but a form of re-creation in the diurnal cycle. Macbeth also seeks to destroy 'the seeds of time' (i.iii.58) in the reproductive cycle, attempting to ensure that Banquo's 'seed' (iii.i.69) will not produce its line of kings, and successfully obliterating Macduff's procreant nest.

Nature reacts by paying Macbeth in kind. He eats his meals in fear and sleeps no more. The rebellious dead rise from their graves to haunt his waking dreams and take from him 'the place reserv'd' (iii.iv.45) at the feast of life. The 'earth-bound root' of Birnam wood unfixes itself and moves to Dunsinane (iv.i.92–5). And there a man untimely ripped from his mother's womb completes the process of even-handed justice, making a mockery of the assurance that 'our high-plac'd Macbeth / Shall live the lease of Nature, pay his breath / To time and mortal custom' (lines 98–100). But even before he dies Macbeth is already a withered tree (v.iii.23), condemned in his own mind to live in a chaos of time where life is a featureless succession of undistinguishable nights and days: process without pattern, motion without rest: 'Tomorrow, and tomorrow, and tomorrow ...'

Others there are in Macbeth's Scotland whose commitment to the bonds of nature is disclosed in a respect for time or time-and-place; their attitudes and actions serve to define Macbeth by contrast and in the end to facilitate the restoration of nature's creative harmony. Duncan is responsive to the 'pleasant seat' and healthy ambience of Macbeth's castle, and Banquo knows that when summer comes the martlet loves to build his procreant cradle in such places. Gracious and unhurried though his manner is, Duncan has decided to stay only one night at the castle and has ordered Macduff 'to call him timely'; for his part, Macduff is agitated because he has '*almost* slipp'd the hour' – the vigorous knocking on the door which grates on the Porter's hangover is evidence of Macduff's determination to act 'timely' (II.iii.44–5; emphasis added). Malcolm's delaying of grief, and his instant flight from Scotland, are indications of a vigilant, foreseeing wisdom which later saves him from rushing with 'overcredulous haste' into the many traps set by Macbeth to 'win' him 'into his power' (IV.iii.117–20) (an obvious contrast to Macbeth's reaction to the witches' assurances). Macduff's refusal to grant credence until after the battle has been fought to rumours that Macbeth's followers are deserting (v.iv.14–16) reflects the same attitude; it is helpfully glossed by his partner-in-arms, Siward, in a manner which comments clearly on Macbeth's credulous impetuosity:

> The time approaches
> That will with due decision make us know
> What we shall say we have, and what we owe.
> Thoughts speculative their unsure hopes relate,
> But certain issue strokes must arbitrate;
> Toward which advance the war. (lines 16–21)

Malcolm's 'royalty of nature' is fully demonstrated in the play's concluding speech. Like Duncan, he bestows honours on the deserving in token of love and gratitude (v.ix.26, 40), and wastes no time in doing so (line 26). Whatever else is to be 'newly planted with the time', he promises to perform 'in measure, time, and place' (where measure denotes both number and limit). And his final emphasis is on the unity of all in Scotland's place of kings: 'So thanks to all at once, and to each one, / Whom we invite to see us crown'd at Scone.'

Those of us who have never lived under the heel of a brutal tyrant are apt to react strongly to Malcom's reference in this speech to the dead butcher and his fiendlike queen. Malcolm, however, is speaking truthfully about one half of the story (when 'o'er the one half-world / Nature seems dead'), and the only half which matters in the end to those who survive the terror. Neither that remark, nor the undoubted slackening of tension when he is present, should blind us to the importance of what Malcolm says in Acts IV and V. Much of it constitutes Shakespeare's considered epilogue to the swelling act of Macbeth's imperial theme. It is perfectly true, however (and herein lies much of the greatness of the tragedy), that Malcolm's concentration on the image of the butcher who would 'confound / All unity on earth' (IV.iii.99–100) in no way obliterates – in fact intensifies – our poignant awareness of the valiant partner, gentle husband, and sensitive man the protagonist once was. The perception voiced in the epilogue to *Doctor Faustus* is implicitly, and far more powerfully, embodied here: 'Cut is the branch that might have grown full straight.'

9

Antony and Cleopatra

I

It is frequently indicated in *Antony and Cleopatra* that its two protagonists are unique – 'rare', 'peerless', 'unmatchable', 'unpara-
llel'd'. And of the play itself the same might be said. Almost everyone
is struck by how greatly it differs from all the other tragedies of
Shakespeare, the Roman ones included. Particularly noticeable is
the absence of violence and a sense of evil: great battles take place,
but they occur off stage and no casualties are reported; and the
anarchic, barbarous potential of the civilised self is ignored. Nor is
there any sense of cruel injustice in the order of things. The lovers
shape their own destiny and are in no sense the victims of error,
mischance, or wicked manipulation. Tragic error in the form of
self-betrayal and a steep fall from the heights of power and prosperity are central to the play's imaginative effect; yet the world
of this tragedy is so inherently and utterly metamorphic that no
change ever seems final or without potential benefit (v.ii.1–2, 125–
6). It is a tragic world in which the spirit of comedy is always at
hand, edged with satire indeed, but buoyant and genial, and so
natural to its environment that it enters with ease upon the great
final scene of Cleopatra's suicide. This scene is what sets the play
off so distinctly from all the other tragedies. The customary sense
of peace and reconciliation is overwhelming here, and suffused too
with a note of ecstasy. The scene leaves us with an impression not of
waste and failure but of fulfilment and triumph. It is a conclusion
which has reminded many of the romances which are soon to follow:
plays where all 'grief is crown'd with consolation' (I.ii.162) in a
vision of life which foregrounds nature's powers of reintegration
and renewal.

Despite its exceptional nature, however, *Antony and Cleopatra* has
important and illuminating links with the other tragedies. The most

obvious are with *Romeo and Juliet* and *Othello*. The sexual relationship at the centre of all three plays is an audacious and precarious union of opposites which reflects the contrary forces at work in society and in nature at large, and its symbolic status is powerfully reinforced by the dichotomous structure of the given play-world: Montague and Capulet, Venice and Cyprus, Rome and Egypt. In *Antony and Cleopatra*, as in *Othello*, this significant design derives additional expressiveness from the warrior role of the hero and a corresponding use of the Mars–Venus myth. In short, the three love tragedies are animated by ideas about the nature of the world which are common to all the other tragedies, the difference being that the union of male and female is so managed as to give special sharpness of impact to the conception of nature as an unstable system of warring opposites.

It has been said that in *Antony and Cleopatra* Shakespeare's 'symbolic treatment of death as apotheosis poised against the usual dramatic significance of death as catastrophe' is an entirely new development.[1] This could be seen, however, as the expansion of a pattern evident in *Romeo and Juliet*. There is 'a glooming peace' and a sense of great waste at the end of that play, but there is also victory, transcendence, and reconciliation. The suicide of the lovers everlastingly affirms the constancy of their love; they are buried in 'a triumphant grave' and honoured with 'a statue of pure gold' – transposed into myth; and the warring families which opposed their union are reconciled. In both tragedies, the world which the lovers abandon is infinitely poorer by their death, but it, like them, has achieved unity through loss; and it is enriched with an inspirational memory.

In a comparison with *Romeo and Juliet*, of course, some of the more idiosyncratic features of *Antony and Cleopatra* are thrown into bold relief. The apotheosis which Antony and Cleopatra enjoy at the end, for example, is not just a consolatory tail-piece but corresponds with the godlike dimension they have frequently assumed in the course of the play. A related and equally important distinction concerns the setting. Although in the early play the polarised setting helps to inject universal significance into the tragedy of young love, nevertheless a Verona split between Montagues and Capulets remains no more than an enclosed and miniature reflection of the great globe itself. In *Antony and Cleopatra*, however, the action is literally about 'half to half the world oppos'd' (III.xiii.9); it moves to and fro between East and West, and the passions and problems of the lovers are hyperbolised accordingly.

A play of global scope about reckless imperial lovers, *Antony and Cleopatra* seems to revitalise the medieval Fall of Princes tragedy, with all its emphasis on the capricious turning of Fortune's wheel and the insecurity of high places. However, although references to Fortune and her wheel are abundant, the goddess is not a personification of blind chance here (whether conceived as an autonomous force or as an instrument of divine retribution). In the conflict between Antony and Octavius, she is firmly committed to Octavius from the start. Antony does not need the Soothsayer to tell him 'whose fortune shall rise higher, Caesar's or mine?', for he has always known that in any competition they had together Fortune would give Octavius all the luck (II.iii.17–39). Fortune in this tragedy is not blind chance at all, but something preordained, an instrument of Fate. And the 'fate' which Antony vainly seeks to 'oppose' (III.iii.169) is not essentially malignant either. It is identifiable with a historical process wherein the triumph of Caesar is inevitable and, in the long run, desirable. 'It was preordained', said Plutarch, 'that the government of all the world should fall into Octavius Caesar's hands'.[2] This was a historiographical commonplace[3] of which Shakespeare is careful to remind his audience: 'Be you not troubled with the time', says Octavius to his sister, 'but let determin'd things to destiny / Hold unbewail'd their way' (III.vi.82–5). Another such commonplace was that Caesar, although ruthless and deceitful in the acquisition of power, used that power for the good of the people throughout his long rule and brought to Rome and to the civilised world a period of great peace and stability.[4] Before Octavius' final clash with Antony, this too is recalled: 'The time of universal peace is near / . . . the three-nook'd world / Shall bear the olive freely' (IV.vi.4–6). Thus although Antony is an infinitely nobler man than Caesar, and although his death is genuinely tragic, the ending of the triumvirate and the placing of supreme power in the hands of his rival is not sensed as part of the tragedy. The action bears witness to the futility of divided rule, and so does Antony himself: 'Equality of two domestic powers / Breed scrupulous faction' (I.iii.47–8). Viewing the tragedy in this wider historical perspective, it is possible to perceive a reassuring ambiguity in Octavia's terrified warning: 'Wars 'twixt you twain would be / As if the world should cleave, and that slain men / Should solder up the rift (III.iv.30–2). The hidden truth is that in this conflict the dead will not lie and rot; they will solder up a rift that has been afflicting Rome for over a century.

This accords with the impression that the historical process which puts Caesar at the top of Fortune's wheel is identifiable with the cycle of Nature.[5] Whereas at the end of *Romeo and Juliet* age is left on stage to mourn the death of the young, the reverse is the case here: 'the boy Caesar' (III.xiii.17) holds the stage and prepares to bury two lovers who were 'wrinkled deep in time' (I.v.29). There is no violent truncation of the natural cycle in *Antony and Cleopatra*, but rather a sense of that cycle being fulfilled. The defeat of Antony pertains to the inevitable displacement of one generation by the next. He is the 'grizzled' warrior of the old school (III.xiii.17) who still believes that great conflicts can be resolved by single combat, and who feels bound in honour to accept any challenge a cunning enemy might issue. Octavius is the cool young strategist and politician who lures his enemy ('the old ruffian') into fighting where he is weakest and who scorns the nonsense of chivalry (IV.i.1–5). The wonderful poetry of the last two acts, with its imagery of fading light and setting suns, confirms the sense of an ending which is profoundly sad, yet natural and not absolute: a 'declining day' (v.i.38).

Of course the idea of renewal is associated primarily with the lovers who represent the old order rather than with the young man who heralds the new: through suffering and death they are purged of their defects, attain the fullness of their natural nobility, and in that way win an undying fame. But we cannot draw an absolute distinction between their regeneration and that which awaits the world when it bears the olive freely, or even between their enduring fame and that of Octavius Augustus Caesar. The apotheosis of the lovers requires a contrasting diminution of Octavius; but Shakespeare knows that Octavius has time on his side – the contrast between what he was before and after he became emperor was and remains one of the marvels of ancient history. We should recall the astute and passionate Cleopatra's reference to her salad days when she was green in judgement and cold in blood and reflect that although 'green' (immature) is a term of contempt it necessarily implies a promise of summer and autumn. We might also recall the cold young prince who said, 'I know thee not, old man. Fall to thy prayers', and went on to become the hero of Agincourt.

Antony and Cleopatra then may be called a tragedy of Fortune, where Fortune is conceived, not a cruel and meaningless mischance, nor as a retributive agent of divine providence, but as a manifestation of inevitable change in the cyclic order of history and nature; and where the tragic effect stems mainly from a perception that what has been swept away in the process of change is irreplaceable – two of Nature's masterpieces 'which not to have been blest withal would have discredited' humanity (i.ii.148–9). This almost serene conception of tragedy might be compared with that expressed by Yeats in 'Lapis Lazuli', where the ruins of time are viewed from above by ancient glittering eyes that are gay. A much more fruitful comparison, however, would be with Shakespeare's (probably) favourite poem, Ovid's *Metamorphoses*; for here we discover not only a large complex of analogies but also, I believe, a profound influence.[6] Ovid, however, is not the only classical author whose work is relevant to an understanding of this tragedy. There is also Plutarch, whose natural philosophy, as expressed in 'Of Isis and Osiris', seems to have contributed much to Shakespeare's imaginative exploration of the material which he borrowed so liberally from the same author's 'Life of Marcus Antonius'. To consider *Antony and Cleopatra* in relation to the *Metamorphoses* and 'Of Isis and Osiris' is not, of course, to question its remarkable originality; it is to acquire a better understanding of its deviations from the strict tragic model, and at the same time to identify a deep structure of ideas about the nature of the world which connects Shakespearian tragedy and romance, so that each is potentially the other.

II

Written during the reign of Augustus, the *Metamorphoses* presents its tales of mortals and immortals within the loose chronological framework of world history, from the beginning up to the time of the Emperor. Starting with the transformation of primal chaos into cosmos, it progresses through Greek mythology towards the Trojan war and the escape of Aeneas and his followers into Italy. Then in the last book (Book xv) comes Pythagoras' great oration on universal change, the poem's binding theme; and that is followed by a rapid synopsis of the history of Rome from its foundation to the fall and apotheosis of Julius Caesar and the rise of his adoptive son. Octavius avenges his father's murder, reduces to an idle boast the promise of Antony's Egyptian queen that she will seize the Capitol, and goes on to bring peace and stability to a violently changing world.

Despite its concluding glorification of stability and permanence, the poem's attitude to change is complex. Many changes, such as becoming speechless or immobile (a bird, beast, or tree), are sensed as terrible; yet they may be a poetically just punishment, or an escape from an even worse fate, or a cause of some special grace in the natural world. Indeed almost everything that is wonderful and glorious seems to presuppose the loss of something uniquely beautiful. Moreover metamorphosis is by implication a sign of the fundamental unity of the natural order (Pythagoras' doctrine of the transmigration of souls is really an elaborate conceit on this idea). In fact nature is seen as a system of 'dynamic permanence' in which things never die but simply take on new forms; an endless dialectic of decay and renewal (xv.277–82).[7] Witness, says Pythagoras, the interconnected fall and rise of great cities and of great men. The destruction of Troy led to the creation of a greater Troy on the banks of the Tiber and so was a good thing for the Trojans (xv.490–503); the heinous murder of Julius Caesar occasioned the rise of Octavius – a greater man – and the glories of Augustan Rome. Moreover fame (apotheosis) immortalises what is mortal. Ovid's world is one where men become gods just as gods become men, so that the distinction between time and the timeless is always receding.

Basic to Ovid's vision of universal flux is the perpetual interchange of the elements. And the element which dominates his imagination is water, that perennial symbol of both change and the life force. Water accounts for some of Ovid's most beautiful descriptions of personal metamorphosis: as in the tale of the nymph Cyane, so lost in tears that she gradually dissolves into the very waters of which she was once the mighty goddess (v.511–44); or the story of Salamacis and Hermaphroditus, where the nymph embraces the youth so passionately in the waters of her pool that they flow into each other, becoming a new creature 'of double shape', neither 'perfect boy / Nor perfect wench' but 'both and none of both' (iv.462–70). More generally, water symbolises both the destructive and the generative powers of nature. Pythagoras' fantastic account of the way in which oceans turn mountains into plains and obliterate the boundaries of nations echoes the tale of Deucalion's Flood in the middle of the first book. Ovid seizes on that universal catastrophe as a different, and perhaps to him a preferable, version of his opening theme of chaos and cosmos. In this version, chaos is a process whereby all solid shapes simply melt away, and the restoration of cosmos one where firm objects and defined shapes gradually emerge from universal slime. Invoking the notion of abiogenesis (the generation of living things from lifeless matter: cf. *Antony and Cleopatra*, I.ii.186–8; II.vii.26), Ovid remarks that one part of the earth – the Nile basin – provides vivid illustration of the process of cosmic renewal he is describing. The opening section of Book I was perhaps the most influential description of the essential nature of the physical world as understood by Shakespeare and his contemporaries; as we shall see, however, this section, with its precise focus on 'the fire / That quickens Nilus' slime', may well have been responsible for the particular cosmological orientation of *Antony and Cleopatra* (I.iii.68–9). I quote the illustrative passage and part of its context (somewhat confusingly, Arthur Golding departs from his original[8] and puts the illustration in the past tense):

The lustie earth of owne accord soone after forth did bring
Assoone as that the moysture once caught heate against the Sunne,
And that the fat and slimie mud in moorish groundes begunne
To swell through warmth of Phebus beames, and that the fruitful seede
Of things well cherist in the fat and lively soyle indeede,
As in their mothers wombe, began in length of time too growe,
To one or other kinde of shape wherein themselves to show.
Even so when that the seven mouthed *Nile* the watrie fieldes forsooke,
And to his auncient chanell eft his bridled streames betooke,
So that the Sunne did heate the mud, the which he left behinde,
The husbandmen that tilde the ground, among the cloddes did finde,
Of sundrie creature sundrie shapes: of which they spièd some
Even in the instant of their birth but newly then begonne,
And some unperfect wanting brest or shoulders in such wise . . .
For when that moysture with the heate is tempred equally,
They do conceyve, and of them twaine engender by and by
All kinde of things. For though that fire with water aye debateth
Yet moysture mixt with equall heate all living things createth.
And so these discordes in their kinde, one striving with the other,
In generation do agree and make one perfect mother. (I.495–518)

Looking at both works in very broad general terms, it can be said that the *Metamorphoses* and *Antony and Cleopatra* both embody an expansive imaginative world which comprehends the human and the divine, the historical and the mythical; a fluid paradoxical world where change and permanence are reconciled and loss in the natural order is counterbalanced by transmutation, transmigration, regeneration, apotheosis. When, however, we come to examine the way in which nature enters into the symbolic structure of the tragedy, the affinities between Ovid's metamorphic vision and

Shakespeare's seem at once intimate and profound. The dramatic action which ushers in the reign of Octavius Augustus Caesar has the whole world as its setting, and it is Ovid's elemental, changing world whose 'sides' (I.ii.186) and 'borders maritime' are forever in process of being reshaped by the ocean's 'varying tide' (I.iv.46, 51).[9] In no other Shakespearian tragedy are we quite so conscious of the interplay of the elements or of their active involvement in the ever-changing human drama. Caesar prays 'the elements' to be 'kind' to his sister (III.ii.40); and Enobarbus reports that when Cleopatra sailed to meet Mark Antony 'the winds were love-sick', the water 'amorous', and the barge 'Burn'd on the water' (II.ii.196–201). Anger 'heats' Antony and makes him glow 'like plated Mars' (I.i.4; I.iii.80); it stirs embers in Caesar (II.ii.13) and cinders in the ashes of Cleopatra's chance (V.ii.172). Antony's powerful heart is both fire and air to Cleopatra's passion, a bellows which heats and a fan which assuages (I.i.6–10). 'The sighs of Octavia blow the fire up in Caesar' and bring 'variance' into his alliance with Antony (II.vi.123–6). Like the associated 'world' motif, the elemental imagery serves to universalise the tragedy. But it also has the effect of placing the two principal characters in the natural order and balancing a sense of their uniqueness with an awareness of their affinities with each other and with all that lives and moves.

As in the *Metamorphoses*, the all-important element is water. It seems to do duty for all the elements, functioning as a symbol of nature's restless and irresistible activity. Here the threat of 'Chaos come again' is not, as in the other tragedies, a great storm-battle between the elements; it is another Flood in which all shapes sink or liquefy, and only the serpent survives in the ocean of slime (I.i.33–5; I.iii.33; II.v.78–9, 93–5). Disaster in the microcosm is imaged similarly. Antony warns Lepidus to keep off the quicksands of drunkenness lest he drown, but urges his other companions to drown their cares in the vats of Bacchus till 'the conquering wine hath steep'd our sense / In soft and delicate Lethe' (II.vii.58, 105–13). He himself is steeped in the waters of oblivion when he throws away his 'absolute soldiership by land' and fights by sea, where his 'fortune sinks ... most lamentably' (III.vii.40–66). Overwhelmed by disaster, he experiences a sense of imminent disintegration which encapsulates all those moments in the play where his identity is in doubt; and it is a sense of liquid metamorphosis, vapoury dissolution. Antony's fate at this point, it seems, is to vanish forever in the river of Lethe, his 'visible shape' lost 'as water is in water' (IV.xiv.2–

14). It is a fate which originates in the grand passion that over-whelmed the lovers and made Cleopatra cry out: 'O, my oblivion is a very Antony, / And I am all forgotten' (i.iii.90–1).

Nature is a threat in this play, not because of its destructive fero-city, but because of its inexhaustible richness. It overflows with bounty and variety, making life a great feast or magnificent pageant at which it is all too easy to become 'a child of the time', forgetting the past and unconscious of anything in the future except some new pleasure. Its supreme symbol is the Nile, the river whose annual inundation renews the earth and brings with it a succession of strange and wonderful creatures: 'The higher Nilus swells / The more it promises; as it ebbs the seedsman / Upon the slime and ooze scatters his grain, / And shortly comes to harvest ... Your serpent of Egypt is bred now of your mud by the operation of your sun ... It lives by that which nourisheth it, and the elements once out of it, it transmigrates' (ii.vii.20–44).

In a world so close to 'the primal state' (i.iv.41), there is an in-evitable blurring of the distinction between the human and the animal. When lost in folly or passion, the protagonists are likened to such creatures as horse, mare, nag, ox, lion, and mallard. Shame-ful and grotesque though it may be, the implied transformation never seems horrifyingly unnatural. Indeed animal similitudes may be used in a laudatory and affectionate manner. Cleopatra is Antony's nightingale (iv.viii.19) and he, to her, is a delighted and delightful dolphin rising above the element it lives in (v.ii.89): in such figures it seems not as if humans are moving down the scale of creation but as if animals are moving up – as if the whole natural order were a single ontological category in which motion, mingling, and change are the norm. Logically, the most important animal image is one which epitomises the fluidity and uncertainty of the natural order, the snake or serpent. Ambiguous as well as am-phibious, it has been regarded not only as uniquely venomous and deadly (*Metam.* 1.526–35) but also as a symbol of nature's arcane wisdom and healing powers – thus it was the form assumed by Aesculapius, god of medicine, when he came to rid Rome of the plague (*Metam.* xv.737–832).[10] Transformation into a serpent is Cleopatra's idea of a horrible curse, and she herself in her least attractive mood is like 'a Fury crown'd with snakes' (ii.v.79, 40). But there is something decidedly serpentine in her 'strong toil of grace', and she is proud to be called 'my serpent of old Nile' by her lover (i.iv.25). In the end, too, the serpent becomes for her 'the pretty worm of Nilus' that 'kills and pains not' (v.ii.241–2); it even turns into a baby that sucks its nurse asleep in a swoon of deliquescent joy (lines 307–8).

The boundaries between the human and the divine are almost as fluid as those between the elemental, the animal, and the human. Apart from giving it an appropriately antique colouring, the play's abundant mythological imagery functions as a kind of extended hyperbole exalting two rare individuals in whom the rich potentialities of human nature are bewitchingly displayed. Antony and Cleopatra are not alone, however, in possessing divine quality. At Antony's side, Scarus fights 'as if a god in hate of mankind had / Destroy'd in such a shape' (iv.viii.25–6). Eros' limitless affection for his master, too, makes his name seem like a literalised metaphor; and the love of Charmian and Iras for their mistress has the same absoluteness. Antony and Cleopatra are semi-divine because they are nature's best pieces, spacious mirrors in which other less gifted mortals can on occasion see themselves (v.i.31–4; v.ii.99).

III

In interpreting the mythological element, the frame of reference provided by Ovid requires extending to include Plutarch; indeed the strongly mythological bias of the play can probably be ascribed to this author.[11] Shakespeare's conception of Antony and Cleopatra as seriously defective yet godlike, worthy of the severest moral censure yet somehow transcending their moral blemishes, can be detected in the *Life*. Plutarch repeatedly criticises the lovers' wanton disregard for 'temperaunce, modestie, and the civil life'. Yet his account of their life together has at times an enthusiasm which seems to endorse their own conviction that 'no life' was 'comparable and matchable with it', and to suggest that they were truly 'rare' individuals (Shakespeare was to make much of this epithet). Particularly revealing is Plutarch's uncritical reference to the old belief that the family of the Antonii were descended from the son of Hercules, and his statement that Antony resembled in his features the Hercules 'commonly seen ... in pictures, stamped or graven in metell'.[12] This ambiguous characterisation of the lovers seems to incorporate the idea of the demi-god or 'daemon' as defined in 'Of Isis and Osiris'. Daemons (who include Isis, Osiris, Bacchus, and Hercules) were midway between gods and men, but the best of them became gods. In 'their puissance they much surmounted our nature:

but that divinitie which they had, was not pure and simple'. Like ordinary mortals, they displayed 'a diversitie and difference of vice and vertue'. Thus they had to be punished and cleansed of their sins and offences before they could 'recover againe the place, estate and degree ... meet for them and according to their nature'.[13]

However the central purpose of 'Isis and Osiris' (ignored by those students of *Antony and Cleopatra* who have looked at it) is 'to reconcile the Aegyptian Theologie with the Greek Philosophy and reduce them to a very good concordance' (p.1307). Osiris, Plutarch explains, is the god of all fructifying moisture and of the Nile in particular (p.1298). Isis, his wife, is the land of Egypt 'which Nilus overfloweth, and by commixtion maketh fertile and fruitfull'; she is the earth, the female principle in nature, and the source of every form of generation (p.1302). For Plutarch, however, the full significance of the myth of Isis and Osiris only becomes apparent when the nature of their son, Orus, and their deadly enemy, Typhon, is taken into account. Orus is 'nothing else but the temperature and disposition of the aire, nourishing and maintaining all things', and Typhon is 'fire and driness ... the very thing that is fully opposite and adverse to humidity' (pp.1302, 1298; cf. p.1303). Thus 'the Muthology of this fable, as it evidently appeareth, accordeth covertly with the trueth of Nature' (p.1302) in a far more comprehensive sense than any other vegetation myth. The Isis–Osiris myth, Plutarch believes, is an eastern equivalent of the myth of Mars ('cruell, grim, quarrellous') and Venus ('milde, lovely, and generative'), from whose union was born 'the goddesse *Harmonia*, that is to say Accord' (p.1306). Both myths symbolise the concordant discord of the elemental world and of life itself; they are vehicles of the contrarious cosmology pioneered by Pythagoras and Heraclitus and perfected by Empedocles (p.1307). They show that 'the generation, composition, and constitution of this world is mingled of contrary powers' (p.1307); that nothing 'that nature produceth and bringeth foorth is pure and simple', and that 'this life is mixt, and the verie world it selfe ... under the Moone is unequall, variable, and subject to all mutations that possibly may be' (pp.1305, 1307). Like Plutarch's own essay, however, the two myths postulate the naturalness of resolving duality and opposition into a complex unity, a very good concordance.

The impact of dualistic thinking on *Antony and Cleopatra* is remarkable even by the standards of *Romeo and Juliet*, *Othello*, and *Macbeth*; and this fact, I feel sure, we must ascribe to Plutarch. What identifies the Plutarchan connection in this respect is Shakespeare's use of certain mythological symbols. Cleopatra is associated mainly with Venus and Isis, Antony with Bacchus and Mars (also Hercules, supreme exemplar of the martial type).[14] The generative aspect of both the Isis and the Venus analogies is emphasised. The first of the play's nine allusions to Isis occurs in a bawdy dialogue about the fertility of women and the Nile; and the reported scene in which Cleopatra appears dressed in 'th' habiliments of the goddess Isis' is a great ceremonial occasion when she and Antony are accompanied by all their children (I.iii.11–70; III.vi.1–18). When Cleopatra got Julius Caesar to 'lay his sword to bed' – 'What Venus did with Mars' – he 'ploughed her and she cropp'd' (II.iii.231–2; I.v.308). And when she sails to meet Mark Antony – 'O'erpicturing that Venus where we see / The fancy outwork nature' (II.ii.204–5) – she is attended not only by boy cupids but also by amorous elements, a figure of procreative as distinct from lustful sensuality. An addition to Plutarch, the elemental imagery seems designed to link the passage with the opening address in Lucretius' *On the Nature of the Universe* to 'life-giving Venus', the deity for whom 'the inventive earth flings up sweet flowers', 'the ocean levels laugh', and 'the sky is calmed and glows with suffused radiance'.[15] At any rate, Shakespeare obviously accepts and reinforces Plutarch's conception of Venus and Isis as one and the same generative deity.

A parallel identification occurs in the Bacchus analogy. In his 'Life of Antony', Plutarch notes that Cleopatra saw herself as a new Isis, but he makes no mention of Osiris. He does record, however, that Antony was generally referred to in Egypt as 'the new Bacchus';[16] and in saying so he must have had Osiris in mind. For in 'Of Isis and Osiris' he explains that Bacchus is not only 'father of oblivion' and god of wine (*The Morals*, p.751). He is also 'the lord and governour ... of every other nature which is moist and liquid' and of all the sacred splendour of the harvest time. He is, therefore, 'no other than Osiris', 'the same god' (p.1301). Plutarch also mentions a tradition which said that 'Isis was ... married unto Bacchus' (p.1302). In Shakespeare, Antony's identification with Bacchus – as understood by Plutarch – is very forceful indeed. It is evident in his habitual feasting and his bounty, that autumn that grew the more by reaping (v.ii.88); in his 'Egyptian Bacchanals' (II.vii.103ff.) (the epithet becomes pointed in a Plutarchan context); and in his association with Lethe and oblivion, the submergence of self in nature's overflowing abundance. Bacchus and Isis, and Mars and Venus, must then be taken as two synonymous mythological sets. Together they bear witness to the underlying unity of East and West and point to the notion of *discordia concors* as essential to an understanding of the protagonists and of the tragedy as a whole.

In her thorough and penetrating account of the play, Janet Adelman has reminded us that there were two quite contradictory interpretations of the Mars–Venus myth: the cosmological one, which is entirely favourable to the lovers; and the moral one, which is the reverse.[17] In the latter, the lovers are seen as furtive adulterers justly exposed to ridicule when caught in Vulcan's net, and the fate of Mars is held up as a warning to the man of action on the debasing effects of sensuality and sloth. Both interpretations are undoubtedly operative in *Antony and Cleopatra* (as they were, to a much lesser degree, in *Tamburlaine the Great* and *Othello*); but I cannot accept Adelman's claim that at the end of the play we are left uncertain as to which interpretation has priority. The implicit linking of the myth with that of Isis and Osiris dictates a mainly positive interpretation. Moreover, the semantically unstable nature of the myth within the play reflects the inherently unstable nature of any union of extreme opposites; given such instability, it is perfectly natural that the myth should carry different signals at different times, and even that at moments the signals should be ambiguous. The crucial question is whether the final effect of the play is to remind us of what is necessarily ignored in moral interpretations of the myth – that the illicit union of the two deities gave birth to a goddess called Harmony. That it does so is, I believe, beyond question and will be argued in detail at a later point in my analysis.

IV

Considered then in relation to Ovid and Plutarch, some of the more remarkable features of *Antony and Cleopatra* – its affirmative, almost serene attitude to tragic change, its sense of renewal in death, of eternity in time, and of the divine in flawed human greatness – appear to have firm roots in pre-modern ways of thinking about the natural order. In addition, and of greater significance here, Plutarch's treatise on 'the trueth of Nature' as made manifest in myth has reminded us that the uniquely firm and pervasive dualistic design which Shakespeare imposed on the material he took from the *Lives* was central to the old cosmology.

Numerous as well as varied, the dualisms of *Antony and Cleopatra* overlap and interweave to produce an iridescent fabric of form and meaning which is the play itself;[18] Egypt and Rome, representing not only East and West but also the totality of nature and experience, is the all-embracing symbolic antithesis. Of the many oppositions which it embraces, the most important is the one which springs directly from nature, that of love and war. As usual in Shakespeare, love includes friendship, loving-kindness, and peace as well as sexual love. War primarily signifies conquest, empire, and public service; but it has secondary suggestions of cruelty and of personal antagonism verging on hatred. This dualism operates within as well as between Egypt and Rome, each place being presented as a dimension of one and the same world, each a partnership of contrary forces. One word provides a key to this dialectic. As many editors observe, the word 'competitor' is used in the play in the now obsolete sense of 'partner', 'comrade', 'equal'. What they do not observe is that the other sense is present too, so that the word functions as an oxymoronic pun pointing to the fact that friendship-and-equality is potential strife-and-domination. In his opening sentence, Caesar declares, 'It is not Caesar's natural vice to hate / Our great competitor' (I.iv.2–3); and though his whole manner at this point suggests that he has begun to give way to that natural vice, his speech on hearing of Antony's death indicates his capacity for the corresponding natural virtue:

> But yet let me lament,
> With tears as sovereign as the blood of hearts,
> That thou, my brother, my competitor
> In top of all design, my mate in empire,
> Friend and companion in the front of war,
> The arm of mine own body, and the heart
> Where mine his thoughts did kindle – that our stars,
> Unreconcilable, should divide
> Our equalness to this. (v.i.40–8)

The essential tragic fact about the relationship between Antony and Caesar is that they are 'two friends / That does afflict each other' (III.vi.77–8), 'noble partners' (II.ii.22) become less than noble antagonists.

The recurrent motif of *game* and *sport* provides metaphoric extension for the 'competitor' paradox. Antony and Caesar have often played games together in the past; but the context in which this is remembered – one of political 'strife' and 'wrangling' which promises civil war – makes clear that those friendly exercises harboured on each side a strong desire to 'o'erpower' the other (II.ii.84, 109; II.iii.33–8). Even when marriage makes the two men brothers in a deeper sense than ever before – 'Let her live / To join our kingdoms and our hearts' – the metaphor tells the same story: 'Come sir, come; / I'll wrestle with you in my strength of love' (II.ii.155–6; III.ii.61–2).

But the *sport* motif discloses the same slippery dialectic at work in the central love relationship. Cleopatra is Antony's 'play-fellow' (III.xiii.125), and their life together has been one long holiday. The games she plays with him, however, are not pure fun. She mocks, teases, and cheats him; she is a 'wrangling queen' (I.i.48) who uses provocation and quarrels in order to keep his attention. Charmian may be wrong in saying that such methods can turn love to hate (I.iii.6–12), but the fact remains that Antony's attitude to Cleopatra swings wildly between love and loathing, idolatry and contempt; a process which culminates in his determination to kill her: 'my heart / Makes only wars on thee' (IV.xii.14–15). In all of this, Shakespeare has gone behind the old metaphor of love's merry and pleasurable wars (II.i.11–12; *Ado*, I.i.51) to elicit complex psychological truth. He has looked at *Venus victrix* and shown how unstable she can be.[19] For much of the play, Cleopatra is victorious love exceeding its limits, enslaving its object, and inviting revolt.

From the dualism of war and love issues that of male and female. As in *Macbeth* and *Coriolanus*, and to a lesser extent *Othello*, attention is directed to the complex interaction of characteristically male and female attributes.[20] Little play is made of the relationship between male ferocity and female tenderness, fire and tears; but, as in the other three tragedies, there is an imbalance in the bisexual nature of the hero prompted by a similar disorder in his sexual opposite (in *Coriolanus*, his mother). Cleopatra's aggressive triumph in love emasculates Antony, consigns him, as an eloquent stage direction indicates, to her band of fanning eunuchs (I.i.9–10 and SD).[21] Less simply, it unbinds the richly feminine element in his nature. Part of his greatness is an affectionate disposition which senses that the nobleness of life lies in human relationships and not just in rule and conquest; a warmth of feeling that can pierce the armour of tough soldiers and make them 'onion-ey'd'; a simple delight in noting 'the qualities of people' and experiencing the enigma of Cleopatra. Liberally indulged, this becomes a way of life which destroys his captainship and justifies Caesar's claim that he 'is not more man-like / Than Cleopatra, nor the queen of Ptolemy / More womanly than he' (I.iv.5–7).

Like *Othello*, the tragedy offers a perfect paradigm of the reason–passion conflict: reason here meaning self-discipline, temperance, and gravity, passion meaning sensuality, intemperance, riot, and levity. This dualism was prompted by Plutarch's 'Life', but Shakespeare develops it in a richly idiosyncratic fashion. He gives us a comic and an anti-comic world, the first characterised by saturnalian revelry, misrule, mockery, feasting, and overflowing bounty, the second by ambition, duty, a prudent respect for limits (especially the limits of time), and a certain meanness of spirit.[22] The antithesis of Epicurean (II.i.24; II.vii.50) and Stoic provides an appropriately classical dimension to this dualism and reminds us that Egypt stands for attitudes which are to be found in Rome itself.

Again there is a quibble which hints that the given dualism is not one of mere contrariety but that the opposites are closely related. As everyone knows, Antony goes east for 'pleasure' (I.i.47; I.iv.32; II.iii.41). But it is also his 'pleasure' to abandon idle pastimes and return to the political arena (I.ii.109, 128, 188); and he reflects on such apparent contradictions: 'the present pleasure, / By revolution low'ring, does become / The opposite of itself' (I.ii.121–3). Caesar on the other hand does not enjoy Alexandrian revels, even in Italy; but he takes considerable pleasure in playing tricks with a cornered enemy. We thoroughly dislike him for this, perhaps forgetting that Antony felt much better when Thyreus was soundly whipped and that he assumed that Caesar would 'at pleasure whip, or hang, or torture' Hipparchus in a *quid pro quo* (III.xiii.150). We might also forget Antony's boasts that 'with half the bulk o' the world' he 'play'd' as he 'pleas'd, making and marring fortunes' (III.xi.64–5), and that he often 'ransom'd lives . . . for jests' (III.xiii.180). The two 'great competitors' both show us that power can mean fun just as fun can mean power. Certainly we are not presented with any simple dichotomy between irresponsible pleasure seeking and pleasureless commitment to military–political ideals. Antony the amiable hedonist and Antony the grave leader are one and the same man; as are his former playfellow and his unrelenting enemy.

Such paradoxes have some bearing on the radical problem of baseness and nobility. That concern for honour which is characteristic of the Renaissance hero is acutely developed in Shakespeare's Roman protagonists, for whom it is an ethnic issue as well as one of personal integrity and class consciousness.[23] Whatever his aberrations, Antony is always aware of his honourable reputation and very insistent that it should be respected. He claims that if he loses his honour he loses himself, and indeed his anguished experience of personal dissolution proceeds largely from his conviction that his military reputation is in ruins. But Cleopatra's status as queen means that the question of nobility and baseness directly concerns her as well as Antony. Thus the play is a continuous and, for some critics, an unresolved debate on whether the term 'noble' or 'base' would be more appropriately applied to the adulterous lovers. To some critics, as to Caesar and sometimes Antony himself, it is a simple matter of the noble Roman allowing himself to be debased by the sensual gipsy. But the foul gipsy is also an Egyptian sovereign with an inbred sense of her own worth that can be called upon in time of crisis. Moreover, the noble ruin of her magic, who has long since begun to conquer by lieutenantry and to deny his surrogates the recognition they deserve, is a hero whose honour is now little more than a name. Antony's honour is badly in need of renewal, and it is the Queen who helps him to bring that about. Before the end, he enjoys with her an Indian summer of 'right royal' nobility.

Whether it is perceived as a transformation of base matter into pure gold, or as a purification of corrupted nature, this final change is the result of a conscious moral endeavour; it is art acting as 'coadiutor to nature'.[24] For most of the play, however, it is easy to see an irreconcilable opposition between nature and art. Nature, signifying (in this antithesis) the free play of instinct and passion, was often associated with Epicureanism; and art, signifying the conscious control of life by reason, was correspondingly associated with Stoicism.[25] Thus the two concepts would seem to be sharply polarised in the conflict between Egypt and Rome. Indeed Caesar, with his unbending self-discipline and politic skills, and Cleopatra, with her passionate spontaneity, could be construed as personifications of Art and Nature respectively. But once we look at Cleopatra in any depth the antithesis begins to break down; or rather it is relocated and resolved in her. It is just right that her soothsayer, with his reverential allusion to 'nature's infinite book of secrecy' (1.ii.28), should postulate the essential oneness of nature and art; for this nature goddess is the supreme artist of the play.[26] In her manipulation of her lover, she is 'cunning past man's thought'; yet as Enobarbus points out, her winds and waters are as natural to her as was (to him) the shower of golden rain into which Jove (the fertility god) turned himself when he would ravish Danae (the earth) (i.ii.141–6). The river pageant in which she plays Venus to Antony's Mars is a perfect partnership of art and nature; and it is the power of her creative imagination which sees in Antony a sublime example of nature's art (ii.iii.195–222; v.ii.76–100). Her suicide, in which she outplays Caesar and identifies herself wholly with Antony, is her masterpiece. It is a majestic spectacle in which she re-enacts her journey on the Cydnus to meet Mark Antony; it is their love's monument (the stage image is emblematic).

No doubt there is an implicit parallel between the artful achievement of Cleopatra and that of the playwright who has helped to immortalise her name. In *A Midsummer Night's Dream*, a play notable for the instability of its lovers and the heterogeneity of its materials, Shakespeare intimated that love and poetry (nature and art) are akin in their quest for 'union in partition', concord in discord, something of great constancy in a world of flux. No less pertinent is the last paragraph of the *Metamorphoses*, where Ovid, having apotheosised the Caesar who turned strife and change into universal peace, makes his own proud boast. When his 'brittle flesh' has decayed, his 'better part' will 'clyme / Aloft above the starrye skye' and his 'lyfe shall everlastingly bee lengthened still' by the fame accorded to his poem. He too has imposed unity on multeity, found permanence in change.

Art being the expression of a timeless order beyond the flux of nature, the nature–art dialectic is closely linked in the play with that of time and eternity. The conflict in Antony between Roman and Egyptian values is a conflict between responsiveness to the ever-changing demands of time and the desire to lose himself in the pleasurable 'stretched' moment that has no end. In his Egyptian mood, he mocks the chimes of midnight and finds eternity in the lips and eyes of Cleopatra. In his Roman mood, he repudiates what these 'poison'd hours' have done and seeks to 'despatch' his neglected business with 'haste' (ii.ii.94, 168–70). The Roman moods, however, are too fitful to enable him to deal with a rival who lives vigilantly in time and moves with astonishing speed when opportunity favours him (i.iv.72–6; iii.vii.56, 75). With remarkable economy, Shakespeare makes Caesar's conduct exemplify to perfection his own well-known motto, *festina lente* ('hasten slowly'), one which became 'the most widely cherished Renaissance maxim'. This was not an exhortation to avoid haste but rather to 'combine speed with patience'; it underpinned the rule of life which dictates that 'ripeness

is achieved by a growth of strength in which quickness and stead-
iness are equally developed'.[27] Caesar triumphs because he is faithful to this motto, and Antony falls because he is not: dilatory at first,
Antony in the end is fatally impulsive (iv.x.1–6).

Unlike Shakespeare's other tragedies, however, *Antony and Cleopatra* goes far beyond the conception of time as an inflexible order
which pitilessly destroys those who ignore or defy its demands. For
the death of the lovers (as already noted) is timely as well as untimely, being part of the generational cycle. And the Egyptian attitude to time contains wisdom as well as folly: it ignores minutes,
hours, and days, yet it promotes a deep awareness of the larger
phases of time's order – spring and harvest, the ebb and flow of the
Nile. Time seen thus is pattern as well as process, a reconciliation
of flux and stasis, a 'moving image of eternity'.[28] In the finally
benign vision of the tragedy, the lovers participate in that eternity
by virtue of the fame which posterity accords them – their 'nobleness in record', their 'place i' th' story' and 'chronicle'. But throughout the play they are given an eternal quality by association with
nature's infinite, and infinitely varied, bounty (the harvest that
grows the more by reaping); and above all, perhaps, by their identification with the heavenly bodies, especially the sun (Antony) and
the moon (Cleopatra).[29] For it was an axiom of cosmography that
although 'the celestial bodies measure the passage of time, yet they
and their patterns are immutable, beyond the reach of *tempus edax*.
They are both timely and timeless'. Moreover, the conjugal union
of sun and moon, the period of one day, was a symbol of 'the diurnal
unit of time ... which by infinite repetition generates eternity'.
Alchemical tradition added to the richness of this symbol, making
the conjunction of sun and moon 'an icon for the completed opus,
another stasis which subsumes all change'.[30]

The alchemical allusion is not far-fetched. European alchemy
originated in Alexandria, and Isis herself was traditionally said
to have taught and written on the subject. It was founded on the
belief that the elemental structure of things makes it possible for
the skilled artist to change any natural substance into another.
In the quest for the philosopher's stone, the great transmuting agent,
the elements of the chosen material were to be separated, then
purified, and then conjoined or 'married' in a perfect unity. The
sexual metaphor is fundamental to alchemic thought, reflecting a
belief that 'the great work' is part of the creative process, an image
in small of cosmos emerging from primal chaos. On the other hand,

alchemy had a strongly mystical dimension, evident primarily in the conception of the alchemical experiment as analogous to the quest for spiritual perfection. Just as the soul is purified by mortification and passes through death and resurrection to the final perfection of the heavenly state, so the alchemist, by nurturing, burning, 'mortifying' and 'killing' his material, and then 'regenerating' it in a purer form, can arrive at the perfect substance, the great transmuting agent.[31]

Early in *Antony and Cleopatra*, Shakespeare's Isis registers her familiarity with this Alexandrian art. Welcoming her messenger back from Rome, she comments excitedly, and in specifically alchemic terms, on the nobly transforming effect which Antony has on others:

> How much unlike art thou Mark Antony!
> Yet, coming from him, that great med'cine hath
> With his tinct gilded thee. (i.v.35–7)[32]

Enobarbus later echoes her sentiment when he acknowledges himself a 'villain of the earth' and perceives that Antony, a 'mine of bounty', has crowned his baseness ('turpitude') with gold (iv.vi.30–4). But Cleopatra's alchemic metaphor seems most relevant when she herself becomes 'fire and air', leaves her 'other elements ... to baser life', and prepares to join her 'golden Phoebus' in eternity (v.ii.287–8, 315). Although Shakespeare himself does not use the term, the word which springs to mind as offering the most appropriate definition of what happens at the end of this tragedy is 'sublimation'. An alchemic and later a chemical term, it denoted (i) the purifying process whereby base metal is changed to silver or gold, and (ii) the ascent of vapour into the air under the action of the sun's rays; in its figurative sense, it meant (iii) the transmutation of anything human or non-material into something higher and more excellent: 'I am sublim'd! Grosse earth / Supports me not. I walk on air'.[33] I would suggest that alchemy – with its basic dualities of base/noble, male/female, Sun/Moon, and King/Queen, and its supreme icon of the Hermaphrodite (Sun-King and Queen-Moon united) – hovers continually as metaphor over the whole of *Antony and Cleopatra*.

Cleopatra reaches her state of sublime perfection when she becomes 'marble-constant' (v.ii.239), an unchanging image, almost an artistic representation of that quality. As I have remarked before, constancy (etymologically, 'standing [or holding] together') was a virtue associated particularly with the Romans. But it is of special significance in Shakespeare's work generally. 'O heaven', declares Proteus,

> were man
> But constant, he were perfect! That one error
> Fills him with faults; makes him run through all th' sins;
> Inconstancy falls off where it begins. (*TGV*, v.iv.110–13)

And a major reason for its importance is that it was identifiable with the perfect functioning of the natural order. Constancy is the psychic and moral manifestation of nature's art of binding things diverse and contrary into a concordant unity. And inconstancy is the universal human flaw because all structures of unity in nature are alliances from which the impulse towards conflict and change can never be eradicated.

Constancy and inconstancy have never been isolated as a specific dualism in *Antony and Cleopatra*, but in my view it is one of the most illuminating. It coincides with the Rome–Egypt and male–female oppositions. The Roman male here sees himself as 'firm' (I.v.43). He claims that whatever change Fortune may have registered on his face she can never make his heart her vassal (II.vi.53–6). He is emphatic that agreements should be honoured and refuses to believe that he could break one (II.ii.85–95). He sees women as weak and unreliable, even when Fortune smiles (III.xii.29–31). He identifies himself with the sure and firm-set earth, and when he ventures on the sea it is to build cities on its back (III.vii.41–66; IV.xiv.58). Nevertheless Roman constancy in this play, as in *Julius Caesar*, is largely a dream of the past. For this is a Rome convulsed with unrest and dissension, caught between the collapse of the republican constitution and the birth of a principate that will last three hundred years. The 'common body' of the people is 'grown sick' with both rest and motion and 'would purge / By any desperate change' (I.ii.53–4; I.iv.44–7). And its leaders are no different. Distrust is universal and no bond endures: allies become enemies and enemies friends with startling ease. The dynamics of this diseased state are omened early in the play in a reference to the war fought between Antony's wife and his brother: 'soon that war had ended, and the time's state / Made friends of them, jointing their force 'gainst Caesar' (I.ii.88–9). But the event of central significance is the new alliance between Caesar and Antony. Extended to include Pompey and Lepidus in an archetypal quadruple unity (unity being binary and quadruple, the triumvirate is of no significance in the play), confirmed by a marriage, written agreements, handshaking, and a comradely feast, this 'band' of 'friendship' (II.v.117) proves no different to the gipsy knot-trick of 'fast and loose' (IV.xiii.28). Antony shows himself to be utterly fickle here, and the man who is destined to unify the state is hardly better. Octavius is constant to his purposes, but not to his friends, breaking the bond with Pompey and Lepidus and perhaps engineering the break with Antony. The time's state is such, it would seem, that anarchy can only be cured by using its own methods.

Of all Shakespeare's tragedies, *Antony and Cleopatra* presents us with the most sustained vision of doubleness and change. In consequence none of the tragedies tends to undermine quite so thoroughly the confidence of audiences and readers in their ability to understand and judge its principal characters. One moment we feel we know Antony, Cleopatra, and Caesar, and are willing to make firm moral judgements on their behaviour, then we see them from an entirely different perspective, or perceive two possible interpretations of this or that action; and so we either change our assessment radically, or begin to question the reality of human identity and the validity of moral judgement. Interpreters whose affinities are with the 'new-critical' tradition (among whom I would class Janet Adelman), a tradition where ambivalence is not only a favourite analytical tool but a criterion of supreme excellence, have tended to isolate this effect of uncertainty and to make it the determinant factor in the play's vision. They present the play as 'an unresolved dialectic between opposed values', one which leaves us free to choose between 'the realistic' (i.e. unfavourable) and 'the lyrical' (i.e. favourable) estimate of the protagonists and their personal tragedy.[34] Where they acknowledge that a critical and ironical attitude is dissolved in the conclusion, they state or imply that this is 'against all probability' and a consequence not of any real moral change which the characters have undergone but of Shakespeare's 'transcendent poetry, which can fuse diverse impressions into a single effect'.[35] What unity they discover in *Antony and Cleopatra* pertains not to the principal characters but to the play itself; it lies in the poise and balance with which Shakespeare sustains his unremittingly double vision.

There are nevertheless a fair number of critics who take it for granted that the dualities in this tragedy are resolved in a genuine harmony at the end;[36] and with these, it will be apparent, I am in agreement. Such critics tend, however, to assert rather than to justify this response, failing to provide enough evidence from the body of the play to show that the resolution is inherent in the total conception. My own account of the play's oppositions, supported by the character analysis which follows, should indicate where such evidence is to be found. Brilliant though its results have often been, the new-critical reading appears to me to be defective in that it produces an essentially static view of a developmental drama (however much emphasis is placed on its oscillating rhythm). It overlooks the whole idea of ennobling interaction, purification, sublimation. It misses the fundamental assumption that in the natural order as imagined by the play opposites are not mere opposites but can be conjoined in a genuine unity, and that so long as that unity lasts – so long as balance and distinction are maintained – then identification, interpretation, and evaluation are possible. The second half of the play dramatises a great change from inconstancy into a noble, constant unity where the self is fully realised and clearly identified. That it requires irreversible calamity to bring about this fullness of noble life is what makes the play a tragedy.

V

A notable feature of the play's design is a sharply defined pattern of contrast and opposition involving the characters of Antony, Octavius, Cleopatra, and Octavia. Octavia was an obvious problem for a dramatist who intended to provide a basically affirmative view of the love tragedy while remaining faithful to his historical source. Shakespeare, however, resisted the temptation to make her an unattractive character and actually used her to advantage with remarkable skill. Modest, gracious, dutiful, and cool, Octavia is Cleopatra's perfect foil. She throws into relief not only the gipsy side of 'Egypt's queen' but also, and more importantly, her magnetic vitality. Antony's marriage to Octavia illustrates the futility of bargain marriages which presume that society creates love rather than love society. It constitutes an impoverishment of his emotional life and makes his return to Cleopatra both inevitable and hard to condemn. At first Octavia is simply a passive instrument for cementing the rebuilt 'fortress' of Roman unity as represented by Caesar and Antony. But later she actively seeks to become the moderating 'mean' between the quarrelling 'extremes' of the two brothers (III.ii.32; III.iv.19–30). Her total failure in this role, and the prompt breakdown of her marriage, is a measure of the extent to which human bonds have been corrupted in Rome. Roman society will be reintegrated only when Caesar overcomes Antony and puts an end to competitive rule; and marriage – amazingly – will be reinstated as the symbol of peace and harmony when the illicit lovers are wedded in death.

Prudently, Shakespeare gives Octavia only three scenes and keeps her out of sight and mind in the latter part of the play. The contrast between Caesar and Antony, on the other hand, becomes progressively more conspicuous, and its effect changes. Caesar in this phase is not just a coldly rational and rather puritanical leader with justifiable objections to his colleague's behaviour; he is mean-spirited, deceitful, and heartless. Thus whereas the earlier contrast served to highlight both the defects and the virtues of Antony, here it is largely a device for magnifying his greatness. But it also lends substance to Caesar's early prediction that he and Antony could not for long 'remain in friendship', their 'conditions so diff'ring in their acts' (II.ii.117–18). The disposal of one partner by the other seems inevitable.

Although Cleopatra is a more subtle character creation than Antony, it is on his character that the tragic quality of the play depends. It is he who presents the spectacle of ruined greatness and endures the anguish of self-betrayal. On one level, he can be seen as a great man with a seriously flawed character.[37] But on a deeper level he is to be understood as a hero whose greatness and weakness alike stem from his intensely double nature. Pulled one way by Rome and another by Egypt, Antony is a man in whom the contrariety of human nature is developed to a unique degree. His soldiership is twice that of his nearest rivals (II.ii.34), and when he fights on land he is invincible. In war his self-discipline is astonishing (I.v.56–70), and he carries within him a fierce, fiery rage – 'as loud as Mars' (II.ii.4–6) and Hercules (IV.xiv.30–49). But hardly less important to his success as a great general is his ability to inspire intense loyalty in his men; and with this we confront the other force in his nature and perceive that when he is truly himself these two forces are interdependent. Antony's men 'follow' him 'close' (IV.iv.34) because they are his 'friends', his 'lads'. In striking contrast to Caesar, he talks compulsively and affectionately to all of them, common soldiers and household servants as well as officers, sharing with them his enthusiasm as a soldier and his happiness as a lover. His lascivious wassails, as Caesar so contemptuously calls them, are an expression of his desire to be at one with others in the joy of living.

A peculiar feature of Antony's wonderfully affable disposition is his generosity of hand and heart. It is shown in the gift of orient pearl sent to Cleopatra from Rome; in the return, 'with bounty overplus', of all Enobarbus' treasures; and in his quickness to blame himself and forgive others when things go wrong. 'Bounty' is the word used to denote this huge generosity of spirit. And it is a strikingly appropriate word. In its usual sense, it meant goodness in giving, and was associated with God or the great. For Shakespeare himself, too, it was synonymous with love, which gives endlessly:

> My bounty is as boundless as the sea,
> My love as deep; the more I give to thee,
> The more I have, for both are infinite. (*RJ*, ii.ii.133–5)

But the word had another sense, almost obsolete even in Shakespeare's time, which he may also have had in mind. It is not a clearly intended sense; but like the word 'gests' ('achievements'), which Shakespeare uses in a context redolent of chivalry (iv.viii.2), it enters the text like the ghost of a nobler age. Commonly met with in chivalric romance, the other sense is 'warlike prowess, valour'.[38] The word bounty, then, crystallises an idea which the action manifests: that Antony's heroic identity constitutes a union of martial valour and loving-kindness.

Of its very nature, Antony's greatness gives him a terrible instability. To keep within limit the impulses with which nature has so generously endowed him, to 'atone' them in a single identity, requires magical control. We must assume that before the present phase of his career he has not attained his full greatness and for that reason has not been greatly at risk; his self-fulfilment has been limited to the context of war and friendship and has not seriously involved his sexuality. In marriage he has been an unsuccessful Theseus, tied to an uncurbable Amazon (ii.ii.65–71). And until after the battle of Actium, his relationship with Cleopatra is of essentially the same kind. In her he finds yet another wrangling woman who feels that domination rather than complementarity is what secures the bond of love. Nevertheless his loving, festive nature has been awakened by Cleopatra as never before, so that the Antony we see in the first scene is an Antony in crisis. His difficulties are compounded by the fact that his youthful friend has turned into a censorious rival who makes public life less attractive to him than hitherto. He has begun to live on his reputation and shows all the touchiness of those who do. Until stabilised by disaster, then, Antony in the time-span of the play is a perfect Proteus, showing now one side of himself, and now another; betraying this person and that. At the end of Act I Cleopatra describes him as a 'heavenly mingle' of opposite qualities, but at that stage Caesar's reference to him as a man of rare 'composure' (composition) is much more appropriate (I.v.59; I.iv.22). Antony will not achieve a heavenly mingle in himself or his relationship with Cleopatra (and the first depends on the second) until after he has been transformed into a doting mallard at Actium.

Instability is the mark of Antony's character from the outset. In the first scene he is provoked into a declaration of absolute commitment to Cleopatra and the Egyptian way of life. In the second he is a grave Roman general, determined to leave Cleopatra and wishing he had never seen her. In the third he buys his departure with the assurance that distance will not separate him from her and that he will make peace or war just as she chooses. The impromptu marriage to Octavia seems to prove that 'the greatest soldier of the world' is 'turn'd the greatest liar' (I.iii.38–9); and it does not stop him turning. He soon decides to go back to Cleopatra and then, with evident sincerity, promises Octavia that his future conduct will be impeccable; he even becomes the indignant Roman when Caesar expresses doubts about his constancy as a husband.

The most important fact about his return to Cleopatra is that it entails complete submission to her. Caesar reports that Cleopatra now threatens Rome and that Antony has given up his 'regiment' to her, assembling on her behalf all the kings of the East and making her absolute ruler of Egypt and other countries. What is said and done at Actium amply bears out the charge of surrendered authority. Cleopatra isolates him from his men, encourages him to fight by sea instead of land, rebukes him in the manner of a military superior, and insists that she will bear a charge in the battle and 'appear there for a man' (III.vii.18). And when she flies, he flies. Before and after this shameful debacle, Antony's men spell out what it signifies; but no one is more eloquent on the subject than Antony himself. He has betrayed his men and everything he stands for; Cleopatra was his 'conqueror' and had 'full supremacy' over his spirit; his sword would obey her on all cause (III.xi.1–68). No expression of tragic self-knowledge in Shakespeare is as complete as this.

Unsteadily, Antony's reintegration begins here, and Cleopatra has everything to do with it. If the candour of his self-criticism wins back much of our respect, so does his treatment of her. He rebukes her in tones of affectionate despair and not of anger; and when she asks forgiveness he grants it instantly, proceeding to the further recognition (voiced in the opening scene, but now tested by experience) that love is the supreme value: 'Fall not a tear, I say; one of them rates / All that is won and lost' (lines 69–70). His rage in the Thyreus incident is caused less by Cleopatra than by Caesar, who has now begun his long endeavour to win her away from him: Antony is furious that she should allow her hand to be kissed by the bearer of a message so base as Thyreus brings. But her powerful protestation of love-unto-death affects him profoundly (never before has she revealed her love to him in this way). Not only does his rage vanish instantly as before; he is filled with a new hope and a knightly enthusiasm for the royal occupation. He is 'Antony again' (IV.xiii.187), but an Antony about to be fulfilled as never before.

Factually, the battle outside Alexandria is a victory of no consequence sandwiched between two major defeats; imaginatively, however, it is Antony's 'lightning before death', an epiphany laden with meaning. It differs from the previous battle in that it is fought on the solid element where 'the firm Roman' and his 'war-mark'd footmen' (III.vii.44) belong. It differs too in that Cleopatra, chastened by the spectacle of his disgrace at Actium, is no longer the wrangling queen who would rule him and displace his men. She accepts her complementary role as woman and queen, providing inspiration, encouragement and reward, and in this way becomes an intrinsic part of a heroic achievement. Antony in consequence is utterly at one with her, with his men, and with himself. Cleopatra inspires him to recover his lost honour as a soldier, his soldiers awaken in him the magnificently generous friend, and the love of war, friends, and mistress are all part of one spiritual continuum. The scene shows the totality of Antony's greatness held in dynamic equilibrium, harmoniously interrelated without confusion or imbalance.

The battle is preceded by a feast designed to lift the spirits of his followers and to celebrate Cleopatra's birthday. It is here that Antony speaks to his men with a warmth of feeling which makes them 'onion-ey'd'; typically, however, he counteracts this immediately with an ebullient heartiness that sets the feast on its way.

Then comes the dawn parting of the lovers – an aubade, but one fit for a soldier and his mistress. Unlike the lady of lyric tradition, Cleopatra does not seek to delay her lover with a lingering farewell and many kisses. Rather she says little and acts as Antony's armourer so that Eros can hasten with his own 'defences' and both men depart promptly; she then accepts a single 'soldier's kiss' from her 'man of steel' – the man of steel she has helped to re-create. Departing, Antony is 'buckled well' in 'riveted trim', an image of soldierly integrity (IV.iv.1–22). The harmonious nature of this parting determines the nature of the reunion. Antony returns in triumph, and an ecstatic union of male and female and of war and love (both friendly and erotic) is enacted. Pointedly, one half of Antony's speech is addressed to his men, the other to Cleopatra:

> We have beat him to his camp. Run one before
> And let the Queen know of our gests. To-morrow,
> Before the sun shall see's, we'll spill the blood
> That has today escap'd. I thank you all;
> For doughty-handed are you, and have fought
> Not as you serv'd the cause, but as't had been
> Each man's like mine; you have shown all Hectors.
> Enter the city, clip your wives, your friends,
> Tell them your feats; whilst they with joyful tears
> Wash the congealment from your wounds and kiss
> The honour'd gashes whole. (IV.viii.1–11)

The last clause, with its metaphoric suggestion of a noble, gashed identity reintegrated through love, is crucial. It prepares for the immediate entry of Cleopatra and Antony's greeting. Graciously, he draws the wounded Scarus into the ritual, commending to the Queen's bounty a soldier who has fought like a god for both of them (compare this with the ignoble treatment of Ventidius and his likes). This gesture enriches the great union of love and soldiership which is postulated in the whole speech and daringly expanded in its erotically suggestive conclusion:

> *Enter* CLEOPATRA *attended*
> [*To* SCARUS.] Give me thy hand –
> To this great fairy I'll commend thy acts,
> Make her thanks bless thee. O thou day o' th' world,
> Chain mine arm'd neck. Leap thou, attire and all,
> Through proof of harness to my heart, and there
> Ride on the pants triumphing. (lines 11–16)

Here indeed is a union of Mars and Venus which begets harmony and is, in consequence, unambiguously admirable. The chivalric colouring of the scene recalls the Knight's Tale, where the code of chivalry, with its twin devotion to love and combat, is identified with the concordant discord of universal nature (including the planets Mars and Venus), and the greatness and instabilities of the noble self defined accordingly (chapter 2). Shakespeare (with Fletcher) will return directly to Chaucer's tragi-comic romance in *The Two Noble Kinsmen*; but this scene is, in effect, his best tribute to the work from which he, Kyd, and Marlowe seem to have learned so much.

Like Lear's reunion with Cordelia, and 'the warlike Moor's' with 'the divine Desdemona' (Mars embracing the Cyprian goddess), that of Antony and Cleopatra after the battle of Alexandria is at once a poignant vision of what might have been had not fate decreed otherwise, and a pointer to the essential structure of Shakespearian tragedy: the sudden shattering of unity and harmony – the destruction of a great bond – and the consequent disintegration of the self. Antony's instability quickly reasserts itself, then his distrust of Cleopatra, and then – with fatal consequence – his wrath. Their tragedy is that the manner of their dying, and not of their living, is what will seal their relationship and create a lasting image of their noble identities. There is, however, a close imaginative connection between their joint victory at Alexandria and their noble deaths; moreover, without that earlier achievement in mutual triumph the claims of the last one would almost certainly ring false.

Antony's death accords with the Roman and Stoic conception of a noble constancy. He punishes sharp fate by seeming to bear it lightly, defeats the conqueror by triumphing over himself, and shuns the baseness of captivity (IV.xiv.135–8; IV.xv.15). Many, however, have felt that his suicide is deficient in Roman nobility because not instantly effective, and some critics even profess to find it comic or bathetic.[39] Yet the text insists that Antony dies exactly as he ought, 'a Roman by a Roman / Valiantly vanquish'd' (lines 57–8). Although this is Antony's own claim, it cannot be construed as self-deception, for it is endorsed not only by Cleopatra ('So should it be, that none but Antony / Should conquer Antony' (lines 17–18)) but also by Dercetas. Offering Antony's bloody sword to Caesar, and defiantly describing his dead master as one who 'best was worthy / Best to be serv'd (v.i.6–7) (an act of courage and love which authenticates what follows), Dercetas announces:

He is dead, Caesar,
Not by a public minister of justice,
Nor by a hir'd knife; but that self hand
Which writ his honour in the acts it did
Hath, with the courage which the heart did lend it,
Splitted his heart. This is his sword;
I robb'd his wound of it; behold it stain'd
With his most noble blood. (lines 20–7)

Part of an iterative pattern, the imagery of this speech confirms the rightness of Antony's death by stressing its redemptive and regenerative effect. Echoed here are the play's many allusions to stained, blemished, and wounded honour; Antony's confession that he was robbed of his sword by a woman who had full supremacy over his heart; and the promise that at Alexandria he would 'bathe' his 'dying honour in the blood / Shall make it live again' (IV.ii.6–7). Stained and stolen honour has been recovered and renewed by valour.

But not by valour alone; nobly Stoic though it is, Antony's death is not a replica of Brutus'. Like Othello's, yet more so, his suicide is a union of both love and valour: 'valiant Eros' (IV.xiv.96) in action. The news that Cleopatra has taken her life, although a lie, is also a prophetic truth, and must be seen as such; for Shakespeare is here advancing the remarkable idea that each lover is inspired by and imitates the other's suicide. The effect of this carefully developed idea will be to intensify the impression – foreshadowed in Mardian's piteous message – of two lovers who 'mingled ... entirely' at the end, the name of each 'buried' in the other (lines 24–5, 34). The idea of mutual imitation is finely complicated and illumined by the suicide of Eros, the squire whose role Cleopatra played so 'rarely' at Alexandria, and whose name makes him her surrogate here. Eros' death is predictive of hers, and, like the fictional suicide, is taken by Antony as a lesson in the courage of love; 'My queen and Eros / Have, by their brave instruction, got upon me / A nobleness in record. But I will be / A bridegroom in my death ... To do thus / I learn'd of thee' (lines 97–103).

VI

Although Cleopatra is one of the polar opposites between which Antony's expansive nature oscillates, she obviously cannot be seen as the embodiment of any one attitude or quality. As Mrs Jameson observed over a century ago, her character is remarkable for its 'antithetical construction', its 'absence of unity and simplicity': it is this which marks her off so distinctly from Shakespeare's other heroines.[40] One very important source of her contradictory impact is an ability to render attractive what is normally perceived as reprehensible for aesthetic or moral reasons: her gracing of things graceless or disgraceful.

Grace, or becomingness, was an effect to which much thought was devoted in humanist and courtly circles during the Renaissance. And while every effort was made to cultivate it in language and action, it was recognised that perfect grace is found only when it is 'planted naturall'. Grace of this kind pleases in no ordinary way; it works on the beholder 'like enchantment';[41] and it may entail defiance of all the rules. Cleopatra is not the first character in Shakespeare to possess this seductive natural art. Hal consciously determines to 'so offend' as 'to make offence a skill', an attempt which reminds us that that is something which Falstaff does by instinct: it is his vocation, his means of survival. More pertinently, it is something which the Poet of the Sonnets finds in the fickle Friend ('lascivious grace, in whom all ill well shows' – no.40; cf. nos.95, 96) and the even more fickle Mistress:

> O from what pow'r hast thou this pow'rful might
> With insufficiency my heart to sway?
> To make me give the lie to my true sight,
> And swear that brightness does not grace the day?
> Whence hast thou this becoming of things ill,
> That in the very refuse of thy deeds
> There is such strength and warrantise of skill
> That in my mind thy worst all best succeeds? (no.150)

The Poet, however, is not habitually seduced by this powerful might. He warns the Friend that, like a knife ill-used, it must lose its edge (no.95); and he tells bitterly how the admirer who wakes to discover that his judgement has been perverted can smell only the stench of festered lilies. He distinguishes between 'external grace' and the grace of truth-constancy, identifying the first as a beauty which decays and the second as one which lasts forever (nos.53, 69, 93). It is when the two graces are one that beauty is perfect, admiration undying, and Time defeated (no.54). Just such a pattern of ideas and experience is embodied in *Antony and Cleopatra*.

The 'becoming of things ill' is something which Antony and Cleopatra have in common: it is part of what makes them so 'rare'. Cleopatra attributes it to Antony ('The violence of either thee becomes' (I.v.60)), and so, in his grudging style, does Caesar: 'Say this becomes him – / As his composure must be rare indeed / Whom these things cannot blemish . . .' (I.iv.21–3). However since Antony is conceived from the start as the victim of Cleopatra's magic, the common gift is pre-eminently hers. Resoundingly, Antony confesses that 'everything becomes' her (I.i.49); and Enobarbus the rationalist agrees: 'vilest things / Become themselves in her', she makes 'defect perfection' (II.ii.242–3, 235). The burden of the tragedy, however, is that her 'becomings' do not always 'eye well' with Antony (I.iii.96–7) or anyone else and that her 'strong toil of grace' (v.ii.345) is permanently binding only when it includes the inner grace of truth-constancy. Perhaps that is what lies behind all Shakespeare's quibbling on 'become', a word whose elusive sense several critics have tried (not with complete success, I think) to pin down.[42] Change, novelty, variety is indeed delightful; but what is truly becoming aspires to and enters the realm of being.

Cleopatra's major contradiction, however, is not that of grace and its opposite but of majesty (or royal nobility) and baseness. Obviously, of course, the first contradiction is integral to the second. Bawdy, boastfully promiscuous, capable of hopping through the public streets, jocular, quarrelsome, and even violent, Cleopatra behaves in a manner which would have struck a Renaissance audience as astoundingly at variance with everything one expects from a great queen (in Daniel's neo-Senecan *Cleopatra*, printed nine times between 1594 and 1611, she is never – despite her moral flaws – anything but stately and grave). But this Cleopatra is also intelligent, proud, and endowed with natural authority. She expects and receives from everyone (including Antony) her titles of respect, and is quick to identify the one and only lapse of ceremony she experiences in personal address (III.xiii.38). Behind all her cavortings and tantrums, there is a deep self-respect which can assert itself just when it seems non-existent: 'These hands of mine do lack nobility, that they strike / A meaner than myself' (II.ii.82–5). This innate sense of her own high nobility – 'fitting for a princess / Descended of so many royal kings' (v.ii.324–5) – is what enables her to unite forever with Antony and to perform a 'noble act' (line 283; cf. line 329) which is eternally becoming.

Cleopatra displays an assured royalty for the first time in the play after the triumph at Alexandria when she responds to her emperor's call for bounty and rewards Scarus with 'an armour all of gold' ('it was a king's') (IV.viii.27). Then she loses it quickly, and is in danger of becoming 'rarely base' (V.ii.177): identified with the fickleness and frailty imputed to all women in Jacobean tragic satire, with the notoriety of the whore, and the degradation of the exhibited freak. After Antony's death, Shakespeare has a second catastrophe to negotiate, and in order to avoid an anti-climax he treats the whole of the last act as a battle of wits between Caesar and Cleopatra. Caesar's competition with his former friend is not in fact over. He resumes his attempt to win Cleopatra from Antony and hopes that with this prize – gracing his chariot wheels in Rome – he will secure at least a posthumous public triumph over him. He bases his hope of success on his own politic skills and on a familiar male estimate of the opposite sex:

> women are not
> In their best fortunes strong; but want will perjure
> The ne'er-touch'd vestal. (III.xii.29–31)

He does admit that there is a Cleopatra who might despise his proffered comforts and 'in her greatness, by some mortal stroke . . . defeat us' (v.i.64–50). But this is less likely to be Caesar speaking in character than Shakespeare pointing to the significance of the last act.

The key issue, then, in Act V is whether Cleopatra will accommodate Caesar and betray Antony's memory, thus depriving his death of all its nobility (he will simply have died for a triple-turned whore). But her fidelity to Antony presupposes fidelity to herself; if she acts as befits a queen, choosing death rather than debased life, then she will become a royal wife ('Husband, I come'). To say, then, that her suicide loses much of its value because it is prompted to a large extent by a fear of personal degradation is to miss the complex nature of their relationship and the significance of their mutual constancy. Shakespeare in fact is at pains to show that Cleopatra's determination to be noble to herself brings her ever closer to Antony. It was he who brought home to her (and Eros) the horrible shame which Caesar's triumphal march would entail for the defeated,[43] he who inspired her to do 'what's brave, what's noble', rather than accept such a fate. Because she commits suicide for the same two reasons as he did, her fortunes and his mingle entirely.

But if the outcome of the struggle between Casear and Cleopatra seemed a foregone conclusion there would be a serious loss of tension in the last act. Shakespeare had to introduce a degree of uncertainty into the duel. This resolves itself into two questions: Will Cleopatra – whose 'fearful sails' at Actium cannot be forgotten – be resolute enough to overcome her natural instinct for life? And will she be cunning enough to outwit the competitor who holds all the best cards? (For the card metaphor see IV.xiv.19.) She herself raises the first question. In the very speech at Antony's death where she determines to do what's brave and noble in the high Roman fashion, she expresses a countervailing awareness of the natural weakness of her sex. Iras may call her, 'Royal Egypt, Empress', but Cleopatra has fainted and seems to herself to be 'No more but e'en a woman, and commanded / By such poor passion as the maid that milks / And does the meanest chares' (IV.xv.71–5). And she sees that common frailty reflected in the faces of her two attendants; 'How do you women? / What, what! good cheer! Why, how now, Charmian. / My noblest girls! Ah women, women, look ... Good sirs take heart' (lines 82–5). It will be observed, however, that the confession of female weakness instantly becomes an urgent attempt to raise the spirits of her women and to set an example in resolution. This marks the beginning of a process wherein Cleopatra becomes 'a queen over her passion'.

Many, however, have argued that her resolution wavers seriously in the last act and that there are clear signs, in her negotiations with Caesar, of an attempt to discover whether it would be possible to stay alive without being taken to Rome. Whether this argument is correct or not does not materially affect the over-all view of Cleopatra's character and the last act which I am following here; but I am not convinced by it. It arises, I believe, from a failure to recognise just how cunning she actually is in coming from the world's great snare uncaught. It is to read her behaviour exactly as Caesar and his emissaries wish to read it.

The scenes in which Cleopatra negotiates with Caesar, both before Antony's death (through Thyreus) and after, have two things in common. They are gross exhibitions of flattering servility edged with an ironic mockery which the complacency of Caesar cannot penetrate, but which satisfies Cleopatra's acute awareness that the role of 'sweet dependency' which he would like her to play is utterly at variance with her nature. In addition, they are almost immediately preceded or followed by impassioned, and unquestionably sincere, speeches in which she expresses a total commitment to Antony or her noble self. The contrasts are so swift and stark that one cannot reasonably infer from the servile speeches that her resolution has begun to waver; had Shakespeare wished to show a wavering resolution he would have made at least some attempt to graduate the shift from one attitude to the other or to interrelate them subtly. The only acceptable explanation for the repeated contradiction is that the scenes with Caesar are scenes of excellent dissembling and that the contrasting speeches show the authentic Cleopatra. At one point, in fact, we are given the clearest indication of a mask suddenly dropping to reveal the truth: when Proculeius talks his way into the Monument with two guards and seizes her, she tries to stab herself and bursts out angrily with the very message that Caesar does not want to receive: 'Say I would die' (v.ii.70). After this, she has to negotiate directly with Caesar, and a piece of rare dissembling is obviously called for.

For many (though not all) the case against Cleopatra rests heavily on the Caesar–Seleucus scene.[44] It is assumed that Cleopatra is here caught out in a genuine attempt to retain half her treasure and that this proves she would like to go on living. To interpret the incident thus, however, is to invert the meaning explicitly given to it by Plutarch and heavily stressed by his Elizabethan translator, Sir Thomas North, in his marginal gloss: 'Cleopatra finely deceiveth Octavius Caesar, as though she desired to live'.[45] Although Shakespeare does not overtly supply this interpretation by making us privy to Cleopatra's intentions, all the signals suggest that it is the only reasonable one and that we must not draw the same conclusion as Caesar. The incident is preceded (at a distance of forty lines) by Cleopatra's sublime panegyric on 'an Emperor Antony', an expression of grief so profound that it strikes Dolabella's Roman heart at root and prompts him to betray his master; and it is followed instantly by her contemptuous comment (a clear reference to someone who has been fooled): 'He words me, girls, he words me that I should not / Be noble to myself' (v.ii.190–1). The whole conduct of the meeting, moreover, suggests that Cleopatra scripted it from start to finish. It was she who asked for the meeting to take place, she who raises the subject of the treasure and asks Caesar to check the inventory, she who sends for Seleucus to verify what she has written – Caesar clearly was not interested in the treasure and is about to leave well satisfied with *his* performance when she raises the matter. Her peremptory, 'Speak the truth, Seleucus', and the histrionics which follow when he apparently betrays her, complete the impression of a well-rehearsed scene. To interpret the incident exactly as Caesar does is not only to deny the superb cunning which Cleopatra shows in her determination to be noble to Antony and herself; it is also to credit her with quite remarkable stupidity. 'Not know me yet?', she might well ask (again).

Despite the delay in committing suicide, and however we interpret it, Cleopatra in the end triumphs morally over change, Fortune, and Fortune's favourite. Although in her servile posture she says she is 'Fortune's vassal' (v.ii.29), that is precisely what she is not. In this and other respects her identification with Antony becomes more and more pronounced as the end approaches. Antony conjured up the horrors of a Roman triumph in order to involve Eros in his suicide, Cleopatra does the same with Iras (even the names rhyme). Antony felt 'base' because Cleopatra (as he believed) and Eros died before him (IV.xiv.57, 95–9); Cleopatra feels the same about Iras' death (v.ii.298). Antony claimed that he did not 'basely die' and proudly recalled that he was once 'the greatest prince o' th' world' (IV.xv.54–5); Cleopatra puts on her robe and crown and dies 'like a queen' (v.ii.178, 226). Antony 'show'd his back / Above the element he liv'd in' (lines 89–90); Cleopatra becomes 'fire and air' and gives her 'other elements . . . to baser life' (lines 287–8) – daringly symbolised here by the earthy clown and his slime-covered leaves from caves of Nile. Like Antony's death, too, Cleopatra's is a union of contraries. But it is a more complex union: it unites courage and love, firmness and sensuousness, Stoicism and Epicureanism, death and birth, gravity and play, tragedy and comedy, becoming and being. And like all perfect unions it suggests transcendence: an escape from the toils of time into the ecstatic peace of eternity, where all that moves, moves still and is still so.

Caesar I would suggest, is not excluded from the powerful effect of unity with which the play ends; indeed he contributes to it. When at the beginning of Act v he magnanimously acknowledged the greatness of his 'friend and companion in the front of war', and lamented that 'our stars / Unreconcilable should divide our equalness to this' (v.i.44–7), he achieved at that moment a posthumous reconciliation with Antony. Now, although he has been grievously frustrated by Cleopatra, he no longer seeks to debase her, but pays tribute to her royal greatness (lines 333–57). He also abandons his sustained attempt to divide the lovers and tacitly solemnises what Cleopatra has claimed to be a marriage:

> She shall be buried with her Antony;
> No grave upon the earth shall clip in it
> A pair so famous. (lines 355–7).

The word 'clip' echoes Antony's triumphant 'clip your wives, your friends'; it is, moreover, the last of a whole range of synonymous verbs ('joint', 'join', 'buckle', 'shackle', 'rivet', 'bolt up', 'cement', 'solder', 'bind', 'tie', 'keep whole', 'mingle', 'atone') which collectively signal an insistent movement (such as Plutarch the mythographical philosopher would have approved) towards oneness in contrariety. To chart that movement is to be acutely aware of the tragic thrust towards division, conflict, confusion, and total self-loss. Yet the fact remains that the movement towards unity succeeds in spite of tragedy – indeed (and here we recall Ovid), because of it.

Caesar's noble attitude to the dead lovers must not be taken as mere form,[46] for the way in which death can turn contempt into admiration and dislike into love has been a recurrent paradox in this most paradoxical of plays. That death can function as a unifying force is, of course, an idea which compels the imagination to transcend the terrible particulars of tragedy and espouse a more comprehensive vision of human experience. Of Shakespeare's Last Plays, in which that vision is developed and perfected, the play which we might look forward to here is one which (rather awkwardly) roots romance in a framework of history. In *Cymbeline*, the self-division of ancient Britain is ended with the death of its wicked Queen and its willing assimilation into the peace of Caesar Augustus, a peace whose harmony is tuned by the fingers of the powers above (v.v.465–9).

VII

Deciding which, or which combination, of the available historical contexts (literary, historiographical, philosophical, religious, economic, political, scientific) is most pertinent to the interpretation of individual texts is frequently problematic. But it seems clear that there are sound textual, canonical, and literary–historical reasons why we should study *Antony and Cleopatra* in the context of Ovid's *Metamorphoses* and Plutarch's 'Of Isis and Osiris'. And to do so, we have seen, is to uncover a kind of intertextuality by which we are reminded, once more, that Shakespeare's tragic art is radically informed by essentialist notions of a transhistorical human nature and of unchanging laws encoded in universal nature. It is to perceive yet again that Shakespeare's tragic contradictions are not necessarily the product of clashing discourses but should be construed rather as intrinsic to a single, ancient discourse whose governing principle is unity in contrariety and vice versa: a discourse which accommodates constancy and process, closure and discontinuity, myth and history. Wherever he looked in tragedy and tragical history, Shakespeare saw 'self against self', 'kin with kin and kind with kind' confounded, human beings declining to their 'confounding contraries', 'half to half the world oppos'd'. From first to last, his preferred discursive practice led him to root these contradictions in the treacherously double nature of nature or 'kind'. It led him to assume too that an answer to the question, 'How shall we find the concord of this discord?' (*MND*, v.i.60) would be found, if at all, in nature: in the differentiation and the binding of opposites; in a radical human instinct for love and justice.

Notes

1 Introduction: 'Nature's fragile vessel'

1 On the theme of Fortune in medieval and Renaissance tragedy, see Willard Farnham, *The Medieval Heritage of Elizabethan Tragedy* (Berkeley, Calif.: University of California Press, 1936); Frederick Kiefer, *Fortune and Elizabethan Tragedy* (San Marino, Calif.: Huntington Library, 1983).
2 *The Life of the Drama* (1964; repr. New York: Atheneum Press, 1975), p.286.
3 See, for example, R.M. Frye, *Shakespeare: the Art of the Dramatist* (1970; rev. edn London: Allen and Unwin, 1982), pp.114, 120–1.
4 On the hero becoming 'his own antithesis', see Maynard Mack, 'The Jacobean Shakespeare: Some Observations on the Construction of the Tragedies', in *Jacobean Theatre*, SUAS 1, ed. Bernard Harris and John Russell Brown (London: Arnold, 1960), p.34.
5 *Touches of Sweet Harmony: Pythagorean Cosmology and Renaissance Poetics* (San Marino, Calif.: Huntington Library, 1974); *The Cosmographical Glass: Renaissance Diagrams of the Universe* (San Marino, Calif.: Huntington Library, 1977).
6 'In few, *there is no constant existence, neither of our being, nor of the objects*. And we, and our judgement, and all mortall things else, do uncessantly rowle, turne, and passe away ... *Heraclitus* averreth that no man ever entered twise one same river' [Montaigne's italics].' – *The Essayes*, trs. John Florio (London: Dent, 1910), vol.II, p.323.
7 Heninger, *The Cosmographical Glass*, pp.102–10, 184–5.
8 John Orrell, *The Quest for Shakespeare's Globe* (Cambridge: Cambridge University Press, 1983), pp.139–57. Orrell notes that although the *ad quadratum* method of design was an eminently practical device for ensuring correct measurement in an age when there were few accurate measuring instruments, 'it must also have appealed because it suggested the mystery of squaring the circle' (p.117) (the squared circle symbolised the revelation of eternity and infinity within the finite, changing, elemental world). Heninger draws attention to the interplay between the circle and the square as a notable feature of church architecture, and

remarks that it probably had cosmic significance (*The Cosmographical Glass*, p.185); since both the tetrad and the sphere had become symbols of the perfection and equilibrium of God's creation (see Leo Spitzer, *Classical and Christian Ideas of World Harmony* (Baltimore: The Johns Hopkins University Press, 1963), p.67), this seems inarguable. On the cosmic conception of Shakespeare's playhouse, see also Frances Yates, *Theatre of the World* (Chicago: University of Chicago Press, 1969); Kent T.van den Berg, *Playhouse and Cosmos: Shakespearean Theater as Metaphor* (Newark: University of Delaware Press; London and Toronto: Associated University Presses, 1985). Van den Berg argues that the concept of the Elizabethan playhouse as 'a theatre of the world' defined it not only as an architectural emblem of cosmos but also as a heterocosm, a world in itself (pp.32–3).

9 *The State in Shakespeare's Greek and Roman Plays* (New York: Columbia University Press, 1940); *Shakespeare and the Nature of Man* (New York: Macmillan, 1942); *The Elizabethan World Picture* (London: Chatto, 1943).

10 Phillips, chs.7–9; Spencer, p.23 and passim; Tillyard, *Elizabethan World Picture*, pp.7–14; E.M.W. Tillyard, *Shakespeare's History Plays* (London: Chatto, 1944), pp.18–20.

11 Rossiter's influential essay, 'Ambivalence: the Dialectic of the Histories', was first published in his *Angel With Horns* (London: Longmans, 1961) ten years after it was delivered as a lecture at Stratford.

12 See Paul Roubiczek, *Thinking in Opposites: an Investigation of the Nature of Man as Revealed in the Nature of Thinking* (London: Routledge, 1952), p.11.

13 The quoted phrase is from an 'entertainment' or pageant by Middleton and Dekker – *The Works of Thomas Middleton*, ed. A.H. Bullen (London: Nimmo, 1885–7), VII.225 (italics added). See p.199. Compare Donne's reference in 'Good Friday 1613: Riding Westward' to the contrary movements of the heavenly spheres which 'Scarce in a year their natural form obey'.

14 *The Fragments*, trs. Charles M. Bakewell, *Source Book in Ancient Philosophy* (New York: Gordian Press, 1973), pp.30–1.

15 Bakewell, *Source Book*, pp.36–7, 44–7. See also John Burnet, *Greek Philosophy, Part I, Thales to Plato* (London: Macmillan, 1920), pp.48–50, 56, 71–4.

16 Leo Spitzer, however, traces the origin of the concept of *discordia concors* (or *concordia discors*) to Heraclitus (*Classical and Christian Ideas of World Harmony*, p.9). This seems reasonable, since Heraclitus maintained that universal strife is measured, a form of justice and harmony. But there can be no doubt that it was the Empedoclean model of nature (both microcosm and macrocosm) which gave the concept its decisive form and imprinted it in Western culture. Perhaps the most famous early use of the phrase *concordia discors* occurs in Ovid's decidedly Empedoclean account of primal chaos and the formation of cosmos at the beginning of the *Metamorphoses*. For consideration of the ways in which the concept

has been used by some medieval and Renaissance authors, see Donald W. Rowe, *O Love! O Charite!: Contraries Harmonized in Chaucer's 'Troilus'* (Carbondale and Edwardsville: Southern Illinois University Press, 1976), ch.1; Rosamund Tuve, 'A Medieval Commonplace in Spenser's Cosmology', *SP*, 30 (1933), 33–47; Leonard Barkan, *Nature's Work of Art: The Human Body as Image of the World* (New Haven and London: Yale University Press, 1975), pp.163, 166–74, 202–4, 208–10, 257–8 (on *The Faerie Queene*); Earl R. Wasserman, *The Subtler Language: Readings of Neoclassical and Romantic Poems* (Baltimore: The Johns Hopkins Press, 1959), pp.53–61 (on Denham's 'Cooper's Hill').

17 John Read, *Prelude to Chemistry: an Outline of Alchemy, its Literature and Relationships* (London: Bell, 1936), pp.18–21.

18 *Of the Interchangeable Course or Variety of Things in the Whole World*, trs. R[obert]. A[shley] (London, 1594), p.5. The Heraclitean element is stressed in John Norden's verse adaptation of Le Roy, *Vicissitudo Rerum: An Elegiacall Poem of the interchangeable courses and varieties of things in this world* (1600). 'Mutual discord', says Norden, produces fruits, enmity creates desirable change (st.47); 'Yet are the Heavens and the Earth maintain'd / By discord excellent' (st.82); discord is a countercheck, a mean (st.89); 'discord seems a friend and not a foe' (st.92). Sir Thomas Browne, too, although he repeatedly laments the violent contrarieties of the human condition, likes to emphasise the positive dimension of conflict: 'contraries, though they destroy one another, are yet the life of one another'; 'The greatest Balsames doe lie enveloped in the bodies of most powerful Corrosives . . . poysons contain within themselves their owne Antidote'; 'the world, whose divided Antipathies and contrary forces doe yet carry a charitable regard to the whole by their particular discords, preserving the common harmony' (*The Major Works*, ed. C.A. Patrides (Harmondsworth: Penguin Books, 1977), pp.140, 152, 146 (*Religio Medici*)).

19 Fulke Greville, *A Treatie of Warres*, ed. G. Bullough, *The Poems and Dramas* (Edinburgh: Oliver & Boyd, 1939), sts.25, 44. Cf. the prayer to Mars in *The Two Noble Kinsmen*, ed. N.W. Bawcutt (Harmondsworth: Penguin Books, 1977), v.i.62–6: 'O great corrector of enormous times, / Shaker of o'er-rank states, thou grand decider / Of dusty old titles, that healest with blood / The earth when it is sick, and curest and world / O' th' plurisy of people'. This conception of war is not voiced in the Knight's Tale (Shakespeare and Fletcher's source), but it is entirely in keeping with the paradoxical temper of that poem. See chapter 2.

20 See my '*Tamburlaine the Great* and *The Spanish Tragedy:* the Genesis of a Tradition', *HLQ*, 45 (1982), 59–81; *English Renaissance Tragedy* (London: Macmillan; Vancouver: University of British Columbia Press, 1986), pp.6–8, 55–81, 92–9. The quoted phrase in the above sentence is from Pierre de La Primaudaye, *The French Academie*, trs. T. Bowes et al. (London, 1618), p.180.

21 'As all things that move within this general globe are maintained by
agreeing discords: even so of necessitie there must be such a harmonie
betweene the bodie and the soul, and that by the help of the one, the
other subsisteth and abideth, and that through their continuall striving
sometimes the one, and then the other be in the end obeyed'. – Pierre de
La Primaudaye, *The French Academie*, p.4. Cf. Bernardus Silvestris
[twelfth century], *The Cosmographia*, trs. Winthrop Wetherbee (New
York and London: Columbia University Press, 1973), ii.iv.97.

22 Confronting the problem of divine foreknowledge and human freedom,
Sir Kenelm Digby (1603–65) writes: '[God] did frame this world and all
that is in it in such an artificial order, that contrariety and disagreeing
qualities is the only knot of this perfect concord ... A more admirable
order and fuller of divine wisdom cannot be conceived, therefore God
hath also used it in superior creatures, the noblest of which are human
souls; in which one may consider an entire liberty with a constrained
necessity which no way hinder or impeach one other.' – *The Private
Memoirs of Sir Kenelm Digby*, ed. N.H. Nicholas (London: Sanders and
Otley, 1827), pp.124–5.

23 See especially, Spencer, *Shakespeare and the Nature of Man*; John F. Danby,
Shakespeare's Doctrine of Nature: a Study of 'King Lear' (London: Faber,
1949); Hiram C. Haydn, *The Counter-Renaissance* (New York: Scribner's,
1950), esp. ch.8, 'The Counter-Renaissance and the Nature of Nature'.
See also, Marion Bodwell Smith, *Dualities in Shakespeare* (Toronto:
University of Toronto Press, 1966), ch.1; Bernard McElroy, *Shakespeare's Mature Tragedies* (Princeton, N.J.: Princeton University Press,
1973), pp.10–14; George C. Herndl, *The High Design: English Tragedy and
The Natural Law* (Lexington, Ky.: University of Kentucky Press, 1970),
ch.2. The most recent examination of the plays from this standpoint is
Graham Bradshaw's *Shakespeare's Scepticism* (Brighton: Harvester Press,
1987); Bradshaw finds in Shakespeare a fundamental scepticism about
values arising from 'mutually exclusive views of human nature and the
nature of Nature' (p.21). In *Nature and Shakespearian Tragedy* (New York:
Collier Books, 1962), Robert Speaight argues that tragic discord stems
simply from a discrepancy between man and nature (where nature
stands unambiguously for a harmonious order).

24 Robert Grudin, *Mighty Opposites: Shakespeare and Renaissance Contrariety*
(Berkeley, Calif.: University of California Press, 1979).

25 See n.20 above.

26 The quotation is from a note cited in J.P. Sterne, *A Study of Nietzsche*
(Cambridge: Cambridge University Press, 1979), p.57. In *Nietzsche and
Tragedy* (Cambridge: Cambridge University Press, 1981), p.209, M.S.
Silk and J.P. Stern specify as a major source for Nietzsche's Dionysus–
Apollo antithesis (the basis of his tragic theory) 'the insistence of his
hero, "the great Heraclitus", on nature as a relationship between
opposites'. Nietzsche, however, puts both Empedocles and Heraclitus

among 'the ideal philosophers' (*The Complete Works* (London: Allen & Unwin, 1923–7), ɪɪ.79). Hegel regarded Heraclitus as a 'profound philosopher' and said of him (after considering earlier Greek philosophers): 'Here we reach land; there is no proposition of Heraclitus which I have not adopted in my logic . . . [he] takes the dialectic itself as principle . . . the unity of opposites'. Of Empedocles, Hegel remarks: '[his] conception of synthesis holds good to this day' (*Lectures on the History of Philosophy*, vol.ɪ, trs. E.S. Haldane (London: Kegan Paul, Trench, Trubner & Co., 1892), pp.279, 313). C.G. Jung explicitly defined as Heraclitean a controlling concept in his own psychological system: '"Old Heraclitus", who was indeed a very great sage, discovered the most marvellous of all psychological laws, the regulative function of opposites . . . a running contrariwise, by which he meant that, sooner or later, everything runs into its opposite' (*Two Essays in Analytical Psychology*, trs. R.F.C. Hall (London: Routledge, 1953), p.71). D.H. Lawrence cites Heraclitus in *Women in Love* (London: Martin Secker, 1921), a novel whose hero is somewhat tiresomely obsessed by the idea of 'unity in tension' (pp.180, 375), the balancing of polar opposites (p.209); Birkin's ideal, however, may be more Empedoclean than Heraclitean: '"I do think . . . that the world is only held together by the mystic conjunction, the ultimate unison between people – a bond. And the immediate bond is between man and woman"' (p.157). (He might be referring to the world of *Antony and Cleopatra*.)

27 *The Major Works*, ed. Patrides, pp.144–5 (*Religio Medici*).
28 See n.11 above.
29 *The Tragic Sense in Shakespeare* (London: Chatto & Windus, 1960), pp.13–14. Cf. Rabkin, *Shakespeare and the Common Understanding* (New York: The Free Press; London: Collier–Macmillan, 1967), p.11: 'The problems of one play are not the problems of the other. The true constant is the dialectical dramaturgy. It may be the most notable constant in Shakespeare's work.'
30 *Shakespeare's Mature Tragedies*, pp.6–7. Cf. Rabkin, p.12. As mentioned above (n.23), irreconcilable conflicts in valuation are the subject of Graham Bradshaw's *Shakespeare's Scepticism*; 'disjunction' rather than 'complementarity' or 'ambivalence' is his preferred term for this phenomenon.
31 *Shakespeare and the Common Understanding*, pp.69–73, 78, n.37.
32 *Ibid.*, p.25.
33 *Timaeus*, 47a, trs. Benjamin Jowett, *The Dialogues of Plato* (London: Sphere Books, 1970), p.251.
34 Bartholomaeus Anglicus, *De Proprietatibus Rerum*, trs. John of Trevisa (Westminster: Wynkyn de Worde, 1495), yɪ; *The Shepardes Kalender* [trs. from *Le Compost et Kalendrier des Bergiers*], (London, 1570?), ɪɪ. The *Kalender* (printed seventeen times in England between 1495 and 1656) reproduces the emblem from Bartholomaeus' encyclopaedic work. For

discussion of this emblem (with illustrations), see Rosamund Tuve, *Seasons and Months: Studies in a Tradition of Middle English Poetry* (Paris, 1933), pp.122–70; Heninger, *The Cosmographical Glass*, pp.110–12.

35 See Heninger, *The Cosmographical Glass*, p.7. I am much indebted in these paragraphs to Heninger's investigations into Renaissance cosmology.

36 *The Shepardes Kalender*, II.

37 *The Shepardes Kalender*, H1, H4, H5; Heninger, *The Cosmographical Glass*, pp.149, 151–3.

38 *The Shepardes Kalender*, 13, K6–L5. See also Peter Brain, *Galen on Blood-letting: a Study of the Origins, Development and Validity of his Opinions, with a Translation of the Three Works* (Cambridge: Cambridge University Press, 1986), pp.7–8 (where the four humours correspond to the four seasons, and each humour increases during the corresponding season).

39 Allen G. Debus, *Man and Nature in the Renaissance*, Cambridge History of Science Series (Cambridge: Cambridge University Press, 1978), pp.2, 11–15. (Brian Vickers, on the other hand, emphasises the paradoxical ability of Renaissance mathematicians and scientists to operate simultaneously within two traditions – occult and non-occult – which have been recognised as incompatible since the first generation after Newton. See *Occult and Scientific Mentalities in the Renaissance*, ed. Brian Vickers (Cambridge: Cambridge University Press, 1984), pp.8–9.)

40 Title of the English translation (London, 1576) of Marcellus Palingenius Stellatus' popular work, *Zodiacus Vitae*. The Latin text was studied in the Elizabethan grammar school. See T.W. Baldwin, *Shakespeare's 'Small Latine and Lesse Greeke'* (Urbana, Ill.: University of North Carolina Press, 1941), Index s.v. 'Palingenius'.

41 L. White, *Medieval Technology and Social Change* (Oxford: Clarendon Press, 1962), p.122.

42 Webster, *The White Devil*, ed. John Russell Brown, 2nd edn (London: Methuen, 1966), I.ii.286–8.

43 For the above points, see my *English Renaissance Tragedy*, pp.31–4, and p.243, ns.2–6.

44 *Shakespearean Tragedy* (London: Macmillan, 1904), p.24.

45 Hesiod, *Theogony*, 125, 212; Plato, *Timaeus*, 38–9.

46 *Hero and Leander*, III.64. Chapman's italics.

47 Plato, *Timaeus*, 31c–32b; Pierre de La Primaudaye, *The French Academie*, p.728; Baldassare Castiglione, *The Booke of the Courtier*, trs. Sir Thomas Hoby (Everyman edn), p.321; Sir Thomas Elyot, *The Book Named the Governor*, ed. S.E. Lehmberg (London: Dent, 1962), p.78; Richard Barckley, *A Discourse of the Felicitie of Man* (London, 1603), p.541.

48 Catherine Belsey, *Critical Practice* (London and New York: Methuen, 1980), ch.4, and *The Subject of Tragedy: Identity and Difference in Renaissance Drama* (London and New York: Methuen, 1985); Jonathan Dollimore, *Radical Tragedy: Religion, Ideology and Power in the Drama of Shakespeare*

and his Contemporaries (Brighton: Harvester Press, 1984). This Marxist position is characteristic of what has been called 'the new historicism'. In her admirable account of the new trend, 'The New Historicism in Renaissance Studies', *ELR*, 16 (1986), 13–43, Jean E. Howard refers to the widespread attack in contemporary thought on the notion that man possesses a transhistorical core of being. The true exemplar of a new historicism, she believes, will find this radical rejection of an essential human nature inscribed in Renaissance texts and will be able to show, on the basis of her or his interpretation of those texts, that there are no human traits which are not the product of social forces at a particular historical juncture (pp.20–1). For less approving responses to the new historicism, see Edward Pechter, 'The New Historicism and its Discontents', *PMLA*, (102) 1987, 292–303; Frank Lentricchia, *Ariel and the Police: Michel Foucault, William James, Wallace Stevens* (Brighton: Harvester Press, 1988), pp.86–102 ('Foucault's Legacy – A New Historicism?').

49 Nevertheless, in the 1987 production of the play by the Royal Shakespeare Company (directed by Deborah Warner, with Brian Cox in the title role) the character of Titus was projected with arresting force and commanded a remarkable degree of imaginative assent.

50 Contrast Robert S. Miola, who says that Shakespeare's conception of Rome evolves dynamically throughout his career and cannot easily be categorised (*Shakespeare's Rome* (Cambridge: Cambridge University Press, 1983), pp.11–6).

51 Plutarch, *The Philosophie Commonly Called the Morals*, trs. Philemon Holland (London, 1603), pp.1305–7; Natalis Comes [Conti], *Mythologiae* (1567; Hanover, 1619), p.162 (11.6). The contribution of this interpretation of the myth to Renaissance Neoplatonism and iconography has been very fruitfully considered by Edgar Wind in his *Pagan Mysteries in the Renaissance* (London: Faber, 1958), pp.78–88.

52 In the course of an extensive discussion of nature's concordant discord, Leone Ebreo makes the following observations on the nature, relationship, and influences of the two planets: 'astrologers suppose a very great amity between these two planets, saying that Venus tempers with her mild aspect all the warlikeness of Mars'; 'Mars and Venus are contrary only in the character of their natures, Mars being dry, hot and ardent, Venus cool, moist and temperate, unlike the Moon, whose coldness and wetness are excessive. Wherefore they ... agree well together like two contraries which, blended, produce temperate effects; especially in the activities of nutrition and generation, one furnishing the heat, which is the active cause of both, and the other the temperate moisture, which is the passive cause thereof. And although the heat of Mars is excessive in ardour, Venus with her sober coolness tempers and proportions him to these operations' (*The Philosophy of Love*, trs. F. Friedeberg-Seeley and Jean H. Barnes (London: Soncino Press, 1937), pp.154, 175–6). A much more widely read expression of this astrological commonplace

is to be found in the encyclopaedia of Bartholomaeus Anglicus. See *Bartholome his Booke De Proprietatibus Rerum*, trs. Stephen Batman (London, 1582), VIII.25–6. See also the passage from Le Roy cited on p.7.

53 In *The German Ideology* (London: Lawrence and Wishart, 1976), p.248, Marx cites *Timon* in support of his attack on private property. He selects from IV.iii those lines in which Timon condemns gold (lines 27–40, 384–6), but ignores the related condemnation of Nature.

54 That is to say, although Shakespeare reveals a relativistic sense of cultural differences and historical change (as, for example, in *Richard II* and the Roman plays), his view of human nature is fundamentally uniformitarian. In both respects he is akin to those sixteenth- and early seventeenth-century writers who contributed most to the evolution of modern historical consciousness – to Machiavelli, Bodin, Bacon, Hobbes, and even Guicciardiani. Says Machiavelli: 'If the present be compared with the remote past, it is easily seen that in all cities and in all peoples there are the same desires and the same passions as there always were' (*The Discourses*, ed. Bernard Crick (Harmondsworth: Penguin Books, 1974), p.207 (I.39), cf. p.266 (II.i)). For Hobbes the clue to history and politics lies in 'a general inclination of all mankind, a perpetual and restless desire of power after power' (*Leviathan*), a 'natural proclivity of men, to hurt each other, which they derive from their passions but chiefly from a vain esteem of themselves' (*De Cive*) (cited in Paul Avis, *Foundations of Modern Historical Thought: From Machiavelli to Vico* (London: Croom Helm, 1986), pp.97–8). The combination of relativist and uniformitarian elements in Bodin's theory is located, like Shakespeare's, in a context of universal nature. Bodin connects history with man, man with his nature, and nature with the cosmic forces working through the elements: see Jean Bodin, *Method for the Easy Comprehension of History*, trs. Beatrice Reynolds (New York: Columbia University Press, 1945), pp.xiv, xxvi. On uniformitarianism and relativism in Guicciardini and Bacon, see Avis, pp.47–8, 74.

2 A medieval approach: Chaucer's tale of love and strife

1 Elizabeth Salter, *Chaucer: 'The Knight's Tale'* (London: Arnold, 1962), p.31. Of all the 'pessimistic' readings, perhaps the most persuasive is that of A.C. Spearing, ed. *The Knight's Tale* (Cambridge: Cambridge University Press, 1966), pp.47–9.

2 *O Love, O Charite!: Contraries Harmonized in Chaucer's 'Troilus'*, pp.31–44. I take it as evidence in favour of our common conclusions about the poem's cosmological frame of reference, and also on Chaucer's philosophical links in this area with Bernardus Silvestris and Alanus, that I reached them quite independently of Professor Rowe. (The account of the Knight's Tale which follows here is based on my article, 'Cosmo-

logy, Contrariety and The Knight's Tale', *MAE*, 55 (1986), 41–57.)

3 *The Consolation of Philosophy*, Book II, met. 8, in *The Works of Geoffrey Chaucer*, ed. F.N. Robinson, 2nd edn (London and Oxford: Oxford University Press, 1957), p.398.

4 *The Cosmographia*, trs. Winthrop Wetherbee (New York and London: Columbia University Press, 1973), pp.117–19.

5 *Cosmographia*, p.76; Chaucer, *Works*, ed. Robinson, A 2031–4. Chaucer remembers the same passage in the Man of Law's Tale (B1 197): see Robinson's note on A 2031.

6 *Cosmographia*, p.5.

7 Alan of Lille, *The Plaint of Nature*, trs. J.J. Sheridan (Toronto: University of Toronto Press, 1980), pp.67, 148–9, 208, 209–11. Cf. Bernardus Silvestris, *Commentary on the First Books of Virgil's 'Aeneid'*, trs. Earl G. Schrieber and Thomas Maresca (Lincoln, Nebraska and London: University of Nebraska Press, 1979), pp.10–11: 'We read that there are indeed two Venuses, one lawful, and the other the goddess of lust. The lawful Venus is the harmony of the world, that is, the even proportion of things, which some call Astraea, and others call natural justice. This subsists in the elements, in the planets, in living things.'

8 For an example of Froissart's attitude to knightly ransoms, see *Chroniques de J. Froissart*, ed. Siméon Luce, *Société de l'histoire de France* (Paris: Renouard, 1869–78), v.64–5.

9 Hyginus, *Fabulae*, XLVII (Hippolytus), in *Auctores Mythographi Latini*, ed. A. van Staveren (Amsterdam: Luchtmans, 1742), p.111.

10 See W.C. Curry, *Chaucer and the Medieval Sciences*, 2nd edn (London: Allen and Unwin, 1960), pp.145–7.

11 This passage echoes the opening lines of the General Prologue. There are many signs in the Prologue of an intention to make the union and conflict of opposites both a basic idea and an organising principle in the whole collection.

12 See, for example, Ben Jonson's 'To Penshurst', lines 8, 15–16.

13 Contrast the 'eyen rede' of the man-eating wolf in the temple of Mars (A 2048). Red (the colour of wrath, war, and Mars) and white (the colour of peace, love, and Venus) are pointedly combined in the banner of Theseus when he goes to war for the sake of the widows (A 975–76). This harmony of opposites is echoed in the 'subtil gerland' woven by Emelye in the garden, 'party white and red' (A 1053–4).

14 The quoted phrase is from Hans Regnell's *Ancient Views on the Nature of Life: Three Studies in the Philosophies of the Atomists, Plato and Aristotle* (Lund: Lund University Press, 1967). Regnell sees 'dynamic permanence' as a fundamental common principle in all Greek speculations on the nature of man and cosmos. The Greeks envisaged 'a permanent system of relations in a stream of continually renewed components. In this way identity and immutability ... are combined with continual change' (p.141). Dynamic permanence is a central theme in Plato's *Timaeus*, a

work whose ideas were disseminated in the Middle Ages by such authors
as Boethius, Macrobius, Chalcidius, and Bernardus.

15 'Hyle' (ῦλη) – i.e. 'wood', 'forest' – is Aristotle's word for unformed
matter (it is also a variant name for 'Silva' in the *Cosmographia*). 'Silva' is
the word for elemental matter in Chalcidius' *Commentary on Plato's
'Timaeus'*, a work with which Bernardus was very familiar. But Paul
Piehler, *The Visionary Landscape: a Study in Medieval Allegory* (London:
Arnold, 1971), p.75, aptly cites Servius, the fourth-century commen-
tator on Virgil's *Aeneid*, as another likely source: says Servius, 'What the
Greeks call *hyle*, the poets call *silva*, that is, the chaotic mass of the
elements out of which all things are created.'

16 *Cosmographia*, p.67.

17 *MED*, s.v. *list*, 4.

18 In the famous Pythagorean table of contraries, as reported by Aristotle
(*Metaphysics*, I.v), the one and the many, good and evil, and light and
darkness come under the heading of limit and the unlimited. For Pythagoras, limit is that which gives form to the unlimited (from which
everything emerges); it is equivalent to the harmonic mean in music and
to the 'tempering' of contraries that produces health in the body (see
John Burnet, *Greek Philosophy. Part I, Thales to Plato* (London: Macmillan,
1920), pp.44–56). In this nucleus of ideas one can see the matrix of that
identification of physical and moral order with limit, form, harmony,
and a mean that was to become fundamental to Greek philosophy.

19 The circle was a common symbol for the system of elemental interaction
and interdependence. See S.K. Heninger, *Touches of Sweet Harmony:
Pythagorean Cosmology and Renaissance Poetics* (San Marino, Calif.: Huntington Library, 1974), p.167. Pierre de La Primaudaye combines the
circle with that other favourite image of cosmic harmony, the dance, in
his account of the elemental order: 'the elements are agreeable one to
another, with their coupled qualities, whereof each retaineth one
peculiar qualitie to it selfe, agreeth in the other, as by a mean with the
next element. So that the fower elements are (as if each one had two
hands, by which they held one another) as in a rounde daunce' (*The
French Academie*, p.728).

20 Bartholomaeus Anglicus, *On the Properties of Things*, trs. John Trevisa, ed.
M.C. Seymour *et al.* (London: Oxford University Press, 1975), I.479,
481, 491.

21 On the self-reflexive nature of the poem, see Charles Muscatine, *Chaucer
and the French Tradition* (Berkeley and Los Angeles: University of California Press, 1957), pp.178–81; Dale Underwood, 'The First of the
Canterbury Tales', *ELH* 36 (1959), repr. in *Discussions of the Canterbury
Tales*, ed. Charles A. Owen, Jr (Boston: Houghton Mifflin, 1961), p.38.

22 Isidore of Seville, *Etymologiae*, III.iv.3 (after Augustine, *De Libero Arbitrio*,
II.xvi). Cited in Russell A. Peck, 'Number as Cosmic Language', in *By
Things Seen: Reference and Recognition in Medieval Thought*, ed. David L.

Jeffrey (Ottawa, Canada: University of Ottawa Press, 1979), p.48, n.3.
It is possible, of course, that the four-part division of the Knight's Tale –
absent from the Hengwrt MS – is not authorial.

23 Macrobius, *Commentary on the Dream of Scipio*, trs. William Harris Stahl
(New York: Columbia University Press, 1952), p.104, following Plato,
Timaeus, 32a–c.

24 According to Pierre de la Primaudaye (*The French Academie*, pp.728–9),
the number four is 'the roote and foundation of all nature' and 'the
foundation of euerie deepe studie and inuention'. Thus in addition to
the four elements, qualities, and humours, there are the four points of
the earth (East, West, etc.), the four seasons, four kinds of creature
(corporal, vegetable, sensitive, reasonable), four kinds of quantity
(point, length, breadth, depth), four faculties, four moral virtues, four
Evangelists etc. etc. 'It then plainely appeareth, that not without great
mysterie the creator setled fower foundations of all this mundane frame.'
This fourfold schematising of things was all very familiar in the Middle
Ages and the Renaissance. See Vincent Hopper, *Medieval Number Symbolism* (New York: Columbia University Press, 1938), pp.42–3; Peck,
'Number as Cosmic Language', p.77; Heninger, *Touches of Sweet
Harmony*, pp.168–76, and *The Cosmographical Glass*, p.107 ('the universe
is one immense collage of interlocking tetrads'), p.200, n.150.

25 Cf. Chauncey Wood, *Chaucer and the Country of the Stars: Poetic Uses of
Astrological Imagery* (Princeton, N.J.: Princeton University Press, 1970),
pp.75–6; Alan T. Gaylord, 'The Role of Saturn in The Knight's Tale',
CR, 8 (1973), 173–7.

26 Wood, *Chaucer and the Country of the Stars*, pp.72–5, also comments on the
doubleness of the stars; he defines it rather differently, however, and
does not draw the same conclusions.

27 It will be apparent that I do not accept W.C. Curry's view that the
mythology of the poem turns on a conflict between Mars and Saturn,
figured on the human level in the confrontation between Emetreus and
Lycurgus. What is important about these two kings is the way in which
they are used by Chaucer to throw the conflict of opposing forces into
the sharpest relief; this contrasts with Boccaccio, where attention is
distributed quite widely among the princely supporters of Palamon and
Arcite.

28 Hyginus, for example, notes that Harmonia was the offspring of Mars
and Venus; but he does not suggest that Harmonia has any symbolical
significance.

29 Bartholomaeus Anglicus, *On the Properties of Things*, 1.479–82.

30 See especially, B.L. Jefferson, *Chaucer and the Consolation of Philosophy
of Boethius* (Princeton, N.J.: Princeton University Press, 1917), pp.120–
32; Curry, *Chaucer and the Medieval Sciences*, pp.154–63; R.M. Lumiansky,
'Chaucer's Philosophical Knight', *TSE*, 3 (1952), 47–68.

31 For an interpretation of the poem which treats this as central, see A.V.

Schmidt, 'The Tragedy of Arcite: a Reconsideration of the *Knight's Tale*', *EIC*, 19 (1969), 107–17.

32 Cf., for further discussion, A.J. Minnis, *Chaucer and Pagan Antiquity* (Cambridge: Cambridge University Press, 1982), esp. ch.4.

33 See M.R. Ridley, ed., New Arden *Antony and Cleopatra* (London: Methuen, 1954), note on II.v.117–18. His gloss on the allusion to a perspective which I have used above is from Henry Mackenzie, *Religio Stoici* (1665).

34 Ann Thompson, *Shakespeare's Chaucer: a Study in Literary Origins* (Liverpool: Liverpool University Press, 1978), p.168. Her evidence is taken from Caroline Spurgeon, *Five Hundred Years of Chaucer Criticism* (Cambridge: Cambridge University Press, 1925).

35   By her [Concord] the heauen is in his course contained,
    And all the world in state unmoued stands,
    As their Almightie maker first ordained,
    And bound them with inuiolable bands;
    Else would the waters ouerflow the lands,
    And fyre deuoure the aire, and hell them quight,
    But that she holds them with her blessed hands. (IV.x.35)

36   As when *Dan Aeolus* in great displeasure,
    For losse of his deare loue by Neptune hent,
    Sends forth the winds out of his hidden threasure,
    Upon the sea to wreake his fell intent;
    They breaking forth with rude unruliment,
    From all the foure parts of heauen doe rage full sore,
    And tosse the deepes, and teare the firmament,
    And all the world confound with wide uprore,
    As if instead thereof they *Chaos* would restore. (IV.ix.23)

37 Important characters in the allegorical narrative are Ate (the Greek goddess of dissension), who holds the House of Discord (i.19–30); Concord, who dwells in the Temple of Venus, and who binds and tempers the brothers Love and Hate (x.31–4); and Venus herself (x.39–58).

38 Alastair Fowler, *Spenser and the Numbers of Time* (London: Routledge, 1964), p.24.

39 Ibid., p.26. See also A.K. Hieatt, *Chaucer Spenser Milton: Mythopoetic Continuities and Transformations* (Montreal and London: McGill–Queen's University Press, 1975), p.79.

40 A.C. Hamilton, *The Structure of Allegory in 'The Faerie Queene'* (Oxford: Clarendon Press, 1961), p.165; Fowler, *Spenser and the Numbers of Time*, p.181.

41 See my *English Renaissance Tragedy*, pp.6–7, 55–81, 92–9.

42 Thompson, *Shakespeare's Chaucer*, p.88.

43 Cf. John Mebane, 'Structure, Source, and Meaning in *A Midsummer Night's Dream*', *TSLL*, 24 (1982), 258, 262, 265. Neither Ann Thompson

nor E. Talbot Donaldson (*The Swan at the Well: Shakespeare Reading Chaucer* (New Haven and London: Yale University Press, 1985)) considers the philosophical connection between the poem and the play.

44 See also Hopper, *Medieval Number Symbolism*, p.39; Heninger, *Touches of Sweet Harmony*, pp.78–9, 201–3.

45 *The Morals*, trs. Philemon Holland, p.812.

46 Fowler, *Spenser and the Numbers of Time*, p.45.

47 Harold F. Brooks, ed. *A Midsummer Night's Dream*, The Arden Shakespeare (London: Methuen, 1979), p.cxxvi.

48 C.S. Lewis, *The Discarded Image: An Introduction to Medieval and Renaissance Literature* (Cambridge: Cambridge University Press, 1964), pp.134–5; John Erskine Hankins, *Backgrounds of Shakespeare's Thought* (Brighton: Harvester Press, 1978), pp.42–7.

49 For an admirable discussion of sources, see Brooks's Arden edn, pp.lviii–lxxxviii. E. Talbot Donaldson (*The Swan at the Well*, pp.34–6) notes the emphasis on Theseus' amorous past as a difference between the play and the poem, but does not draw the same conclusions from this emphasis as I do; nor does he consider Theseus' future.

50 In the Legend of Ariadne (*The Legend of Good Women*), Theseus swears repeatedly to everlasting truth and constancy in his love for Ariadne, and promises to marry her (Chaucer, *Complete Works*, ed. Robinson, F 2053–74, 2103–23, 2139). But when he has escaped from the labyrinth with her help, he promptly 'as a traytour stal his wey' (F 2174). In the last lines of the poem Ariadne condemns him as a 'false lover [that] can begyle / His trewe love' (F 2226–7). As Chaucer indicates (F 2220), this view of Theseus derives from Ovid's Epistle of Ariadne in the *Heroides*. In Book VIII of the *Metamorphoses*, too, Ovid comments on the cruelty with which Theseus abandoned Ariadne.

51 See David Ormerod, '*A Midsummer Night's Dream*, the Monster in the Labyrinth', *ShakS*, 11 (1978), 39–52; M.E. Lamb, '*A Midsummer Night's Dream*: the Myth of Theseus and the Minotaur', *TSLL*, 31 (1979), 479–91.

52 As, for example, in Ovid's *Heroides* (Epistle of Phaedra to Hippolytus).

53 In Seneca's *Hippolytus* Phaedra complains: 'Behold, fled is my love afar and keeps his bridal bed as is the wont of Theseus . . . there in the depths of Acheron he seeks adultery and an unlawful bed, this father of Hippolytus.' – *Seneca's Tragedies* ed. and trs. Frank Justus Miller, Loeb Classical Library (London: Heinemann; New York: Putnam, 1916), I.327. The Elizabethan translation of John Studley gives added emphasis to Theseus' infidelities. Accusing him of 'lawless wedlock's ravishments', Phaedra complains: 'My husband lo, a runnagate is gon from mee his Wyfe, / Yet Theseus still performes his Othe alike unto his spouse / As earst to Ariadne, when hee falsifide his vowes.' – *Seneca, His Tenne Tragedies*, ed. Thomas Newton, The Tudor Translations (London: Constable; New York: Knopf, 1927), I.139–40.

54 *Lives of the Noble Grecians and Romans*, trs. Sir Thomas North, The Tudor Translations (London: Nutt, 1895), 1.58–9. In his summary comparison of Theseus and Romulus, Plutarch speaks harshly of the former's sexual relations. His 'faults touching women and ravishments' had 'no shadowe and culler of honestie' (p.116). His 'mariages did get neither love nor kynred of any one person, but rather they procured warres, enmities, and the slaughter of their citizens [i.e. the Athenians]'. Plutarch thus ends his biography with the ironical observation that Theseus' reputation would be well served *if* many of his deeds could be found 'false, and but fables' (p.117). This may account for the lofty and (dramatically ironic) manner in which Shakespeare's Theseus expresses disbelief in 'These antique fables' (v.i.3).

55 *Seneca's Tragedies*, ed. and trs. Miller, 1.423.

56 Ed. *A Midsummer Night's Dream*, pp.lxii–lxiii, 139–44.

57 Ed. *A Midsummer Night's Dream*, p.39, note on II.i.195.

58 Ibid., p.19 (note on I.i.247–51), p.141.

59 Ibid., p.lxiii.

60 See my *English Renaissance Tragedy*, ch.2.

61 See Harriet Hawkins, *Likenesses of Truth in Elizabethan and Jacobean Drama* (Oxford: Clarendon Press, 1972), pp.27–38.

62 *English Renaissance Tragedy*, pp.195–8.

63 Ibid., Index, s.v. 'labyrinth'.

3 *Romeo and Juliet*

1 Giulio Ferretti, *Equitis et comitis lateranensis Palatii consilia et tractatus* (1562), cited in Frederick R. Bryson, *The Sixteenth Century Italian Duel* (Chicago: University of Chicago Press, 1938), p.xxiii. Cf. M.H. Keen, *The Laws of War in the Late Middle Ages* (London: Routledge, 1965), pp.8–9.

2 Marion Bodwell Smith, *Dualities in Shakespeare* (Toronto: Toronto University Press, 1966), pp.79–109.

3 Robert Grudin, *Mighty Opposites: Shakespeare and Renaissance Contrariety* (Berkeley, Calif.: University of California Press, 1979), pp.36–40.

4 For discussion of the comic element, see Nicholas Brooke, *Shakespeare's Early Tragedies* (London: Methuen, 1968), pp.87–94, 98, 104; Rosalie L. Colie, *Shakespeare's Living Art* (Princeton, N.J.: Princeton University Press, 1974), pp.56–70; Susan Snyder, *The Comic Matrix of Shakespeare's Tragedies* (Princeton, N.J.: Princeton University Press, 1979), pp.56–70.

5 Philip Edwards, *Shakespeare and the Confines of Art* (London: Methuen, 1968), p.80.

6 The play's relation to lyric and Petrarchan tradition has been much discussed. See especially Colie, *Shakespeare's Living Art*, pp.56–70; A.J. Earl, '*Romeo and Juliet* and the Elizabethan Sonnets', *English*, 27 (1978), 99–119; Jill L. Levenson, 'The Definition of Love: Shakespeare's

Phrasing in *Romeo and Juliet*', *ShakS*, 15 (1979), 21–36; Brian Gibbons, ed. *Romeo and Juliet* (London: Methuen, 1980), pp.42–52.

7 *The Icy Fire: Six Studies in European Petrarchism* (Cambridge: Cambridge University Press, 1969), p.8. For examples of this paradox, see Spenser's *Amoretti*, Sonnets XIV, XLIX, LXIX.

8 Cf. Harry Levin, 'Form and Formality in *Romeo and Juliet*', *SQ*, 10 (1960), 6–9.

9 The whole conception of this scene derives from Kyd's *Spanish Tragedy*, II.ii, II.iv. See my *English Renaissance Tragedy* (London: Macmillan; Vancouver: University of British Columbia Press, 1986), pp.74–5, and below, p.147.

10 The gentle and the violent hands are important images also in *Julius Caesar* (p.84), *Macbeth* (p.203.), and *Titus Andronicus*.

11 T.J.B. Spencer, ed. *Romeo and Juliet* (Harmondsworth: Penguin Books, 1967), p.30.

12 I.v.132–3; III.ii.138; v.iii.92–6, 102–8.

13 See Ovid, *Metamorphoses*, v.386–571. The agreement whereby Proserpina (Persephone) was allowed to return to her mother Ceres from the underworld for six months of each year constitutes a mythical explanation of seasonal change.

14 The nineteenth-century critic, Bernhard Ten Brink, gives an excellent account of this aspect of the play's technique. See his *Five Lectures on Shakespeare*, trs. Julia Franklin (London: Bell, 1895), pp.130–8.

15 For an elucidation of the poem's complex numerological design, see A.K. Hieatt's pioneer study, *Short Time's Endless Monument: the Symbolism of Numbers in Spenser's 'Epithalamion'* (New York: Columbia University Press, 1960).

16 Martin Ingram, *Church Courts, Sex and Marriage in England 1570–1640* (Cambridge: Cambridge University Press, 1988), pp.136–8.

17 'Violence' in the sense of 'haste', 'speed', is not recorded in *OED*; for examples, see Chapman, *Hero and Leander*, III.59–64; *Hamlet*, v.ii.289–90; Middleton and Rowley, *The Changeling*, ed. N.W. Bawcutt (London: Methuen, 1961), I.i.191. For discussion of *Romeo and Juliet* as a tragedy of 'the unguarded haste of youth', see Brents Stirling, *Unity in Shakespearian Tragedy: the Interplay of Theme and Character* (New York: Gordian Press, 1966), pp.10–25. As suggested below, however, the haste / patience polarity is not identical with that of youth and age.

18 See Gary M. McCown, '"Runnawayes Eyes" and Juliet's Epithalamium', *SQ*, 27 (1976), 165–70. McCown details several inversions of epithalamic convention in the soliloquy, but does not touch on the whole notion of timeliness. Brooke, *Shakespeare's Early Tragedies*, p.101, points out that there is a notable absence in Juliet's epithalamium of all reference to fertility and growth.

19 McCown, pp.150–9, argues against identifying Juliet's 'runaway' as Phaeton, pointing out that 'runaway' or 'fugitive' was an epithet

conventionally applied to Cupid. I would contend, however, that in its poetic and dramatic context 'runaway' functions as a pun linking blind Cupid with reckless Phaeton..

20 See M.C. Bradbrook, *Shakespeare and Elizabethan Poetry* (London: Chatto & Windus, 1951), p.109.

21 On this aspect of the play's meaning, see especially M.M. Mahood, *Shakespeare's Wordplay* (London: Methuen, 1957), pp.66–9, 72.

22 The problem of fate and character, innocence and guilt, is closely related to the 'curious wavering between moralistic and romantic interpretations of love suicides' found in much of the fiction and drama of the Elizabethan and Jacobean period. See Rowland Wymer, *Suicide and Despair in the Jacobean Drama* (Brighton: Harvester Press, 1986), pp.113–18.

4 *Julius Caesar*

1 John Nichols, *The Progresses and Public Processions of Queen Elizabeth* (London: Nichols, 1823), III.552–3.

2 Peter Clark, ed. *The European Crisis of the 1590's* (London: Allen & Unwin, 1985), p.6. Concerning the year 1599, M.C. Bradbrook says: 'Unease, discouragement and above all suspense and tension must have been the mood', *Shakespeare the Craftsman* (London: Chatto & Windus, 1969), p.115.

3 R.B. Outhwaite, 'Dearth, the English Crown and the "Crisis of the 1590's"', in Clark, ed. *The European Crisis of the 1590's*, p.27.

4 See Mervyn James, *English Politics and the Concept of Honour, 1485–1642*, Past and Present, Supplement no. 3 (Cambridge: Cambridge University Press, 1978); repr. in James, *Society, Politics and Culture: Studies in Early Modern England* (Cambridge: Cambridge University Press, 1986), pp.308–415.

5 See Arthur B. Ferguson, *The Chivalric Tradition in Renaissance England* (Washington: Folger Shakespeare Library; London and Toronto: Associated University Presses, 1986), esp. ch.4.

6 See Mervyn James, 'At the Crossroads of the Political Culture: the Essex Revolt of 1601' in his *Society, Politics and Culture*, p.423.

7 William Camden, *Historie of Elizabeth the Queene of England* (London, 1630), p.170.

8 James, *Society, Politics and Culture*, p.332.

9 Thomas Birch, *Memoirs of the Reign of Queen Elizabeth* (London: Millar, 1754), II.481.

10 Malcolm Vale, *War and Chivalry: Warfare and Aristocratic Culture in England, France and Burgundy at the End of the Middle Ages* (London: Duckworth, 1981), pp.19, 23.

11 T.J.B. Spencer, 'Shakespeare and the Elizabethan Romans', *SQ*, 10 (1957), 28; Peter Ure, ed. *Shakespeare: Julius Caesar: a Casebook* (London:

Macmillan, 1969), p.13; A.D. Nuttall, *A New Mimesis: Shakespeare and the Representation of Reality* (London and New York: Methuen, 1983), pp.98–113; Bradbrook, *Shakespeare the Craftsman*, p.101.

12 T.S. Dorsch, ed. *Julius Caesar*, New Arden Shakespeare (London: Methuen, 1955), p.xxvi. Richard G. Moulton, *Shakespeare as a Dramatic Artist* (Oxford: Clarendon Press, 1897) found quadruple character grouping (statuesque and pictorial in effect) to be an outstanding feature of the play: 'the four leading figures, all on the grandest scale, have the elements of their characters thrown into relief by comparison with one another' (pp.168–9).

13 Ugo Ruggieri, *Dürer*, trs. Murtha Baca (New York: Barron, 1979), p.56 and plate 39. It was Dürer's friend and first biographer, Johannes Neudörffer, who first explained that the intention in this diptych was to depict 'a sanguine, a choleric, a phlegmatic, and a melancholic' individual. The individualised types are easily identifiable (left to right: sanguine, phlegmatic, choleric, melancholic). This tense and compact painting communicates a superb impression of human difference and variety.

14 Shakespeare picked up the suggestion for his humoral pattern from Plutarch, who describes Cassius as choleric and Brutus as melancholic. Shakespeare's portrayal of the four leading characters directly or indirectly accommodates the following points, all made in standard descriptions of the humours and humoral types: (1) the melancholy man suffers from fear and sleeplessness, aggravates his distemperature by exposing himself to the unhealthy night air; shuns all company (even of those near to him), seeks out deserted places such as orchards and gardens, and walks moodily with his arms crossed; (2) the choleric man is lean, shrewd, envious, eloquently bitter in his speech, 'by nature hot and burning, like to fire' (La Primaudaye), impatient, and vengeful; (3) the sanguine is amiable, magnanimous, cheerful, fond of music – although when corrupt, his humour is the most dangerous of all; (4) the phlegmatic is often fat and subject to palsies and feebleness of the limbs; he is sluggish and 'not ... easily mooued' (La Primaudaye), and since his humour has the nature of water, 'he dreameth and hath sodain appearance of waters and rain, and of ... swimming in cold water' (Batman). Phlegm is usually dominant in age. See Levinus Lemnius, *The Touchstone of Complexions*, trs. Thomas Newton (London, 1581), fols. 65, 99, 143; *Bartholome His Booke De Proprietatibus*, trs. Batman, fols. 29–33; La Primaudaye, *The French Academie*, pp.457, 524; Timothy Bright, *A Treatise of Melancholy* (London, 1586), pp.33–8, 132, 214; Robert Burton, *The Anatomy of Melancholy*, ed. Holbrook Jackson, Everyman Library (London: Dent, 1932; repr. 1961), 1.9, 237–62, 395–6. See also John W. Draper, *The Humors and Shakespeare's Characters* (Durham, N.C.: North Carolina University Press, 1945); Lawrence Babb, *The Elizabethan Malady: a Study of Melancholia in English Literature*

from 1580 to 1642 (East Lansing: State University of Michigan Press, 1951).

15 The relevant section of Platter's account of his visit to England is reprinted (from *Anglia* XXII [1899], 458) in the Arden edition of the play, p.166, and in the Oxford *Julius Caesar*, ed. Arthur Humphreys (Oxford: Oxford University Press, 1984), p.1. (This chapter incorporates material on the humours and the symbolism of number that is more fully developed in my article, 'The Numbering of Men and Days: Symbolic Design in *The Tragedy of Julius Caesar*', *SP*, 81 (1984), 372–93.)

16 T.S. Dorsch, ed. *Julius Caesar*, p.lxx; Bernard Beckermann, *Shakespeare at the Globe* (New York: Macmillan, 1962) p.95; Andrew Gurr, *The Shakespearean Stage* (Cambridge: Cambridge University Press, 1970), pp.98–100.

17 *Lives of the Noble Grecians and Romans*, trs. Sir Thomas North, v.30, 71; VI.237; 'The Fortune of the Romans', *Moralia*, ed. Frank Cole, Loeb Classical Library (Cambridge, Mass.: Harvard University Press, 1936), IV.341–2, 363. The idea that Fortune and divine power collaborated in making Augustan Rome a source of stability in a world of change does not originate with Plutarch but can be found in earlier historians: see C.P. Jones, *Plutarch and Rome* (Oxford: Clarendon Press, 1971), pp.67–71. The idea is also enshrined in Ovid's panegyric address to Augustus at the end of the *Metamorphoses* – a fact of enormous importance in any consideration of Renaissance attitudes to Octavius and the events which brought him to power. See chapter 9.

18 *Shakespeare's Appian*, ed. Ernest Schanzer (Liverpool: Liverpool University Press, 1956), pp.5–9.

19 *The Roman Histories*, trs. E.M.B.[olton] (London, 1619), pp.439, 448–9.

20 *The thre bokes of Cronicles*, trs. Walter Lynne (London, 1550).

21 *An Historicall Collection of the Continuall Factions, Tumults, and Massacres of the Romans and Italians during the Space of one hundred and twentie yeares next before the peaceable Empire of Augustus Caesar* (London, 1601), pp.13, 18, 209. This work was completed in 1584 and 'of others some times read' (Preface).

22 Parallel to the citizens is the conspirator Ligarius, his 'heart new fir'd' by Brutus – 'To do I know not what' (II.i.332–3).

23 Cf. G. Wilson Knight, *The Imperial Theme* (London: Methuen, 3rd edn, 1951), p.78: '"evil" ... [derives] its existence from the clash of two positive goods: love and honour'.

24 Ligarius is by no means the last recruit in Plutarch.

25 Cf. Antony's reference in *Antony and Cleopatra* to 'the mad Brutus' (III.xi.38).

26 Reuben Brower, *Hero and Saint: Shakespeare and the Graeco-Roman Heroic Tradition* (Oxford: Clarendon Press, 1971), pp.171–7.

27 *The Book of the Courtier*, trs. Sir Thomas Hoby, p.69.

28 *The Renaissance Hamlet: Issues and Responses in 1600* (Princeton, N.J.: Princeton University Press, 1984), pp.171–7.

29 For a full account of the subject see Curtis Brown Watson, *Shakespeare and the Renaissance Concept of Honor* (Princeton, N.J.: Princeton University Press, 1960). Brown (pp.5, 11–12) finds 'a basic duality, a deep seated ambivalence' at the heart of Renaissance attitudes to honour, this arising from the twin notions of honour as self-esteem and as social esteem. The two are compatible, but the individual may come to feel that honour's self-esteem is a priceless personal possession which can only be preserved by resisting society's judgements. See also Norman Council, *When Honour's at the Stake: Ideas of Honour in Shakespeare's Plays* (London: Allen & Unwin, 1973), pp.27–9.

30 Brutus' domineering will can be detected in Plutarch's narrative but is nowhere acknowledged by him. He contrasts the motives of Antony and Octavius unfavourably with those of Brutus, saying that whereas their sole desire was 'to overcome, and raigne, Brutus sought only to restore freedom to his country' (*Lives*, VI.229).

31 In Plutarch this disagreement is between Cassius and Brutus, not Antony and Octavius (*Lives*, VI.222).

32 With characteristic economy and adroitness, Shakespeare has transferred to the conspirators a contradiction imputed by Plutarch to the people. Referring to their applause when Caesar refuses the crown, he remarks: 'And this was a wonderfull thing, that they suffered all things subjects should doe by commaundment of their kings; and yet they could not abide the name of a king, detesting it as the utter destruction of their liberty' (VI.13).

33 See Kenneth Muir, *Shakespeare's Sources* (London: Methuen, 1977), p.123; Humphreys, ed., *Julius Caesar*, p.119, note on lines 9–28.

34 See R.G. Moulton, *Shakespeare as a Dramatic Artist*, pp.185–201.

35 Plutarch imputed this particular change to Calphurnia and not to Caesar. Again, Shakespeare appropriates and redistributes Plutarch's details to fit his own interpretation.

36 The pun is another Plutarchan morsel, this time endowed with a totally un-Plutarchan meaning. Plutarch says that the citizens were delighted when Flavius and Marullus pulled the diadems off Caesar's statues, and 'called them Brutes: bicause of Brutus, who had in old time driven the kinges out of Rome'. Caesar, however, was displeased with the tribunes 'and called them Bruti, and Cumani, to witte, beastes and fooles' (V.62–3). Although notably scrupulous in acknowledging both the virtues and defects of the principal characters (especially Caesar, Antony, and Cassius), Plutarch would never have allowed the noble Brutus to be the object of such a pun.

37 Plutarch, *Lives*, VI.188. In *Tragic Form in Shakespeare* (Princeton, N.J.: Princeton University Press, 1972), pp.106–9, Ruth Nevo argues persuasively on grounds of dramatic consistency against interpreting

Cassius' soliloquy as the expression of a cynical determination to corrupt Brutus' nobility.

38 See I.ii.79, 256; I.iii.79 (cf. 86); II.i.234; II.ii.28; III.ii.216 (cf. III.iii.131); IV.iii.128. The recurrent question is about meaning in the sense both of significance and intention; this reflects Brutus' problem – how to infer from Caesar's past and present performance his likely response to kingship. The problem is introduced in I.ii. as a distinctively semiotic one, replete with a reporter who suffered from ignorance of Greek. (This fine and famous point was improbably inspired by Plutarch's remark [*Lives*, v.67] that Casca *spoke* Greek just before the assassination.)

39 I.ii.215–86; I.iii.32–78, 132–3; II.i.2–3, 42–58, 72–5, 234–308; III.15–26; IV.ii.15–27; V.i.1–12; V.iii.15–35, 80–4.

40 See Macrobius, *Commentary on the Dream of Scipio*, trs. Stahl, p.98; Vincent Hopper, *Medieval Number Symbolism* (New York: Columbia University Press, 1938), pp.77–8, 101, 112, 114; Russell A. Peck, 'Number as Cosmic Language', p.78; Alistair Fowler, *Spenser and the Numbers of Time* (London: Routledge, 1964), p.53, *Triumphal Forms: Structural Patterns in Elizabethan Poetry* (Cambridge: Cambridge University Press, 1970), pp.151–4.

41 The exact number of conspirators is not indicated in Plutarch, but it far exceeds eight. Appian names fifteen conspirators, Suetonius speaks of more than sixty.

42 According to Plutarch, Caesar's triumph celebrating the victory over Pompey's sons took place in October.

43 On Night, Erebus, and Chaos, see pp.16 and 151.

44 Humphreys, ed., *Julius Caesar*, p.135 (note on line 107) observes that there are two errors in Casca's speech: dawn does not break in the south in mid-March (as Casca asserts) but in the east; and it does not break before 3 a.m. Humphreys ascribes these errors to Shakespeare rather than to Casca.

45 'But the ordinaunce of the kalender, and reformation of the yeare, to take away all confusion of time, being exactly calculated by the Mathematicians, and brought to perfection, was a great commoditie unto all men. For the Romanes using then the auncient computacion of the yeare, had not only such incertainty and alteration of the moneth and times, that the sacrifices and yearly feastes came by little and little to seasons contrary for the purpose they were ordained: but also in the revolution of the sunne (which is called Annus Solaris) no other nation agreed with them in account: and of the Romaines them selves, only the priests understood it. And therefore when they listed, they sodainley (no man being able to controll them) did thrust in a moneth, above their ordinary number ... But Caesar committing this matter unto the Philosophers, and best expert Mathematicians at that time, did set foorth an excellent and perfect Kalender, more exactly calculated, then any other that was before: the which the Romanes do use until this

present day, and doe nothing erre as others, in the difference of the time. But his enemies notwithstanding that envied his greatness, did not sticke to finde fault withall' (*Lives*, v.60).

46 *Shakespeare's Appian*, ed. Schanzer, p.52; Carion, *Cronicles*, fol. lxxxiv. Cf. Sir Thomas Elyot, *The Governor*, p.86, where Caesar is lauded as the learned emperor who 'first found the order of our calendar'.

47 See Achsah Guibbory, *The Map of Time: Seventeenth Century English Literature and Ideas of Pattern in History* (Urbana and Chicago: University of Illinois Press, 1986). Guibbory finds that there were three major conceptions of the shape of history in the seventeenth century: the idea of decay; the cyclical conception; and the idea of progress (p.5). Among the various exponents of the cyclical theory cited by Guibbory are Jean Bodin and Machiavelli. Says Bodin: 'By some eternal law of nature the path of change seems to go in a circle' – *Method for the Easy Comprehension of History*, trs. Beatrice Reynolds (New York: Columbia University Press, 1945), p.302. According to Leonard F. Dean, the *Methodus* 'was probably read by most serious students of history between 1580 and 1625' ('Bodin's *Methodus* in England before 1625', *SP*, 39 (1942), 166). And as I pointed out in 'The Numbering of Men and Days: Symbolic Design in the Tragedy of *Julius Caesar*', (*SP*, 81 (1984), 377), 'Bodin's consciousness of the tide of mutability with which all nations must contend is balanced by a belief that mutability follows a cyclical pattern, and that to some extent the pattern is intelligible and therefore predictable in the light of Pythagorean numerology.' See *Method*, pp.147–52, 222–36, 316–19. *Julius Caesar* hints at no such belief in prediction by numerology; but it is pertinent nonetheless to note that a well-known theorist of history linked historical change and pattern to cosmic number.

48 Guibbory, *The Map of Time*, pp.10–11.

5 Hamlet

1 The phrase is William Empson's and refers to Hamlet's inability to decide why he delays – '*Hamlet* When New', *SR* 61 (1953), 21.

2 For recent accounts of the critical history of the play, see Michael Hattaway, *Hamlet*, The Critics' Debate Series (London: Macmillan, 1987), pp.11–65; Cedric Watts, *Hamlet*, Harvester New Critical Introductions Series (Hemel Hempstead: Harvester-Wheatsheaf, 1988), pp.xxiii–xlvi.

3 iii.ii.135. Consider also: 'What does this mean, my lord?' (i.iii.7); 'What may this mean . . .?' (i.iv.51); 'That's not my meaning' (ii.i.31); 'What means your lordship?' (iii.i.106); 'Do you think I meant country matters?' (iii.ii.112); 'What means this, my lord?' (line 133); 'Belike this show imports the argument of the play' (line 136); 'There's matter in these sighs, these profound heaves, / You must translate; 'tis fit we

understand them' (IV.i.1–2); 'what imports this song?' (IV.v.26); 'when they ask you what it means, say you this' (lines 44–5); 'What should this mean?' (IV.vii.48); 'Is't not possible to understand in another tongue? ... What imports the nomination of this gentleman?' (V.ii.123–7).

4 The significance of the parallel between Brutus and Hamlet located in the 'brute' pun has been noted by Harold C. Goddard, *The Meaning of Shakespeare* (Chicago and London: Chicago University Press, 1951), pp.339–40.

5 Cf. Peter Alexander, *Hamlet, Father and Son* (Oxford: Clarendon Press, 1955), pp.142–3. (Alexander mentions the union of opposites in Hamlet's character, but ignores the conflict.)

6 We have already seen Shakespeare's keen interest in this conception of revenge in Antony's funeral oration in *Julius Caesar* (pp.83–4).

7 The force of an appeal to filial affection in the call for revenge is something which interested Shakespeare as early as *Titus Andronicus*. Grotesquely foregrounded, the appeal functions there as part of Shakespeare's attempt to locate the origins of tragedy in the treacherous doubleness of nature or 'kind' (see pp.21–3). Says Tamora to her sons: 'Revenge it, as you love your mother's life, / Or be ye henceforth not call'd my children.' Having stabbed Bassianus, Demetrius responds: 'This is witness that I am thy son' (II.iii.114–16).

8 Cf. *MND*, I.i.14–15: 'Turn Melancholy forth to funerals ... The pale companion is not for our pomp.'

9 Cf. *Tro*.v.ii.137–58.

10 Cf. Maurice Charney, *Style in 'Hamlet'* (Princeton, N.J.: Princeton University Press, 1969), pp.6–30.

11 The frown of Mars and the martial man was as conventional as his anger and his association with blood, fire, and the colour red. See *MV*, III.ii.85 ('frowning Mars') and *Tamburlaine the Great*, ed. Gill, Pt.I,II.i.21; III.ii.68.

12 Cf. Peter Mercer, *'Hamlet' and the Acting of Revenge* (London: Macmillan, 1987), pp.227–37.

13 Cf. Nigel Alexander, *Poison, Play and Duel: a Study of Hamlet* (London: Routledge, 1971), p.81. Much of my interpretation echoes Alexander's emphasis on 'the conflict of interest between the aggressive drives and the power of affection and human love and understanding'.

14 Watts, *Hamlet*, p.34.

15 John Lawlor, *The Tragic Sense in Shakespeare* (London: Chatto & Windus, 1960), p.57.

16 Cf. Alexander, *Poison, Play and Duel*, p.64; Watts, *Hamlet*, pp.54–5.

17 See p.48 above. The labyrinth was a favourite symbol in the Renaissance for error and moral and intellectual perplexity. See John M. Steadman, *The Maze and the Labyrinth: Discourse and Certitude in Milton and His Near-Contemporaries* (Berkeley/Los Angeles/London: University of California Press, 1984), pp.6–7, 12–13. There may be some dramatic

irony in Hamlet's reply ('Very like, very like') to Horatio's comment on the appearance of the ghost: 'It would have much amaz'd you' (I.ii. 235–6): he could hardly realise just how 'amaz'd' he will be. For further references to 'amazement' see II.ii.558 and III.ii.318. Hamlet's predicament recalls a remark of the Bastard in *King John*: 'I am amaz'd, methinks, and lose my way / Among the thorns and dangers of the world' (IV.iii.140–1).

18 *Shakespeare's Scepticism*, p.123.

19 Charney, *Style in 'Hamlet'*, p.120, citing Florio and Cotgrave.

20 Charney, *Style in 'Hamlet'*, p.133, n.6, pertinently observes that *Hamlet* has more 'o'er' and 'over' prefixes than any other play of Shakespeare's; they are indicative mostly of excess.

21 George T. Wright, 'Hendiadys in *Hamlet*', *PMLA*, 96 (168–93). Earlier discussions of hendiadys in *Hamlet* are R.A. Foakes, '*Hamlet* and the Court of Elsinore', *ShS*, 9 (1956), 36, 43 (n.5); Harry Levin, *The Question of 'Hamlet'* (New York: Oxford University Press, 1959), p.49; Andrew Gurr, *Hamlet and the Distracted Globe* (Edinburgh: Sussex University Press, 1978), pp.47–8, 63. Foakes notes that there are at least 240 doublets in *Hamlet* and says that they give weight, amplification, and a slight pompousness to the style, thus contributing to an impression of the court as a place 'of ostensible stateliness and nobility'. Levin says 'they are doubtless more ornamental than functional', but adds that 'they charge the air with overtones of wavering and indecision'. Gurr regards the hendiadys 'scourge and minister' as of central significance. Following a well-known distinction made by Fredson Bowers, he argues that the two terms in this figure are ostensibly complementary but are in fact antithetical (as in 'blood and judgement') – a scourge was a wicked instrument of God's will, a minister a virtuous one. Bowers's distinction, however, has been shown to be false to Elizabethan usage. See R.W. Dent, 'Hamlet: Scourge and Minister', *SQ*, 29 (1978), 82–4.

22 On the logical and ethical confusions of this soliloquy, see G.K. Hunter, 'The Heroism of Hamlet', in *Hamlet*, ed. John Russell Brown and Bernard Harris (London: Arnold, 1963), p.95; T. McAlindon, *Shakespeare and Decorum* (London: Macmillan, 1973), pp.67–70; Walter N.King, *Hamlet's Search for Meaning*, (Athens, Ga.: University of Georgia Press, 1982), pp.94–8; Peter Mercer, *Hamlet and the Acting of Revenge* (London: Macmillan, 1986), pp.228–30; Watts, *Hamlet*, pp.43–6.

23 I have already discussed in *Shakespeare and Decorum* (pp.53–79), and from a different perspective, the semiotic interrelation in *Hamlet* of language, rite, and play. For a recent consideration of the language-ritual nexus, see Malcolm Evans, *Signifying Nothing: Truth's True Contents in Shakespeare's Plays* (Brighton: Harvester, 1986), pp.129–33. Evans notes that Jacques Lacan has recently drawn attention to this nexus in the play.

24 See Roland Mushat Frye, *The Renaissance 'Hamlet'* (Princeton, N.J.: Princeton University Press, 1984), pp.82–102.

25 Bridget Gellert Lyons, *Voices of Melancholy: Studies in Literary Treatments of Melancholy in the Renaissance* (London: Routledge, 1971), pp.93–4.

26 Tentative gloss from Harold Jenkins, ed. *Hamlet* (London: Methuen, 1982), p.260 (note on II.ii.397).

27 On Hamlet's use of words as a weapon, see Grigori Kozintsev, *Shakespeare: Time and Conscience*, trs. Joyce Vining (New York: Hill and Wang, 1966), pp.133–42; Alexander, *Poison, Play and Duel*, pp.28, 72; Bernard McElroy, *Shakespeare's Mature Tragedies* (Princeton, N.J.: Princeton University Press, 1973), pp.63–4.

28 Among those who have argued the latter view, are A.C. Bradley, *Shakespearean Tragedy* (London: Macmillan, 1904), pp.144–5; D.G. James, *The Dream of Learning* (Oxford: Clarendon Press, 1951), p.194; H.B. Charlton, *Shakespearian Tragedy* (Cambridge: Cambridge University Press, 1948), p.112. It has become a curiously unfashionable view.

29 Psycho-physical order is identified with timeliness in Hamlet's claim that his 'pulse ... doth temperately keep time, / And makes as healthful music' as his mother's (III.iv.140–1).

30 Cf. Gurr, *Hamlet and the Distracted Globe*, p.30.

31 On constancy and time, see Frederick Turner, *Shakespeare and the Nature of Time* (Oxford: Clarendon Press, 1971), p.76.

32 *Poison, Play and Duel*, p.200.

6 Othello

1 For a classic expression of the orthodox view, see A.C. Bradley, *Shakespearean Tragedy* (London: Macmillan, 1904), pp.185–6. Cf. M.C. Bradbrook, 'The Jacobean Shakespeare', in *A New Companion to Shakespeare Studies*, ed. Kenneth Muir and S. Schoenbaum (Cambridge: Cambridge University Press, 1971) pp.146, 149, 154; Norman Sanders, ed. *Othello*, The New Cambridge Shakespeare (Cambridge: Cambridge University, Press, 1984), pp.18–20. The symbolic and universal implications of the tragedy, moreover, have been persuasively unfolded by (among others) Robert B. Heilman in *Magic in the Web: Action and Language in 'Othello'* (Lexington, Ky.: University of Kentucky Press, 1956), and Alvin B. Kernan in the Introduction to his Signet edition of the play (New York and Toronto: New American Library, 1963).

2 'No real attempt is made whatever to relate Othello's disorder to the entire order of nature. The mirror is held up only to limited aspects of nature, not to nature itself.' – V.K. Whitaker, *The Mirror Up To Nature: the Technique of Shakespeare's Tragedies* (San Marino: Huntington Library, 1965), p.124. Cf. Theodore Spencer, *Shakespeare and the Nature of Man* (New York: Macmillan, 1942), p.124 ('Since *Othello* is a personal tragedy, we do not find in it, as we do in *Hamlet* and *Troilus*, much use of the political and cosmological hierarchies'); Norman Rabkin, *Shakespeare and the Common Understanding* (New York: The Free Press; London:

Collins–Macmillan, 1967), p.61 ('Of all Shakespeare's tragedies, it is the least concerned with the evocation of a cosmic universe').

3 'The Noble Moor', *PBA*, 41 (1955), repr. in *'Othello': a Selection of Critical Essays*, ed. John Wain (London: Macmillan, 1971), p.149.

4 Richard Knolles, *The Generall Historie of the Turkes*, 2nd edn (London, 1610), p.1. Cf. Anon., *The Policy of the Turkish Empire* (London, 1597), sig. A3: 'The terrour of their name doth even now make the kings and princes of the West ... to tremble and quake through fear of their victorious forces.' Knolles's book resounds continually with 'a dark foreboding of euill fortune' that seës to have found its way into *Othello*. He claims that while most Christians seem lost in 'the dead sleepe of carelesse negligence and securitie', this 'barbarous nation ... now triumpheth ouer the best part of the world' and 'so mightily swelleth, as it would ouerflow all' (pp.iv–v,1,185).

5 *Historie of the Turkes*, pp.iii, 122–3, 130, 349, 904–5. This is also a major theme in the 'Historie of the Turkes' contained in John Foxe's immensely popular *Actes and Monuments* (London, 1583): see pp.735, 737, 748, 755. And in *The English Mirror. A regard wherein al estates may behold the Conquests of Envy* (London, 1586) p.69, George Whetstone claims: 'The contention that enuie set between [Christian princes] ... was the first grounde and sure foundation of the great Turkes Empire ... such dissentions and hostility Sathan hath sent amongst us, that Turkes bee not more enemies to Christians then Christian to Christian.'

6 *Historie of the Turkes*, p.839.

7 Ibid., pp.847, 853, 857, 887, 902.

8 *Othello*, New Variorum Shakespeare, ed. Horace Howard Furness (Philadelphia: Lippincott, 1886), pp.357–8; Samuel C. Chew, *The Crescent and the Rose: Islam and England during the Renaissance* (1937; repr. New York: Octagon Books, 1965), p.496. In *'Othello*, Lepanto and the Cyprus Wars', *ShS*, 21 (1968), repr. in *Aspects of 'Othello'*, ed. Kenneth Muir and Philip Edwards (Cambridge: Cambridge University Press, 1977), p.65, Emrys Jones points out that Shakespeare's Senator is correctly informed by his letters about the number of galleys in the Turkish fleet. He cites Knolles, *Historie* (2nd edn 1610), pp.846, 863.

9 George Hibbard, *'Othello* and the Pattern of Shakespearian Tragedy', *ShS*, 21 (1968), repr. in *Aspects of 'Othello'*, ed. Muir and Edwards, pp.67–73. Emrys Jones (n.8 above) argues that the historical allusions in the play were intended as a compliment to King James, author of a poem on the Christian victory at Lepanto. Reminding James of the Christian loss of Cyprus would seem to me to have been a somewhat infelicitous way of complimenting him on his Lepanto poem. My argument, however, is that the primary purpose of the historical details is much more serious than (although it does not necessarily exclude) that of royal compliment.

10 In the circumstances, Shakespeare did not have to point to the error

with any great degree of emphasis, but point to it he did. His method is the simple one of parallelism, verbal echo, and strong contrast. The previous scene opens with the Duke's words, 'There is no composition in these news/That gives them credit' (I.iii.1–2). There follows a discussion in which the Duke and his colleagues deduce from conflicting reports the size, position, and intentions of the Turkish fleet; they seem determined that their natural desire to hope for the best will not 'secure' them to 'error' (line 10). At line 19 of the next scene (at Cyprus), a gentleman reports, 'News, lads! Your wars are done', and adds that 'most part' of the enemy fleet has perished. Governor Montano asks, 'Is this true?', and on being told that Cassio was on the ship which sighted the sinking, asks no more. When Cassio appears, he says nothing about the fleet. The only person to endorse the Third Gentleman's momentous piece of news is Othello: in the twenty-eight rapturous lines he speaks on landing, he gives one line to the Turks: 'News, friends: our wars are done; the Turks are drown'd' (line 200). No one speaks who claims to have seen the sinking; no one is puzzled that almost two hundred enemy ships sank when all three of the Venetian vessels survived; and Montano's original thought that the fleet might be 'enshelter'd and embay'd' (line 18) does not recur. Othello's remark that he is prattling out of fashion and doting in his own comforts seems doubly ironical.

11 Foxe, *Actes and Monuments*, pp.737, 753–4, 758. Cf. Chew, *The Crescent and the Rose*, pp.141, 375–83.

12 *Historie of the Turkes*, p.847. Adds Knolles: 'There was not ... any valiant or renowned captaine, who as the danger of the time required, should have taken upon him the charge'.

13 The idea is given special emphasis in the couplet pronounced by Agamemnon as he leaves the stage at the end of v.ix: 'If in his death the gods have us befriended; / Great Troy is ours, and our sharp wars are ended.'

14 *Religio Medici*, ed. Patrides, *The Major Works*, pp.144–5.

15 On Othello's 'Farewell' to the big wars, Susan Snyder comments: 'War is individual passion subordinated to a larger plan, martial harmony, formal pageantry, imitation of divine judgement ... majestic order.' – *The Comic Matrix of Shakespeare's Tragedies*, (Princeton, N.J.: Princeton University Press, 1979) p.82. On the positive conception of strife, see above p.6.

16 See chapter 1, n.51. The contrarious design of *Othello* has been duly emphasised in critical commentary. Three critics, moreover, have considered the play in relation to the Mars–Venus myth: Heilman, *Magic in the Web*, pp.182–4; Rosalie Colie, *Shakespeare's Living Art* (Princeton, N.J.: Princeton University Press, 1974), pp.150–9; Robert G. Hunter, *Shakespeare and the Mystery of God's Judgements* (Athens, Ga.: University of Georgia Press, 1976), pp.127–50. Hunter alone attends to the cosmological implications of the myth. I take the cosmological approach

much further than he, and find myself in disagreement, moreover, with some important aspects of his interpretation: (1) the identification of love and strife with good and evil; (2) the assumption that the process by which 'Chaos is come again' differs in *Othello* and the other tragedies; (3) the use of a theological rather than a naturalistic explanation for the predominance of strife in the *Othello* world.

17 Knolles, *Historie of the Turkes*, p.843. Rosalie Colie (*Shakespeare's Living Art*, pp.156–7) seems to have been the first critic of *Othello* to recall the association of Venus with Cyprus. As well as poems by Petrarch and Ronsard, she cites Surrey's sonnet beginning, 'In Cypres springes, whereas dame Venus dwelt'. Chaucer frequently uses 'Cipris' or 'Cipride' ('the Cypriot') as another name for Venus: see, for example, *The House of Fame*, 1.518; *Troilus and Criseyde*, III.725, v.208.

18 Foxe, *Actes and Monuments*, pp.758–9; Fulke Greville, *A Treatie of Warres*, ed. Bullough, stanza 68 ('these Turkes ... leave us as to the Iewish bondage heirs, / A Sabaoth rest for self-confusion fit').

19 Behind the bond solemnly struck between Othello and Iago lies the familiar paradigm of the Satanic compact or deed of gift (see Dieter Mehl, *Shakespeare's Tragedies* (Cambridge: Cambridge University Press, 1986), p.70). Associated mainly with Doctor Faustus of Wittenberg, this myth was familiar in many different forms from medieval times. It was a popular vehicle for the conception of sin as a state of bondage into which the erring mortal is tricked by the devil's promises of freedom from the constraints imposed by the bond with God. The presence of this mythical paradigm in *Othello* connects it both with *Macbeth* and with earlier and later tragedies such as Marlowe's *Doctor Faustus*, Heywood's *A Woman Killed with Kindness*, Webster's *The White Devil*, and Middleton and Rowley's *The Changeling*.

20 Robert B. Heilman, *Magic in the Web: Action and Language in 'Othello'*, pp.169–70; Alvin Kernan, ed. *Othello*, The Signet Shakespeare (New York and Toronto: New American Library, 1963), Introduction, p.xxiv; Robert Grudin, *Mighty Opposites* (Berkeley, Calif.: University of California Press, 1979), p.132.

21 Antony Low points out that Cassio's 'infirmity' is a comic parallel to Othello's: his often amusing deterioration from sober, responsible officer to carousing drunkard parallels Othello's tragic fall from kindly, loving husband to jealous murderer. See 'Othello and Cassio: "Unfortunate in the Infirmity"', *Archiv*, 121 (1970), 428–33.

22 Norman Sanders, ed. *Othello*, Introd., p.54.

23 Chew, *The Crescent and the Rose*, p.104.

24 Cf. Heilman, *Magic in the Web*, p.139.

25 Helen Gardner, 'The Noble Moor', in *'Othello': a Collection of Critical Essays*, ed. Wain, pp.151–2.

26 A reference to the proverb, 'Catch Occasion by the front, for she is bald behind.' In an age which reverenced timeliness in human affairs,

'Occasion' (i.e. the opportune moment) was a familiar emblematic icon. See Erwin Panofsky, *Studies in Iconology: Humanistic Themes in the Art of the Renaissance* (1939; New York: Harper and Row, 1972), p.72. As Panofsky points out, 'Occasion' is synonymous with 'Opportunity' (see n.39).

27 Mehl, *Shakespeare's Tragedies*, pp.63–4.

28 Derek Traversi, *An Approach to Shakespeare*, 2nd edn (London: Sands, 1957), pp.127, 131–2.

29 See my *English Renaissance Tragedy* (London: Macmillan, 1986), pp.17–25, 48.

30 Helen Gardner, '*Othello*: a Retrospect, 1900–67', *ShS*, 21 (1968), repr. in *Aspects of 'Othello'*, ed. Edwards and Muir, p.7.

31 Prominent among those who have argued against this view are John Holloway, *The Story of the Night: Studies in Shakespeare's Major Tragedies* (London: Routledge, 1961), pp.55–6 and pp.155–65 (Appendix A, 'Dr. Leavis and Diabolic Intellect'); Barbara Everett, 'Reflections on the Sentimentalist's *Othello*', *CQ*, 3 (1961), 127–39; and Helen Gardner in the articles cited above. See also Kenneth Muir, *Shakespeare's Tragic Sequence* (London: Hutchinson, 1972), pp.99–103; Ruth Nevo, *Tragic Form in Shakespeare* (Princeton, N.J.: Princeton University Press, 1972), pp.210–13; Mehl, *Shakespeare's Tragedies*, pp.63–4.

32 On the failure of Leavis and Eliot to appreciate the dramatic convention to which Othello's last speech relates, see Holloway, *The Story of the Night*, p.55.

33 Maud Bodkin, *Archetypal Patterns in Poetry* (London: Oxford University Press, 1934), p.221.

34 See G.M. Matthews, '*Othello* and the Dignity of Man', in *Shakespeare in a Changing World*, ed. Arnold Kettle (London: Lawrence and Wishart, 1964), pp.123–45. Matthews argues that the play is not about how Othello reverts to barbarism but about 'how a white barbarian . . . tries to make a civilised man in his own image'.

35 *English Renaissance Tragedy*, pp.74–5.

36 See Norman Sanders, ed. *Othello*, p.81, note on I.iii.315–16.

37 T. McAlindon, *Shakespeare and Decorum*, (London: Macmillan, 1973), pp.87–8; Wylie Sypher, *Shakespeare and the Ethic of Time* (New York: Seabury Press, 1976), pp.115, 122.

38 Vincenzo Cartari, *The fountaine of ancient fiction*, trs. Richard Linche (London, 1599) p.24. See also the characterisation of Janus in Book I of Ovid's *Fasti*, a lengthy poem on 'the times' or festivals of the Julian (solar) year. Janus originates in Chaos but is now wholly identified with the order of nature and society in their temporal dimension. He is 'the origin of the silent year rolling on', presides over the seasons, looks forth upon East and West; and the whole world would be thrown into confusion were it not for his confining powers (trs. Henry T.Riley (London: Bell, 1879), pp.7, 11–12). Janus was often depicted holding the number 300 in one hand and 65 in the other in order to show that he

presides over the year.

39 The word 'importune' (or 'importunity') occurs five times in the play. It has to be taken as the antonym of 'opportunity' (as in 'I will do this if I can bring it to any opportunity' (I.iii.275)), signifying the appropriate moment. Like 'Occasion', for which it is really another name, 'Opportunity' was often personified and was central to all discussions on timeliness in human behaviour: see George Puttenham, *The Arte of English Poesie* (Menston, Yorks: The Scolar Press Facsimile Reprint, 1968), pp.223–4, and cf. Cicero, *De Officiis*, ed. and trs. W. Miller, Loeb Classical Library (London and Cambridge: Heinemann and Harvard University Press, 1947), 1.142–4. On the artistic representations of Opportunity, see Panofsky, *Studies in Iconology*, pp.71–2.

40 Terry Eagleton's remarks on an aspect of *King Lear* are pertinent here: 'The paradox which *King Lear* explores is that it is "natural" for the human animal to transcend its limits, yet this creative tendency to exceed oneself is also the source of destructiveness . . . The problem [is] of respecting a norm or measure while simultaneously going beyond it'. – *William Shakespeare* (Oxford: Blackwell, 1986) p.81.

41 *Magic in the Web*, pp.68–9.

42 On Iago as agent and embodiment of chaos, see G. Wilson Knight, *The Wheel of Fire* (1930; London: Methuen, 1960), p.116; Theodore Spencer, *Shakespeare and the Nature of Man* (New York: Macmillan, 1942), pp.129–30; and (especially) Heilman, *Magic in the Web*, pp.91, 121–2. No one, however, has seen Iago as a figure of chaos in its temporal aspect.

43 For discussion of the dramatic significance of speech in the play, see Matthew N. Proser, *The Heroic Image in Five Shakespearean Tragedies* (Princeton, N.J.: Princeton University Press, 1965), pp.135–8; McAlindon, *Shakespeare and Decorum*, pp.1–3, 82–6, 105–31; Terence Hawkes, *Shakespeare's Talking Animals* (London: Arnold, 1973), pp.132–42; Patricia Parker, 'Shakespeare and Rhetoric: "dilation" and "delation" in *Othello*', in *Shakespeare and the Question of Theory*, ed. Parker and Geoffrey Hartman (Methuen: New York and London, 1985), pp.54–74; Eamonn Grennan, 'The Women's Voices in *Othello*: Speech, Song, Silence', *SQ*, 37 (1986), 277–92; James L. Calderwood, 'Speech and Self in *Othello*', *SQ*, 37 (1986), 293–303.

44 Cicero, *De Oratore*, ed. and trs. G.L. Hendrickson and H.M. Hubbell, Loeb Classical Library (London and Cambridge, Mass.: Heinemann and Harvard University Press, 1942), III.55, *De Inventione*, ed. and trs. H. Hubbell, 1.4–5; Foster Watson, *Vives on Education: A Translation of the 'De Tradendis Disciplinis' of Juan Luis Vives* (Cambridge: Cambridge University Press, 1913), p.177.

45 *Ben Jonson*, ed. C.H. Herford and P. and E. Simpson (Oxford: Clarendon Press), VI.620–1 (*Timber, or Discoveries*).

46 See my *Shakespeare and Decorum*, pp.128–30.

47 Eamonn Grennan (see n.43) remarks that Emilia's speech in the last act 'functions as a moral measure for the world of the play, morality being implicitly identified here with honest feeling and plain speech' (p.285). Cf. my *Shakespeare and Decorum*, p.85.

48 'The order of God's creatures in themselves is not only admirable and glorious, but eloquent.' – John Hoskins, *Directions for Speech and Style*, ed. H. Hudson (Princeton, N.J.: Princeton University Press, 1935), p.2. See also Pierre de La Primaudaye, *The French Academie*, p.379 (II.ii).

49 *Shakespeare's Ovid: being Arthur Golding's Translation of the 'Metamorphoses'*, ed. W.H.D. Rouse (London: Centaur Press, 1961), Epistle, lines 521–6. See further Kirsty Cochrane, 'Orpheus Applied: Some Instances of his Importance in the Humanist View of Language', *RES*, NS, 19 (1968), 1–13.

50 For this interpretation of Kyd's play (and its influence on Shakespeare), see my *English Renaissance Tragedy*, pp.64–81.

51 'Shakespeare's "Dull Clown" and Symbolic Music', *SQ*, 17 (1966), 107–8.

52 *The Hidden God: A Study of the Tragic Vision in the 'Pensées' of Pascal and the Tragedies of Racine*, trs. Philip Thody (London: Routledge, 1964), pp.19–20.

7 *King Lear*

1 *Timaeus*, 28c. See *OED*, 'all', B3: 'Whole system of things, τὸ πᾶν, the Universe'. On 'nothing' (chaos as the void), S.K. Heninger, *The Cosmographical Glass: Renaissance Diagrams of the Universe* (San Marino, Calif.: Huntington Library, 1977), p.26, cites Du Bartas, *Devine Weekes*, trs. Sylvester (1605), p.2: 'But all this *All* did once (of nought) begin.' Heninger refers to a similar pun in Cleopatra's 'All's but nought' (IV.xv.78), adding pertinently that it paraphrases Othello's realisation that without love 'Chaos is come again.'

2 Folio reading. Alexander follows Q2, 'domestic-door particulars'.

3 Rosalie Colie, *Paradoxica Epidemica: the Renaissance Tradition of Paradox* (Princeton, N.J.: Princeton University Press, 1966), p.472, remarks that 'Lear's "all" invokes cosmic totality'. She seems, however, to have been unaware of the cosmological meaning of the word and to have been responding rather to its imaginative impact within the play.

4 John F. Danby, *Shakespeare's Doctrine of Nature; a Study of 'King Lear'* (London: Faber, 1949), pp.46–53, 186–8. In a Marxist analysis, however, John Turner argues that the true subject of *King Lear* 'is not an old order succumbing to a new but an old order succumbing to its own internal contradictions'. See Graham Holderness, Nick Potter, and John Turner, *Shakespeare: the Play of History* (London: Macmillan, 1987), p.101. I would prefer this reading myself.

5 Alvin B. Kernan, '*King Lear* and the Pageant of History', in *On 'King*

Lear', ed. Lawrence Danson (Princeton, N.J.: Princeton University Press, 1981), p.11.

6 Rosalie L. Colie, 'Reason and Need: *King Lear* and the Crisis of the Aristocracy', in *Some Facets of 'King Lear'*, ed. Colie and F.T. Flahiff (London: Heinemann, 1974), pp.185–219.

7 Stephen Greenblatt, 'Shakespeare and the Exorcists', in *Shakespeare and the Question of Theory*, ed. Patricia Parker and Geoffrey Hartman (New York and London: Methuen, 1985), pp.163–87. Repr. in Greenblatt, *Shakespearean Negotiation: the Circulation of Social Energy in Renaissance England* (Oxford: Clarendon Press, 1988).

8 *Shakespeare and the Nature of Man* (New York: Macmillan, 1942), p.135.

9 Emphasis on this aspect of the play's design goes back to Dr Johnson (who noted 'its striking opposition of contrary characters') and to A.C. Bradley (see n.12 below). It has received most attention from Robert Heilman (*This Great Stage: Image and Structure in 'King Lear'* (Baton Rouge, La.: Louisiana State University Press, 1948)) and Robert Grudin (*Mighty Opposites: Shakespeare and Renaissance Contrariety* (Berkeley, Calif.: University of California Press, 1979)). Heilman finds that the play's patterns of idea and symbol are all presented dualistically (pp.284–6). Grudin analyses both the parallels and the oppositions in the tragedy, and on the basis of this analysis concludes, most interestingly, that *King Lear* is one of the most intricately contrived of Shakespeare's plays. He also claims that whereas the parallels universalise meaning, the oppositions complicate (p.139). My own view is that the oppositions both universalise and complicate.

10 John Norden, *Vicissitudo Rerum* (London: 1600), Preface and stanzas 9, 33–6, 40–6; Godfrey Goodman, *The Fall of Man* (London: 1616), pp.34–7, 51–2, 123–5, 206.

11 Compare Shakespeare's symbolic use of quadruple character grouping (as an image of threatened or violated unity) in *A Midsummer Night's Dream* (above, p.46); *Romeo and Juliet*, I.i.32–54; *Richard II*, I.i; and *Julius Caesar* (above, pp.79–82). See also my *English Renaissance Tragedy* (London: Macmillan, 1986), pp.75, 96, 196, 231, 251, 252, 263.

12 *Shakespearean Tragedy* (London: Macmillan, 1904), p.263. E. Catherine Dunn develops Bradley's hint in her article, 'The Storm in *King Lear*', *SQ*, 3 (1952), 329–33. She sees in the storm scenes not only 'a cosmic strife of the four elements' but also 'a cosmic chaos of the Empedoclean type, a destruction of the universe by Strife' – where Strife symbolises the effect of ingratitude. However she does not take her argument beyond the storm scene and the theme of ingratitude.

13 Ed. Geoffrey Bullough, *Narrative and Dramatic Sources of Shakespeare*, vol.VII, *Major Tragedies* (London and New York: Routledge and Columbia University Press, 1973), lines 2122–3, 195–6. See also lines 1994–5, 2087–8, 2172–3.

14 In *Shakespeare's Mature Tragedies* (Princeton, N.J.: Princeton University

Press, 1973), Bernard McElroy considers violently opposed extremes to be one of the characteristic features of the *Lear* world: 'nothing is done either in leisure or in moderation' (pp.149, 151).

15 See Kenneth Muir, ed. *King Lear* (London: Methuen, 1966), pp.164–5.

16 *Shakespeare's Living Art* (Princeton, N.J.: Princeton University Press, 1974), p.315. (She is adapting the distinction made between 'hard' and 'soft' primitivism by Arthur O. Lovejoy and George Boas in *Primitivism and Related Ideas in Antiquity* (New York: Octagon Books, 1973), pp.9–11). Maynard Mack, on the other hand, has described *Lear* as 'the greatest anti-pastoral ever penned' (*King Lear in Our Time* (London: Methuen, 1966), p.65), an idea developed at length by Turner in *Shakespeare: the Play of History*, pp.96–118.

17 On Kyd, see p.54.

18 Enid Welsford, *The Fool: His Social and Literary History* (London: Faber, 1936), p.264.

19 *The Wheel of Fire* (London: Methuen, 1936), pp.160–76.

20 See my *English Renaissance Tragedy*, pp.37–41.

21 See, for example, John Lawlor, *The Tragic Sense in Shakespeare* (London: Chatto & Windus, 1960), pp.181–2 ('the power of the natural bond is the only final reality'); Maynard Mack, *King Lear in Our Time*, pp.100–6 ('human reality' in *Lear* is 'a web of ties commutual'); David Horowicz, *Shakespeare: an Existentialist View* (London: Tavistock Press, 1968), pp.123–31.

22 Says Boethius (*Consolation of Philosophy*, Book II, met.8, trs. Chaucer): 'the contrarious qualities of elementz holden among hemself allyaunce perdurable ... all this accordaunce of thynges is bounde with love, that governeth erthe and see, and hath also comaundement to the hevene ... This love halt togidres peoples joyned with an holy boond, and knytteth sacrement of mariages of chaste loves; and love enditeth lawe to trewe felawes' (Chaucer, *Works*, ed. F.N. Robinson (London: Oxford University Press, 1974)). In Spenser's 'Hymn in Honour of Love', Love is similarly conceived as a benign ruler whose law turns chaos into cosmos: when the elements threatened 'their own confusion and decay', Love 'relented their rebellious ire', separated them, and compelled them 'To keep themselves within their sundry reigns, / Together linkt with adamantine chains.' See also La Primaudaye, *The French Academie*, p.728, and above, p.266, n.7.

23 *English Renaissance Tragedy*, p.50.

24 *Paradoxica Epidemica*, pp.470, 472, 474.

25 George Puttenham, *The Arte of English Poesie*, facsimile repr. (Menston, Yorks.: Scolar Press, 1968), p.189.

26 Concerning 'the enterchaunging course' of the elements, Ovid says (in the famous speech of Pythagoras near the end of the *Metamorphoses*):

> The earth resolving leysurely dooth melt too water sheere,
> The water fyned turnes to aire. The aire eeke purged cleere

> From grossnesse, spyreth up aloft, and there becommeth fyre.
> From thence in order contrary they backe ageine retyre.
> Fyre thickening passeth intoo Aire, and Ayër wexing grosse
> Returnes to water: Water eek congealing into drosse,
> Becommeth earth. No kind of thing keepes ay his shape and hew.

(Trs. Arthur Golding, xv.263, 270–6.) See also Spenser, 'The Mutability Cantos', vii.xxv.

27 '"Love" in *King Lear*', *RES*, ns 10 (1959), 178–81.

28 See especially lines 1240–82 and 2150–226 (ed. Bullough). See also lines 146, 167, 233. 613, 869, 912, 914, 917, 920, etc. etc. In all of this, the *Leir* playwright is echoing a comment in Holinshed's version of the story: 'such was the unkindness, or (as I maie saie) the unnaturalnesse which he found in his two daughters' (Bullough, p.318).

29 *OED*, 'natural', iii.13, 13c.

30 See the Glossary in the New Shakespeare *King Lear*, ed. G.L. Duthie and J. Dover Wilson (Cambridge: Cambridge University Press, 1960).

31 Danby, *Shakespeare's Doctrine of Nature*, pp.15–53. The germ of this approach can be found in the admirable account of the play given in Enid Welsford's *The Fool*, pp.257–80.

32 Heilman, *This Great Stage*, p.133. Cf. G. Wilson Knight, *The Wheel of Fire*, pp.177–8.

33 *Radical Tragedy*, pp.192–3.

34 Hiram C. Haydn, *The Counter-Renaissance* (New York: Scribner's, 1950), pp.468–96; Edward William Tayler, *Nature and Art in Renaissance Literature* (New York: Columbia University Press, 1964).

35 Montaigne, *Essayes*, trs. Florio, 1.220, 225, 229.

36 Clothes symbolism has been considered in detail (with emphasis on its negative implications) by Heilman in *This Great Stage*, pp.67–79, and by Maurice Charney in '"We Put Fresh Garments on Him": Nakedness and Clothes in *King Lear*', in *Some Facets of 'King Lear'*, ed. Colie and Flahiff, pp.77–88.

37 Arthur Sewell, *Character and Society in Shakespeare* (Oxford: Clarendon Press, 1951), p.110; Nicholas Brooke, *Shakespeare: 'King Lear'* (London: Arnold, 1963), p.31.

38 On Edgar's dramatic art see also Elton, *'King Lear' and the Gods* (San Marino, Calif.: The Huntington Library, 1966), pp.87–8, 112,; Robert Egan, *Drama Within Drama: Shakespeare's Sense of his Art in 'King Lear', 'The Winter's Tale, and 'The Tempest'* (New York and London: Columbia University Press, 1975), pp.21–30; Alvin Kernan, *The Playwright as Magician: Shakespeare's Image of the Poet in the English Public Theatre* (New Haven and London: Yale University Press, 1979), pp.120–5.

39 *Shakespeare: 'King Lear'*, pp.42–45, 59. Cf. Elton, *'King Lear' and the Gods*, pp.114; Egan, *Drama Within Drama*, pp.21, 26, 29. Contrast Kernan, who observes that 'the fall from the cliff in Edgar's play ends in miraculous survival and thus dramatizes the truly miraculous survival found by the

wanderers and outcasts on the heath. All their lives are miracles in the sense that ... they discovered their human reality in a way they never expected' (*The Playwright as Magician*, p.128).

40 'Its purpose is humane', says John Bayley, *Shakespeare and Tragedy* (London: Routledge, 1981), p.33.

41 *Shakespeare: 'King Lear'*, p.43.

42 On Plato, Aristotle, and Cicero as anti-primitivists, see Lovejoy and Boas, *Primitivism and Related Ideas in Antiquity*, pp.166, 189–90, 246–8. In the *Laws* (890 d), Plato says that 'law and also art exist by nature'; in other words – as Lovejoy and Boas point out – he regards the antithesis of art and nature to be a spurious one, and so anticipates Shakespeare's 'The art itself is nature' (*Winter's Tale*, iv.iv.97). Aristotle and Cicero take a similar position: art completes or complements nature; but that process is nature completing itself. (There is in consequence no justification for Jacques Derrida's claim – in *Of Grammatology*, Part ii – that the whole of Western metaphysics from Plato to Rousseau and Lévi-Strauss privileges the first term in the nature–culture antithesis.)

43 Peter Brain, *Galen on Bloodletting: a Study of the Origins, Development and Validity of his Opinions, with a Translation of the Three Works* (Cambridge: Cambridge University Press, 1986), pp.2–4. Sixteenth-century medical writings continually echo this idea; says Jacques Guilleameau, *The French Chirugery*, trs. A.M. (1597): 'We recommende such things unto Nature, and follow her instructions' (8/2).

44 'Now art thou sociable. Now art thou Romeo. Now art thou what thou art, by art as well as Nature' (ii.iv.87–90).

45 'A conjuring trick with words' is how Nicholas Brooke describes it (*Shakespeare: 'King Lear'*, p.49). See also S.L. Goldberg, *An Essay on 'King Lear'* (Cambridge: Cambridge University Press, 1974), pp.85–6; Ruth Nevo, *Tragic Form in Shakespeare* (Princeton, N.J.: Princeton University Press, 1972), pp.302–3. Elton (*'King Lear' and the Gods*, p.107) argues that Edgar's sententia is ironically subverted in the next scene when 'the young and most unripe Cordelia is carried onstage dead in her father's arms'. I would draw the opposite conclusion: her death is a most terrible reminder that ripeness *is* all, a supreme value.

46 Martha Andresen, '"Ripeness is All": Sententiae and Commonplaces in *King Lear*', in *Some Facets of 'King Lear'*, ed Colie and Flahiff, pp.148–50.

47 Cf. Andresen, p.158. On time, truth, and justice, see above, p.15.

48 *The Ethic of Time: Structures of Experience in Shakespeare* (New York: Seabury Press, 1976), pp.169, 174.

49 Brooke, *Shakespeare: 'King Lear'*, pp.53, 59–60; McElroy, *Shakespeare's Mature Tragedies*, p.162.

50 In *Shakespeare: 'King Lear'* (Harmondsworth, Middlesex: Penguin Books, 1986), Kenneth Muir remarks that Edgar's (anachronistic) status as Lear's godson makes it appropriate for him to succeed Lear (p.114). He also draws attention to F.T. Flahiff's point that the historical King

Edgar was honoured in Shakespeare's time as a ruler who brought unity, peace, and civility to a divided and barbarous realm (*Some Facets of 'King Lear'*, ed. Colie and Flahiff, pp.228–31). It should be acknowledged, of course, that in the Quarto text the final speech of the play is given to Albany, so that he rather than Edgar appears as Lear's successor. The Folio version may indicate a change of mind on Shakespeare's part, but more likely it points to an error in the Quarto text. The phrase 'we that are young' (v.iii.326) fits Edgar better than Albany; moreover, Albany's earlier reference to Edgar's 'royal nobleness' of conduct in the lists (l.176; Quarto and Folio) seems designed, with the royal-godson role, to prepare for his succession.

51 Knight, *The Wheel of Fire*, p.189.

52 Kent's reference to Juno – 'By Juno, I swear, ay' – is simply a stychomythic extension of Lear's oath, 'By Jupiter, I swear, no' (II.iv.20–1).

53 I am by no means the first to adopt this position. It is apparent in the interpretations of Sewell, *Character and Society in Shakespeare*, pp.91–121; John Holloway, *The Story of the Night: Studies in Shakespeare's Major Tragedies* (London: Routledge, 1961), pp.75–98; Maynard Mack (n.16); McElroy, *Shakespeare's Mature Tragedies*, esp. pp.203–4; Michael Long, *The Unnatural Scene: a Study in Shakespearean Tragedy* (London: Methuen, 1976), pp.158–219.

54 Brooke, *Shakespeare: 'King Lear'*, pp.37–43; Sypher, *The Ethic of Time*, p.161. John Turner sees *both* plots as derivatives of romance which engender and shockingly frustrate expectations of renewal – *Shakespeare: the Play of History*, pp.95–7.

55 I cannot conceive that this repeated exclamation indicates anything but sudden excitement; and for that the only explanation must be that he thinks (rightly or wrongly) that Cordelia's lips have moved. See also Bradley, *Shakespearean Tragedy*, p.291; Phyllis Rackin, 'Delusion as Resolution in *King Lear*', *SQ*, 21 (1970), 33–4; McElroy, *Shakespeare's Mature Tragedies*, p.201.

56 Here and throughout this chapter my position is close to that of Arthur Sewell, who remarked that 'the characters are imagined not only as members of each other but also as members of a nature which is active both within themselves and throughout the circumambient universe. Man is nowhere so certainly exhibited as a member of all organic creation and of the elemental powers' (*Character and Society in Shakespeare*, p.117).

8 Macbeth

1 Text in Christopher Marlowe, *The Plays*, ed. Roma Gill (London: Oxford University Press, 1971).

2 See my *English Renaissance Tragedy* (London: Macmillan; Vancouver: University of British Columbia Press, 1986), pp.92–9.

3 John Russell Brown, 'Afterword', in *Focus on 'Macbeth'*, ed. Brown (London: Routledge, 1982), p.249.

4 Cf. Peter Hall, 'Directing *Macbeth*: an Interview with John Russell Brown', in *Focus on 'Macbeth'*, ed. Brown. Duncan is very gracious and courteous, but also adroit and in control; anything but senile (pp.234–5).

5 See p.259, n.13. James's peaceful reign unites not only the Four Elements but also the Four Kingdoms (England, Scotland, Wales, Ireland) – 'by Brute divided, but by ... [James] alone ... again united and made one' (pp.225–6). Hindsight might point to the Gunpowder Plot (1605) as one of many historical ironies bearing on the idealisation of James's gift for unity and peace. But Middleton's pointed (and characteristic) emphasis on the naturalness of conflict deflects such criticism.

6 Malcolm Evans, *Signifying Nothing: Truth's True Contents and Shakespeare's Text* (Brighton: Harvester Press, 1986), pp.113–20. For a comparable attempt to show that *Macbeth* contradicts its own 'conservative ideology', see Alan Sinfield, '*Macbeth*: History, Ideology and Intellectuals', *CQ*, 28 (1986), 63–77. This 'oppositional analysis' of the play (reading it 'against the grain') is designed 'to expose, rather than to promote, State ideologies' – the promotion of such ideologies being a fault of both Shakespeare and his conservative and liberal critics. The analysis leads to the conclusion that although Macbeth is 'certainly ... a murderer and an oppressive ruler ... he is but one version of the Absolutist ruler, not the polar opposite' of Duncan and Malcolm. Sinfield adds that 'by conventional standards, the present essay is perverse' (pp.70, 74–5).

7 Thomas Aquinas, *Summa Theologica*, I–II, qq.82, 85; Alain de Lille, *The Plaint of Nature*, prose 3, metre 5, prose 8, Pierre de La Primaudaye, *The French Academie*, pp.418 (I.xi), 528 (I.lxv); Milton, *Paradise Lost*, VII.192ff., x.640ff.

8 Gunnar Qvärnstrom, *Poetry and Numbers: On the Structural Use of Symbolic Numbers* (Lund: Gleerup, 1966), p.18.

9 See *Macbeth*, New Variorum Edition, ed. Horace Howard Furness, Jr (Philadelphia and London: Lippincott, 1915), p.38; George Lyman Kittredge, ed. *Macbeth* (Boston: Ginn, 1939), p.98; James. M Nosworthy '*Macbeth, Doctor Faustus*, and the Juggling Fiends', in *Mirror up to Shakespeare: Essays in Honour of G.R. Hibbard*, ed. J.C. Gray (Toronto: University of Toronto Press, 1984), pp.218–22; Antony L. Johnson, 'Number Symbolism in *Macbeth*', *Analysis*, 4 (1986), 25–41.

10 Johnson, 'Number Symbolism in *Macbeth*', pp.25–8 and passim. Apart from the fact that they are intrinsic to a large frame of reference and a total view of the play, my own conclusions about number symbolism in *Macbeth* are essentially very close to Johnson's. They were arrived at independently shortly after I did my study of number symbolism in *Julius Caesar* (see p.275, n.15). That we have reached similar conclusions independently is, I take it, a point in their favour.

11 On the use of antithesis in the play, see Kenneth Muir, ed. *Macbeth*, the Arden Shakespeare (9th edn, London: Methuen, 1962), pp.xxxi–xxxii; G.L. Duthie, 'Antithesis in *Macbeth*', *ShS*, 19 (1966), 25–32. See also Margaret D. Burrell, '*Macbeth*: a Study in Paradox', *SJ*, 90 (1954), 167–90. Burrell enumerates examples of antithesis, equivocation, paradox, riddling, oxymoron, chiasmus, and hysteron proteron. They are symptomatic of the 'murky ambiguity of morality' in the play (p.166).

12 Vincent Hopper, *Medieval Number Symbolism* (New York: Columbia University Press, 1938), pp.4–8, 11, 122–3. The association of witchcraft with trinities ante-dates Christianity and is to be found in the role of 'triple Hecate' (*MND*, v.i.373) as goddess of the black art. The 'three formed Goddesse' is invoked by Medea in Ovid's *Metamorphoses* (trs. Golding, vii.142), a passage echoed several times in Shakespeare, most notably by Claudius' *alter ego* Lucianus: 'Thou mixture rank, of midnight weeds collected, / With Hecat's ban thrice blasted, thrice infected' (*Ham.*, iii.ii.251–2).

13 Kenneth Muir, ed. *Macbeth*, p.118 (note on iv.i.121).

14 The Porter says he caroused 'till the second cock' (ii.iii.24), which is 3 a.m. Cf. *RJ*, iv.iv.3–4: 'The second cock hath crow'd / The curfew bell hath rung, 'tis three o'clock'. Re-living the moment when she signalled to Macbeth to go to Duncan's chamber, Lady Macbeth says, 'One, two; why then 'tis time to do't' (v.i.33–4). This seems to suggest that the unspoken number which follows completes the signal. Cf. her 'Glamis thou art, and Cawdor; and shalt be / What thou art promis'd' (i.v.13–14) (to give but one example of the ominously unspecified third). Some editors, however, have concluded from Lady Macbeth's 'One, two . . .' that Duncan was murdered at 2 a.m.: e.g. Kittredge, ed. cit. (n.9, above), p.211.

15 See R.A. Foakes, 'Images of Death: Ambition in *Macbeth*', in *Focus on 'Macbeth'*, ed. Brown, p.18.

16 With an item missing from the last triple unit. However, Nosworthy ('*Macbeth, Faustus*, and the Juggling Fiends', p.219) and Johnson ('Number Symbolism in *Macbeth*', p.27) suggest that 'hereafter' might be intended as two words.

17 On the Renaissance concept of 'condign' or fitting punishment, and its effect on this play, see Paul A. Jorgensen, *Our Naked Frailties; Sensational Art and Meaning in 'Macbeth'* (Berkeley: University of California Press, 1971), pp.32–9 and *passim*.

18 'My dearest partner of greatness' (i.v.9); 'my dearest love' (line 55); 'Love' (iii.ii.29), 'dear wife' (line 36), 'dearest chuck' (line 45).

19 The subject of true and false manhood in the play has been much discussed. See especially, Eugene M. Waith, 'Manhood and Valor in Two Shakespearean Tragedies', *ELH*, 17 (1950), 262–73; Wilbur Sanders, *The Dramatist and the Received Idea: Studies in the Plays of Marlowe and Shakespeare* (Cambridge: Cambridge University Press, 1968), pp.272–4;

Jarold Ramsey, 'The Perversion of Manliness in *Macbeth*', *SEL*, 13 (1973), 285–300; Coppelia Kahn, *Man's Estate: Masculine Identity in Shakespeare* (Berkeley and Los Angeles: University of California Press, 1981), pp.172–89.

20 'A word ... designed to stir reverberations in the mind as the play goes on' – Marvin Rosenberg, *The Masks of 'Macbeth'* (Berkeley and Los Angeles: University of California Press, 1978), p.253 (on *done-do-deed* in 'If it were done ...'). See also M.M. Mahood, *Shakespeare's Wordplay* (London: Methuen, 1957), pp.137–9; Jorgensen, *Our Naked Frailties*, p.151; James L. Calderwood, *If It Were Done: 'Macbeth' and Tragic Action* (Amherst: University of Massachusetts Press, 1986), pp.32–70.

21 See my article, 'The Ironic Vision: Diction and Theme in Marlowe's *Doctor Faustus*', *RES*, 22 (1981), 137–9.

22 The significance of time in *Macbeth* is another topic which has attracted much attention. See especially Mahood, *Shakespeare's Wordplay*, pp.131–7; Frederick Turner, *Shakespeare and the Nature of Time*, (Oxford: Clarendon Press, 1971), pp.128–45; G.F. Waller, *The Strong Necessity of Time* (The Hague: Mouton, 1976), pp.130–5; Wylie Sypher, *The Ethic of Time: Structures of Experience in Shakespeare* (New York: Seaburg Press, 1976), pp.90–108; Donald W. Foster, 'Macbeth's War on Time', *ELR*, 16 (1986), 319–42.

23 Director Peter Hall comments: 'it has a feverish rhythm. It's very, very quick, and its movement is very economical ... In modern performance you really can't put an interval anywhere without loss' ('Directing *Macbeth*', in *Focus on 'Macbeth'*, ed. Brown, p.247).

9 *Antony and Cleopatra*

1 Julian Markels, *The Pillar of the World: 'Antony and Cleopatra' in Shakespeare's Development* (Columbus, Ohio: Ohio State University Press, 1968), p.150.

2 *Narrative and Dramatic Sources of Shakespeare*, vol.v, *The Roman Plays*, ed. Geoffrey Bullough (London: Routledge, 1964), p.292.

3 See, for example, John Carion, *The three bokes of Cronicles*, trs. Lynne, fol. xxxvii. On the origins of this idea in pre-Plutarchan historiography (mainly Polybius), see above pp.82 and 275 (n.17).

4 See *The Cambridge Ancient History*, vol.x, ed. S.A. Cook, F.E. Adcock, and M.P. Charlesworth (Cambridge: Cambridge University Press, 1934), pp.5 and 590; Robert P. Kalmey, 'Shakespeare's Octavius and Elizabethan Roman History', *SEL*, 18 (1978), 275–87. Robert S. Miola, *Shakespeare's Rome* (Cambridge: Cambridge University Press, 1983), p.162, cites Seneca's *De Clementia* as a *locus classicus* for the dual conception of Octavius.

5 See Matthew Proser, *The Heroic Image in Five Shakespearean Tragedies*, (Princeton, N.J.: Princeton University Press, 1965), p.205; Marion Bodwell Smith, *Dualities in Shakespeare* (Toronto: Toronto University

Press, 1966), pp.205–6. See also above, p.101, on the cycle of nature and history in *Julius Caesar*.

6 In *Hero and Saint: Shakespeare and the Graeco-Roman Heroic Tradition* (Oxford: Clarendon Press, 1971), Reuben Brower remarks in passing that the ennobling of Cleopatra through her love for Antony is 'a metamorphosis worthy of Ovid' (p.339); but he does not pursue this thought. Nor does James Hill consider the possibility of an Ovidian connection in 'The Marriage of True Bodies: Myth and Metamorphosis in *Antony and Cleopatra*', *REALB*, 2 (1984), 211–37. For Shakespeare's general indebtedness to Ovid (especially the *Metamorphoses*), see R.K. Root, *Classical Mythology in Shakespeare's Plays* (New York: Holt, 1903), p.3 ('the whole character of Shakespeare's mythology is essentially Ovidian') and passim; J.A.K. Thomson, *Shakespeare and the Classics* (London: Allen & Unwin, 1952), p.155 ('Shakespeare was regarded by his contemporaries as . . . the new Ovid') and passim.

7 For the term, 'dynamic permanence', see pp.36 and 266 (n.14).

8 *Metamorphoses*, ed. F.J. Miller, 2nd edn (London: Heinemann, 1921–2), 1.420–9. The passage quoted is from *Shakespeare's Ovid: being Arthur Golding's Translation of the 'Metamorphoses'*, ed. W.H.D. Rouse, (London: Centaur Press, 1961). All subsequent references to the *Metamorphoses* in my text follow the line numbering of this translation.

9 Compare Sonnet 64, lines 5–10. The connection of the Sonnets with the *Metamorphoses* (in relation to the theme of time and change) is a scholarly commonplace. See Sidney Lee, 'Ovid and Shakespeare's Sonnets', *Quarterly Review*, 210 (1909), 455–67 (repr. in his *Elizabethan and Other Essays* (Oxford: Clarendon Press, 1929)); J.W. Lever, *The Elizabethan Love Sonnet* (London: Methuen, 1966), pp.166, 201, 248–72.

10 The dual significance of the serpent image in *Antony and Cleopatra* has been stressed by G. Wilson Knight, *The Imperial Theme* (London: Methuen, 3rd edn, 1951), pp.227–8; Maurice Charney, *Shakespeare's Roman Plays: the Function of Imagery in the Drama* (Cambridge, Mass.: Harvard University Press, 1961), pp.96–101; Marion Bodwell Smith, *Dualities in Shakespeare*, pp.210–12.

11 The rest of this paragraph borrows from my *Shakespeare and Decorum* (London: Macmillan, 1973), pp.187–9.

12 *Narrative and Dramatic Sources*, vol.v, ed. Bullough, pp.269, 275, 257.

13 Plutarch, *The Philosophie Commonly Called the Morals*, trs. Philemon Holland (London, 1603), pp.1296–8.

14 Shakespeare's use of the Mars–Venus myth in this play has been explored by Raymond B. Waddington in 'Antony and Cleopatra: "What Venus did with Mars"', *ShakS*, 2 (1966), 210–37, and by Janet Adelman, in *The Common Liar: an Essay on 'Antony and Cleopatra'* (New Haven and London: Yale University Press, 1973), pp.78–101. On the Cleopatra–Isis analogy, see Michael Lloyd, 'Cleopatra as Isis', *ShS*, 12 (1959), 89–94, and Adelman, pp.30, 80, 81, 97 (neither critic anticipates

the principal points made in my own account of the way in which the Isis–Osiris myth impinges on the symbolic design of the play). The Mars–Hercules association seems to have been instinctive with Shakespeare: 'his martial thigh,/The brawns of Hercules' (*Cym.*, IV.ii.311–12); 'The beards of Hercules and frowning Mars' (*MV*, III.ii.85). In Marlowe's *Tamburlaine the Great*, as in *Antony and Cleopatra*, the Herculean parallel serves to intensify and complicate the martial analogy (see my *English Renaissance Tragedy*, pp.93–99 and p.251, n.13). In *The Herculean Hero in Marlowe, Chapman, Shakespeare, and Dryden* (London: Methuen, 1962), Eugene M. Waith treats the Herculean analogy as primary in both plays, and ignores the cosmological myth of Mars and Venus.

15 *On the Nature of the Universe*, trs. R.E. Latham (Harmondsworth: Penguin Books, 1951), p.26. The context of Lucretius' invocation is relevant. He asks Venus to bring peace to the people of Rome: 'grant that this brutal business of war by sea and land may elsewhere be lulled to rest. For you alone have power to bestow on mortals the blessings of quiet peace. In your bosom Mars himself, supreme commander in this brutal business, flings himself down at times, laid low by the irremediable wound of love' (p.28). Subsequently (V.1008ff.) Lucretius imputes the origin and continuance of civilised society to Venus, symbol of both human-kindness and the generative impulse (p.202).

16 *Narrative and Dramatic Sources*, V.291, 295 (cf.308, 274).

17 *The Common Liar*, pp.78ff. Raymond B. Waddington (n.14) was the first to show that the myth functions in this play as a symbol of nature's concordant discord; he recognised that the moral interpretation is also relevant to the play, but did not attach the same importance to it as does Adelman. Neither Waddington nor Adelman has treated Venus as a symbol of love in the large, general sense as nature's binding force, signifying friendship and loving-kindness as well as erotic love; in consequence they have not shown just how deeply embedded is the Mars–Venus myth in the imaginative structure of the play.

18 I am necessarily covering some familiar critical territory here, although from my own point of view; ever since G. Wilson Knight's brilliantly sympathetic essays in *The Imperial Theme*, the dualistic aspect of the tragedy has received much attention.

19 On *Venus victrix* (signifying the power of love), see Edgar Wind, *Pagan Mysteries in the Renaissance* (London: Faber, 1958), pp.85–6.

20 'The interplay of the sexes, their respective weaknesses and strengths, is always finely pictured. The play throughout shows not only the blending of sex, but also its necessary antagonism and mutual hindrance.' – Knight, *The Imperial Theme*, p.302.

21 Charney, *Shakespeare's Roman Plays*, p.107.

22 Ernest Schanzer, *The Problem Plays of Shakespeare* (London: Routledge, 1963), pp.162–6; J.L. Simmons, *Shakespeare's Pagan World* (Brighton: Harvester Press, 1973), pp.151–3.

23 See Miola, *Shakespeare's Rome*, p.17.

24 George Puttenham, *The Art of English Poesie*, facsimile repr. (Menston, Yorks.: Scolar Press, 1968), p.254.

25 Hiram C. Haydn, *The Counter-Renaissance*, (New York: Scribners, 1950), p.472.

26 See Robert Ornstein, 'The Ethic of the Imagination: Love and Art in *Antony and Cleopatra*', in *Later Shakespeare*, ed. John Russell Brown, SUAS, 8 (1966), pp.31–46; Ruth Nevo, *Tragic Form in Shakespeare* (Princeton, N.J.: Princeton University Press, 1972), pp.350–3.

27 Wind, *Pagan Mysteries in the Renaissance*, pp.90–1.

28 Plato, *Timaeus*, 37d.

29 Knight, *The Imperial Theme*, pp.240–2; Wolfgang Clemen, *The Development of Shakespeare's Imagery* (London: Methuen, 1951), pp.162–4.

30 S.K. Heninger, Jr, *The Cosmographical Glass: Renaissance Diagrams of the Universe* (San Marino, Calif.: Huntington Library, 1977), pp.13, 5.

31 *The Mirror of Alchimy. Composed by the thrice-famous and learned Fryer, Roger Bachon ... With certaine other worthie Treatises of the like Argument* (London, 1597), pp.17, 20, 25–6; Elias Ashmole, *Theatrum Chemicum Britannicum. Containing Severall Poeticall Pieces of our Famous English Philosophers who have written the Hermetique Mysteries in their Ancient Language* (1602), rpt from the 1652 edn (New York and London: Johnson Reprint Corporation, 1967;, pp.8, 21, 57–61, 85, 90–2, 116, 133, 148, 178–9; Paracelsus, *The Hermetic and Alchemic Writings*, trs. Arthur Edward Waite (London: Elliott, 1894), 1.40, 84–6, 120; John Read, *Prelude to Chemistry: an Outline of Alchemy, its Literature and Relationships* (London: Bell, 1936), pp.4–5, 17, 38–9.

32 The terms 'medicine' and 'tinct' (or 'tincture') both refer to the transmuting agent which is the goal of alchemical experiment – the magisterium or philosopher's stone which turns base metal to gold. Cf. *AWW*, v.iii.102–4: 'Plutus himself, / That knows the tinct and multiplying medicine, / Hath not in nature's mystery more science'.

33 Massinger, *The City Madam*, ed. Philip Edwards and Colin Gibson, *The Poems and Plays of Philip Massinger* (Cambridge: Cambridge University Press, 1980), iii.iii.43–4 (cf. lines 12–15).

34 Norman Rabkin, *Shakespeare and the Common Understanding* (New York: The Free Press; London: Collier–Macmillan, 1967), p.188; D.A. Traversi, *An Approach to Shakespeare*, 2nd edn (London: Sands, 1957), p.249.

35 Traversi, *An Approach to Shakespeare*, p.254 (cf. p.258). See also J.F. Danby, *Poets on Fortune's Hill* (London: Faber, 1952), p.145; Adelman, *The Common Liar*, pp.12, 15, 30, 88, 99; Simmons, *Shakespeare's Pagan World*, pp.124, 136; Robert Grudin, *Mighty Opposites: Shakespeare and Renaissance Contrariety* (Berkeley, Calif.: University of California Press, 1979), pp.178–9; Hill, 'The Marriage of Two Bodies: Myth and Metamorphosis in *Antony and Cleopatra*', p.235.

36 M.W. MacCallum, *Shakespeare's Roman Plays and their Background* (London: Macmillan, 1910), pp.450–3; Knight, *The Imperial Theme*, pp.318, 321, 322; Smith, *Dualities in Shakespeare*, pp.212–13; Markels, *The Triple Pillar of the World*, pp.9–10, 130, 132, 147–8; Nevo, *Tragic Form in Shakespeare*, pp.308, 337.

37 See Willard Farnham, *Shakespeare's Tragic Frontier: the World of his Final Tragedies* (Berkeley and Los Angeles: University of California Press, 1950), pp.139–97. In contrast to the heroes of Shakespeare's middle period, Antony, Macbeth, Timon, and Coriolanus are seen as deeply flawed – 'self-centred individualists' who draw from us 'reactions which vary widely between profound antipathy and profound sympathy'. Being inseparable from their flaws, their nobility is inherently paradoxical (pp.7–10).

38 *OED*, 'bounty', 1b.

39 No one who has seen this tragedy performed (other than by rude mechanicals) could find Antony's suicide amusing or ridiculous in any way. It is harrowing to behold. Even the neo-Senecan Robert Garnier saw that it should be so (see *The Tragedie of Antonie*, trs. Mary Herbert [1595] lines 1610ff., in Bullough, p.397). Antony's anguish, of course, makes his response to the news that Cleopatra has tricked him all the more heroic.

40 Excerpt in *'Antony and Cleopatra': a Selection of Critical Essays*, ed. John Russell Brown (London: Macmillan, 1968), p.35.

41 Spenser, *The Faerie Queene*, v.i.2–3. Book II of Castiglione's *The Book of the Courtier* is the most important source for Renaissance thinking on the subject of grace (fitness, propriety, decorum).

42 Grudin, *Mighty Opposites*, pp.169–71; Michael Goldman, *Acting and Action in Shakespearean Tragedy* (Princeton, N.J.: Princeton University Press, 1985), pp.124–6.

43 See IV.xii.32–9; IV,xiv.72–7; IV.xv.22–31.

44 M.R. Ridley accepted that the Seleucus affair is 'a put-up job' while at the same time arguing against 'the supporters of an unwavering purpose'. See his New Arden edn of the play (London: Methuen, 1954), pp.xl–xlii.

45 Bullough, *Narrative and Dramatic Sources*, vol.v, p.314.

46 Caesar's sincerity in these speeches has been accepted by Knight, *The Imperial Theme*, pp.267–8, and Schanzer, *The Problem Plays of Shakespeare*, p.143.

Index